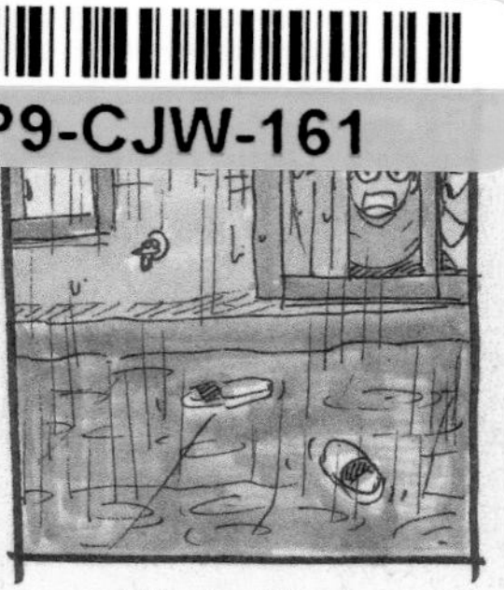

岸本斉史

The other night, during a bad rainstorm, I happened to peer out the window. "Look at all that rain... *What...?!!*" It wasn't just the rain! Rainwater had started accumulating on my veranda, forming a pool of water! The drain had gotten clogged, and it created a scene similar to the one in *Ponyo!* I was afraid for the first time in a while...

—*Masashi Kishimoto, 2010*

Author/artist Masashi Kishimoto was born in 1974 in rural Okayama Prefecture, Japan. After spending time in art college, he won the Hop Step Award for new manga artists with his manga **Karakuri** (Mechanism). Kishimoto decided to base his next story on traditional Japanese culture. His first version of **Naruto**, drawn in 1997, was a one-shot story about fox spirits; his final version, which debuted in **Weekly Shonen Jump** in 1999, quickly became the most popular ninja manga in Japan.

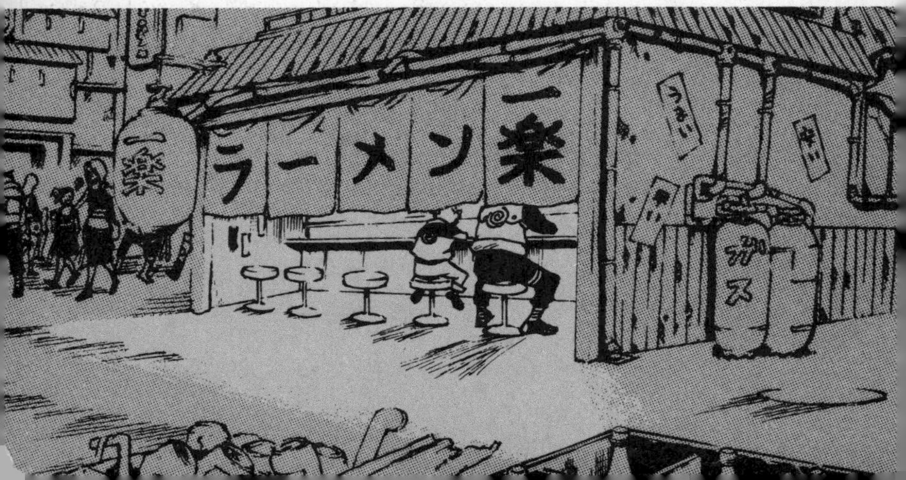
一楽
ラーメン一楽

NARUTO VOL. 54
SHONEN JUMP Manga Edition

This graphic novel contains material that was originally published in English
in SHONEN JUMP #102–105. Artwork in the magazine may have been
slightly altered from that presented here.

STORY AND ART BY MASASHI KISHIMOTO

Translation/Mari Morimoto
Touch-up Art & Lettering/Inori Fukuda Trant, Sabrina Heep
Design/Sam Elzway
Series Editor/Joel Enos
Graphic Novel Editor/Megan Bates

Published by VIZ Media, LLC
P.O. Box 77010
San Francisco, CA 94107

10 9 8 7 6 5 4 3 2 1
First printing, January 2012

www.viz.com

THE WORLD'S
MOST POPULAR MANGA

www.shonenjump.com

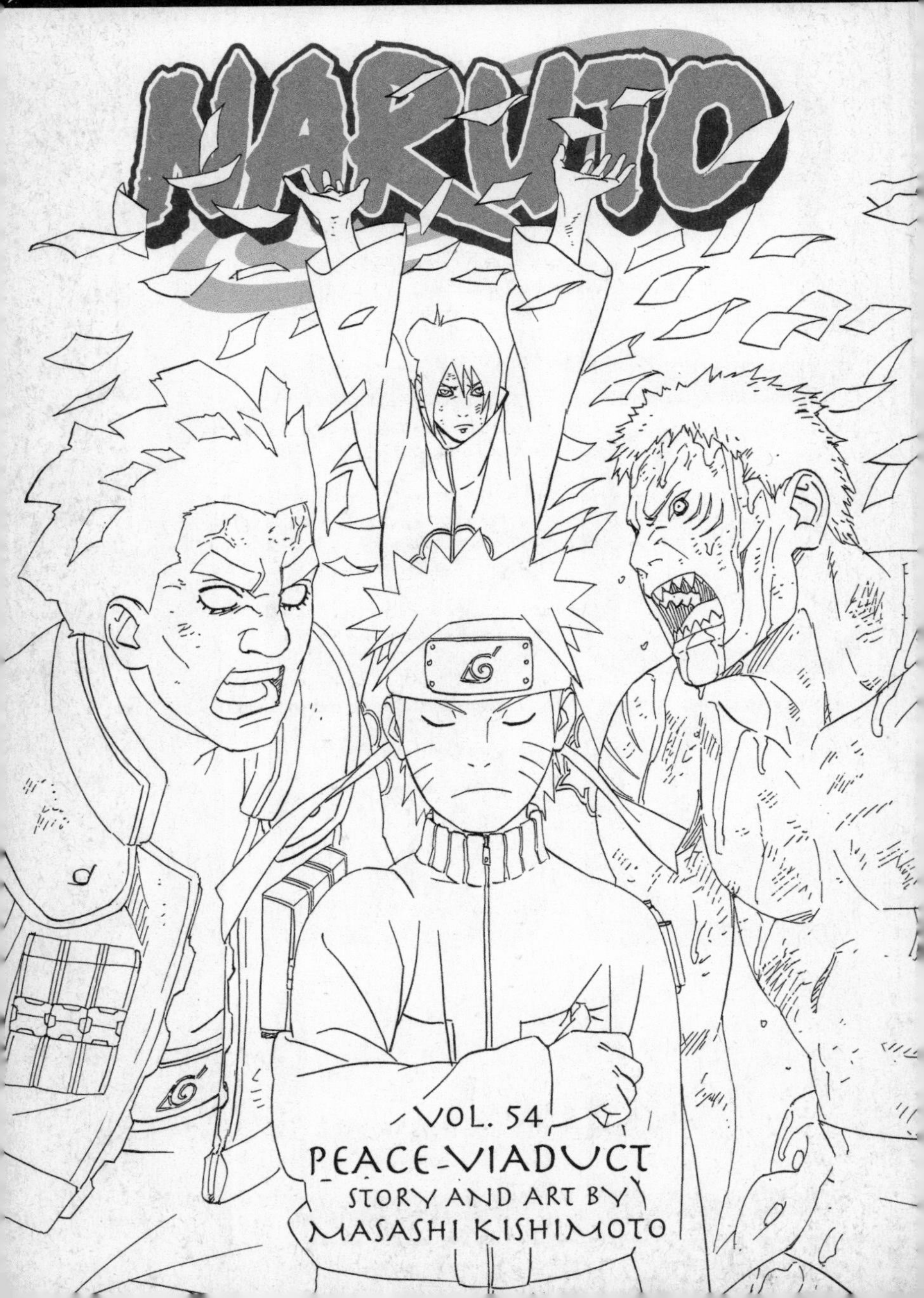

NARUTO

VOL. 54

PEACE-VIADUCT

STORY AND ART BY
MASASHI KISHIMOTO

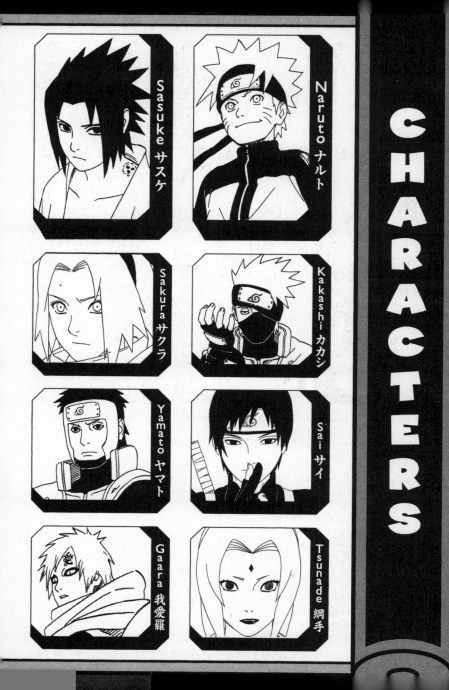

CHARACTERS

Sasuke サスケ

Naruto ナルト

Sakura サクラ

Kakashi カカシ

Yamato ヤマト

Sai サイ

Gaara 我愛羅

Tsunade 綱手

Mizukage 水影

Tsuchikage 土影

Raikage 雷影

Kisame 鬼鮫

Zetsu ゼツ

Madara マダラ

Motoi モトイ

Killer Bee キラービー

Kabuto カブト

THE STORY SO FAR...

Naruto, the biggest troublemaker at the Ninja Academy in the Village of Konohagakure, finally becomes a ninja along with his classmates Sasuke and Sakura. They grow and mature through countless trials and battles. However, Sasuke, unable to give up his quest for vengeance, leaves Konohagakure to seek Orochimaru and his power...

Two years pass. Naruto grows up and engages in fierce battles against the Tailed Beast-targeting Akatsuki. Elsewhere, after winning the heroic battle against Itachi and learning his older brother's true intentions, Sasuke allies with the Akatsuki and sets out to destroy Konoha.

Upon Madara's declaration of war, an Allied Shinobi Force is formed. Naruto, sent away in the name of protecting the jinchûriki, succeeds in taking in Nine Tails' chakra. Plus, when his mother reappears to explain the secrets of his birth, Naruto accepts his parents' hopes and renews his vow to become Hokage!

NARUTO

VOL. 54
PEACE VIADUCT

CONTENTS

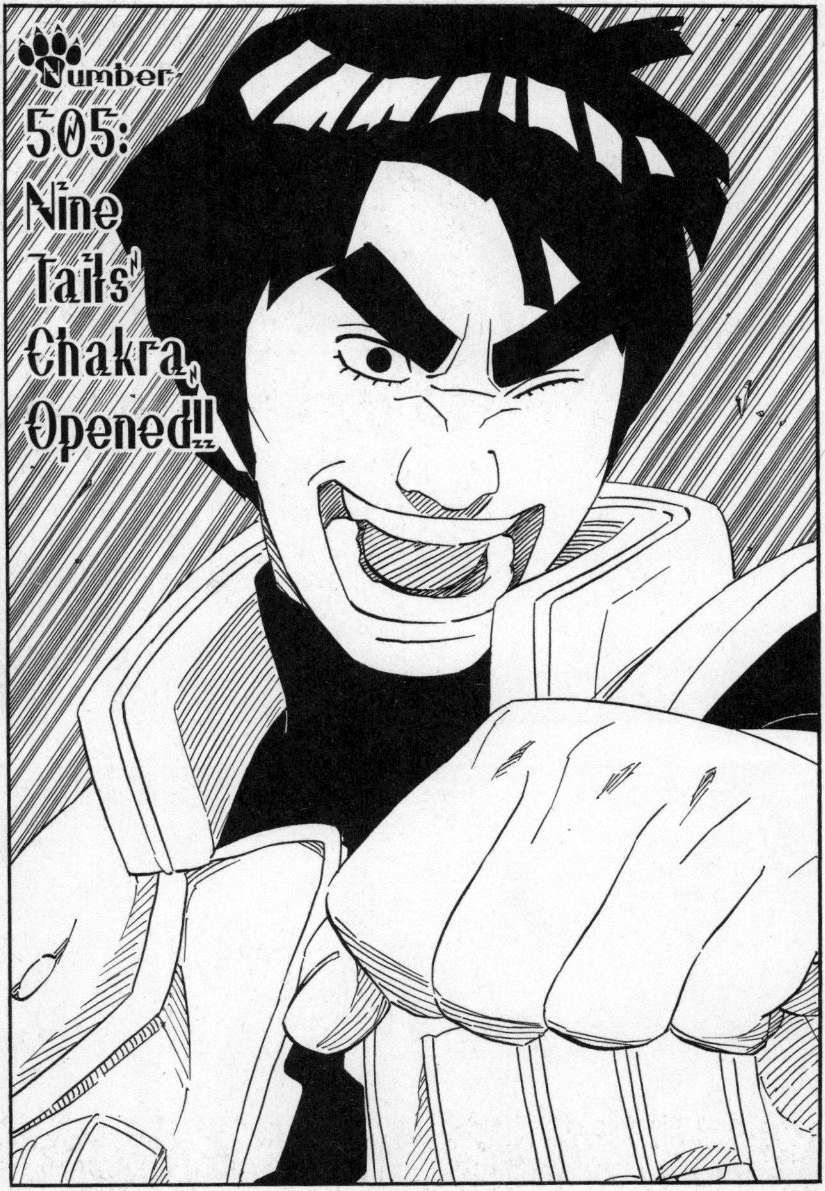
Number 505: Nine Tails' Chakra Opened!!

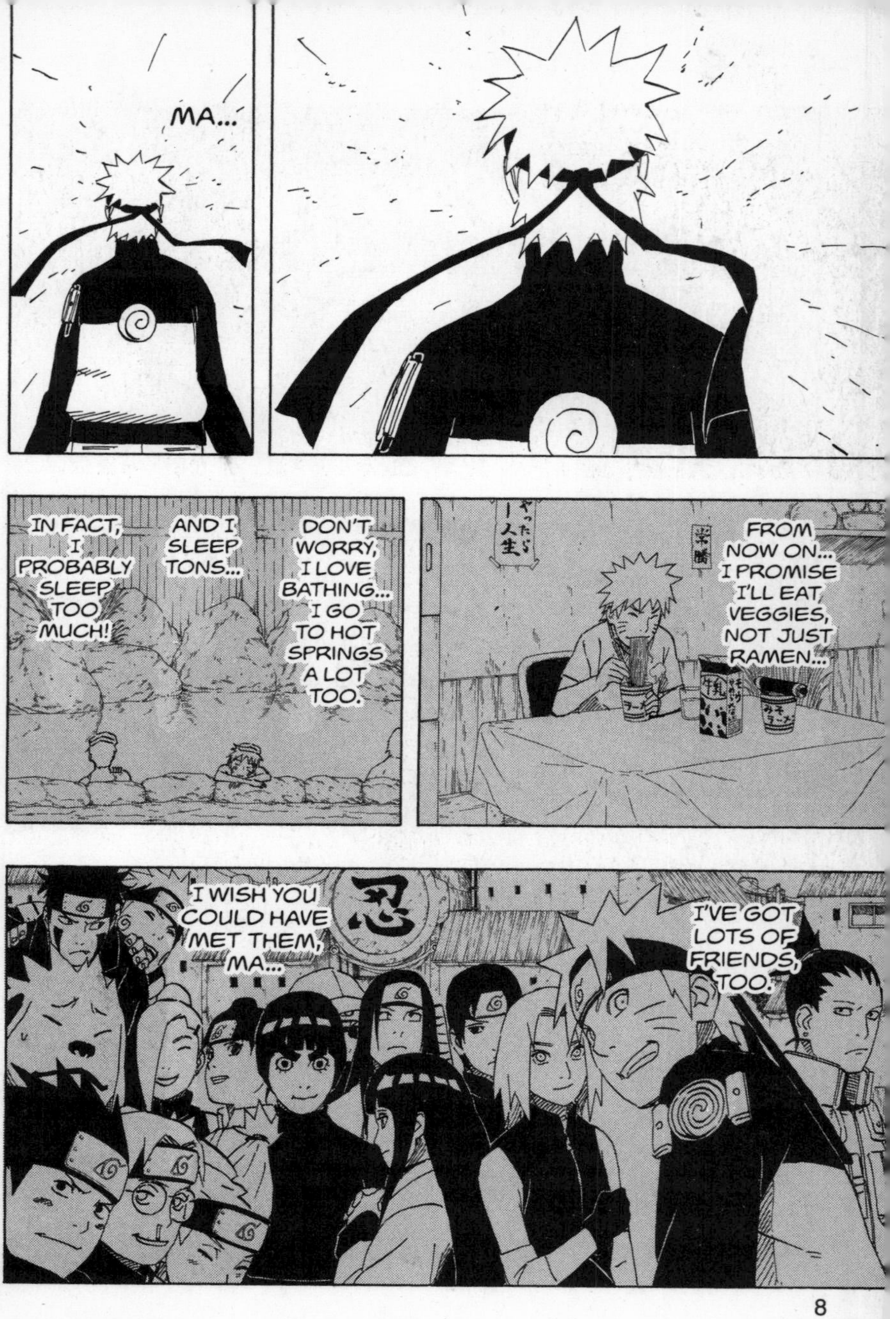
MA...
FROM NOW ON... I PROMISE I'LL EAT VEGGIES, NOT JUST RAMEN...
DON'T WORRY, I LOVE BATHING... I GO TO HOT SPRINGS A LOT TOO.
AND I SLEEP TONS...
IN FACT, I PROBABLY SLEEP TOO MUCH!
I'VE GOT LOTS OF FRIENDS, TOO.
I WISH YOU COULD HAVE MET THEM, MA...

READ THIS WAY

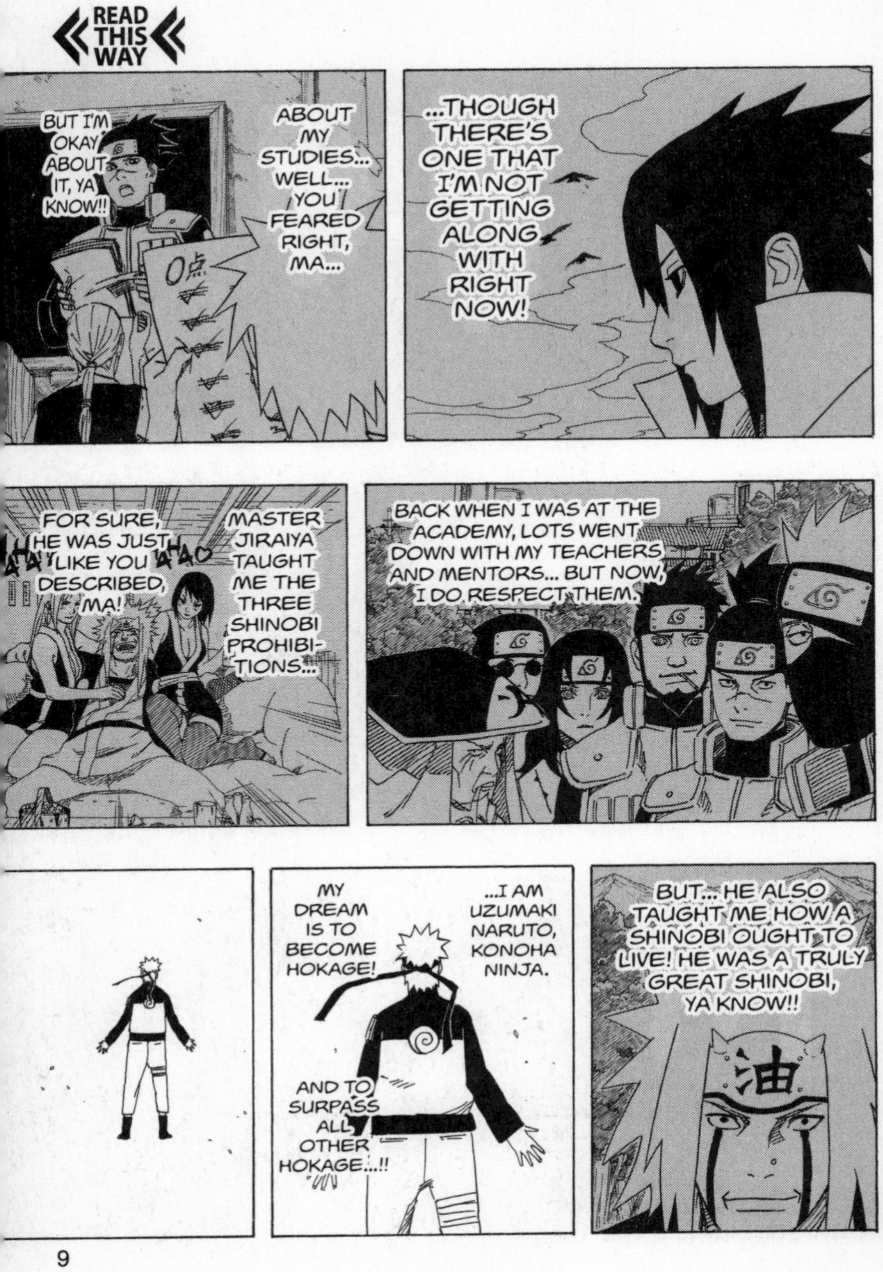
...THOUGH THERE'S ONE THAT I'M NOT GETTING ALONG WITH RIGHT NOW!
ABOUT MY STUDIES... WELL... YOU FEARED RIGHT, MA...
0点
BUT I'M OKAY ABOUT IT, YA KNOW!!
BACK WHEN I WAS AT THE ACADEMY, LOTS WENT DOWN WITH MY TEACHERS AND MENTORS... BUT NOW, I DO RESPECT THEM.
MASTER JIRAIYA TAUGHT ME THE THREE SHINOBI PROHIBITIONS...
FOR SURE, HE WAS JUST LIKE YOU DESCRIBED, MA!
BUT... HE ALSO TAUGHT ME HOW A SHINOBI OUGHT TO LIVE! HE WAS A TRULY GREAT SHINOBI, YA KNOW!!
油
...I AM UZUMAKI NARUTO, KONOHA NINJA.
MY DREAM IS TO BECOME HOKAGE!
AND TO SURPASS ALL OTHER HOKAGE...!!

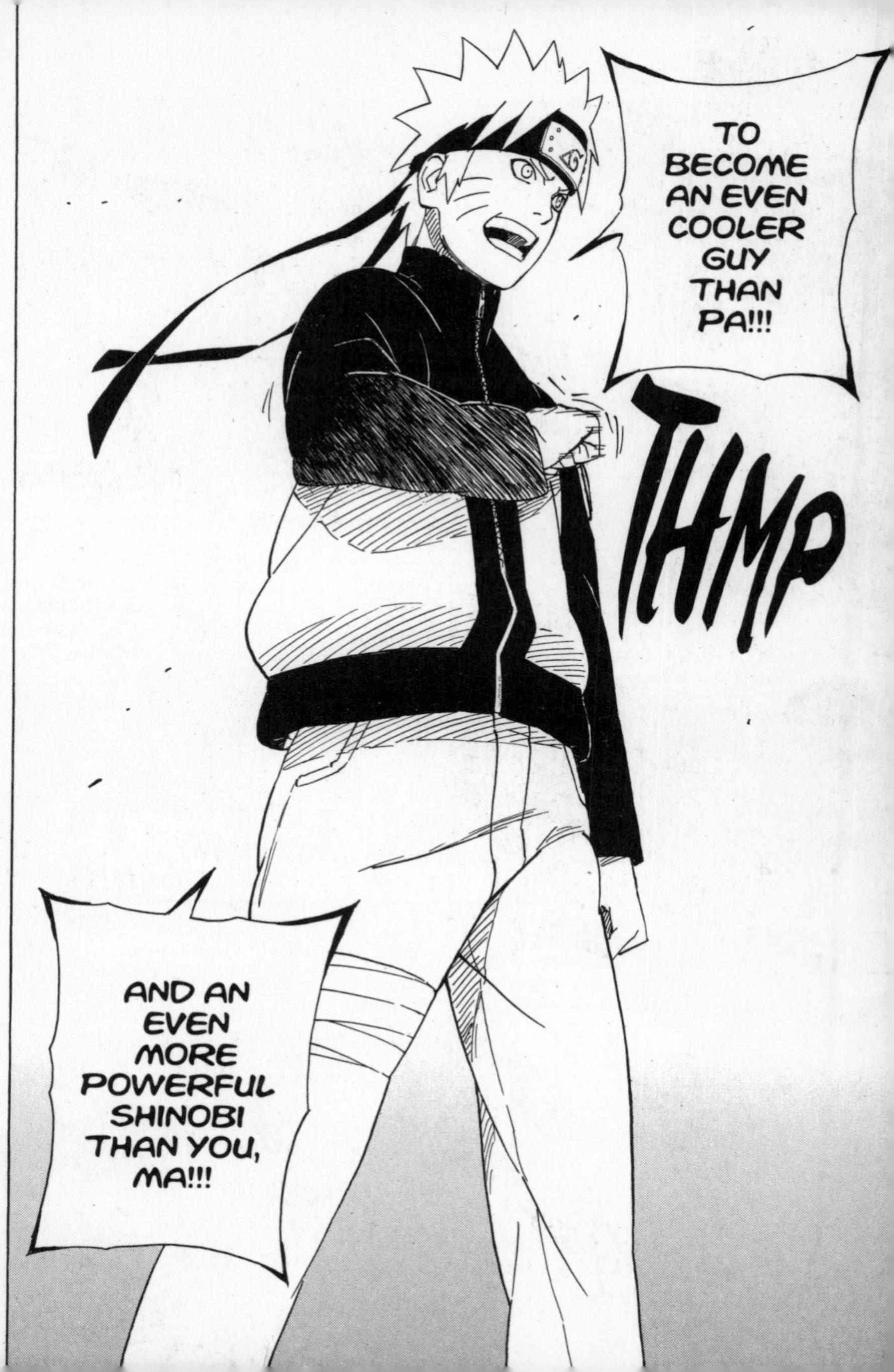
TO BECOME AN EVEN COOLER GUY THAN PA!!!
THMP
AND AN EVEN MORE POWERFUL SHINOBI THAN YOU, MA!!!

READ THIS WAY

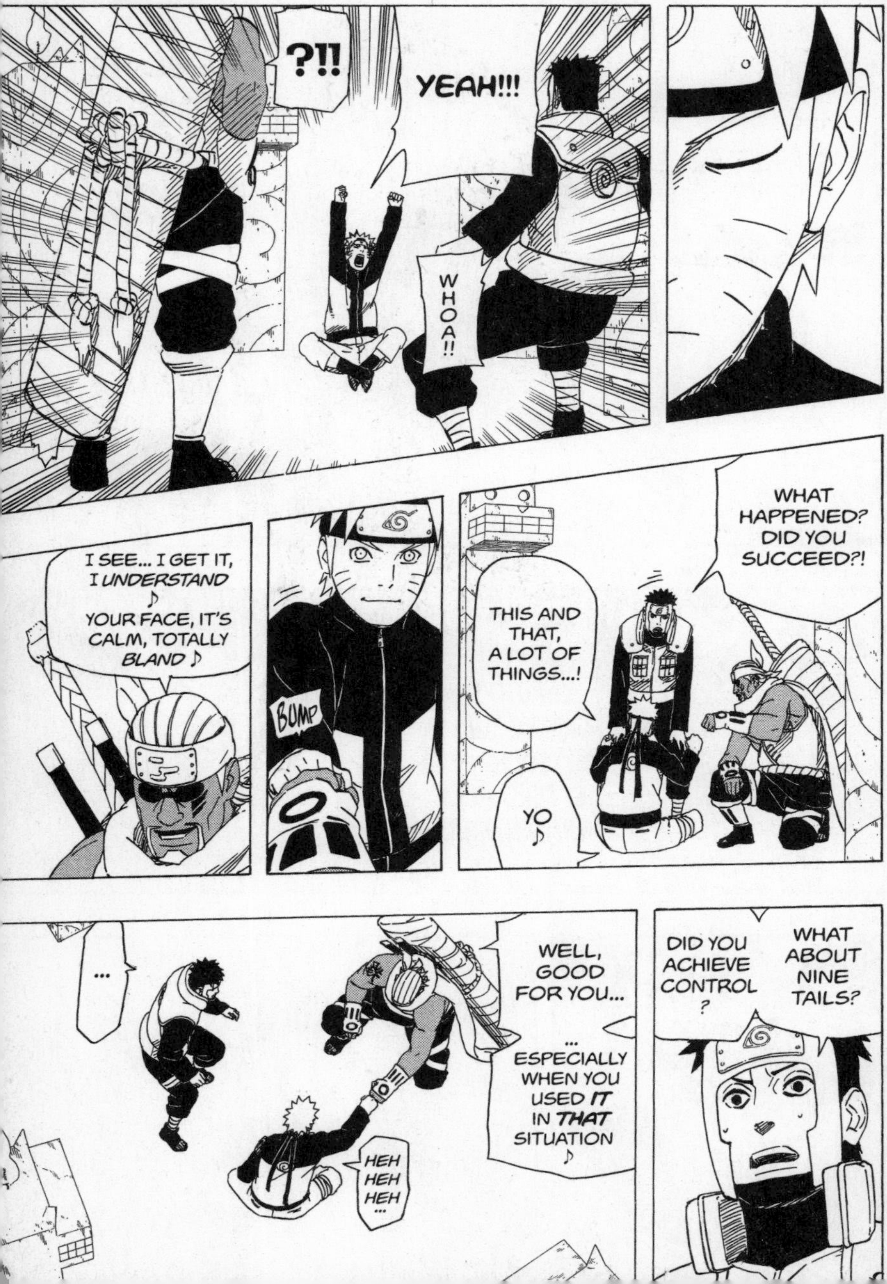
YEAH!!!
?!!
WHOA!!
WHAT HAPPENED? DID YOU SUCCEED?!
THIS AND THAT, A LOT OF THINGS...!
YO ♪
BUMP
I SEE... I GET IT, I UNDERSTAND ♪ YOUR FACE, IT'S CALM, TOTALLY BLAND ♪
WHAT ABOUT NINE TAILS?
DID YOU ACHIEVE CONTROL ?
WELL, GOOD FOR YOU...
... ESPECIALLY WHEN YOU USED IT IN THAT SITUATION ♪
...
HEH HEH HEH ...

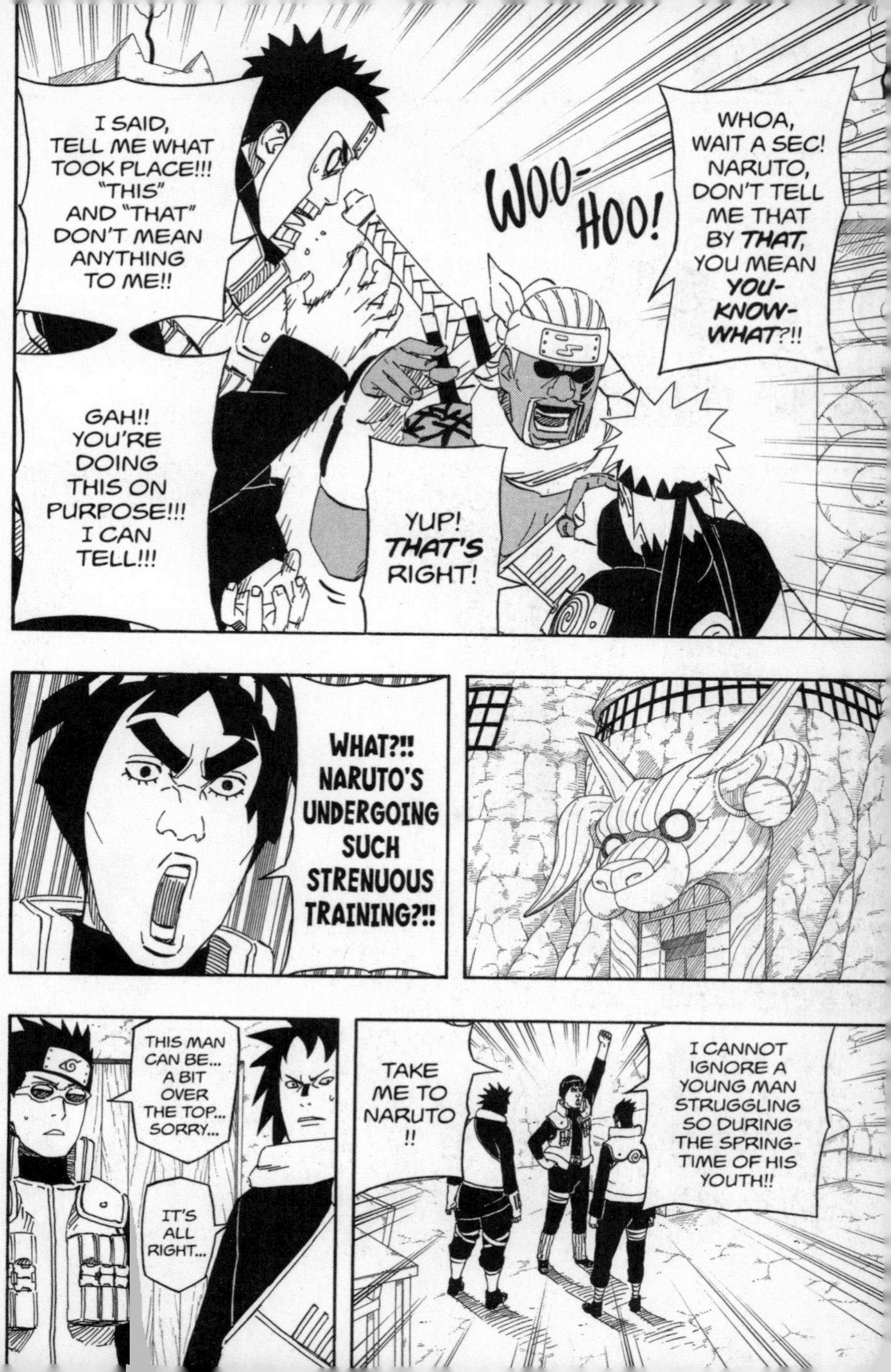
WHOA, WAIT A SEC! NARUTO, DON'T TELL ME THAT BY *THAT*, YOU MEAN *YOU-KNOW-WHAT*?!!
WOO-HOO!
I SAID, TELL ME WHAT TOOK PLACE!!! "THIS" AND "THAT" DON'T MEAN ANYTHING TO ME!!
YUP! *THAT'S* RIGHT!
GAH!! YOU'RE DOING THIS ON PURPOSE!!! I CAN TELL!!!
WHAT?!! NARUTO'S UNDERGOING SUCH STRENUOUS TRAINING?!!
I CANNOT IGNORE A YOUNG MAN STRUGGLING SO DURING THE SPRING-TIME OF HIS YOUTH!!
TAKE ME TO NARUTO!!
THIS MAN CAN BE... A BIT OVER THE TOP... SORRY...
IT'S ALL RIGHT...

READ THIS WAY

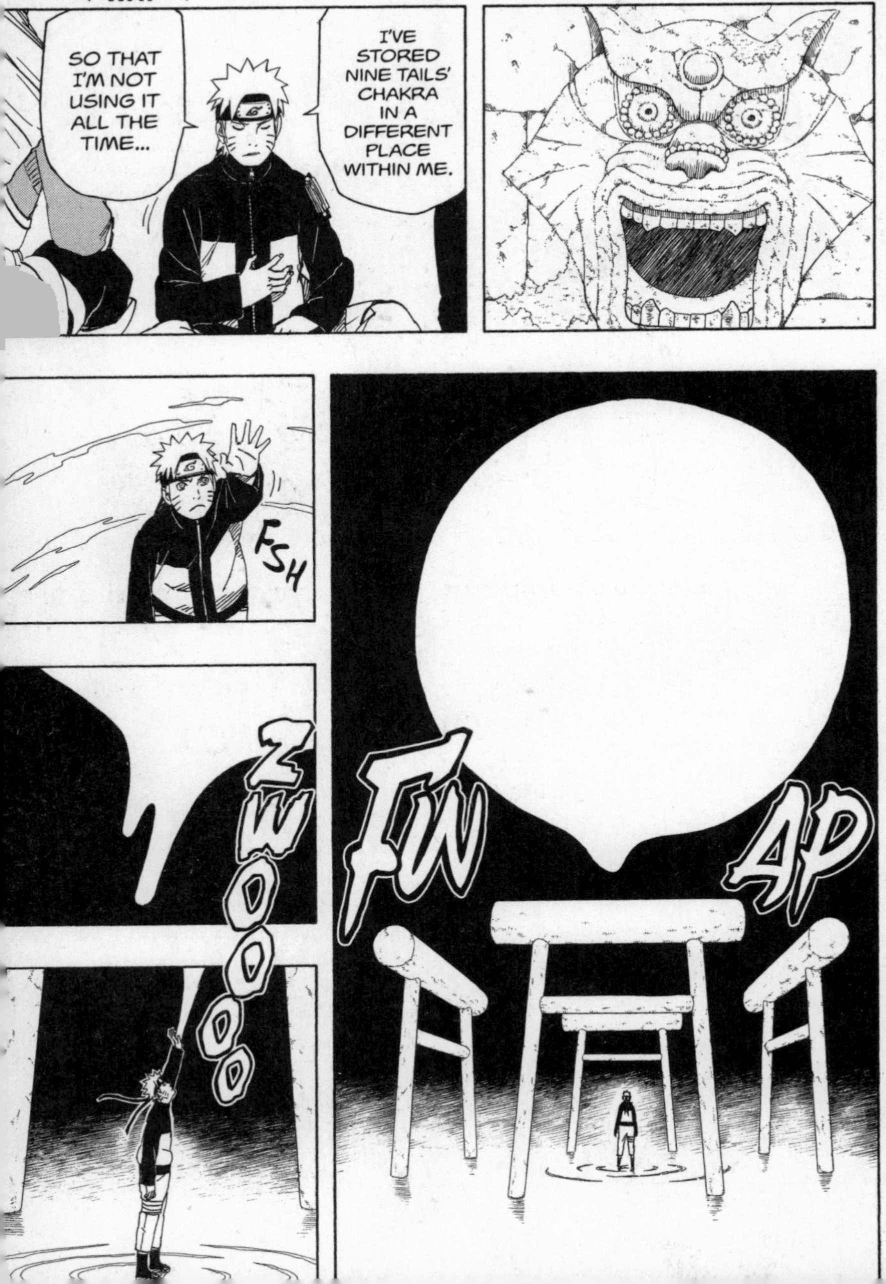
I'VE STORED NINE TAILS' CHAKRA IN A DIFFERENT PLACE WITHIN ME.
SO THAT I'M NOT USING IT ALL THE TIME...
FWAP
FSH
ZWOOOO

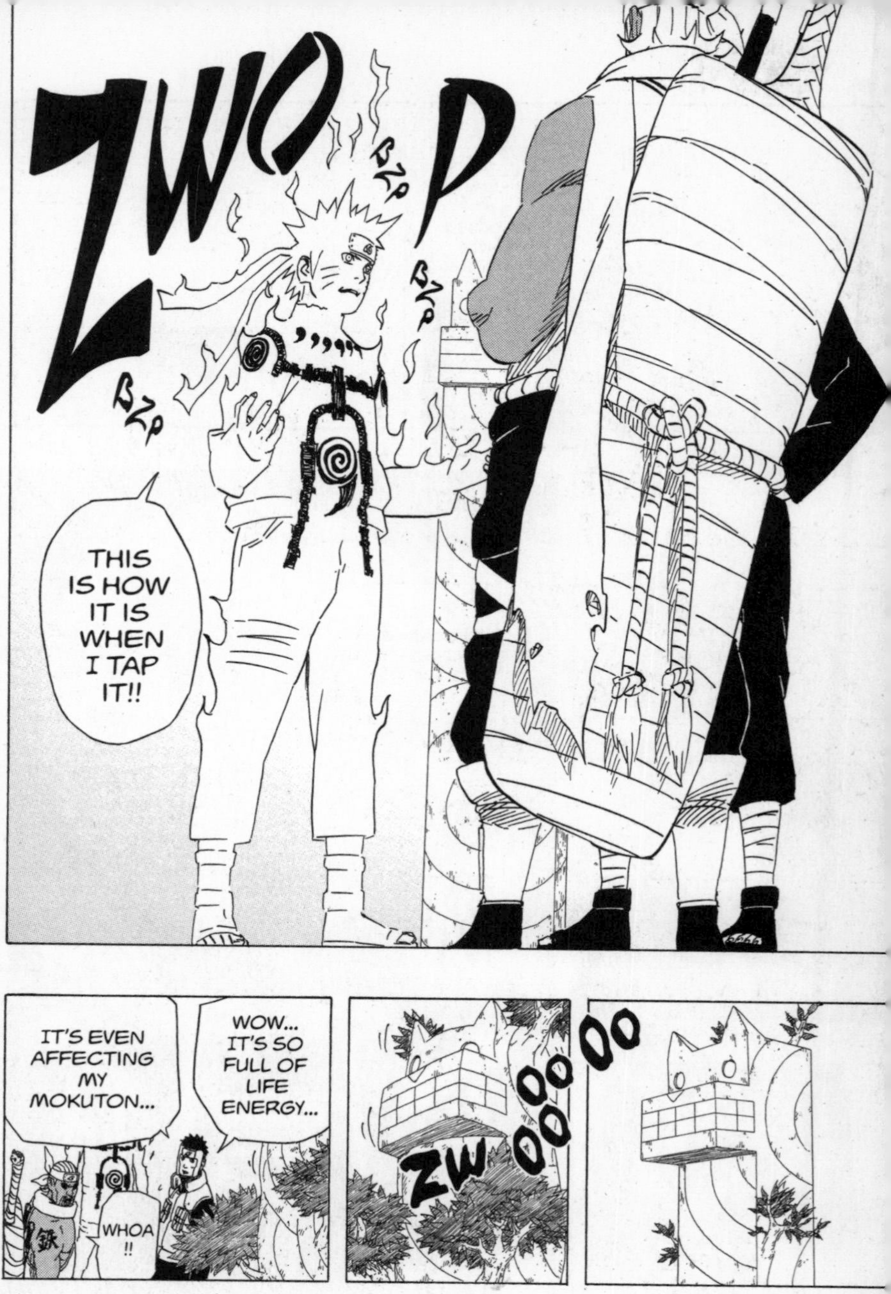
ZWOP
BZP
BZP
BZP
THIS IS HOW IT IS WHEN I TAP IT!!
ZWOOOOOOOO
WOW... IT'S SO FULL OF LIFE ENERGY...
IT'S EVEN AFFECTING MY MOKUTON...
WHOA!!

READ THIS WAY

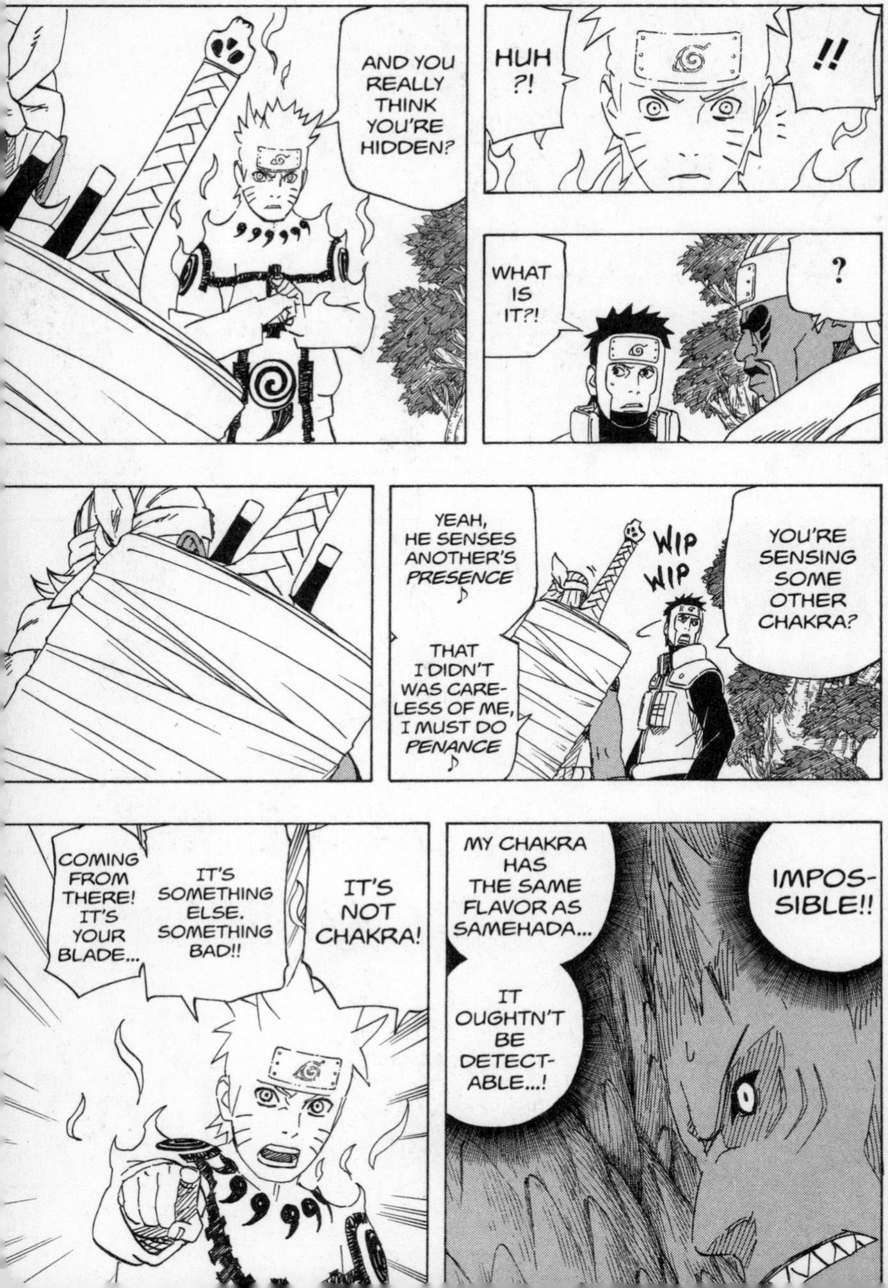
HUH ?!
!!
WHAT IS IT?!
?
AND YOU REALLY THINK YOU'RE HIDDEN?
YOU'RE SENSING SOME OTHER CHAKRA?
WIP WIP
YEAH, HE SENSES ANOTHER'S *PRESENCE* ♪
THAT I DIDN'T WAS CARELESS OF ME, I MUST DO *PENANCE* ♪
IMPOSSIBLE!!
MY CHAKRA HAS THE SAME FLAVOR AS SAMEHADA...
IT OUGHTN'T BE DETECTABLE...!
IT'S NOT CHAKRA!
IT'S SOMETHING ELSE. SOMETHING BAD!!
COMING FROM THERE! IT'S YOUR BLADE...

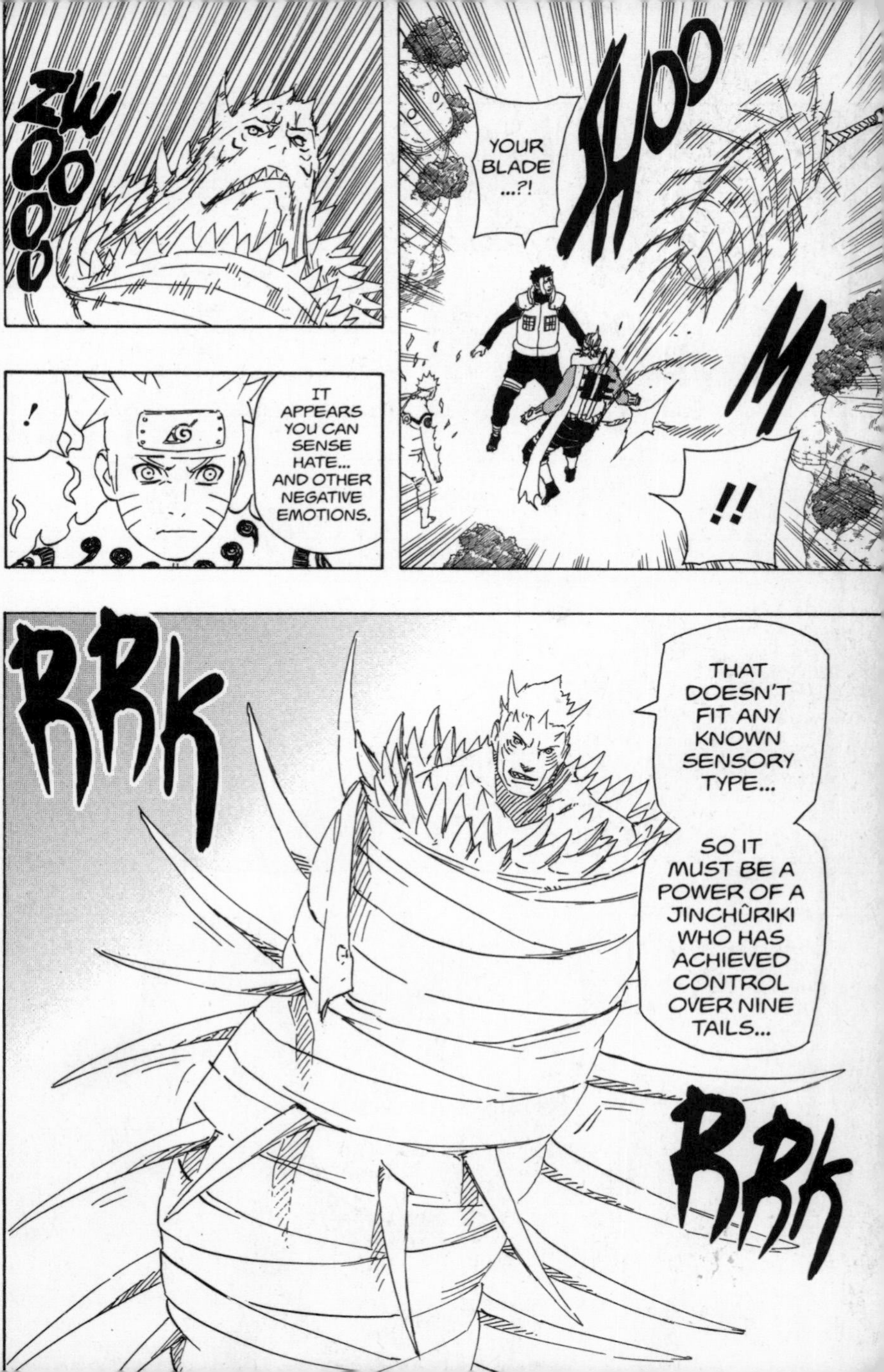

YOUR BLADE ...?!
SHOOM
!!
ZWOOOO
IT APPEARS YOU CAN SENSE HATE... AND OTHER NEGATIVE EMOTIONS.
!
THAT DOESN'T FIT ANY KNOWN SENSORY TYPE...
SO IT MUST BE A POWER OF A JINCHÛRIKI WHO HAS ACHIEVED CONTROL OVER NINE TAILS...
RRK
RRK

READ THIS WAY

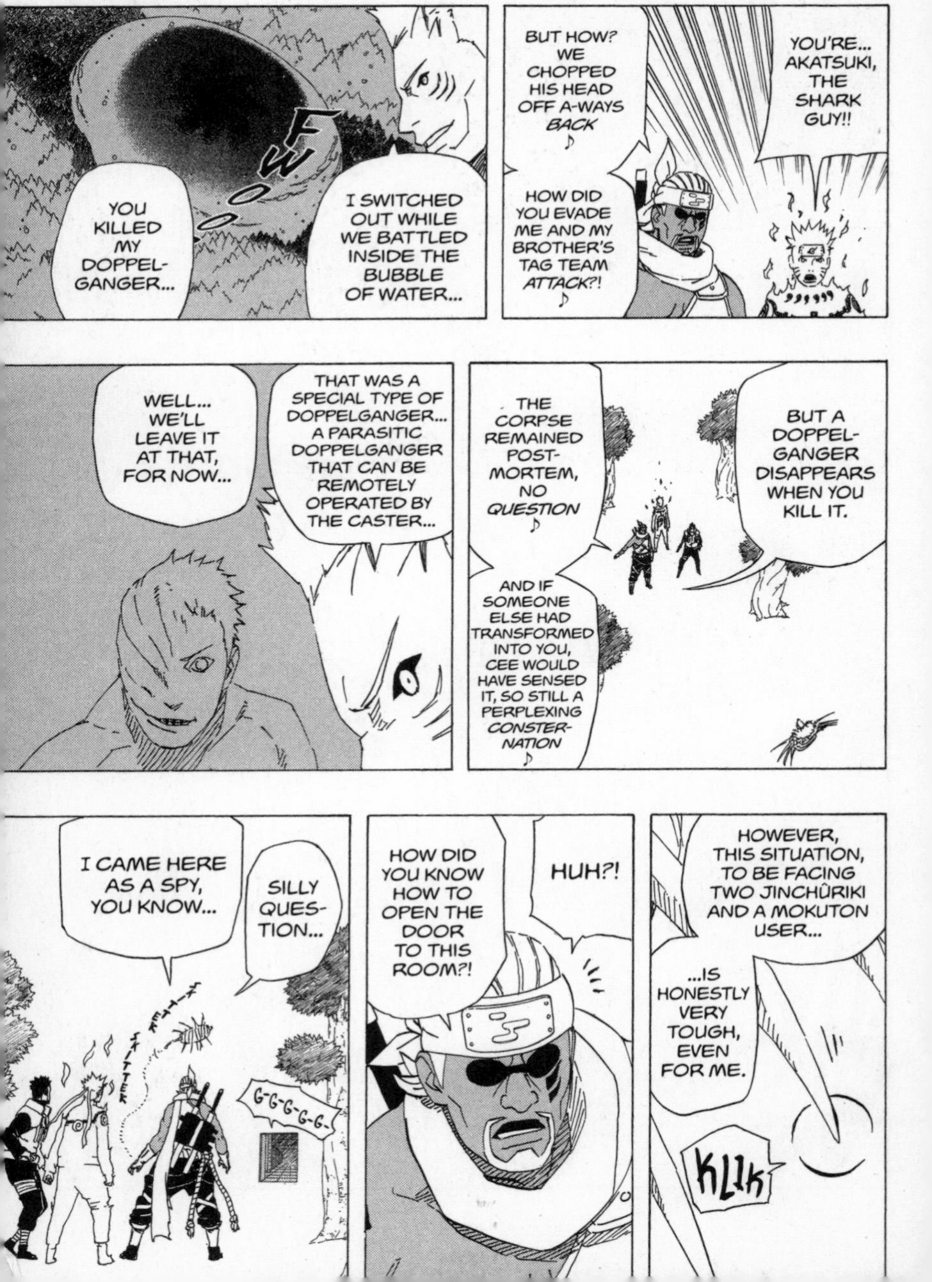

YOU'RE... AKATSUKI, THE SHARK GUY!!
BUT HOW? WE CHOPPED HIS HEAD OFF A-WAYS *BACK* ♪
HOW DID YOU EVADE ME AND MY BROTHER'S TAG TEAM *ATTACK*?! ♪
FWOOO
I SWITCHED OUT WHILE WE BATTLED INSIDE THE BUBBLE OF WATER...
YOU KILLED MY DOPPEL-GANGER...
BUT A DOPPEL-GANGER DISAPPEARS WHEN YOU KILL IT.
THE CORPSE REMAINED POST-MORTEM, NO *QUESTION* ♪
AND IF SOMEONE ELSE HAD TRANSFORMED INTO YOU, CEE WOULD HAVE SENSED IT, SO STILL A PERPLEXING *CONSTER-NATION* ♪
THAT WAS A SPECIAL TYPE OF DOPPELGANGER... A PARASITIC DOPPELGANGER THAT CAN BE REMOTELY OPERATED BY THE CASTER...
WELL... WE'LL LEAVE IT AT THAT, FOR NOW...
HOWEVER, THIS SITUATION, TO BE FACING TWO JINCHÛRIKI AND A MOKUTON USER...
...IS HONESTLY VERY TOUGH, EVEN FOR ME.
KLIK
HUH?!
HOW DID YOU KNOW HOW TO OPEN THE DOOR TO THIS ROOM?!
SILLY QUES-TION...
I CAME HERE AS A SPY, YOU KNOW...
SKITTER
G-G-G-G-G

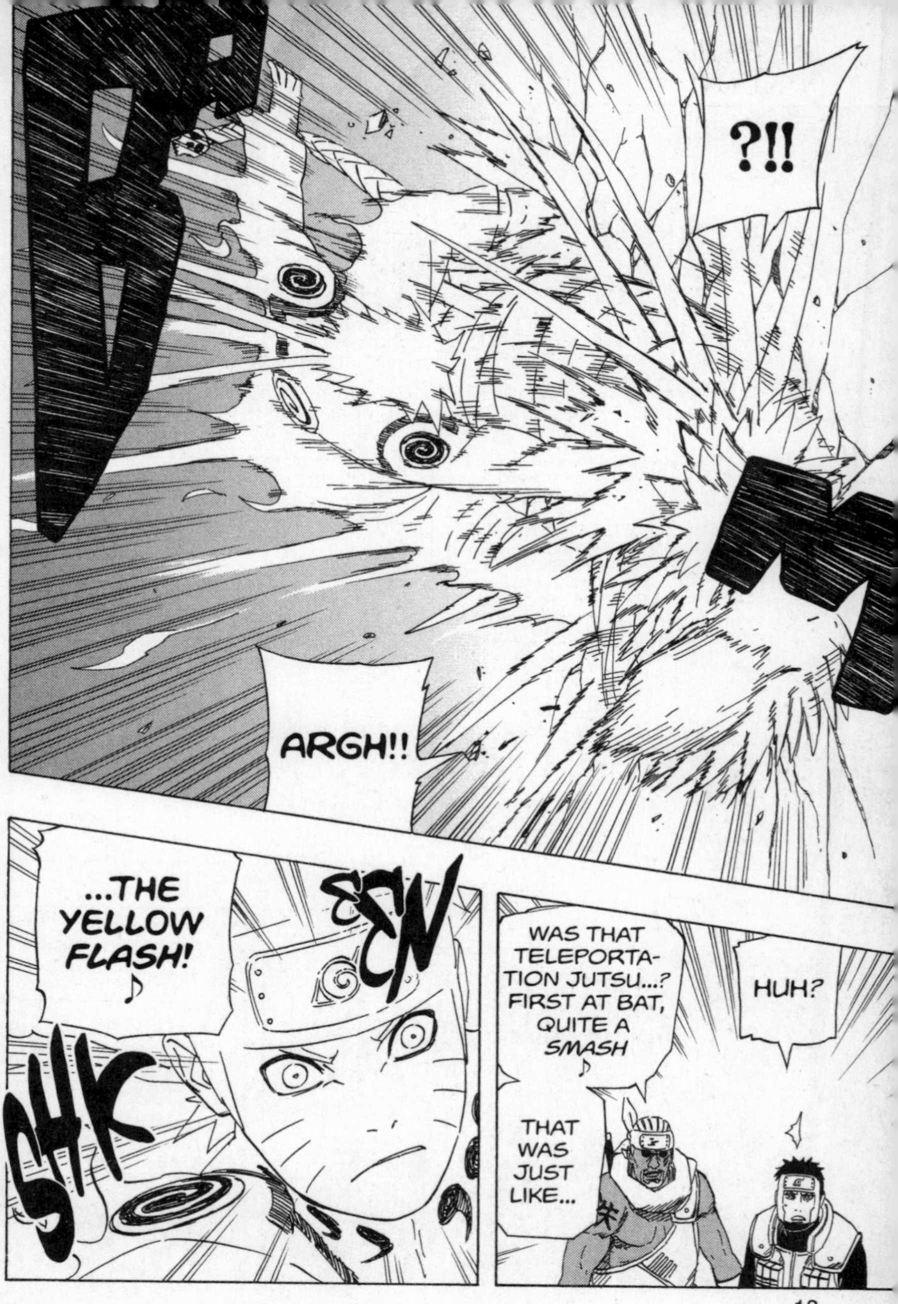
?!!
ARGH!!
HUH?
WAS THAT TELEPORTATION JUTSU...? FIRST AT BAT, QUITE A SMASH ♪
THAT WAS JUST LIKE...
...THE YELLOW FLASH! ♪
SHK

READ THIS WAY

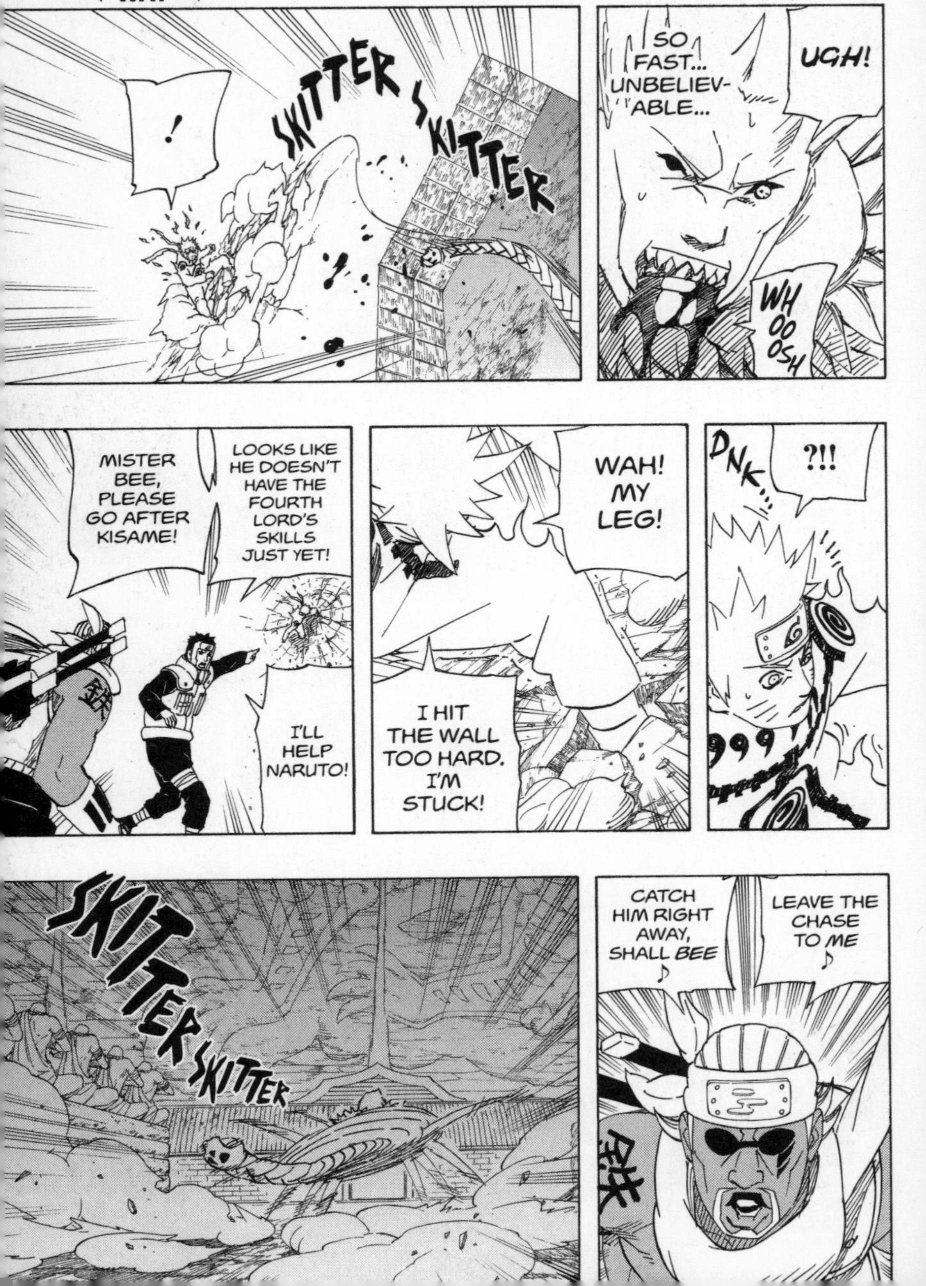
UGH!
SO FAST... UNBELIEV-ABLE...
WHOOOSH
!
SKITTER SKITTER
?!!
DNK...
WAH! MY LEG!
I HIT THE WALL TOO HARD. I'M STUCK!
LOOKS LIKE HE DOESN'T HAVE THE FOURTH LORD'S SKILLS JUST YET!
MISTER BEE, PLEASE GO AFTER KISAME!
I'LL HELP NARUTO!
LEAVE THE CHASE TO ME ♪
CATCH HIM RIGHT AWAY, SHALL *BEE* ♪
SKITTER SKITTER

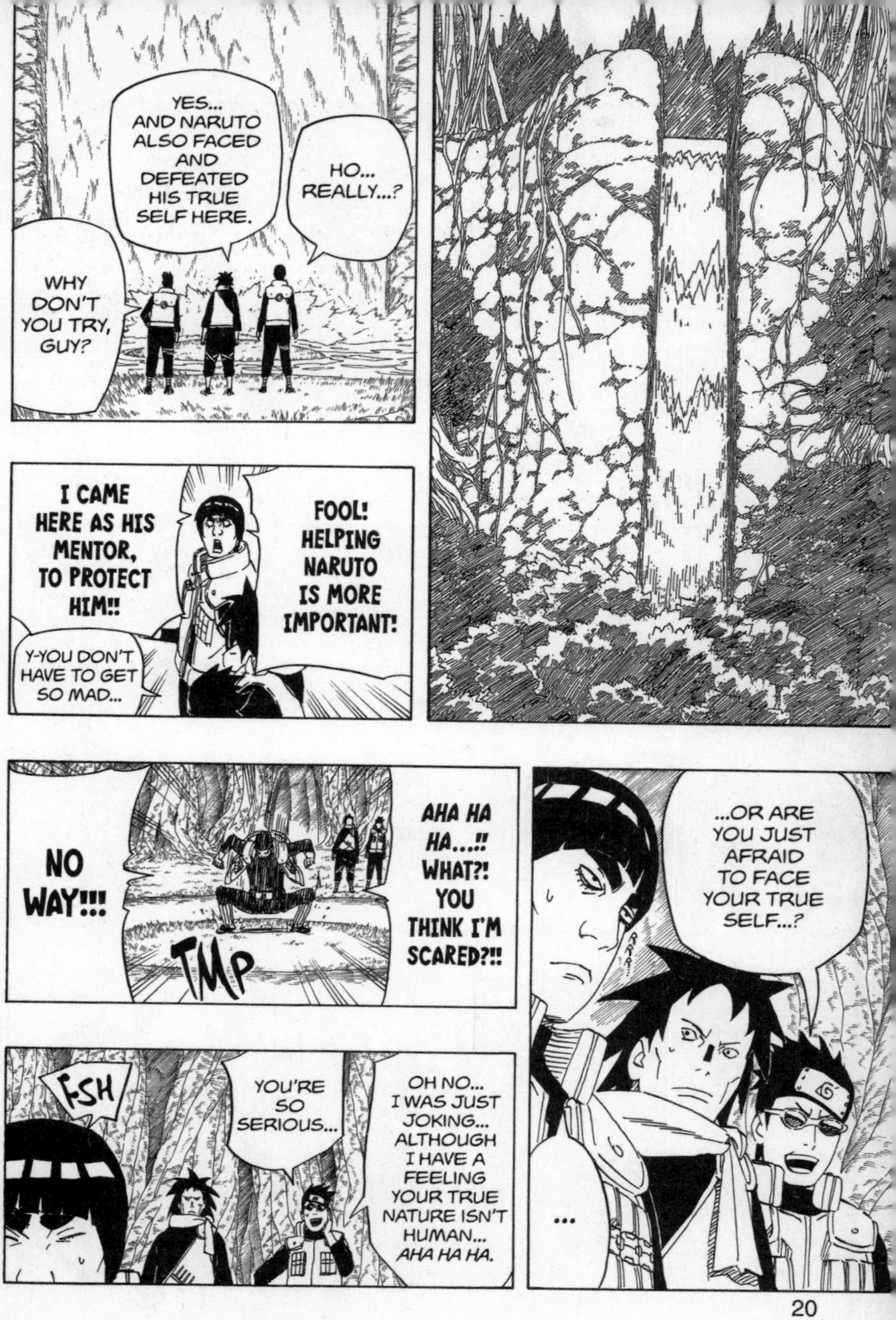
HO... REALLY...?
YES... AND NARUTO ALSO FACED AND DEFEATED HIS TRUE SELF HERE.
WHY DON'T YOU TRY, GUY?
FOOL! HELPING NARUTO IS MORE IMPORTANT!
I CAME HERE AS HIS MENTOR, TO PROTECT HIM!!
Y-YOU DON'T HAVE TO GET SO MAD...
...OR ARE YOU JUST AFRAID TO FACE YOUR TRUE SELF...?
RRR...
...
AHA HA HA...!! WHAT?! YOU THINK I'M SCARED?!!
TMP
NO WAY!!!
OH NO... I WAS JUST JOKING... ALTHOUGH I HAVE A FEELING YOUR TRUE NATURE ISN'T HUMAN... *AHA HA HA.*
YOU'RE SO SERIOUS...
FSH

READ THIS WAY

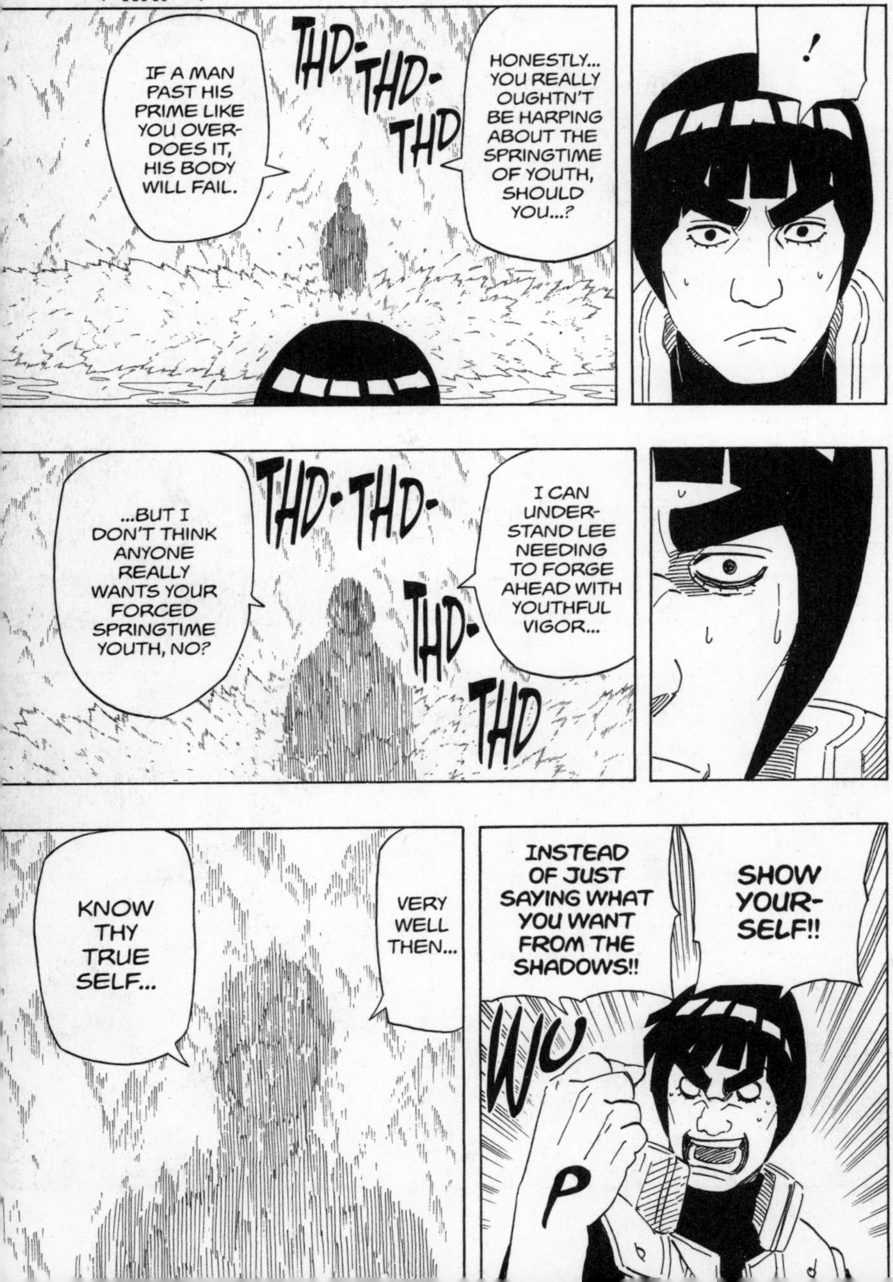
!
HONESTLY... YOU REALLY OUGHTN'T BE HARPING ABOUT THE SPRINGTIME OF YOUTH, SHOULD YOU...?
THD-THD-THD
IF A MAN PAST HIS PRIME LIKE YOU OVER-DOES IT, HIS BODY WILL FAIL.
I CAN UNDER-STAND LEE NEEDING TO FORGE AHEAD WITH YOUTHFUL VIGOR...
THD-THD-THD-THD
...BUT I DON'T THINK ANYONE REALLY WANTS YOUR FORCED SPRINGTIME YOUTH, NO?
SHOW YOUR-SELF!!
INSTEAD OF JUST SAYING WHAT YOU WANT FROM THE SHADOWS!!
WUP
VERY WELL THEN...
KNOW THY TRUE SELF...

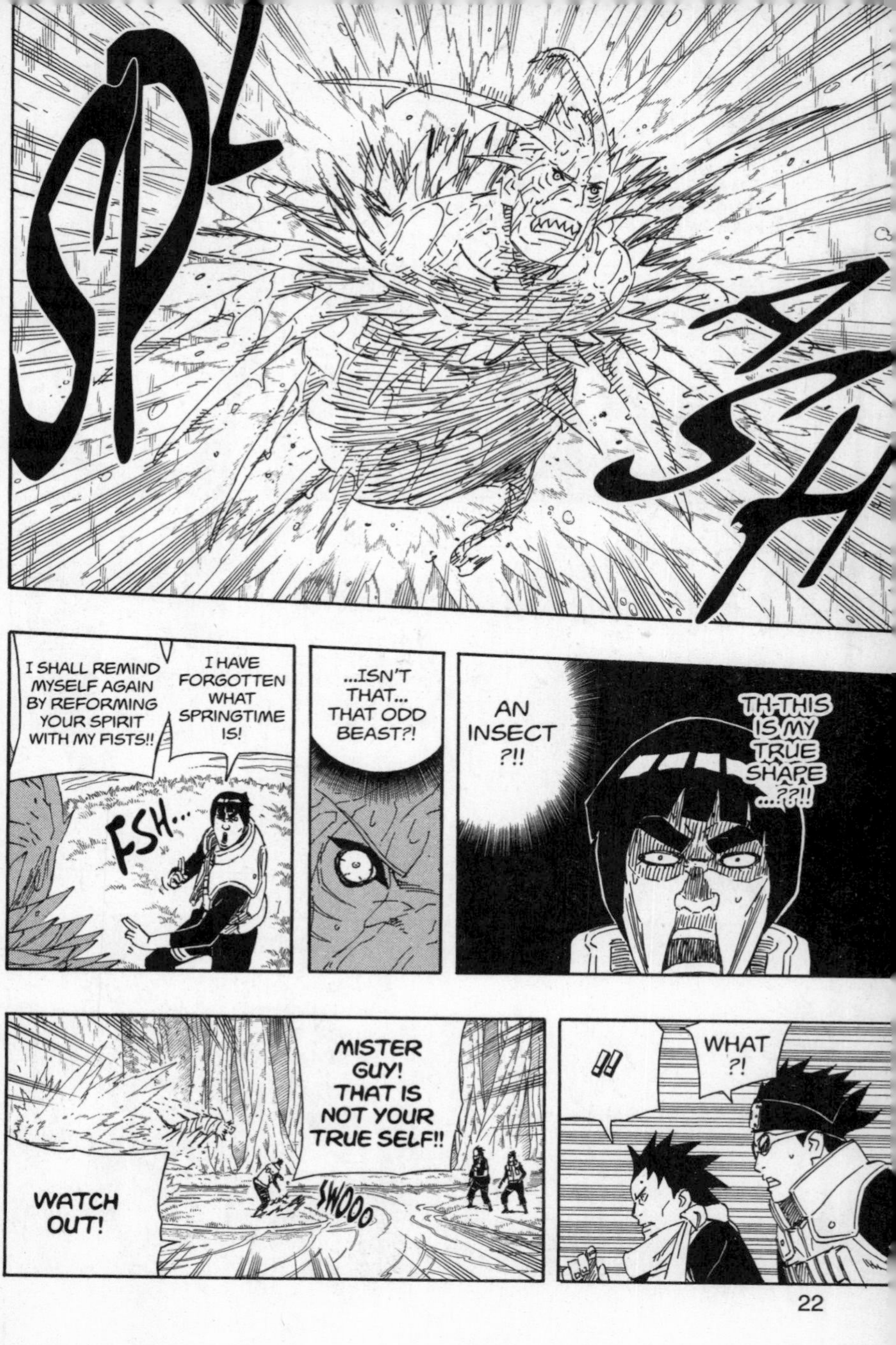
SPLASH
TH-THIS IS MY TRUE SHAPE...??!!
AN INSECT?!!
...ISN'T THAT... THAT ODD BEAST?!
I HAVE FORGOTTEN WHAT SPRINGTIME IS!
I SHALL REMIND MYSELF AGAIN BY REFORMING YOUR SPIRIT WITH MY FISTS!!
FSH...
WHAT?!
!!
MISTER GUY! THAT IS NOT YOUR TRUE SELF!!
SWOOO
WATCH OUT!

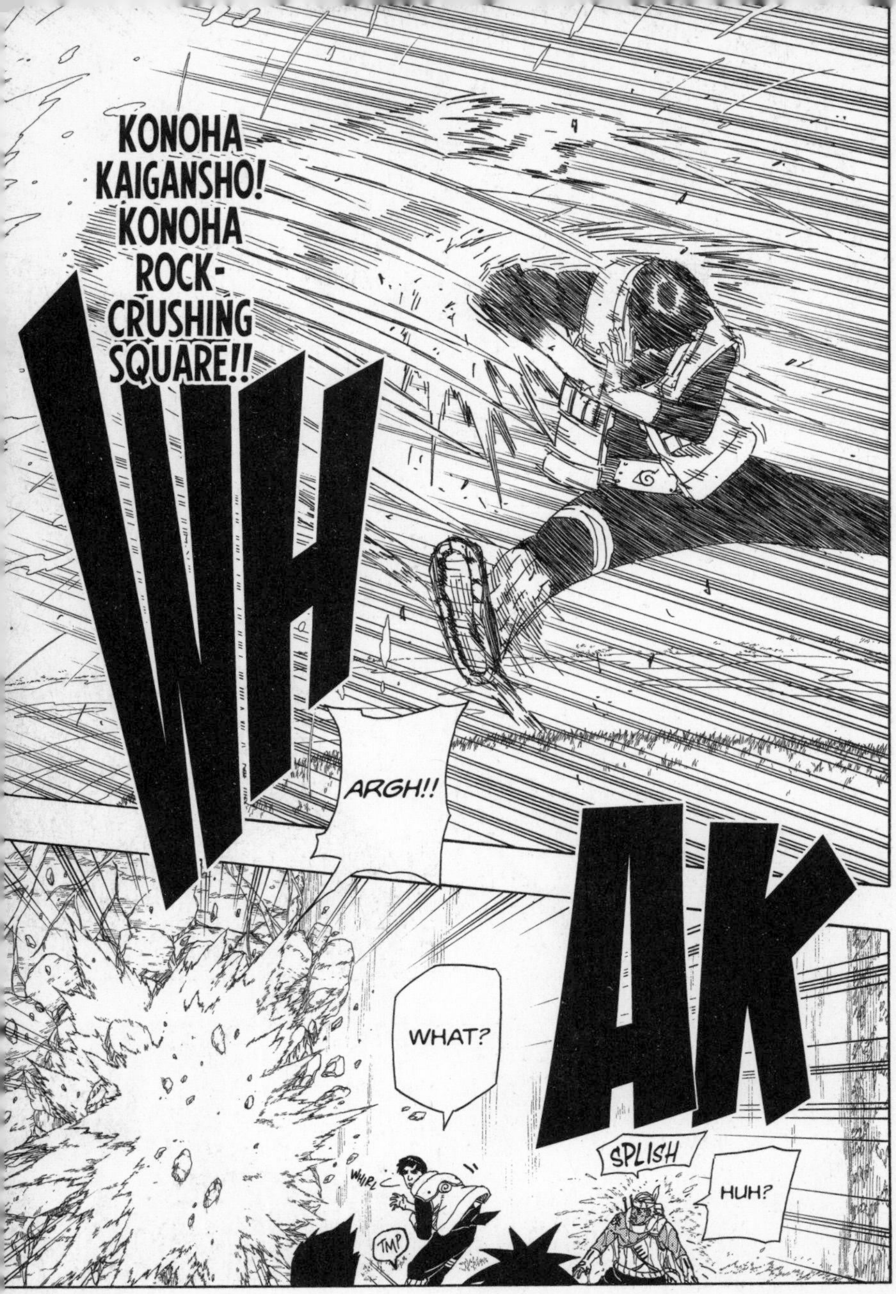
KONOHA KAIGANSHO! KONOHA ROCK-CRUSHING SQUARE!!
WHAK
ARGH!!
SPLISH
HUH?
WHAT?
WHIRL
TMP

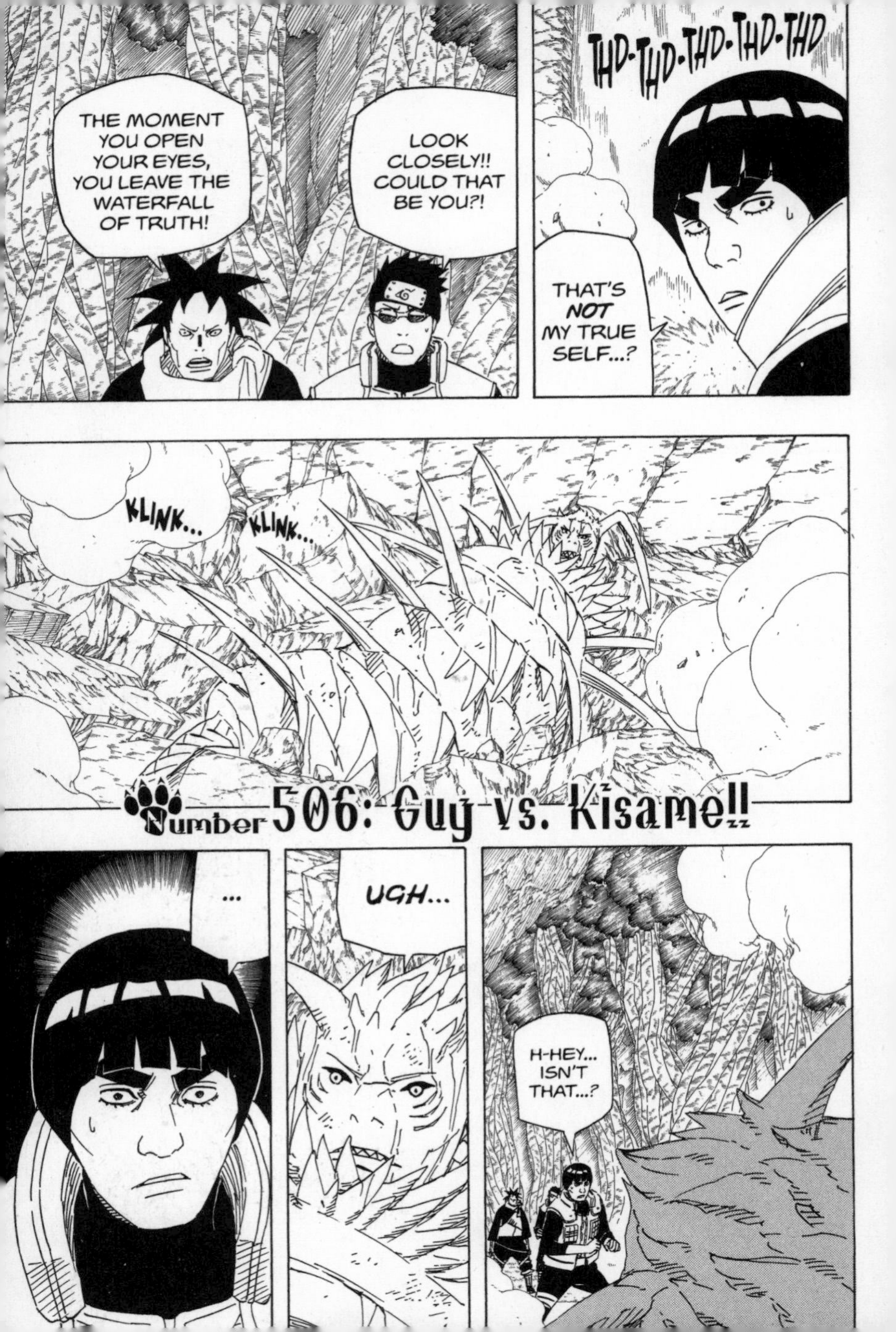
THD-THD-THD-THD-THD
THAT'S NOT MY TRUE SELF...?
LOOK CLOSELY!! COULD THAT BE YOU?!
THE MOMENT YOU OPEN YOUR EYES, YOU LEAVE THE WATERFALL OF TRUTH!
KLINK...
KLINK...
Number 506: Guy vs. Kisame!!
H-HEY... ISN'T THAT...?
UGH...
...

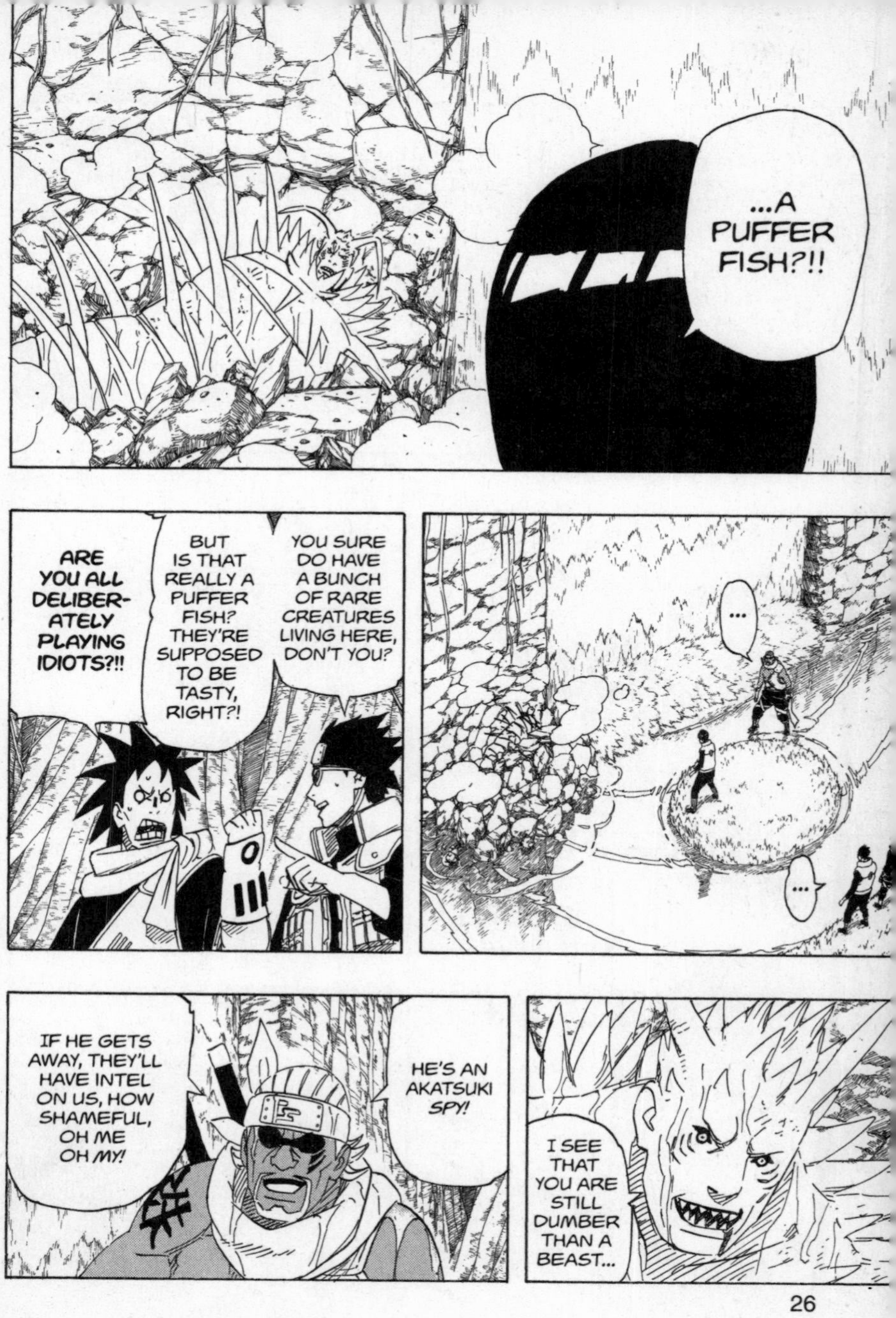
...A PUFFER FISH?!!
...
...
YOU SURE DO HAVE A BUNCH OF RARE CREATURES LIVING HERE, DON'T YOU?
BUT IS THAT REALLY A PUFFER FISH? THEY'RE SUPPOSED TO BE TASTY, RIGHT?!
ARE YOU ALL DELIBERATELY PLAYING IDIOTS?!!
I SEE THAT YOU ARE STILL DUMBER THAN A BEAST...
HE'S AN AKATSUKI SPY!
IF HE GETS AWAY, THEY'LL HAVE INTEL ON US, HOW SHAMEFUL, OH ME OH MY!

READ THIS WAY

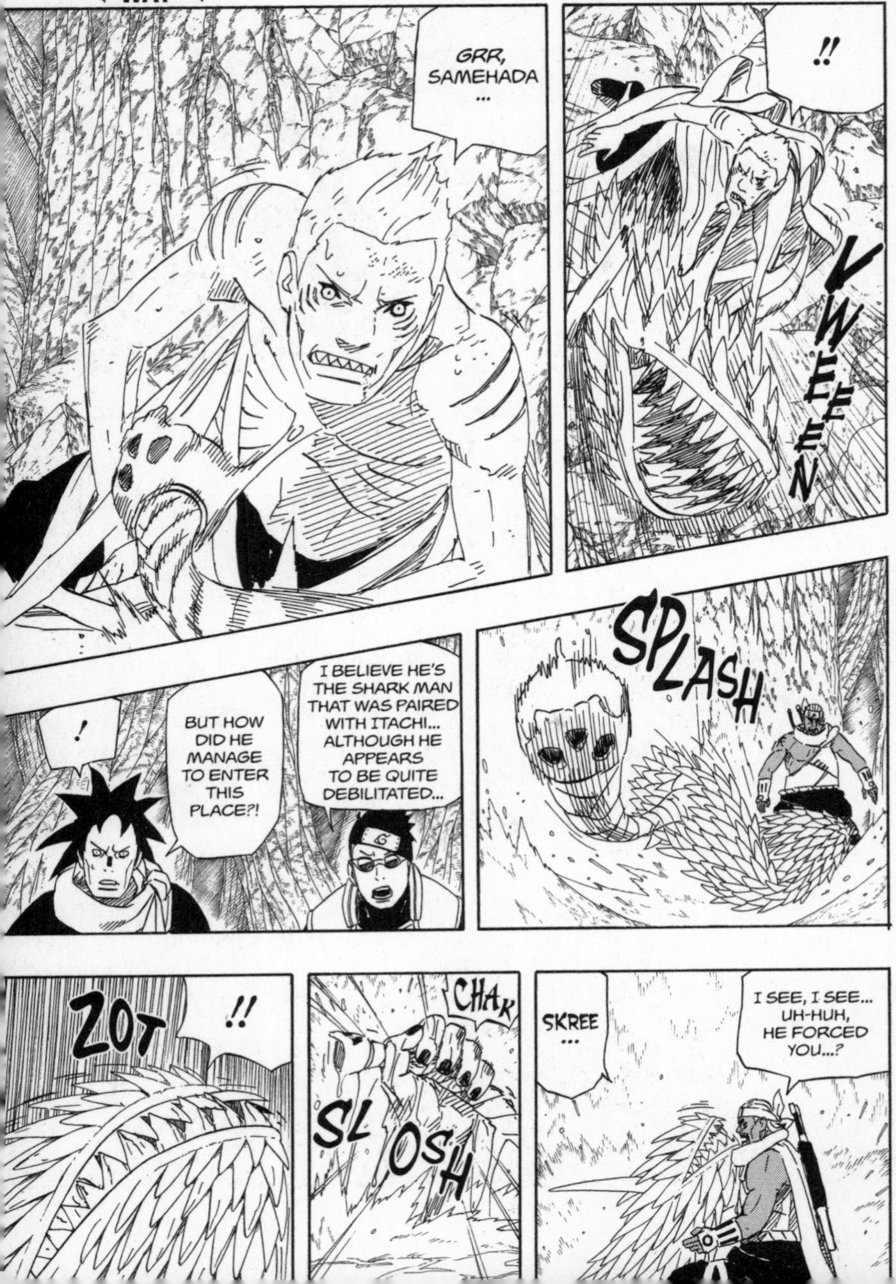
!!
VWEEEN
GRR, SAMEHADA ...
SPLASH
I BELIEVE HE'S THE SHARK MAN THAT WAS PAIRED WITH ITACHI... ALTHOUGH HE APPEARS TO BE QUITE DEBILITATED...
BUT HOW DID HE MANAGE TO ENTER THIS PLACE?!
!
I SEE, I SEE... UH-HUH, HE FORCED YOU...?
SKREE ...
CHAK
SLOSH
!!
ZOT

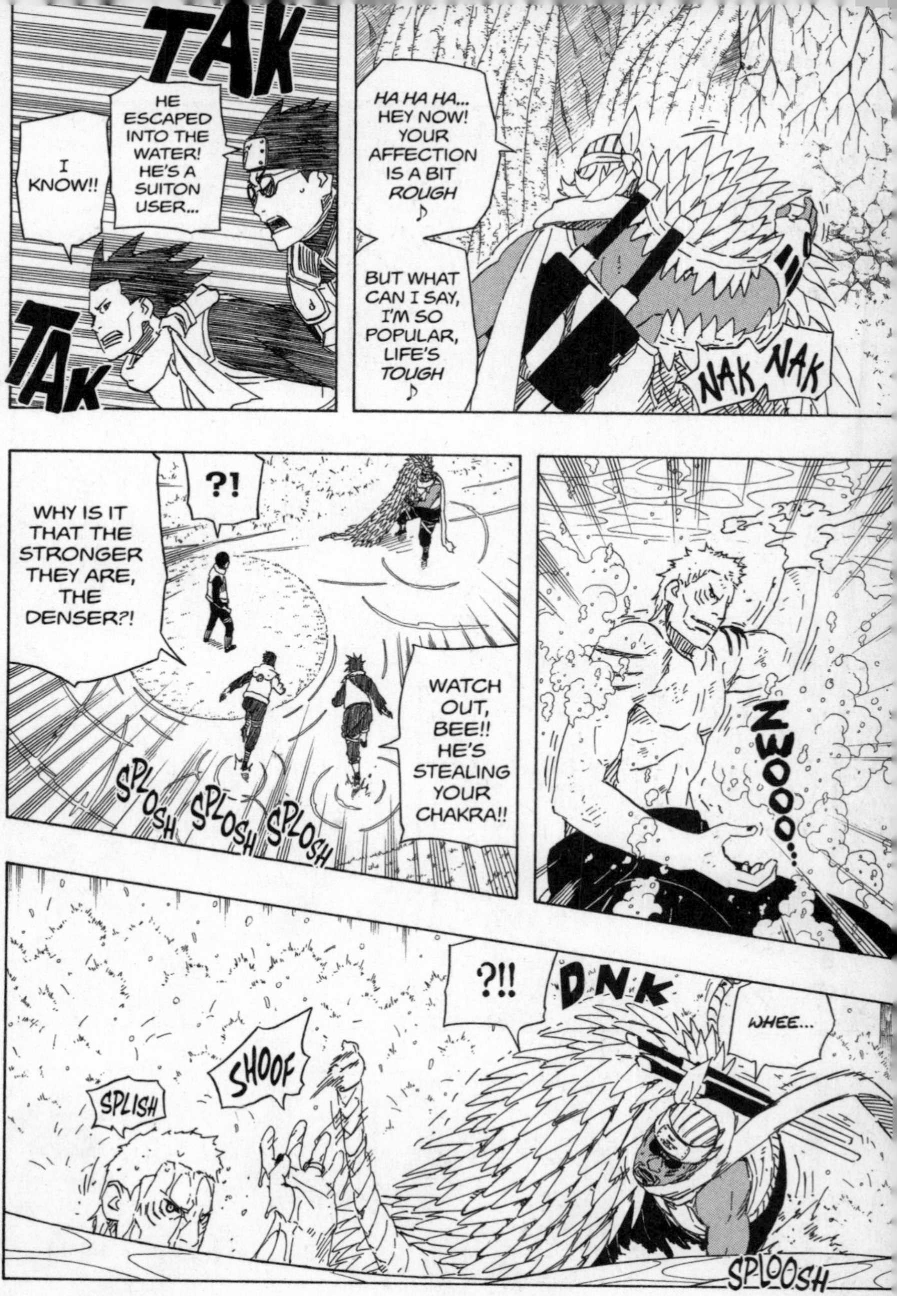
HA HA HA... HEY NOW! YOUR AFFECTION IS A BIT ROUGH ♪
BUT WHAT CAN I SAY, I'M SO POPULAR, LIFE'S TOUGH ♪
NAK NAK
TAK
HE ESCAPED INTO THE WATER! HE'S A SUITON USER...
I KNOW!!
TAK
ZWOOO...
?!
WHY IS IT THAT THE STRONGER THEY ARE, THE DENSER?!
WATCH OUT, BEE!! HE'S STEALING YOUR CHAKRA!!
SPLOSH SPLOSH SPLOSH
WHEE...
DNK
?!!
SHOOF
SPLISH
SPLOOSH

READ THIS WAY

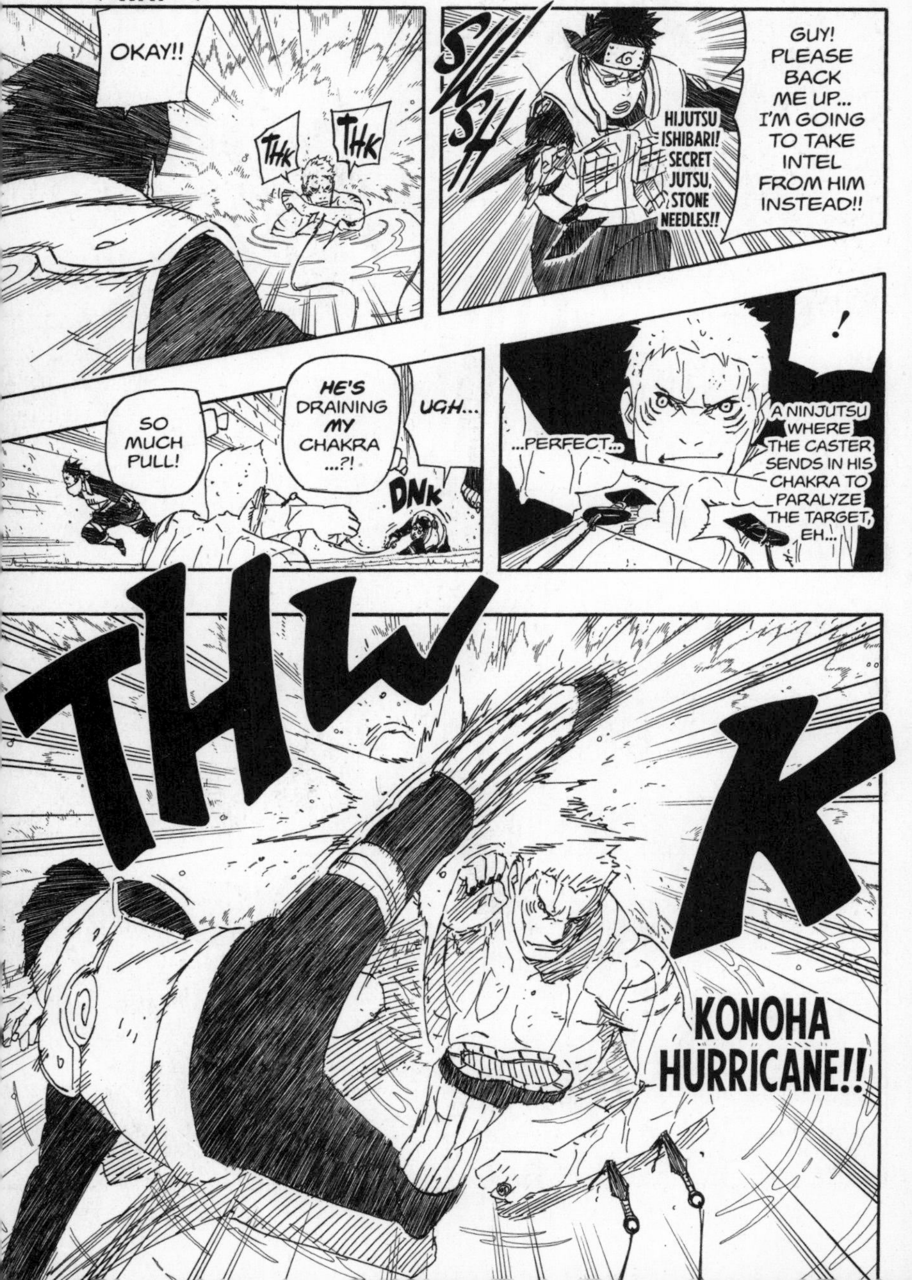
SWSH
GUY! PLEASE BACK ME UP... I'M GOING TO TAKE INTEL FROM HIM INSTEAD!!
HIJUTSU ISHIBARI! SECRET JUTSU, STONE NEEDLES!!
OKAY!!
THK
THK
!
A NINJUTSU WHERE THE CASTER SENDS IN HIS CHAKRA TO PARALYZE THE TARGET, EH...
...PERFECT...
UGH...
HE'S DRAINING MY CHAKRA ...?!
DNK
SO MUCH PULL!
THWK
KONOHA HURRICANE!!

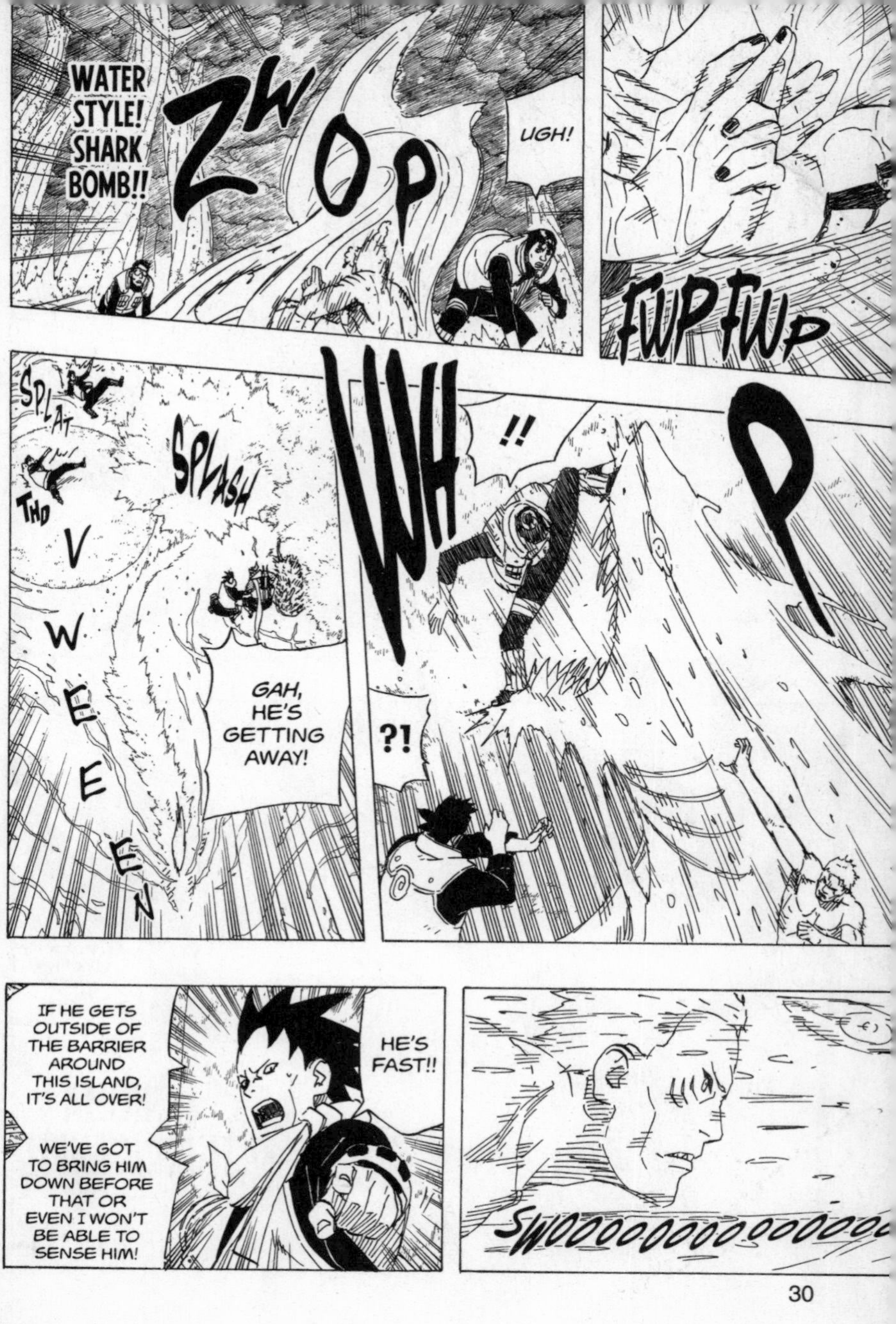
FWP FWP
UGH!
ZWOP
WATER STYLE! SHARK BOMB!!
!!
WHUP
?!
SPLASH
SPLAT
THD
GAH, HE'S GETTING AWAY!
VWEEEEN
SWOOOOOOOOOOOOOO
HE'S FAST!!
IF HE GETS OUTSIDE OF THE BARRIER AROUND THIS ISLAND, IT'S ALL OVER!
WE'VE GOT TO BRING HIM DOWN BEFORE THAT OR EVEN I WON'T BE ABLE TO SENSE HIM!

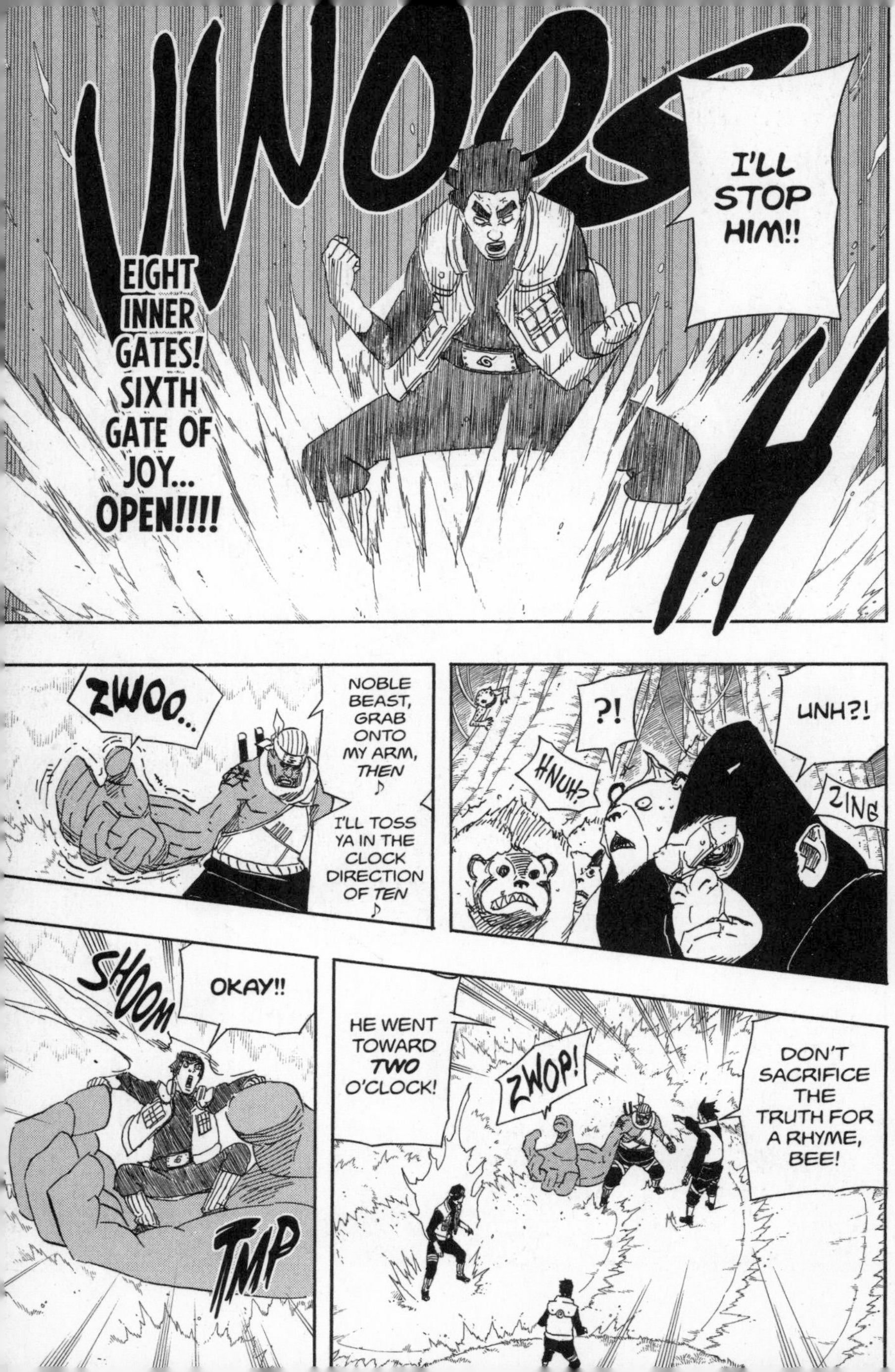
WOOSH
I'LL STOP HIM!!
EIGHT INNER GATES! SIXTH GATE OF JOY... OPEN!!!!
UNH?!
?!
ZING
HNUH?
NOBLE BEAST, GRAB ONTO MY ARM, THEN ♪
ZWOO...
I'LL TOSS YA IN THE CLOCK DIRECTION OF TEN ♪
HE WENT TOWARD TWO O'CLOCK!
DON'T SACRIFICE THE TRUTH FOR A RHYME, BEE!
ZWOP!
OKAY!!
SHOOM
TMP

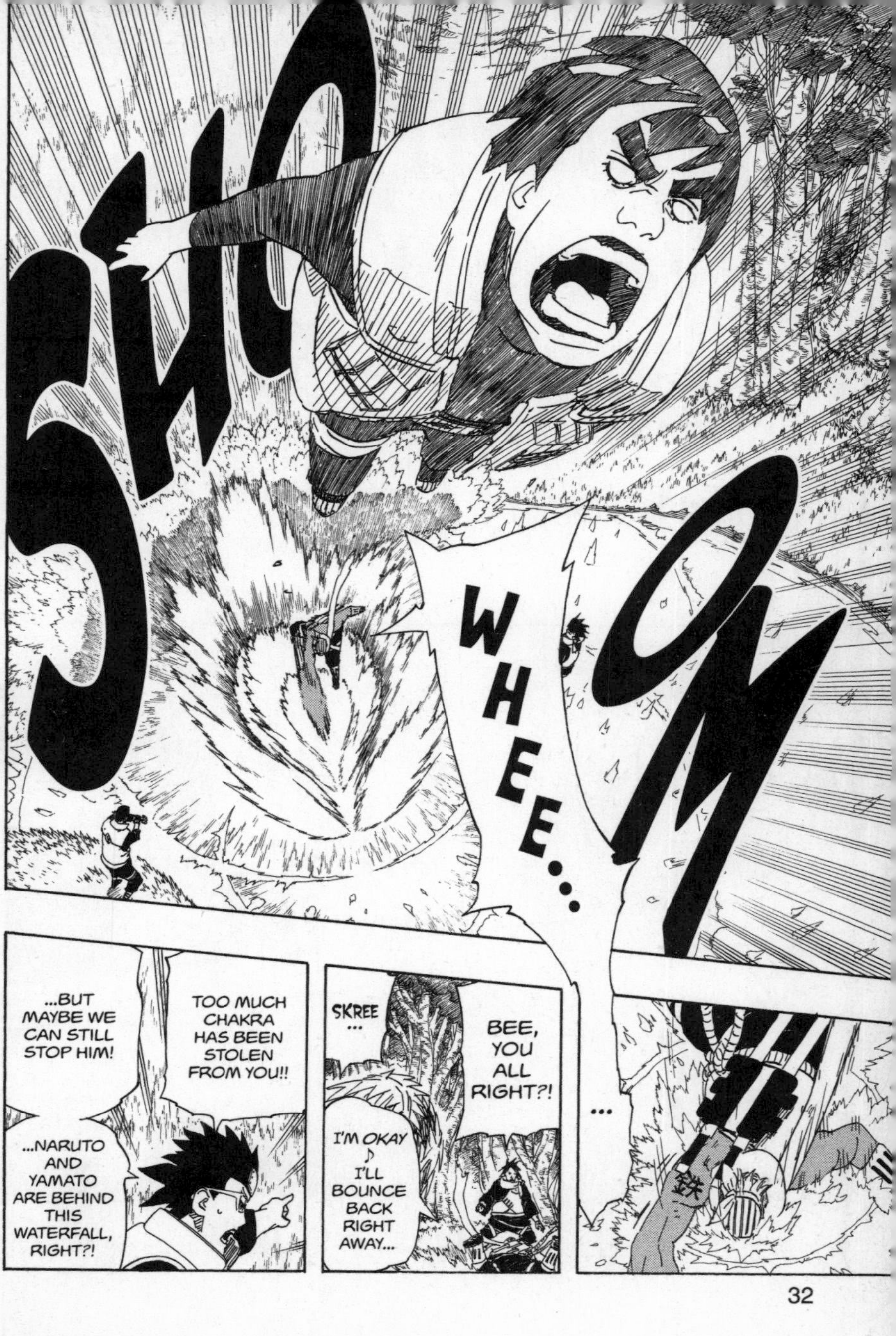
SHOOM
WHEE...
...
BEE, YOU ALL RIGHT?!
SKREE ...
I'M OKAY ♪ I'LL BOUNCE BACK RIGHT AWAY...
TOO MUCH CHAKRA HAS BEEN STOLEN FROM YOU!!
...BUT MAYBE WE CAN STILL STOP HIM!
...NARUTO AND YAMATO ARE BEHIND THIS WATERFALL, RIGHT?!

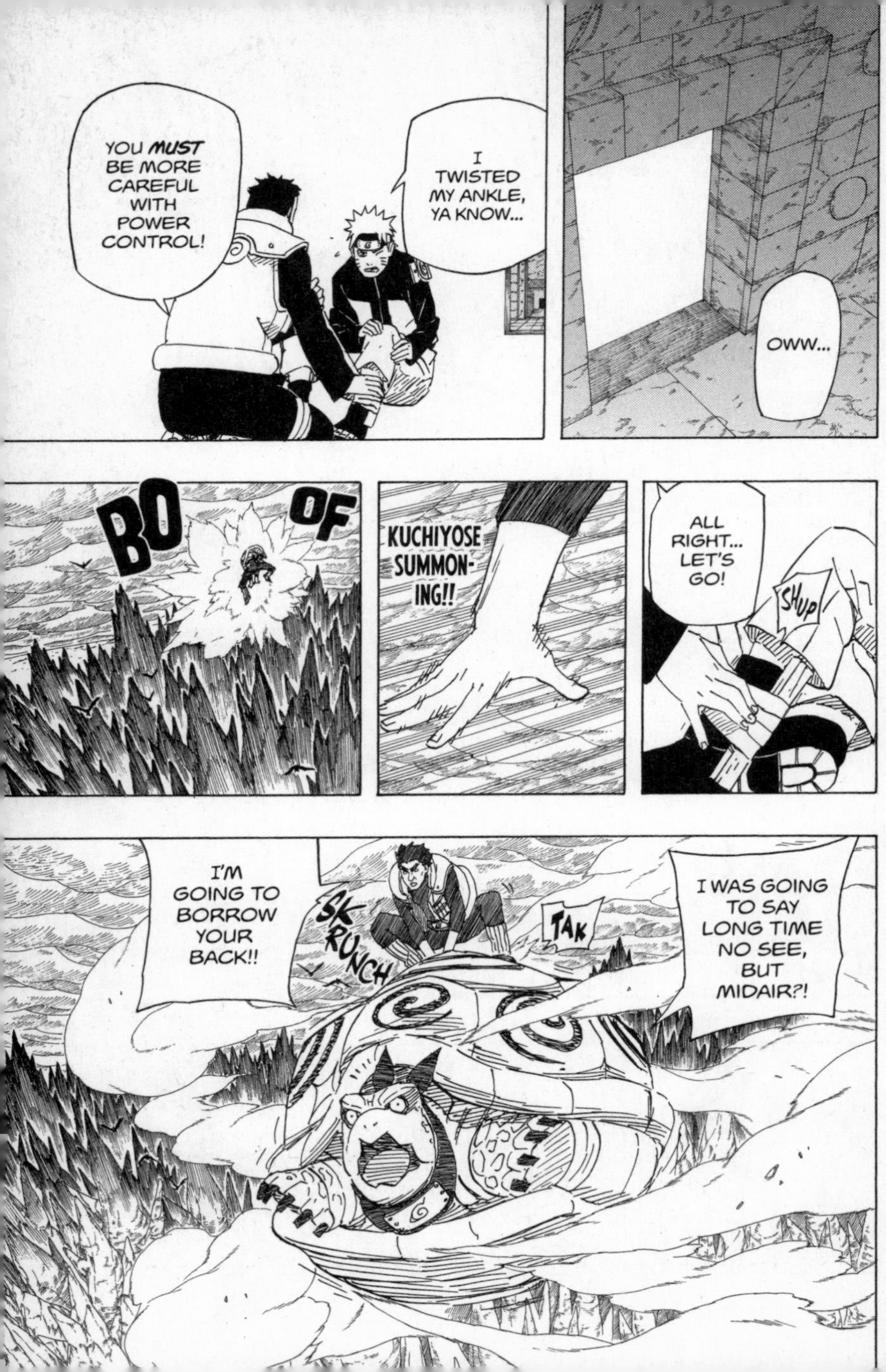
OWW...
I TWISTED MY ANKLE, YA KNOW...
YOU MUST BE MORE CAREFUL WITH POWER CONTROL!
ALL RIGHT... LET'S GO!
SHUP
KUCHIYOSE SUMMONING!!
BO OF
I WAS GOING TO SAY LONG TIME NO SEE, BUT MIDAIR?!
TAK
I'M GOING TO BORROW YOUR BACK!!
SKRUNCH

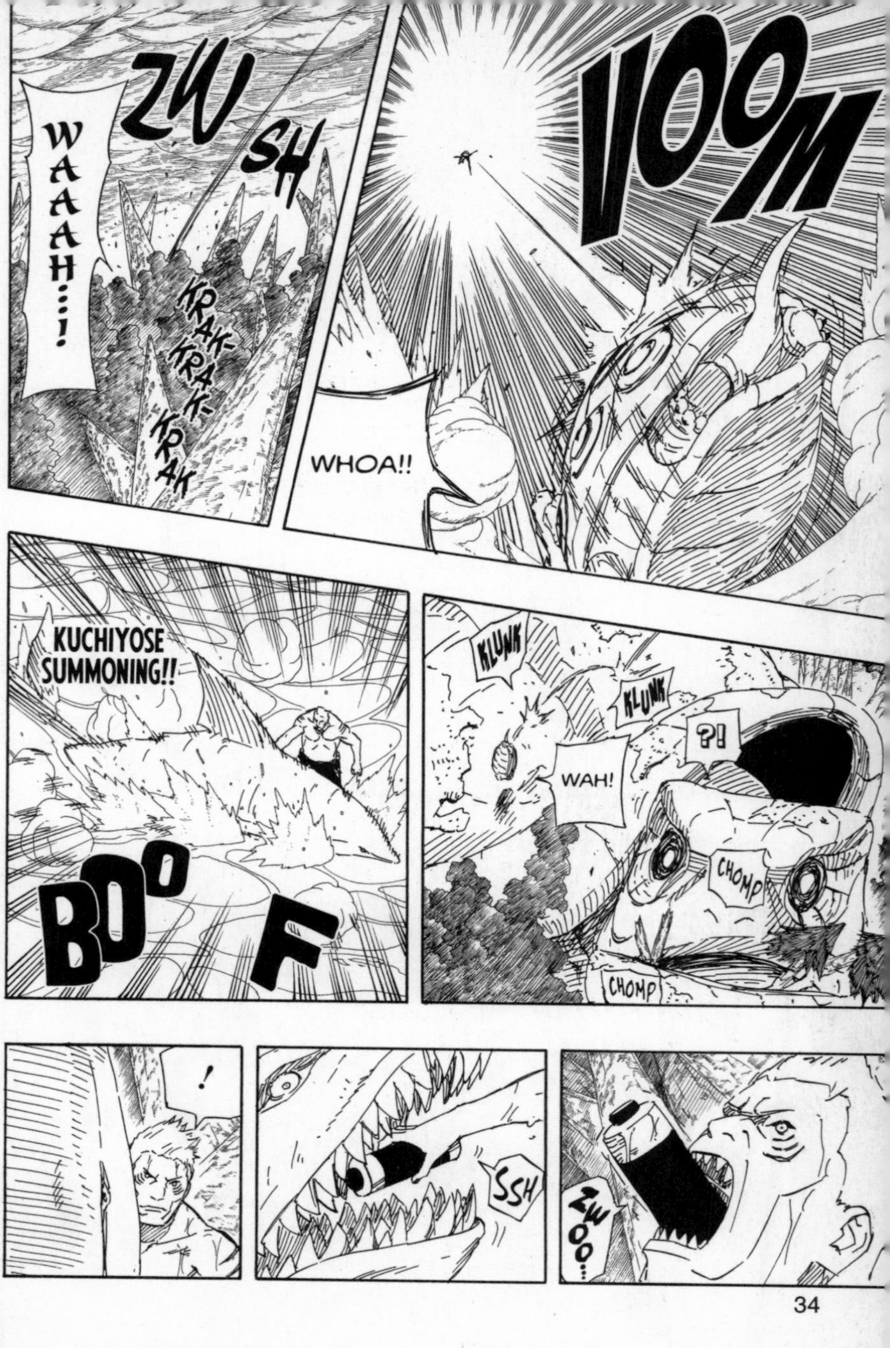
VOOM
WHOA!!
ZWSH
WAAAAH...!
KRAK-KRAK-KRAK
KLUNK
KLUNK
?!
WAH!
CHOMP
CHOMP
KUCHIYOSE SUMMONING!!
BOOF
ZWOO...
SSH
!

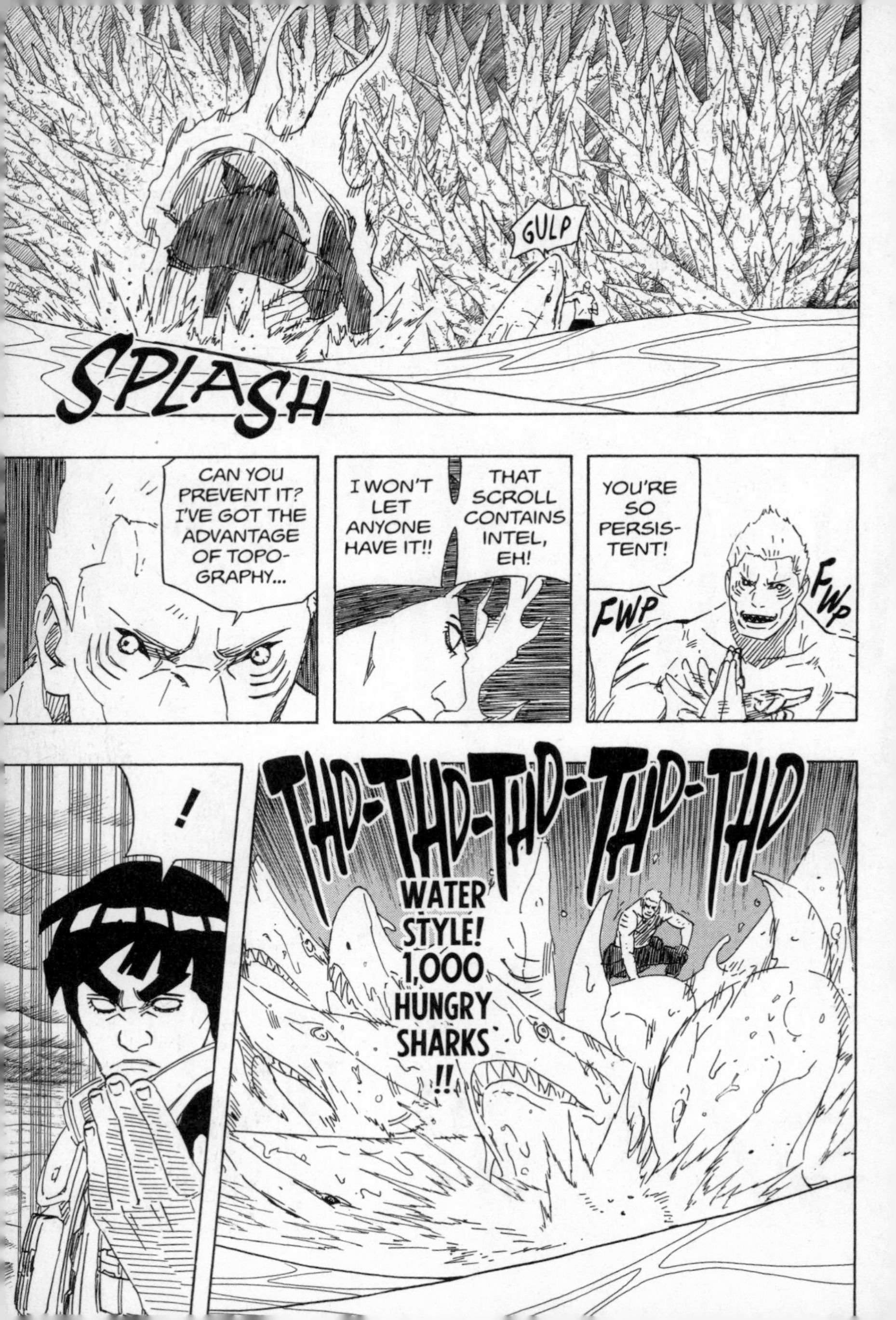
GULP
SPLASH
YOU'RE SO PERSIS-TENT!
FWP
FWP
THAT SCROLL CONTAINS INTEL, EH!
I WON'T LET ANYONE HAVE IT!!
CAN YOU PREVENT IT? I'VE GOT THE ADVANTAGE OF TOPO-GRAPHY...
THD-THD-THD-THD-THD
WATER STYLE! 1,000 HUNGRY SHARKS!!
!

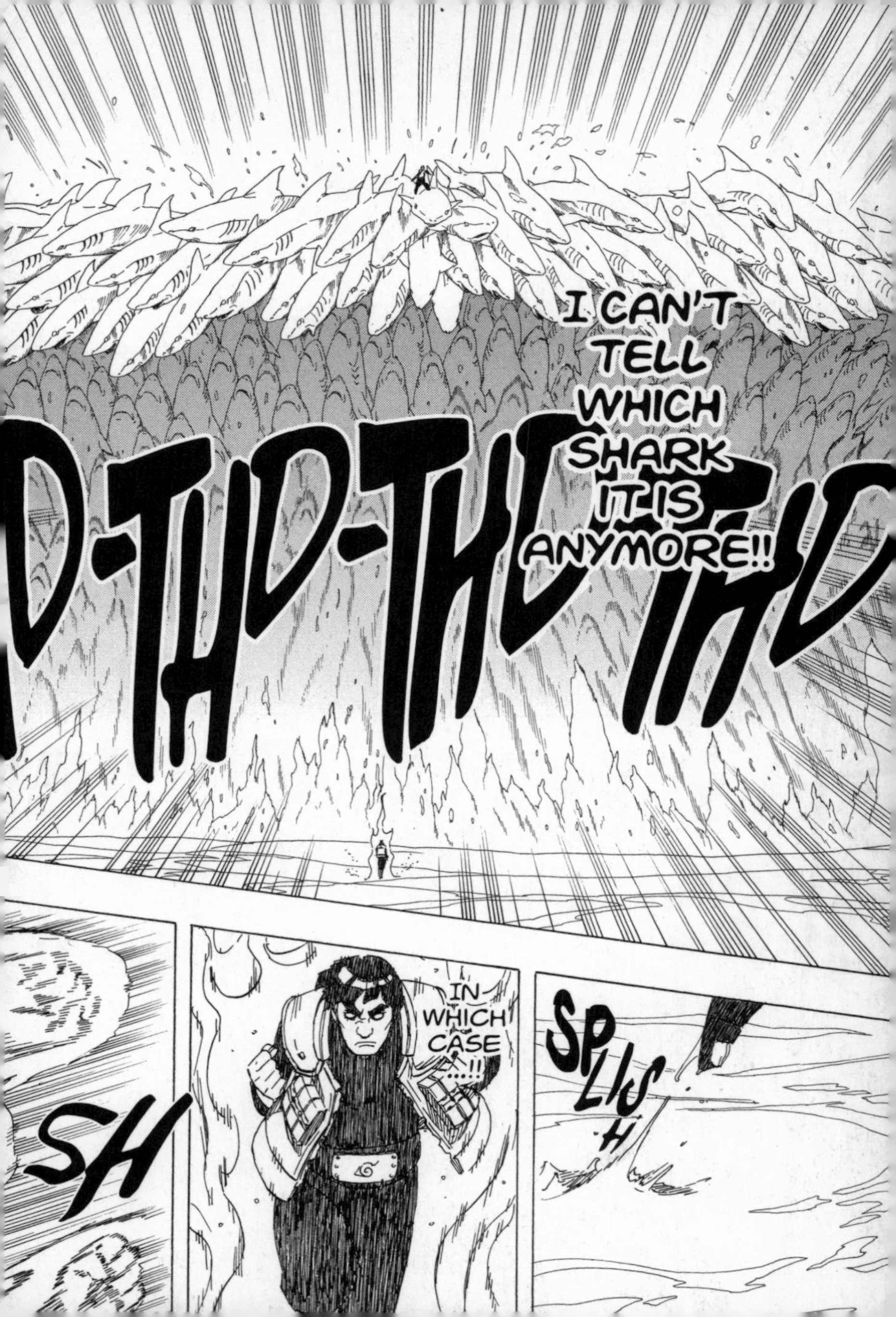
I CAN'T TELL WHICH SHARK IT IS ANYMORE!!
D-THD-THD-THD
SPLISH
IN WHICH CASE...!!
SH

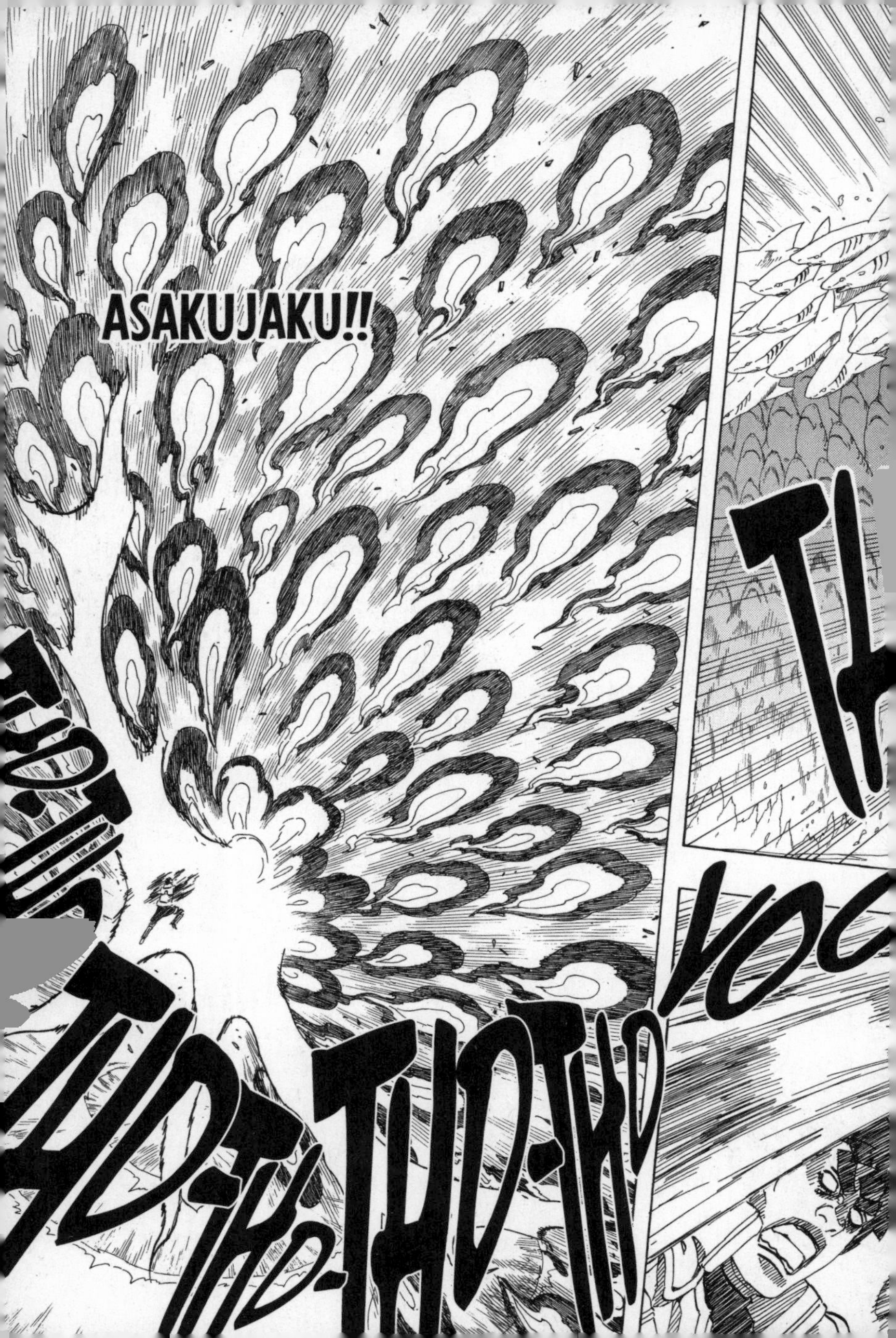
ASAKUJAKU!!
THD-THD-THD-THD

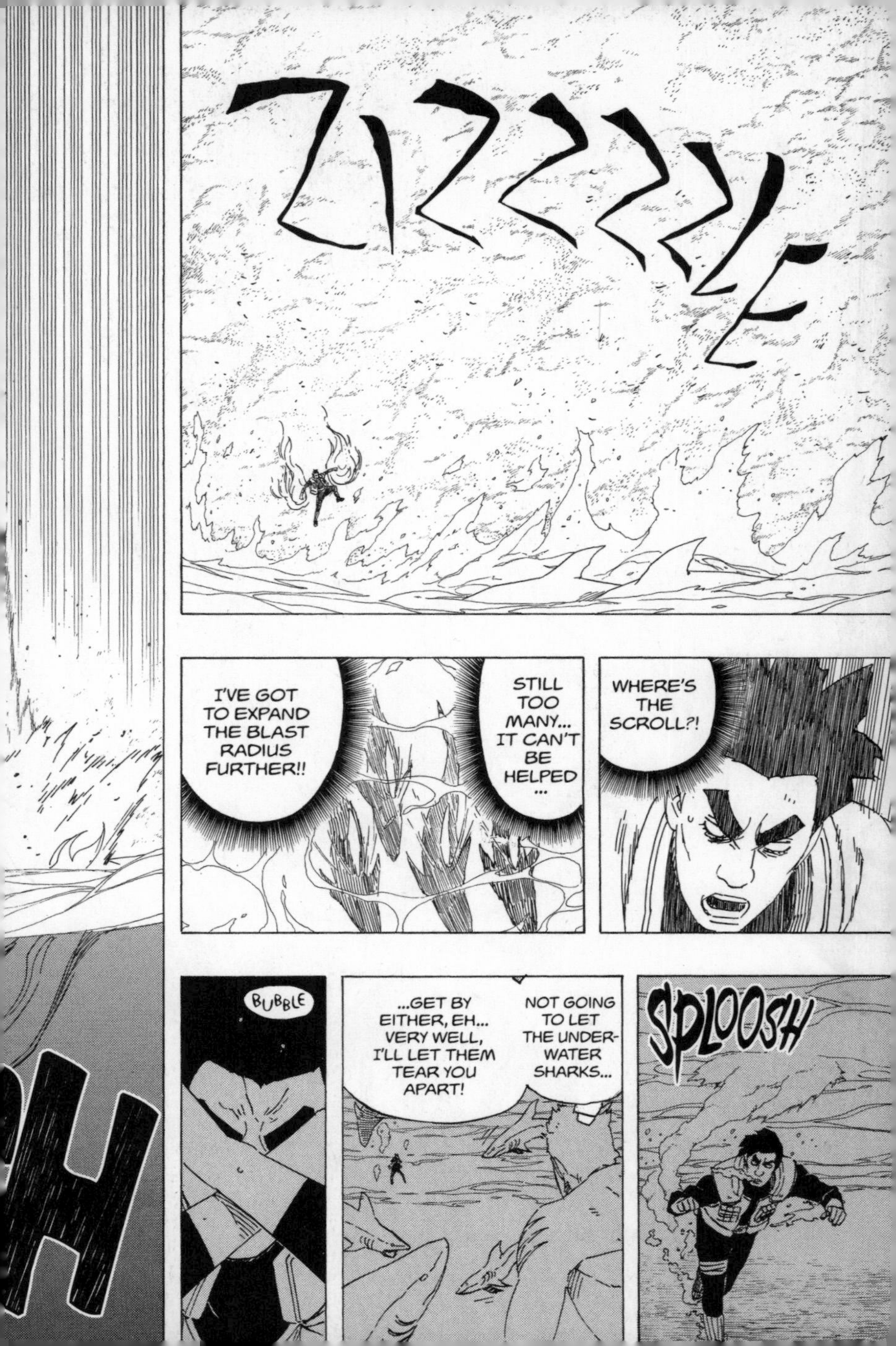
ZIZZZZLE
WHERE'S THE SCROLL?!
STILL TOO MANY... IT CAN'T BE HELPED...
I'VE GOT TO EXPAND THE BLAST RADIUS FURTHER!!
SPLOOSH
NOT GOING TO LET THE UNDER-WATER SHARKS...
...GET BY EITHER, EH... VERY WELL, I'LL LET THEM TEAR YOU APART!
BUBBLE

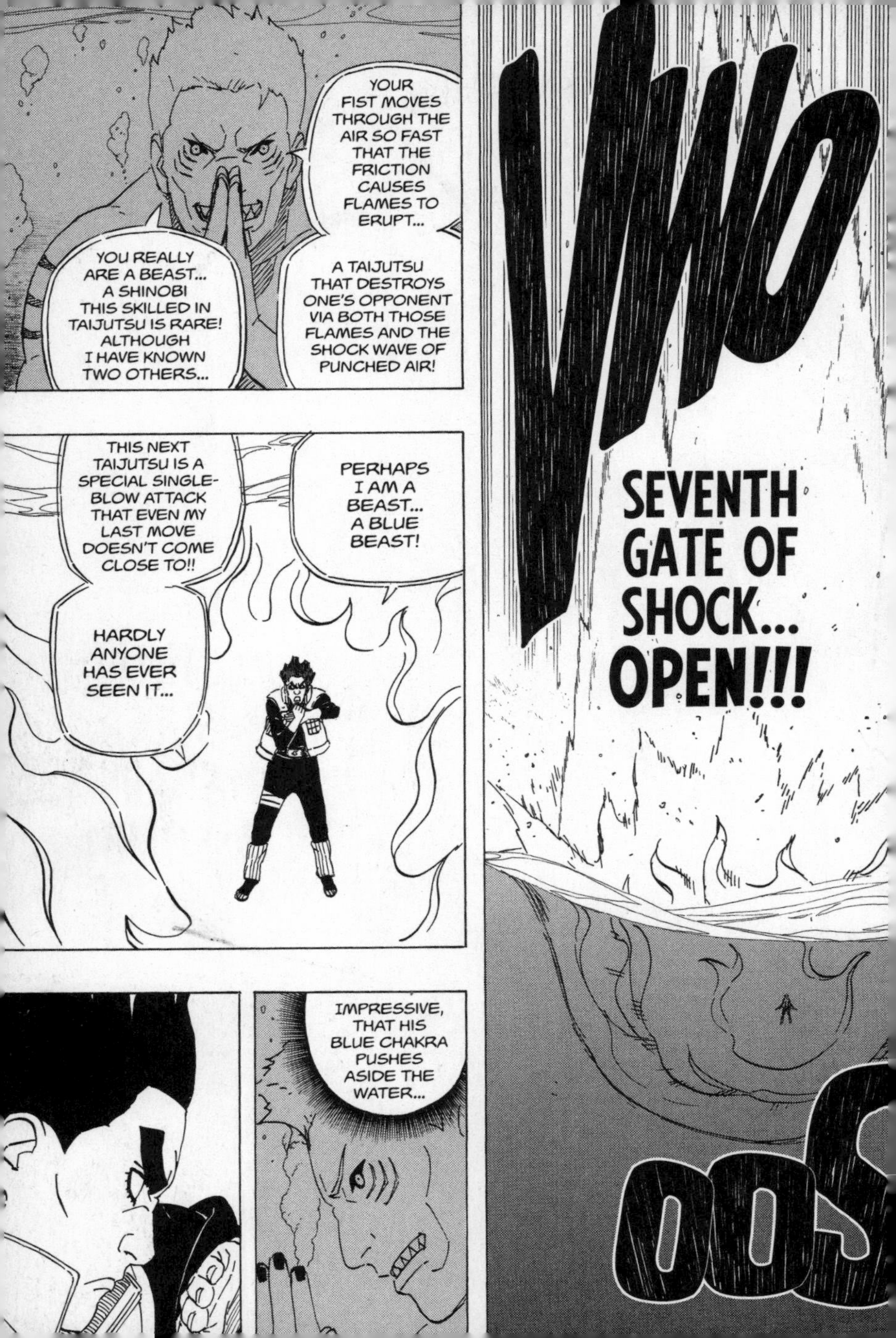
VWO
SEVENTH GATE OF SHOCK... OPEN!!!
YOUR FIST MOVES THROUGH THE AIR SO FAST THAT THE FRICTION CAUSES FLAMES TO ERUPT...
A TAIJUTSU THAT DESTROYS ONE'S OPPONENT VIA BOTH THOSE FLAMES AND THE SHOCK WAVE OF PUNCHED AIR!
YOU REALLY ARE A BEAST... A SHINOBI THIS SKILLED IN TAIJUTSU IS RARE! ALTHOUGH I HAVE KNOWN TWO OTHERS...
PERHAPS I AM A BEAST... A BLUE BEAST!
THIS NEXT TAIJUTSU IS A SPECIAL SINGLE-BLOW ATTACK THAT EVEN MY LAST MOVE DOESN'T COME CLOSE TO!!
HARDLY ANYONE HAS EVER SEEN IT...
IMPRESSIVE, THAT HIS BLUE CHAKRA PUSHES ASIDE THE WATER...

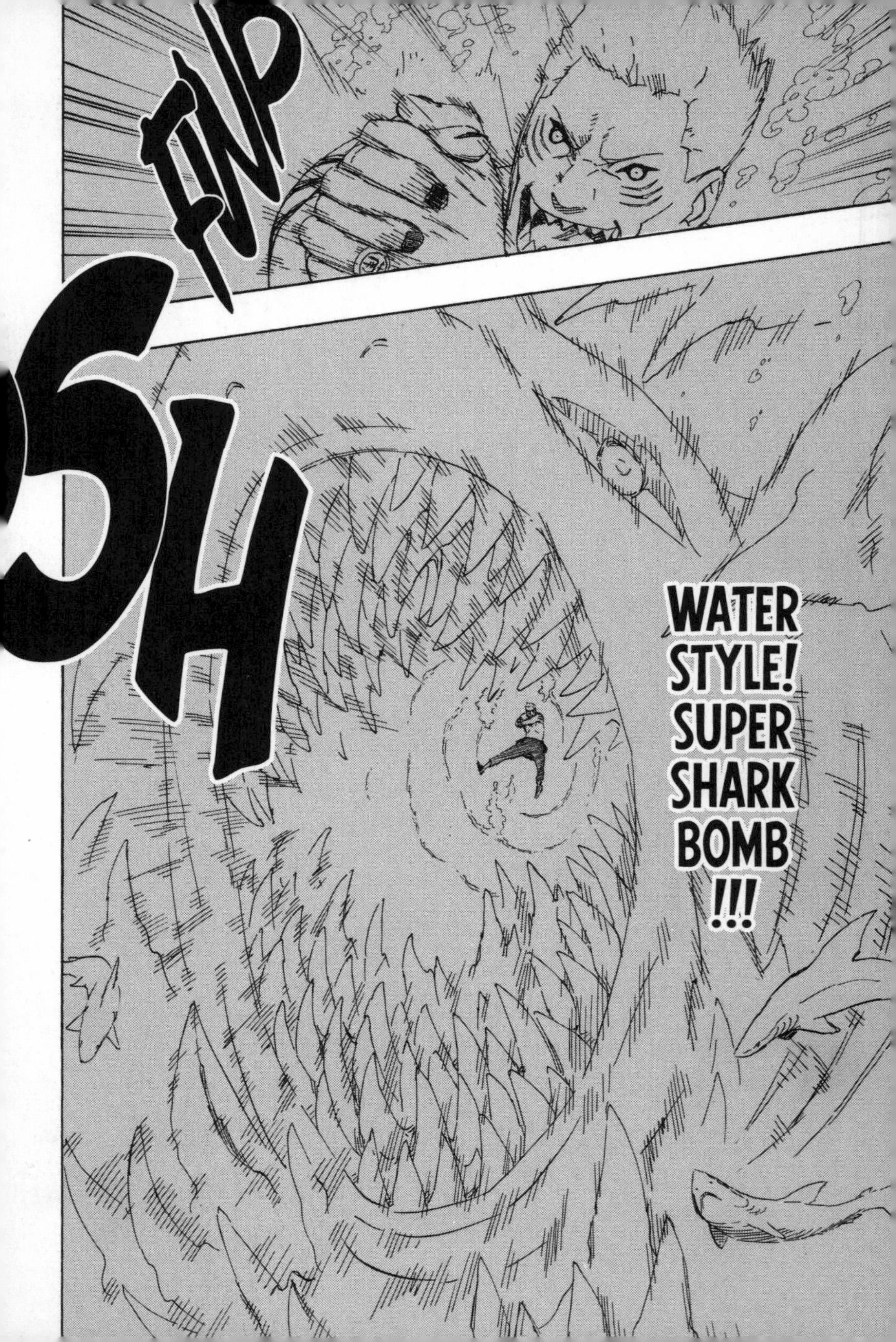
FWP
SH
WATER STYLE! SUPER SHARK BOMB !!!

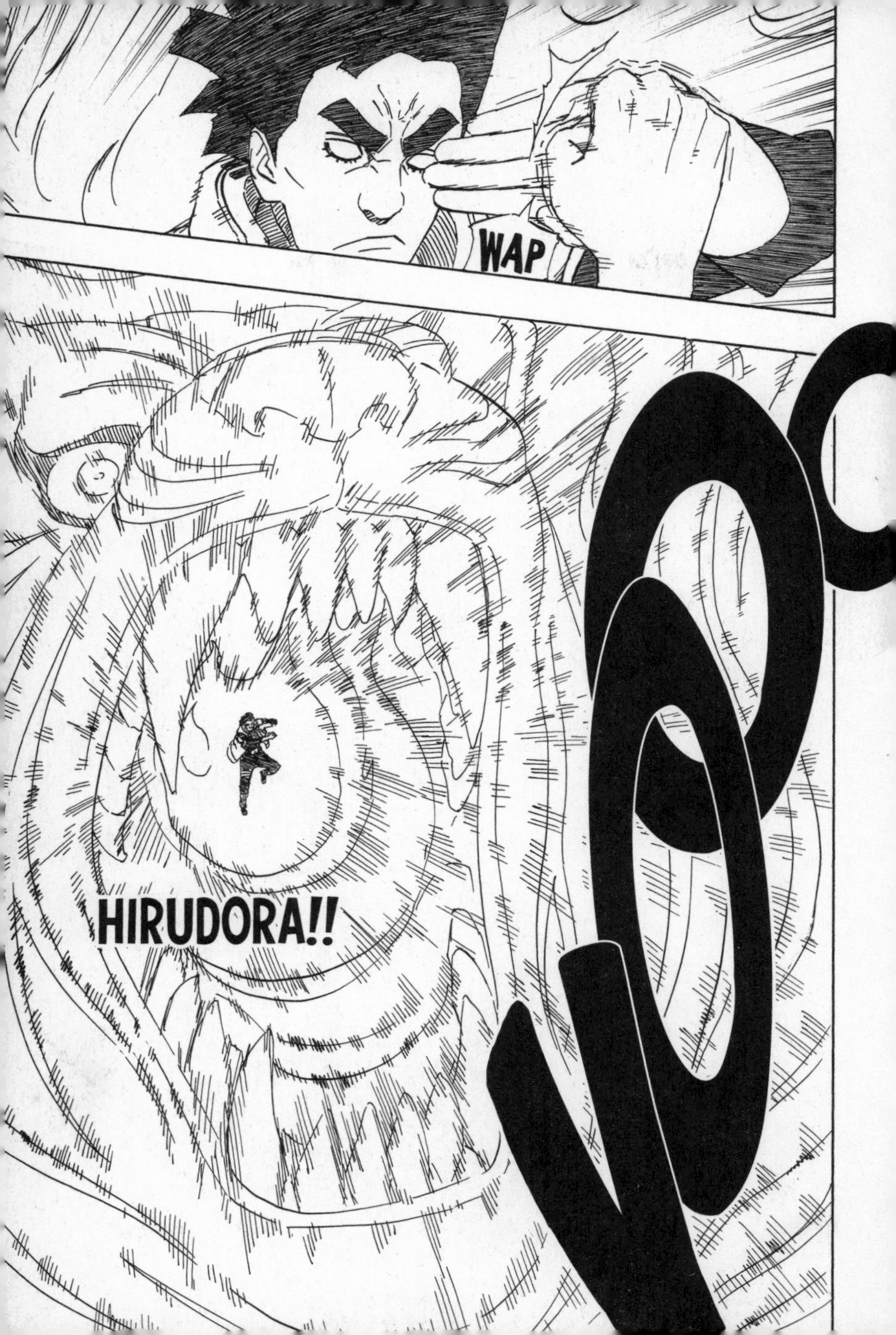
WAP
HIRUDORA!!

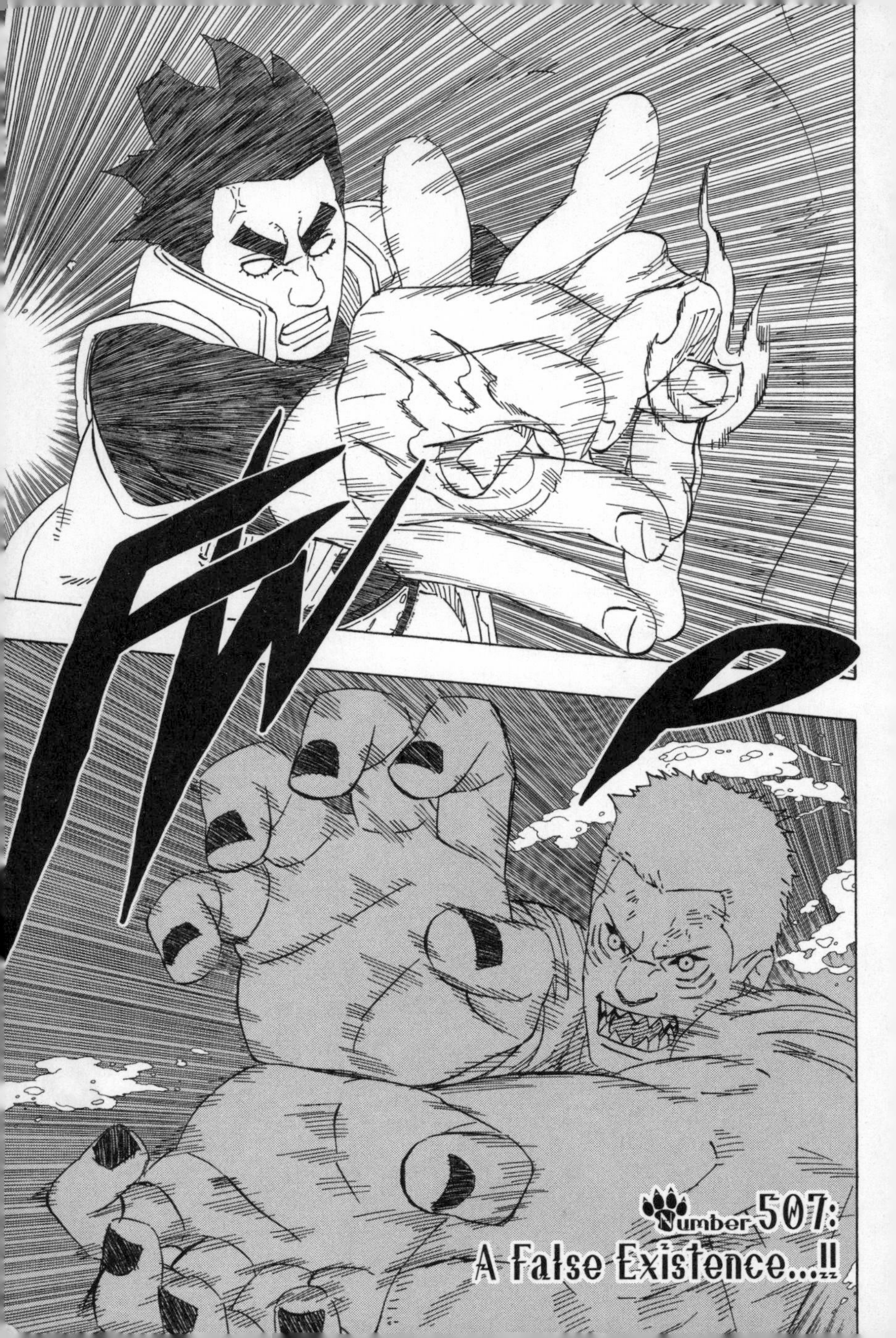
FWP
Number 507:
A False Existence...!!

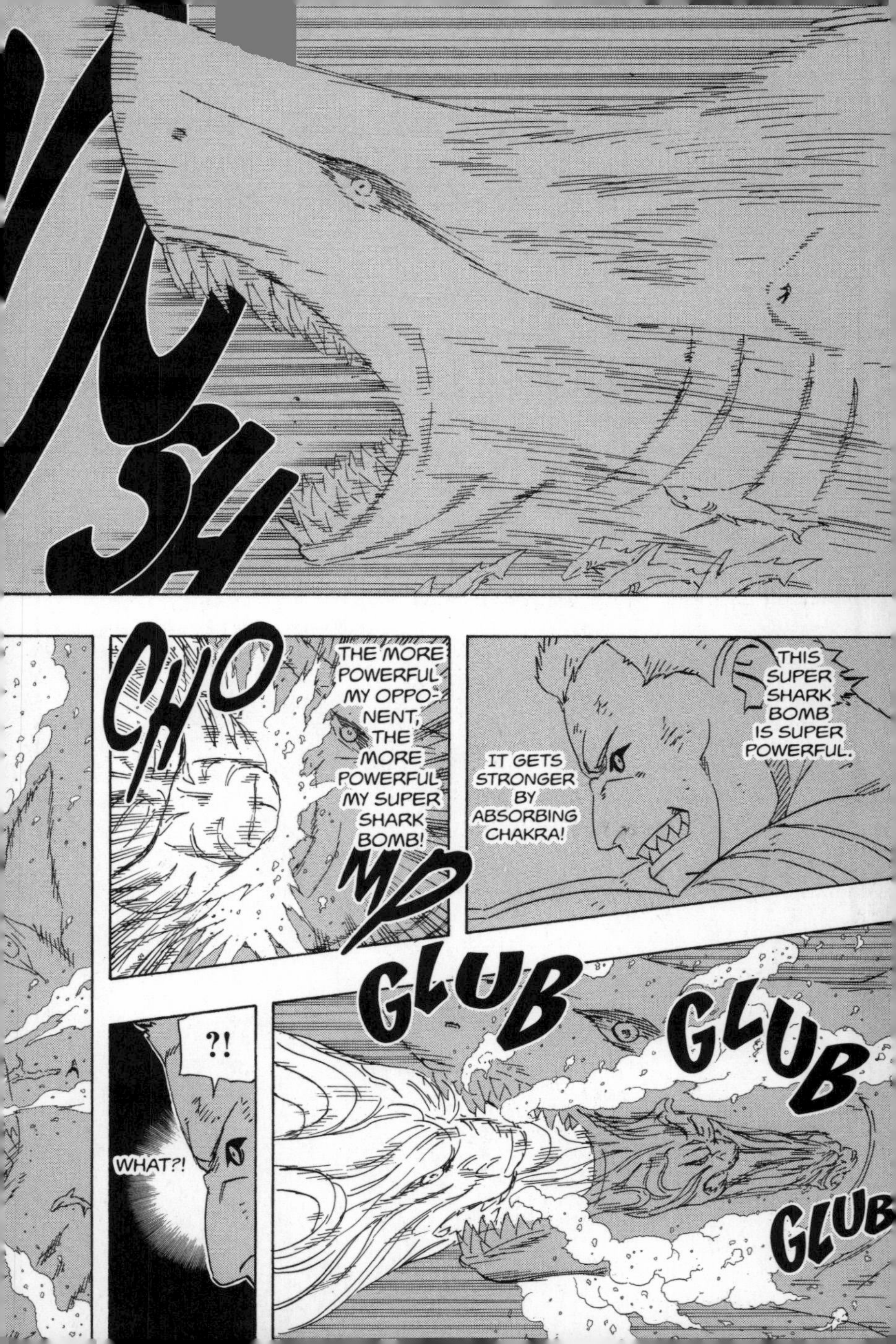
THIS SUPER SHARK BOMB IS SUPER POWERFUL.
IT GETS STRONGER BY ABSORBING CHAKRA!
CHOMP
THE MORE POWERFUL MY OPPONENT, THE MORE POWERFUL MY SUPER SHARK BOMB!
GLUB
GLUB
GLUB
?!
WHAT?!

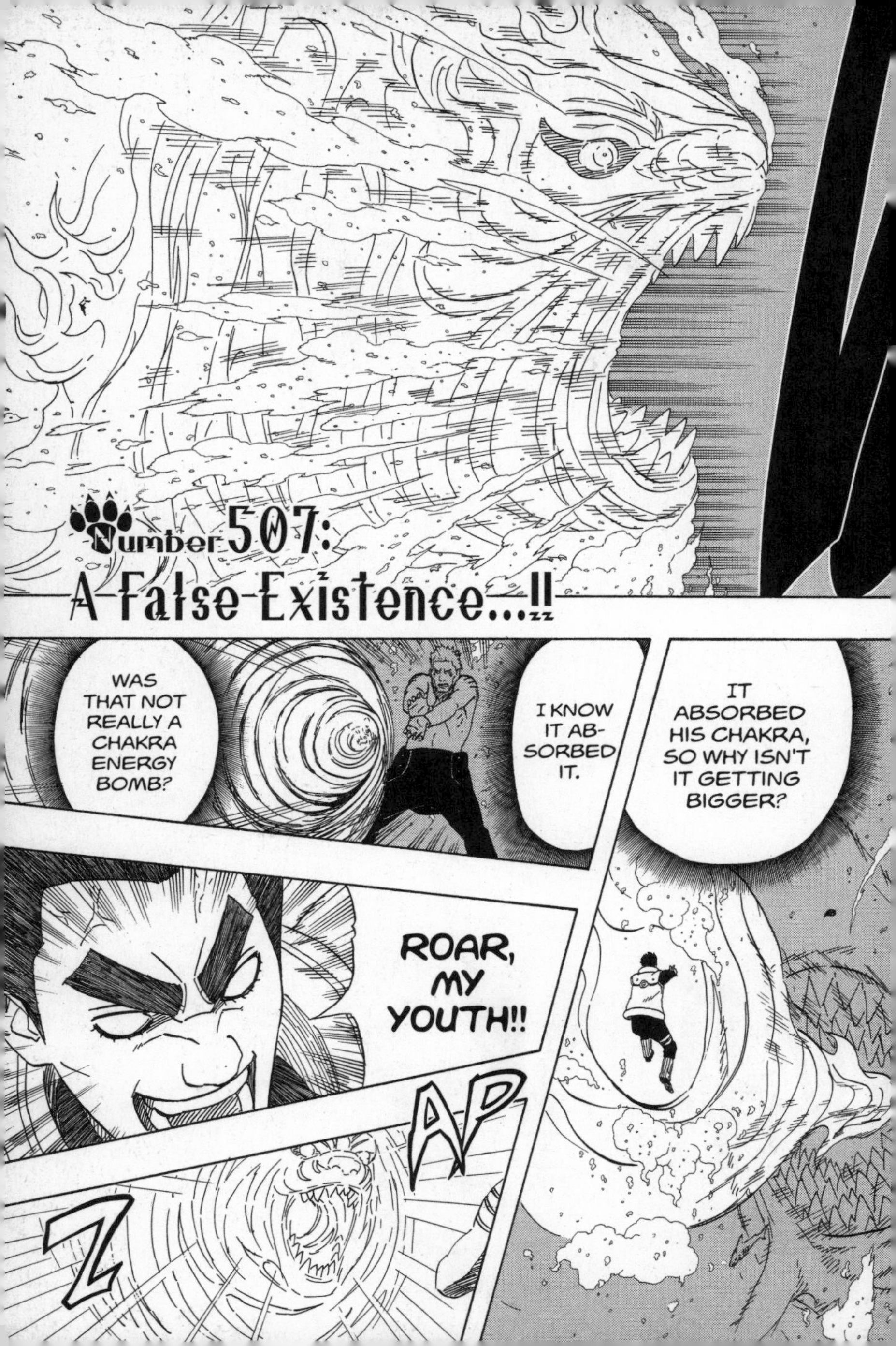
Number 507:
A False Existence...!!
IT ABSORBED HIS CHAKRA, SO WHY ISN'T IT GETTING BIGGER?
I KNOW IT ABSORBED IT.
WAS THAT NOT REALLY A CHAKRA ENERGY BOMB?
ROAR, MY YOUTH!!
ZAP

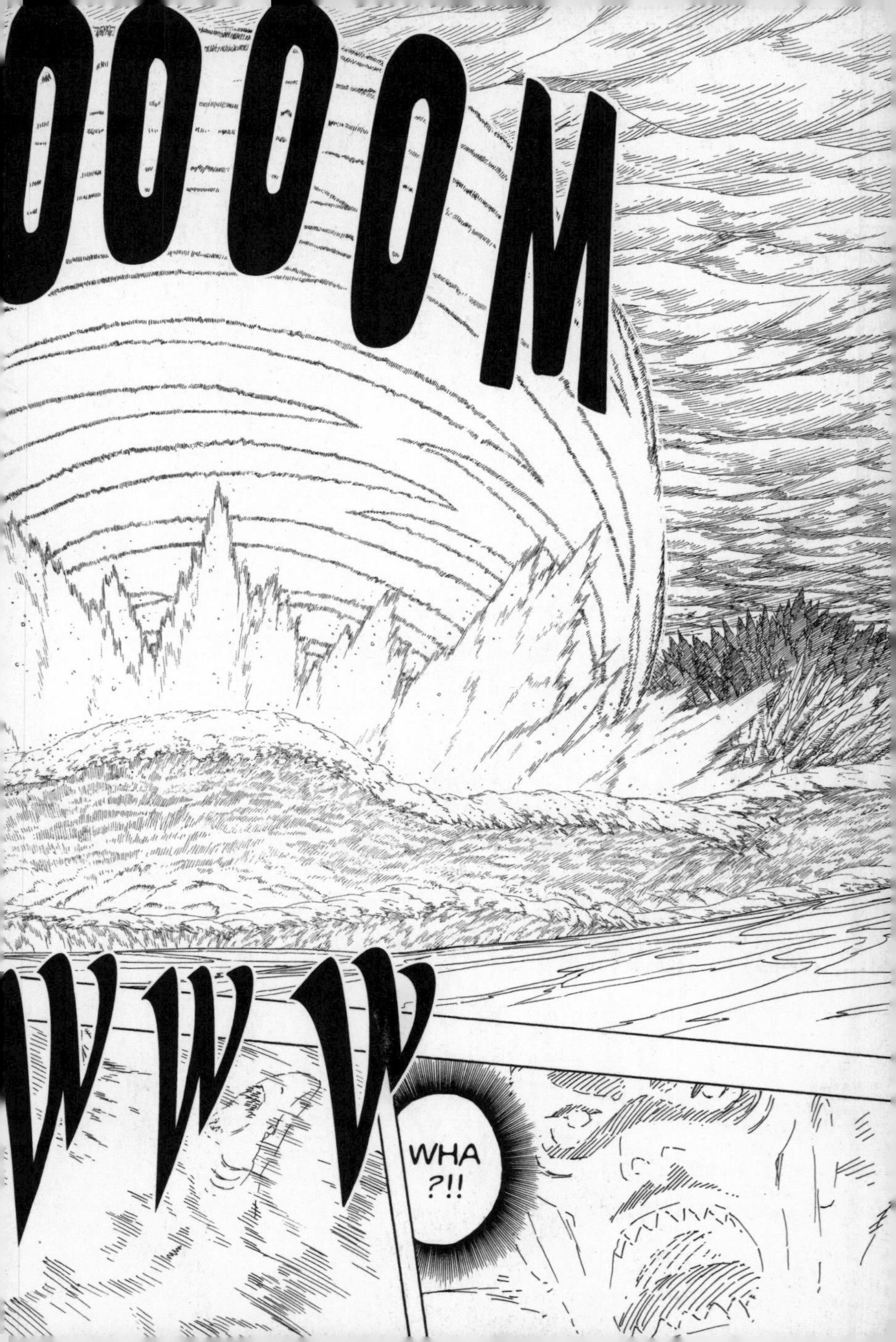
OOOOM
WWW
WHA ?!!

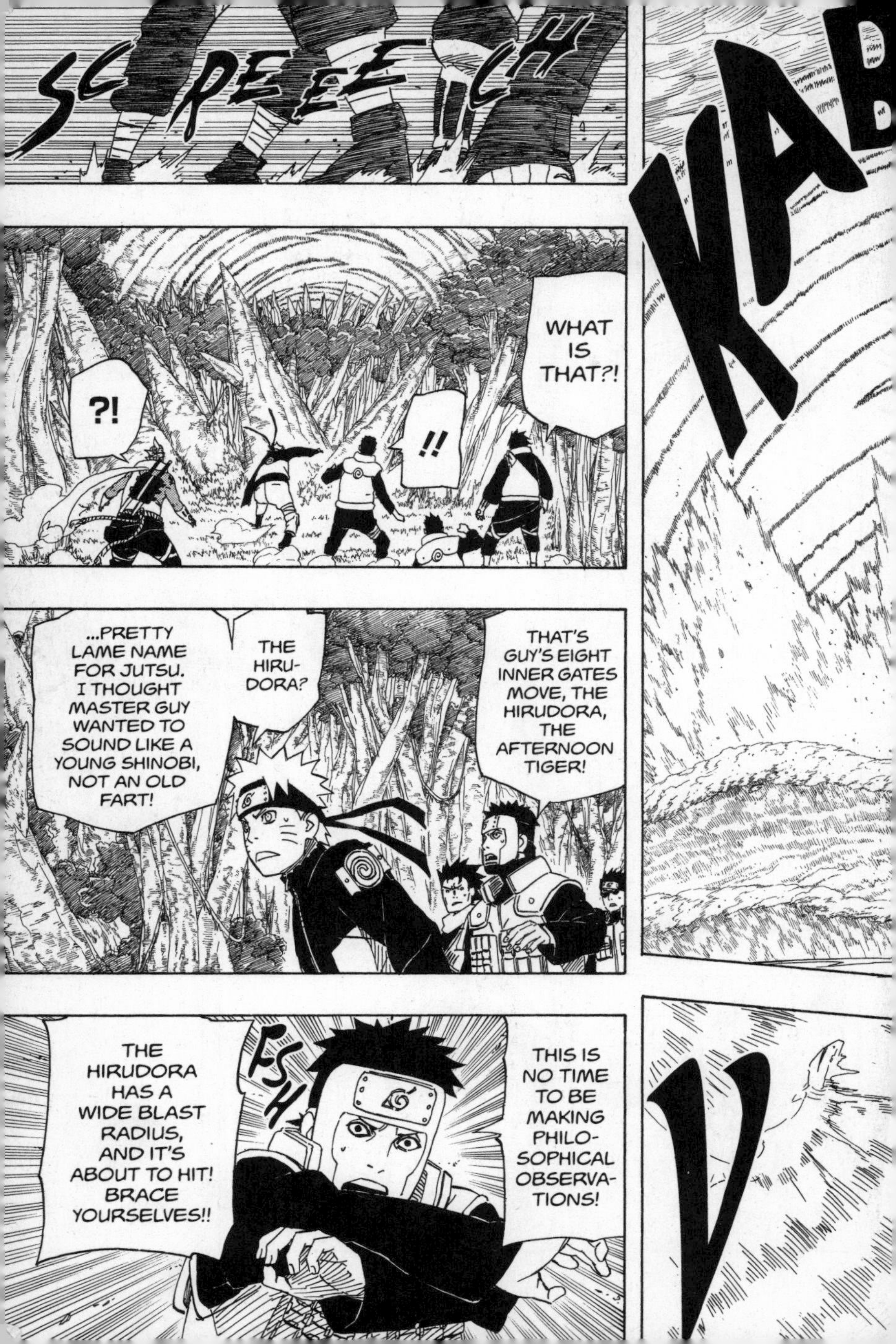
KAB
SCREEECH
WHAT IS THAT?!
!!
?!
THAT'S GUY'S EIGHT INNER GATES MOVE, THE HIRUDORA, THE AFTERNOON TIGER!
THE HIRUDORA?
...PRETTY LAME NAME FOR JUTSU. I THOUGHT MASTER GUY WANTED TO SOUND LIKE A YOUNG SHINOBI, NOT AN OLD FART!
V
THIS IS NO TIME TO BE MAKING PHILOSOPHICAL OBSERVATIONS!
FSH
THE HIRUDORA HAS A WIDE BLAST RADIUS, AND IT'S ABOUT TO HIT! BRACE YOURSELVES!!

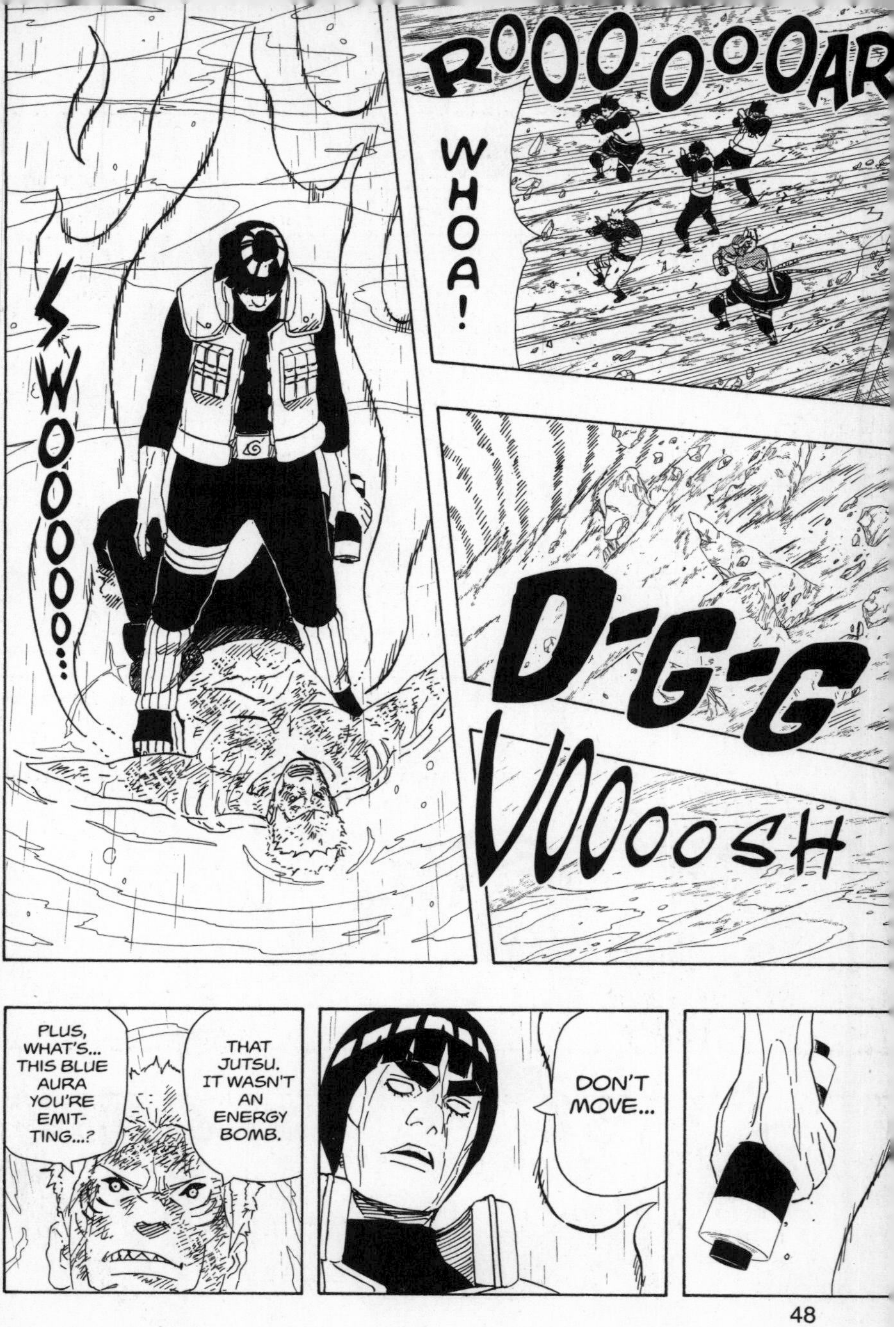
ROOOOOOAR
WHOA!
D-G-G
VOOOOSH
SWOOOOOO...
DON'T MOVE...
THAT JUTSU. IT WASN'T AN ENERGY BOMB.
PLUS, WHAT'S... THIS BLUE AURA YOU'RE EMIT-TING...?

READ THIS WAY

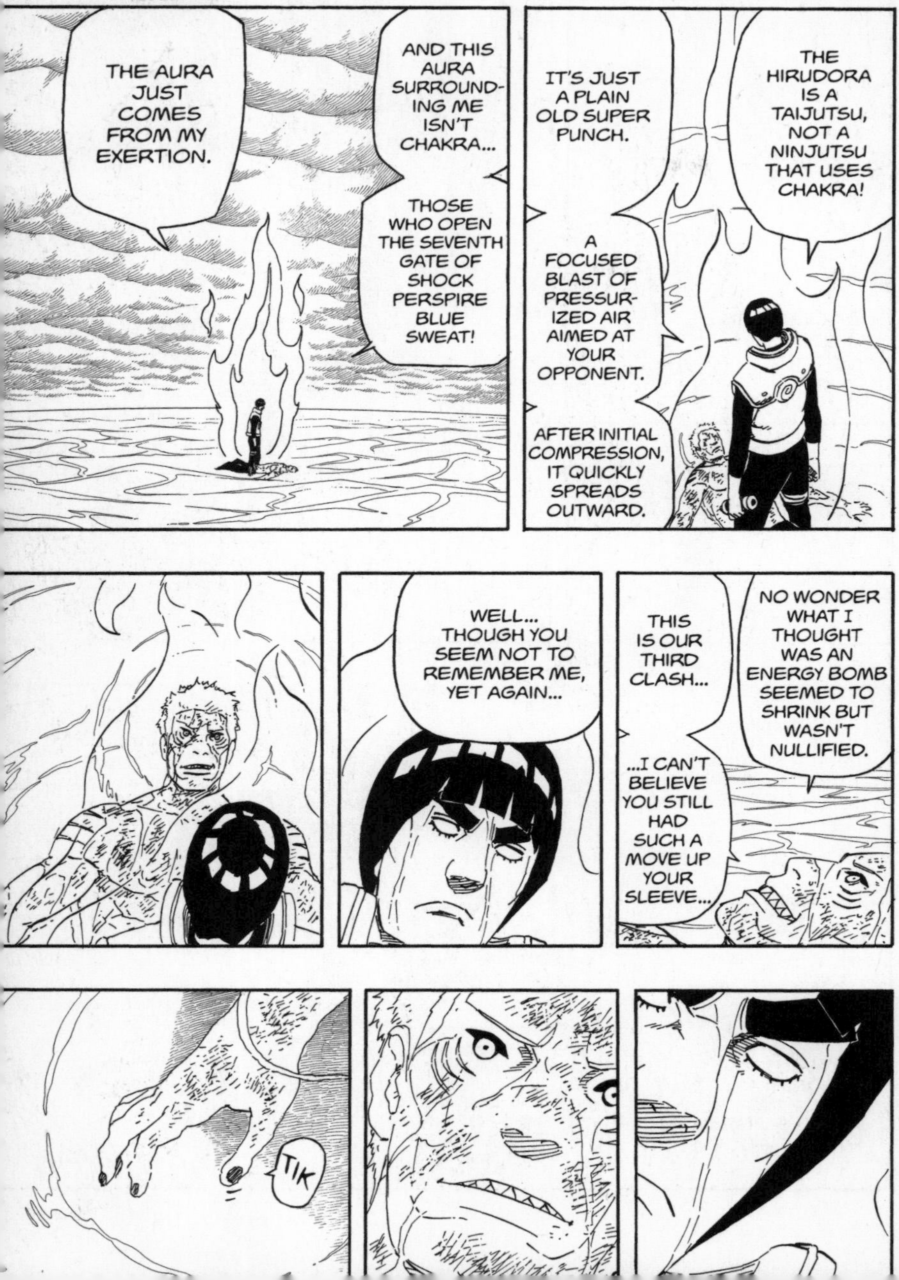
THE HIRUDORA IS A TAIJUTSU, NOT A NINJUTSU THAT USES CHAKRA!
IT'S JUST A PLAIN OLD SUPER PUNCH.
A FOCUSED BLAST OF PRESSURIZED AIR AIMED AT YOUR OPPONENT.
AFTER INITIAL COMPRESSION, IT QUICKLY SPREADS OUTWARD.
AND THIS AURA SURROUNDING ME ISN'T CHAKRA...
THOSE WHO OPEN THE SEVENTH GATE OF SHOCK PERSPIRE BLUE SWEAT!
THE AURA JUST COMES FROM MY EXERTION.
NO WONDER WHAT I THOUGHT WAS AN ENERGY BOMB SEEMED TO SHRINK BUT WASN'T NULLIFIED.
THIS IS OUR THIRD CLASH...
...I CAN'T BELIEVE YOU STILL HAD SUCH A MOVE UP YOUR SLEEVE...
WELL... THOUGH YOU SEEM NOT TO REMEMBER ME, YET AGAIN...
TIK

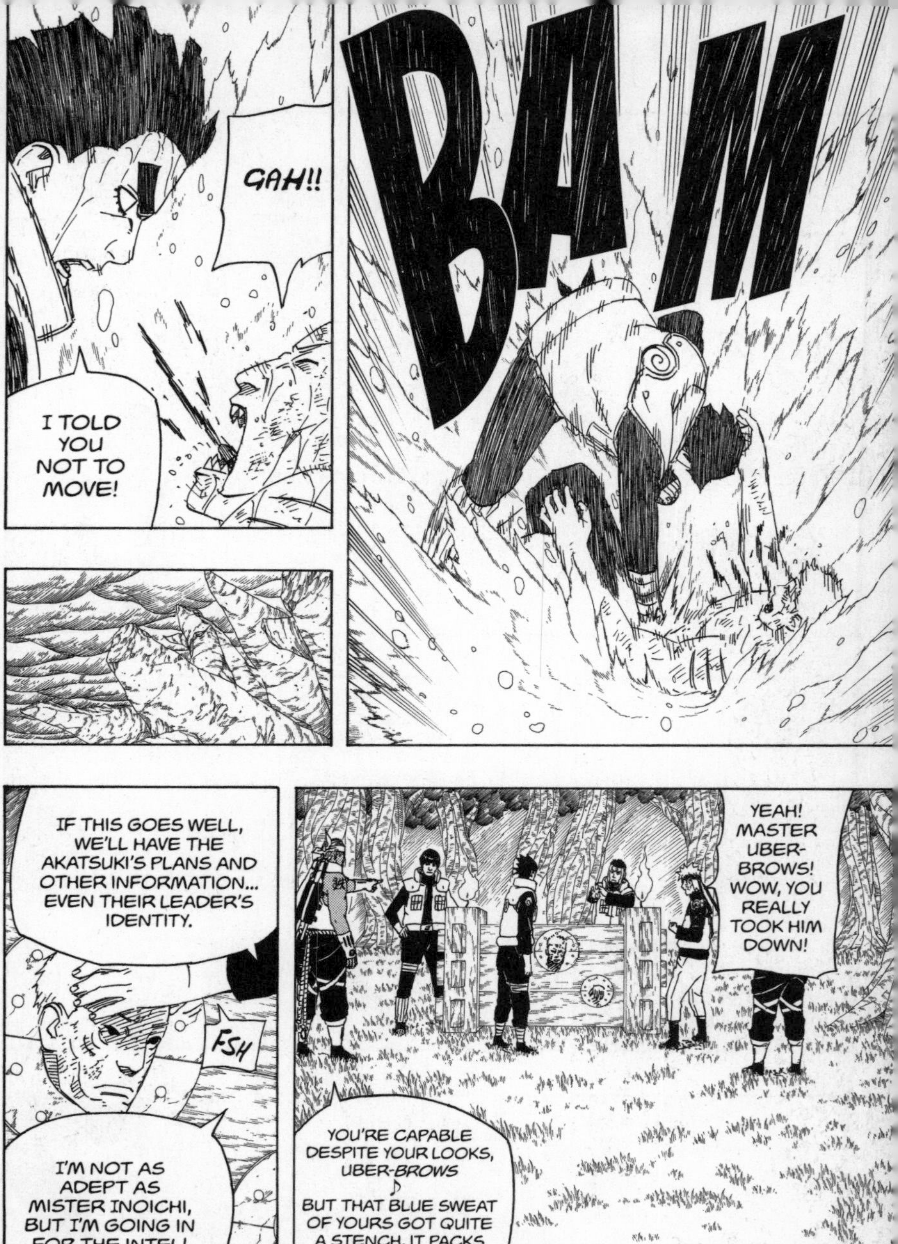
BAM
GAH!!
I TOLD YOU NOT TO MOVE!
YEAH! MASTER UBER-BROWS! WOW, YOU REALLY TOOK HIM DOWN!
YOU'RE CAPABLE DESPITE YOUR LOOKS, UBER-*BROWS* ♪ BUT THAT BLUE SWEAT OF YOURS GOT QUITE A STENCH, IT PACKS SOME *POWS* ♪
IF THIS GOES WELL, WE'LL HAVE THE AKATSUKI'S PLANS AND OTHER INFORMATION... EVEN THEIR LEADER'S IDENTITY.
FSH
I'M NOT AS ADEPT AS MISTER INOICHI, BUT I'M GOING IN FOR THE INTEL!

READ THIS WAY

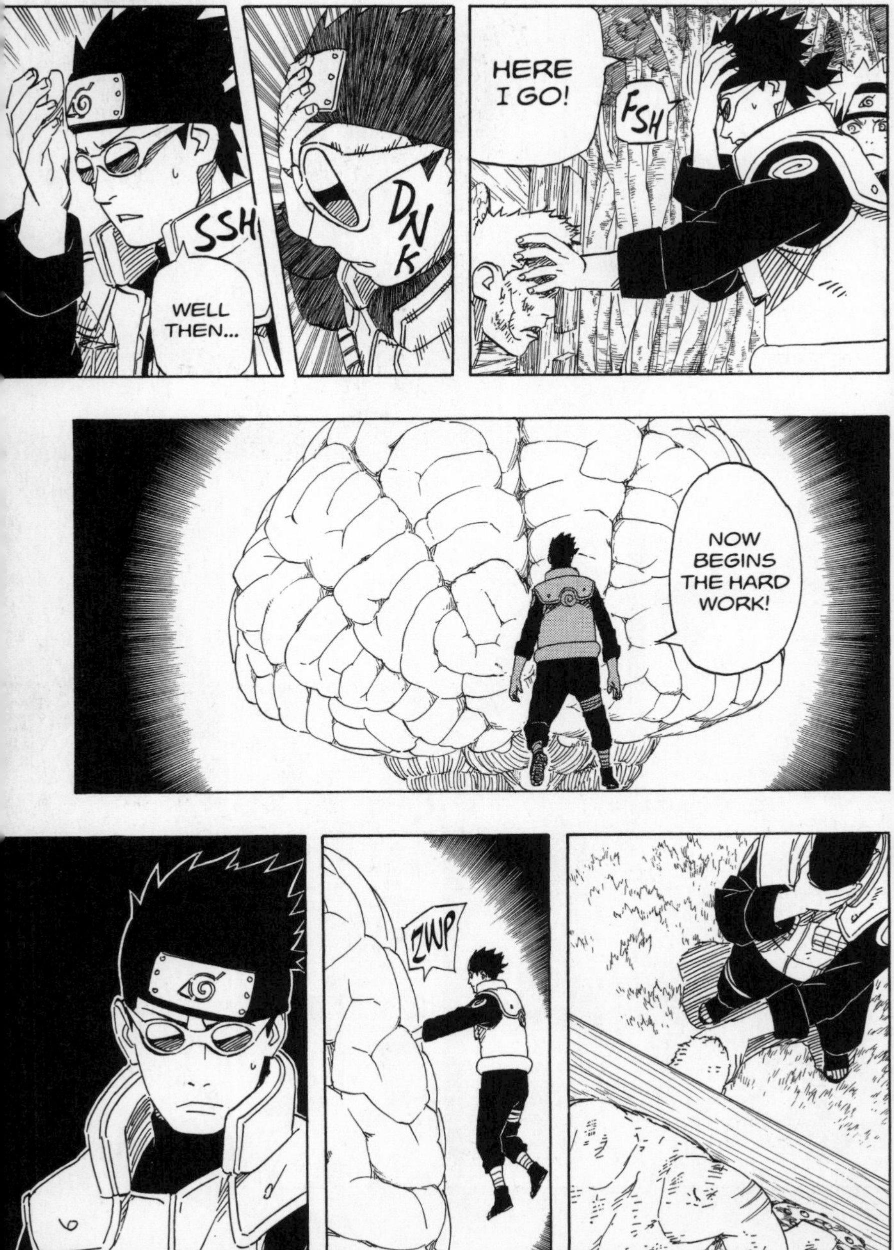
HERE I GO!
FSH
DNK
SSH
WELL THEN...
NOW BEGINS THE HARD WORK!
ZWP

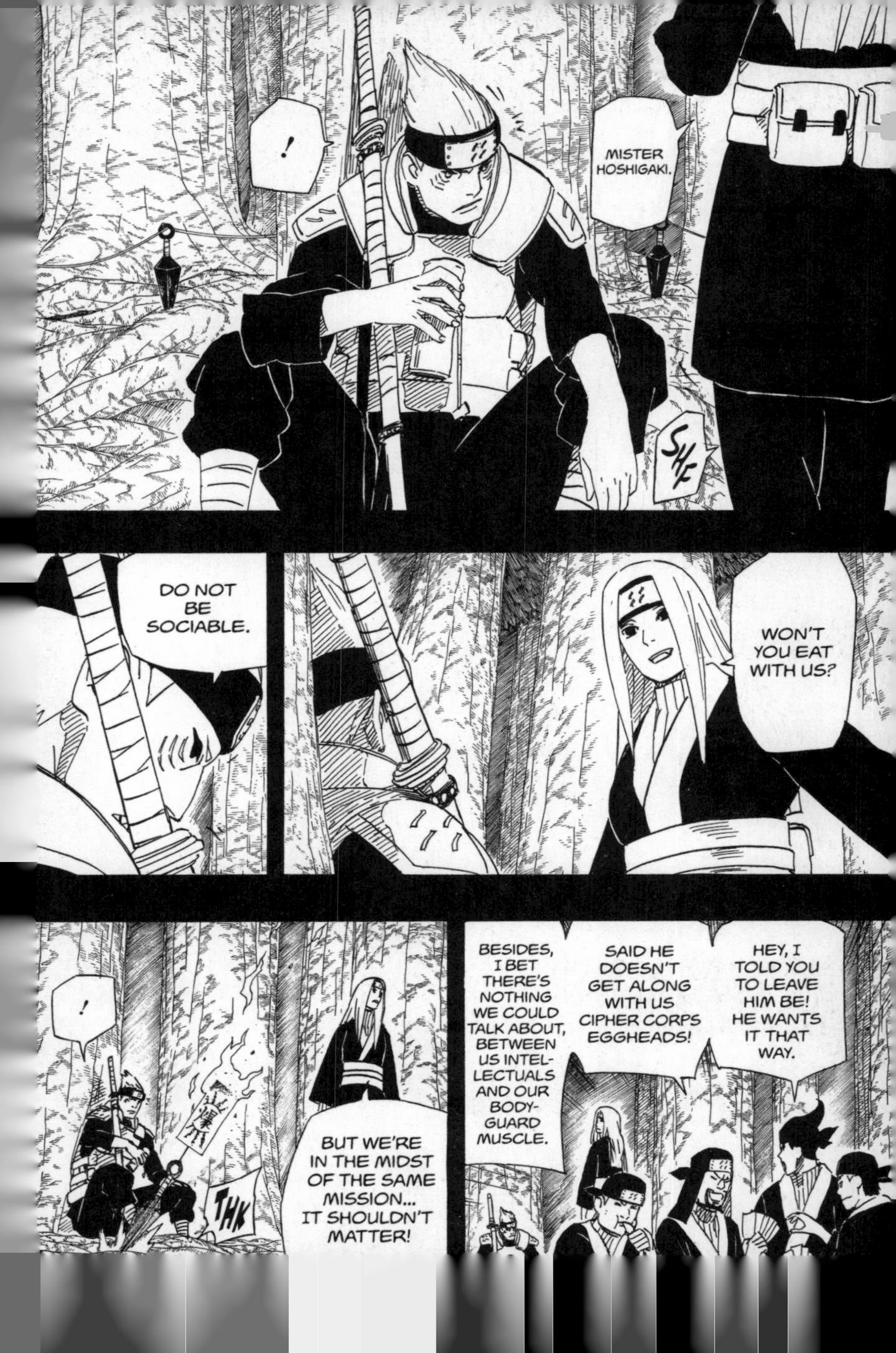
MISTER HOSHIGAKI.
SHF
!
WON'T YOU EAT WITH US?
DO NOT BE SOCIABLE.
HEY, I TOLD YOU TO LEAVE HIM BE! HE WANTS IT THAT WAY.
SAID HE DOESN'T GET ALONG WITH US CIPHER CORPS EGGHEADS!
BESIDES, I BET THERE'S NOTHING WE COULD TALK ABOUT, BETWEEN US INTELLECTUALS AND OUR BODYGUARD MUSCLE.
BUT WE'RE IN THE MIDST OF THE SAME MISSION... IT SHOULDN'T MATTER!
!
THK

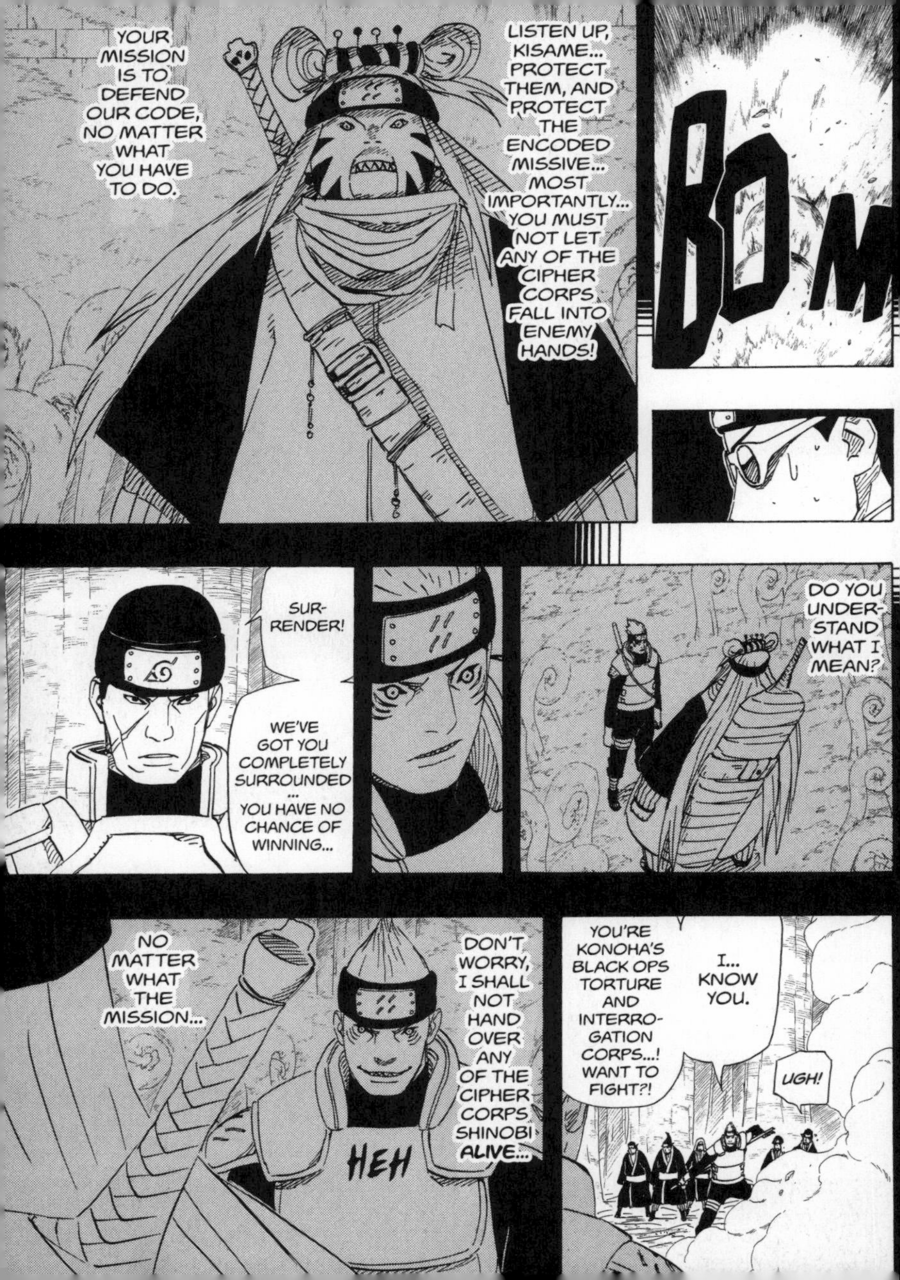
BOOM
LISTEN UP, KISAME... PROTECT THEM, AND PROTECT THE ENCODED MISSIVE... MOST IMPORTANTLY... YOU MUST NOT LET ANY OF THE CIPHER CORPS FALL INTO ENEMY HANDS!
YOUR MISSION IS TO DEFEND OUR CODE, NO MATTER WHAT YOU HAVE TO DO.
DO YOU UNDERSTAND WHAT I MEAN?
SUR-RENDER!
WE'VE GOT YOU COMPLETELY SURROUNDED... YOU HAVE NO CHANCE OF WINNING...
I... KNOW YOU.
YOU'RE KONOHA'S BLACK OPS TORTURE AND INTERROGATION CORPS...! WANT TO FIGHT?!
UGH!
DON'T WORRY, I SHALL NOT HAND OVER ANY OF THE CIPHER CORPS SHINOBI ALIVE...
HEH
NO MATTER WHAT THE MISSION...

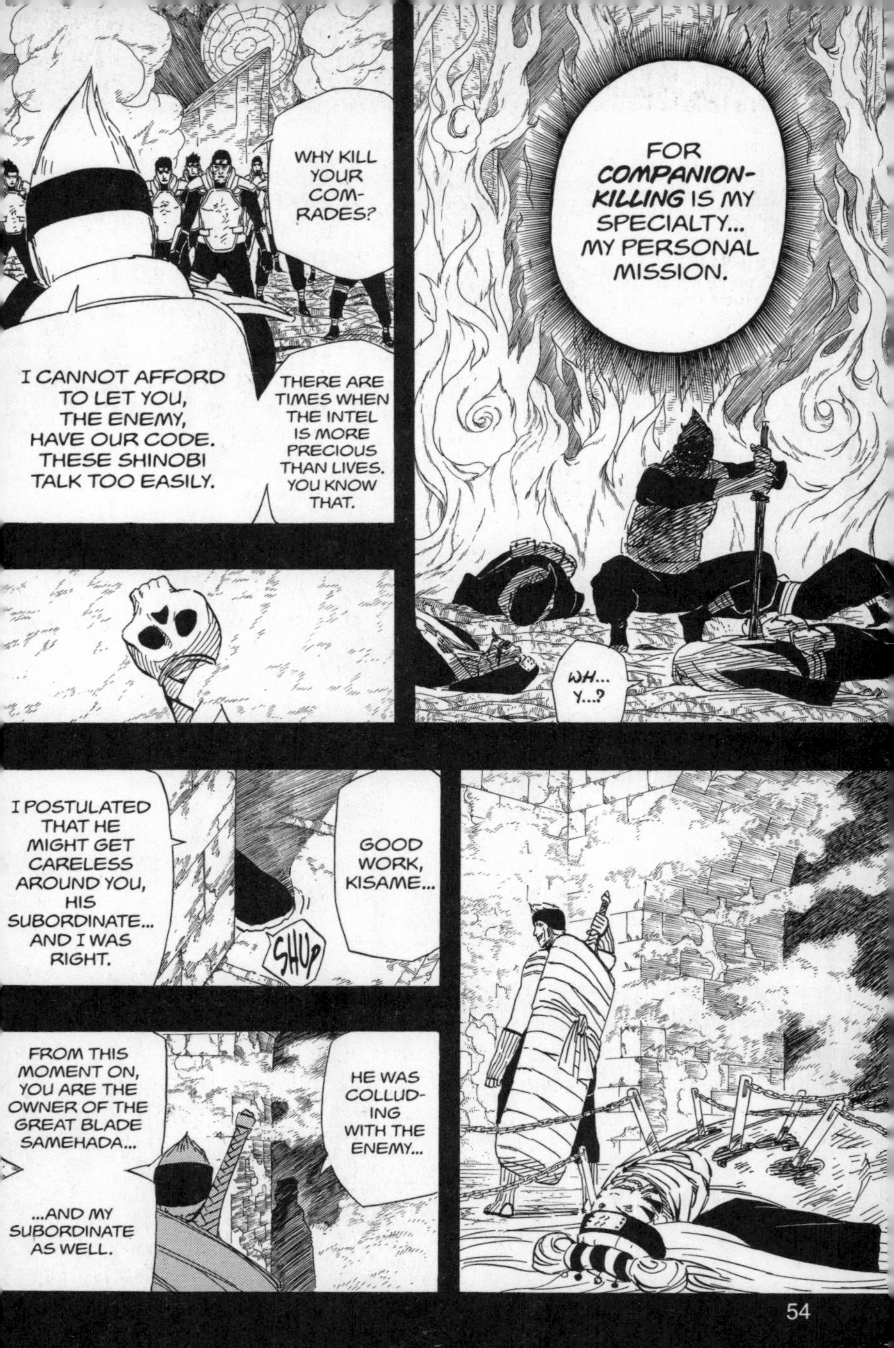

FOR COMPANION-KILLING IS MY SPECIALTY... MY PERSONAL MISSION.
WH... Y...?
WHY KILL YOUR COM-RADES?
THERE ARE TIMES WHEN THE INTEL IS MORE PRECIOUS THAN LIVES. YOU KNOW THAT.
I CANNOT AFFORD TO LET YOU, THE ENEMY, HAVE OUR CODE. THESE SHINOBI TALK TOO EASILY.
GOOD WORK, KISAME...
SHUP
I POSTULATED THAT HE MIGHT GET CARELESS AROUND YOU, HIS SUBORDINATE... AND I WAS RIGHT.
HE WAS COLLUD-ING WITH THE ENEMY...
FROM THIS MOMENT ON, YOU ARE THE OWNER OF THE GREAT BLADE SAMEHADA...
...AND MY SUBORDINATE AS WELL.

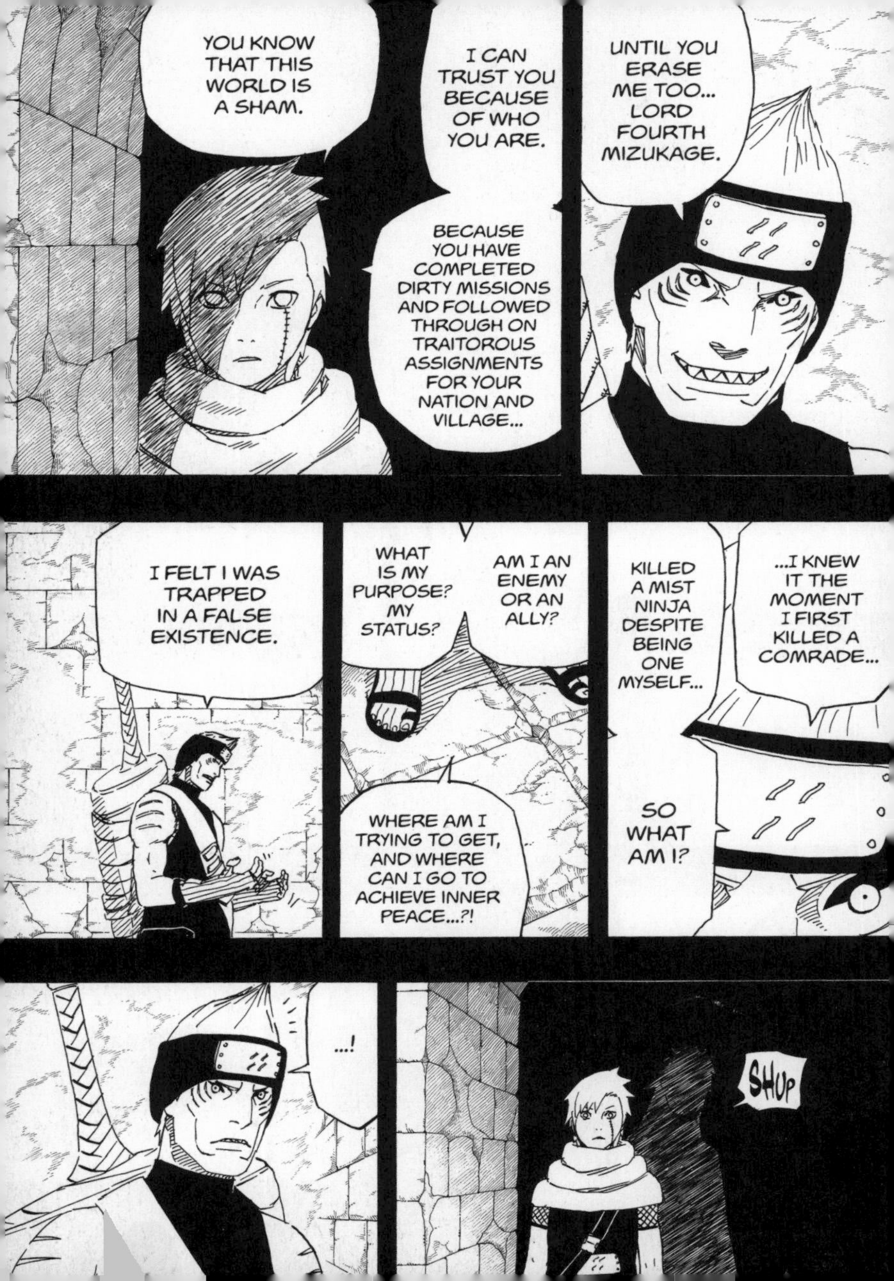
UNTIL YOU ERASE ME TOO... LORD FOURTH MIZUKAGE.
I CAN TRUST YOU BECAUSE OF WHO YOU ARE.
YOU KNOW THAT THIS WORLD IS A SHAM.
BECAUSE YOU HAVE COMPLETED DIRTY MISSIONS AND FOLLOWED THROUGH ON TRAITOROUS ASSIGNMENTS FOR YOUR NATION AND VILLAGE...
...I KNEW IT THE MOMENT I FIRST KILLED A COMRADE...
KILLED A MIST NINJA DESPITE BEING ONE MYSELF...
SO WHAT AM I?
AM I AN ENEMY OR AN ALLY?
WHAT IS MY PURPOSE? MY STATUS?
WHERE AM I TRYING TO GET, AND WHERE CAN I GO TO ACHIEVE INNER PEACE...?!
I FELT I WAS TRAPPED IN A FALSE EXISTENCE.
SHUP
...!

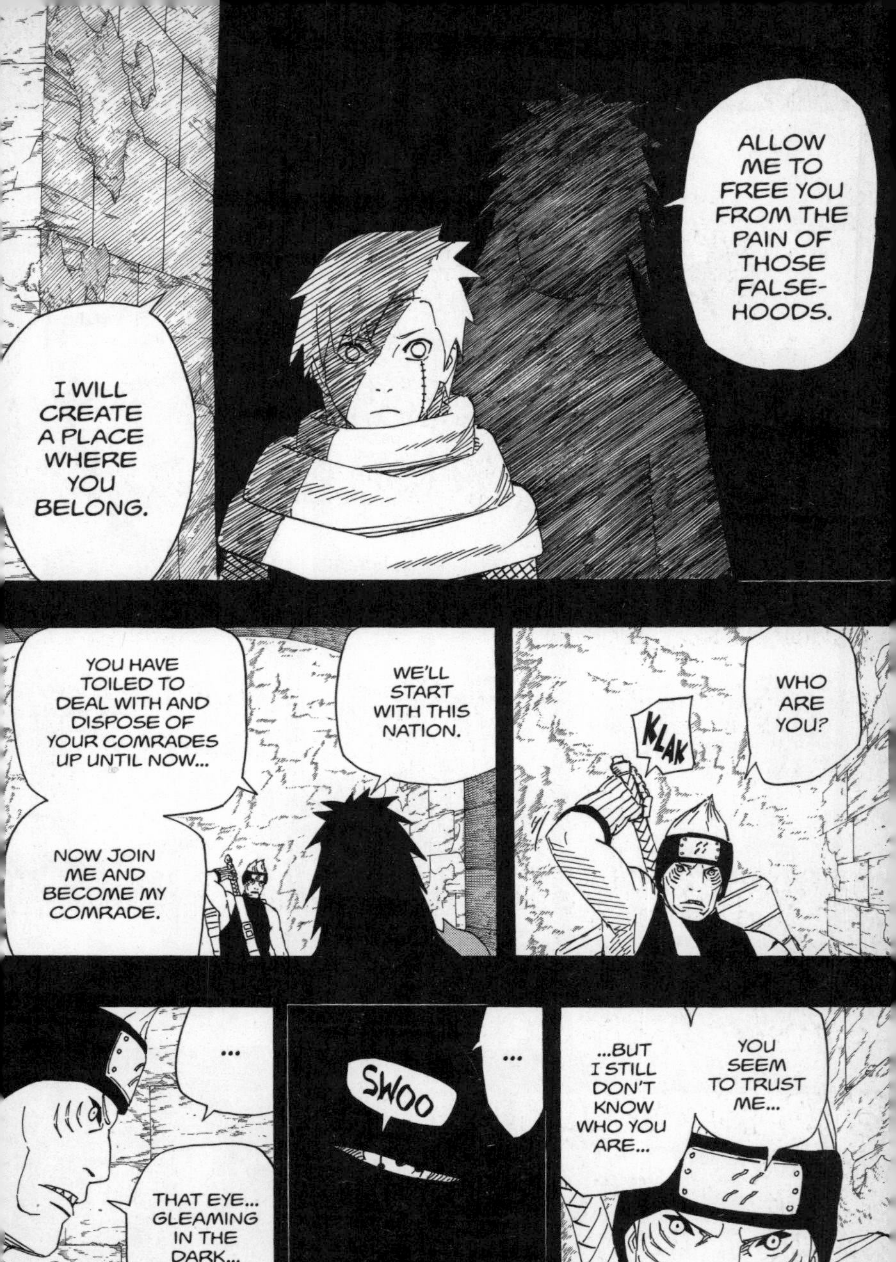
ALLOW ME TO FREE YOU FROM THE PAIN OF THOSE FALSEHOODS.
I WILL CREATE A PLACE WHERE YOU BELONG.
WHO ARE YOU?
KLAK
WE'LL START WITH THIS NATION.
YOU HAVE TOILED TO DEAL WITH AND DISPOSE OF YOUR COMRADES UP UNTIL NOW...
NOW JOIN ME AND BECOME MY COMRADE.
YOU SEEM TO TRUST ME...
...BUT I STILL DON'T KNOW WHO YOU ARE...
...
SWOO
...
THAT EYE... GLEAMING IN THE DARK...

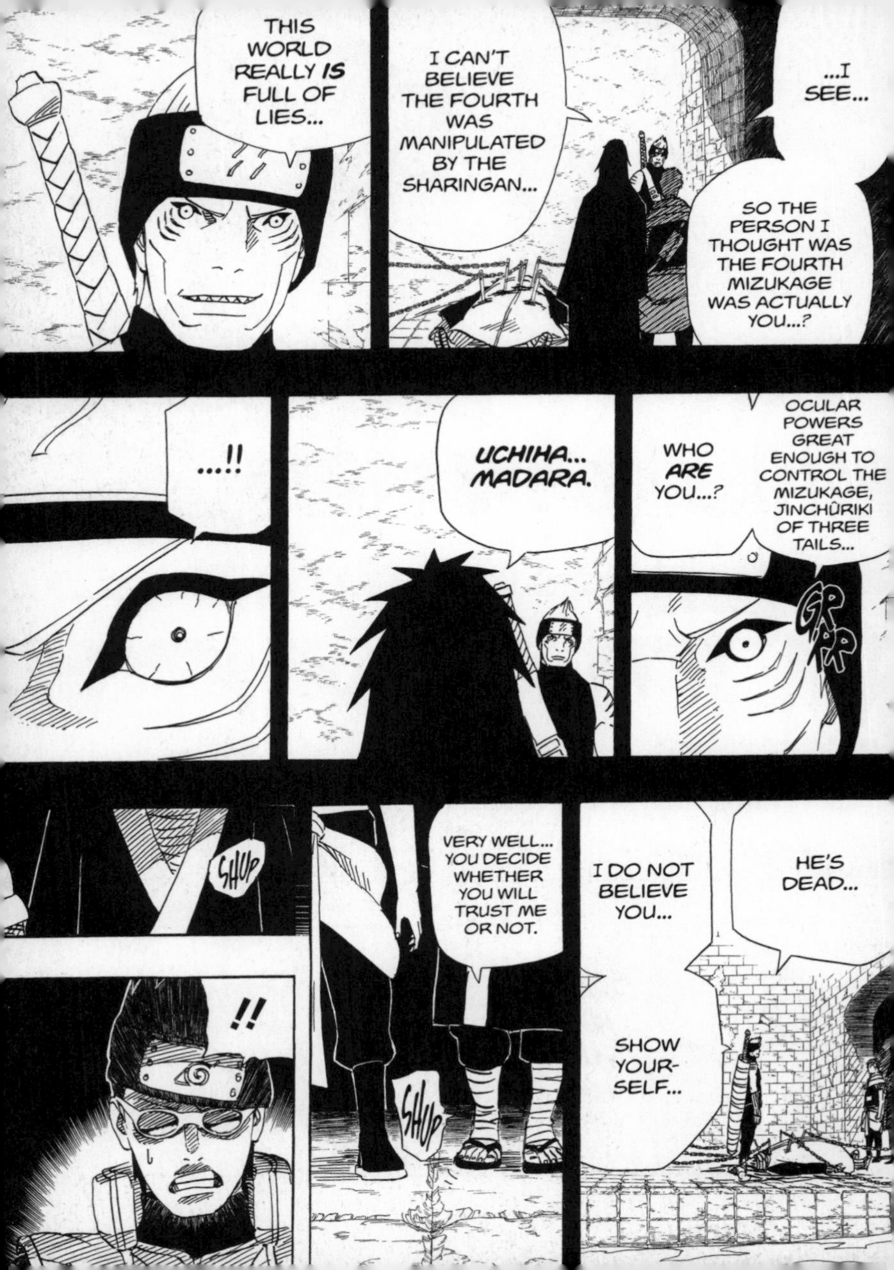
...I SEE...
SO THE PERSON I THOUGHT WAS THE FOURTH MIZUKAGE WAS ACTUALLY YOU...?
I CAN'T BELIEVE THE FOURTH WAS MANIPULATED BY THE SHARINGAN...
THIS WORLD REALLY *IS* FULL OF LIES...
OCULAR POWERS GREAT ENOUGH TO CONTROL THE MIZUKAGE, JINCHÛRIKI OF THREE TAILS...
WHO *ARE* YOU...?
GRRR
UCHIHA... MADARA.
...!!
HE'S DEAD...
I DO NOT BELIEVE YOU...
SHOW YOURSELF...
VERY WELL... YOU DECIDE WHETHER YOU WILL TRUST ME OR NOT.
SHUP
SHUP
!!

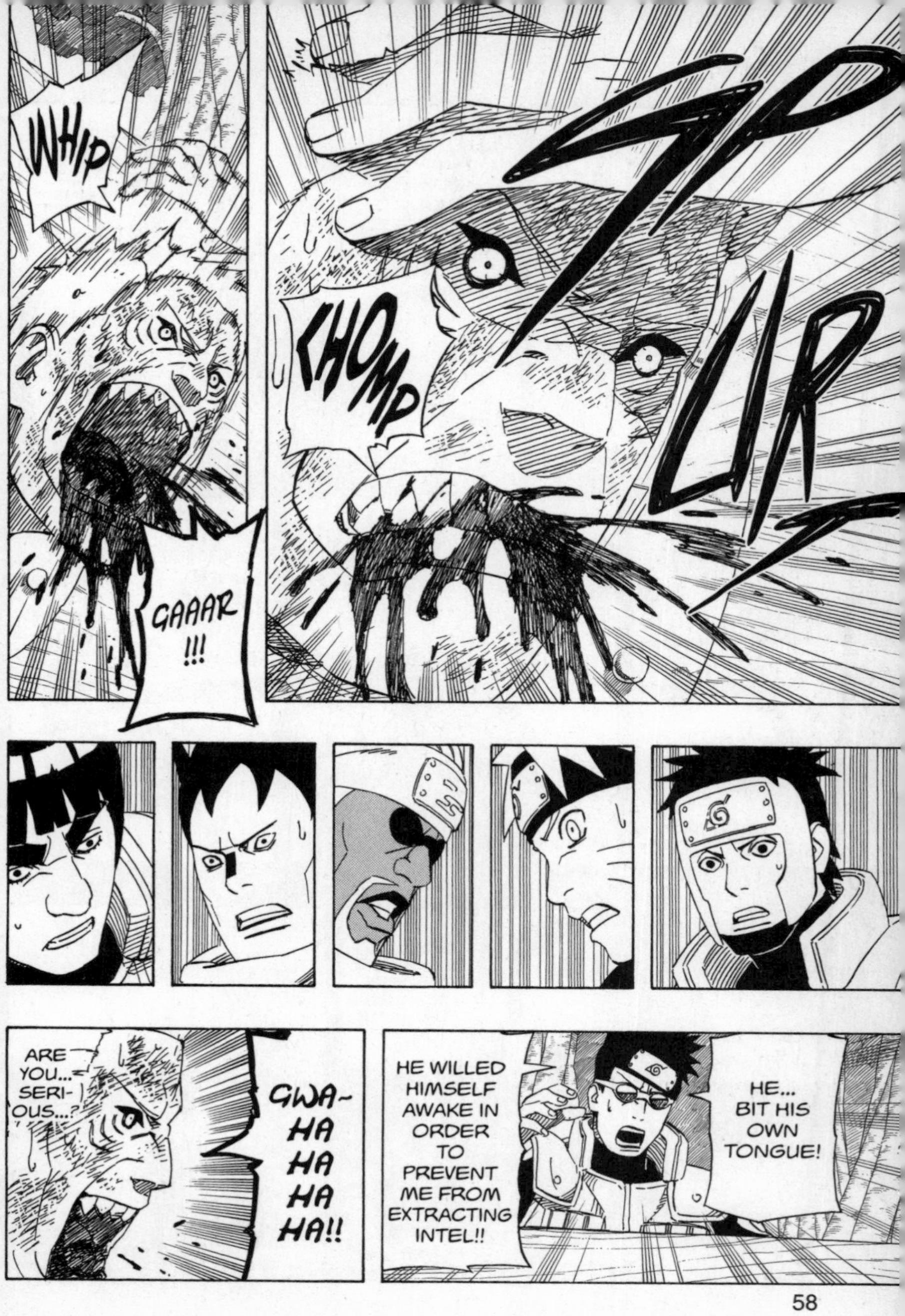
CHOMP
WHIP
GAAAR !!!
HE... BIT HIS OWN TONGUE!
HE WILLED HIMSELF AWAKE IN ORDER TO PREVENT ME FROM EXTRACTING INTEL!!
GWA-HA HA HA HA!!
ARE YOU... SERI-OUS...?

READ THIS WAY

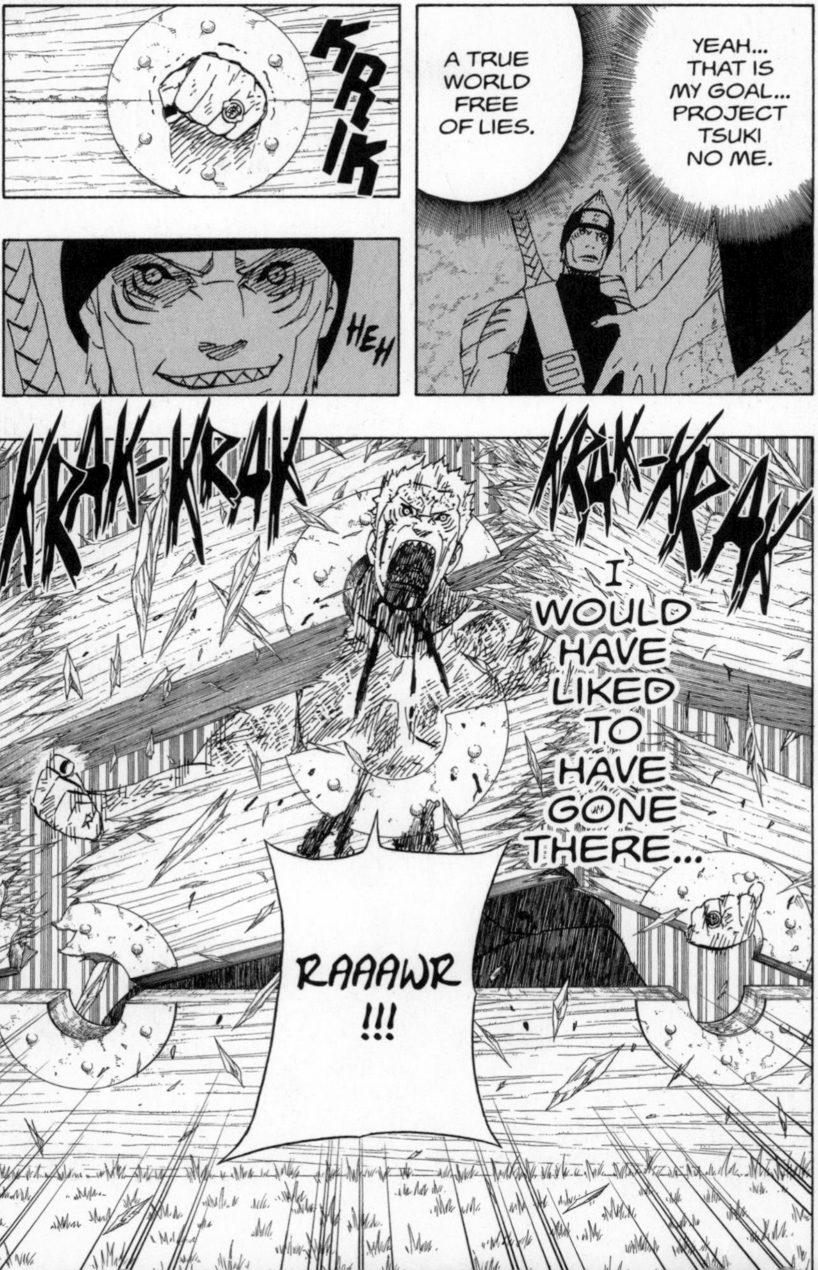
YEAH... THAT IS MY GOAL... PROJECT TSUKI NO ME.
A TRUE WORLD FREE OF LIES.
KRIK
HEH
KRAK-KRAK
I WOULD HAVE LIKED TO HAVE GONE THERE...
KRAK-KRAK
RAAAWR !!!

NARUTO

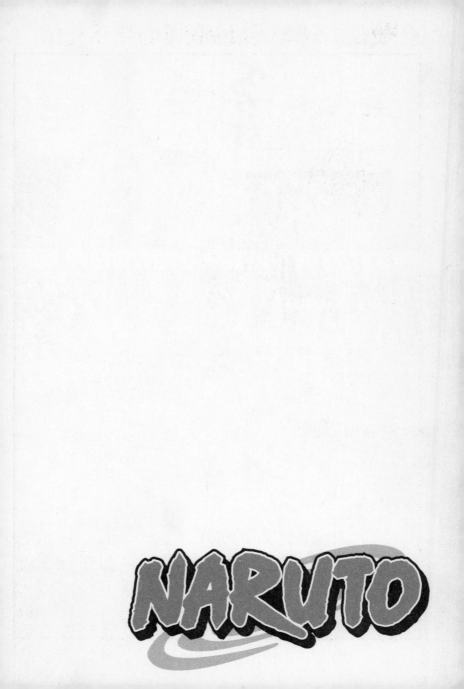

Number 508: Shinobi Death Style

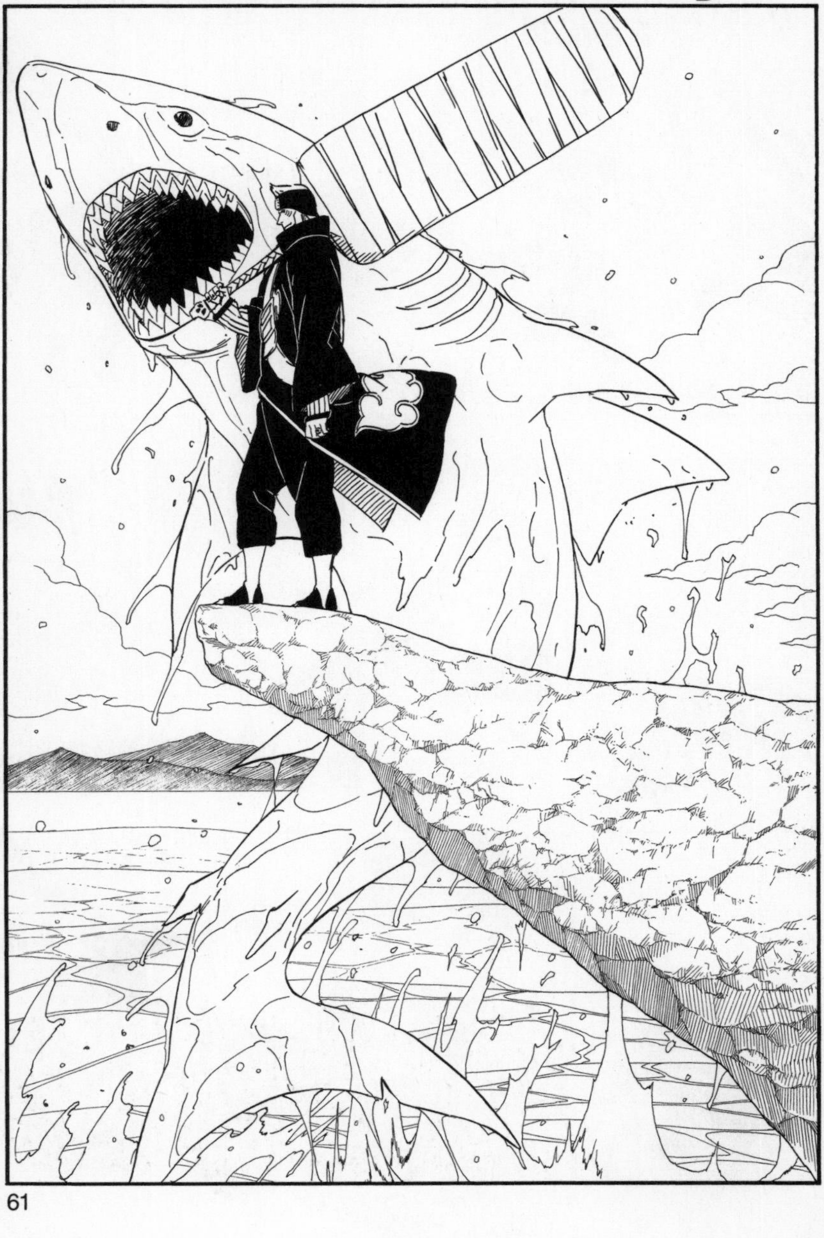

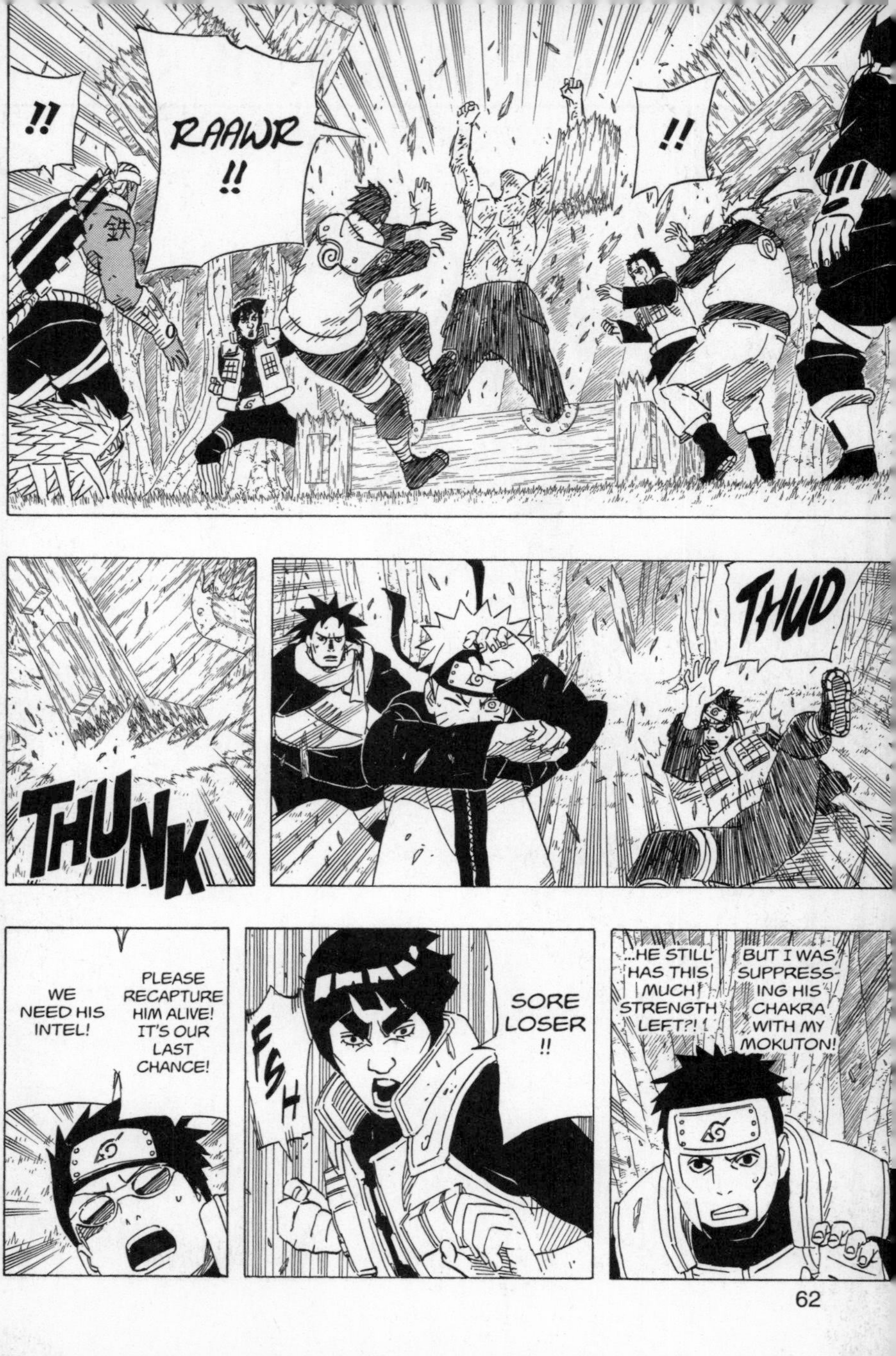
!!
RAAWR !!
!!
THUD
THUNK
BUT I WAS SUPPRESSING HIS CHAKRA WITH MY MOKUTON!
...HE STILL HAS THIS MUCH STRENGTH LEFT?!
SORE LOSER !!
FSH
PLEASE RECAPTURE HIM ALIVE! IT'S OUR LAST CHANCE!
WE NEED HIS INTEL!

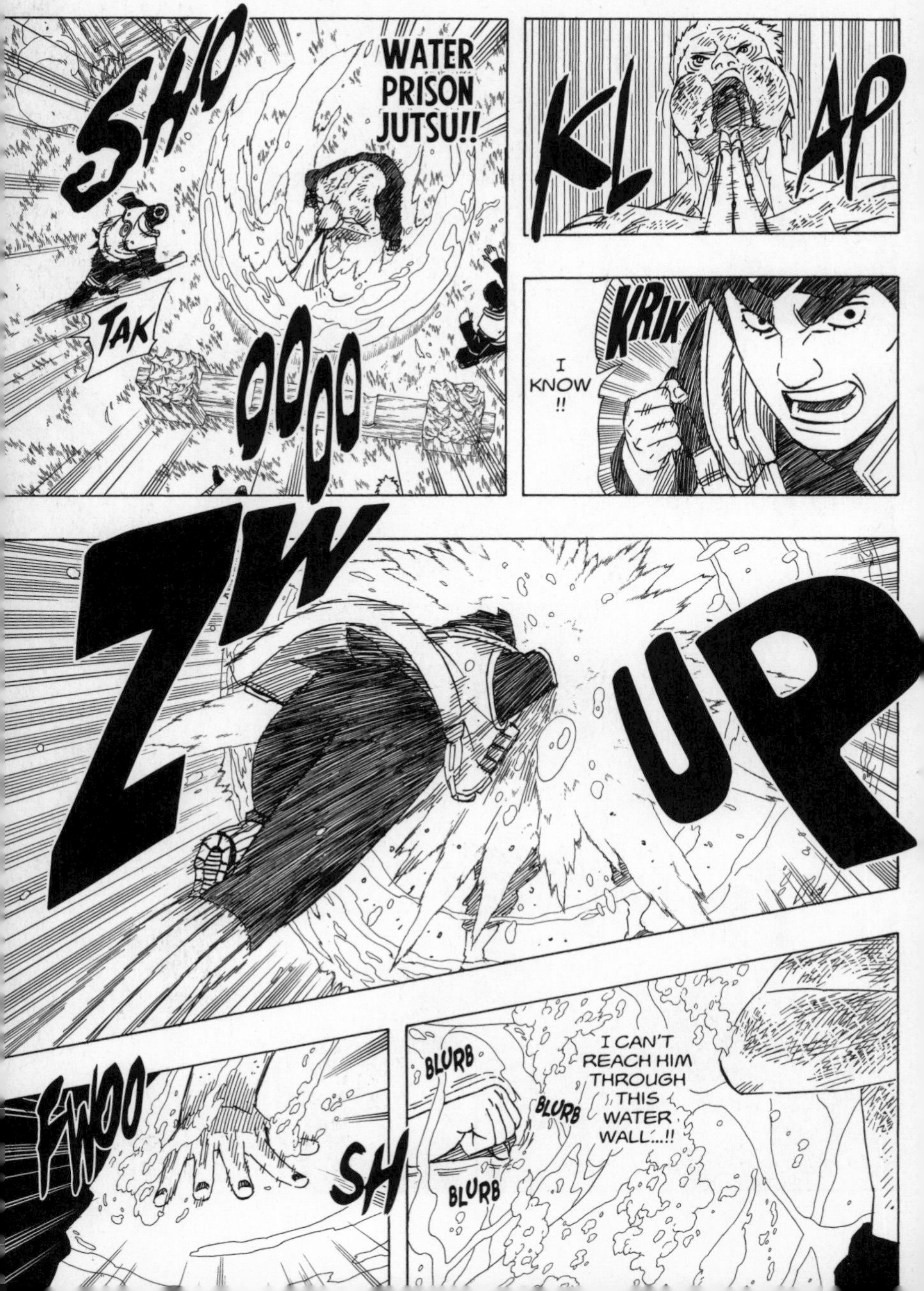
KL AP
KRIK
I KNOW !!
SHO
WATER PRISON JUTSU!!
TAK
OOOO
ZW UP
BLURB
I CAN'T REACH HIM THROUGH THIS WATER WALL...!!
BLURB
BLURB
SH
FWOO

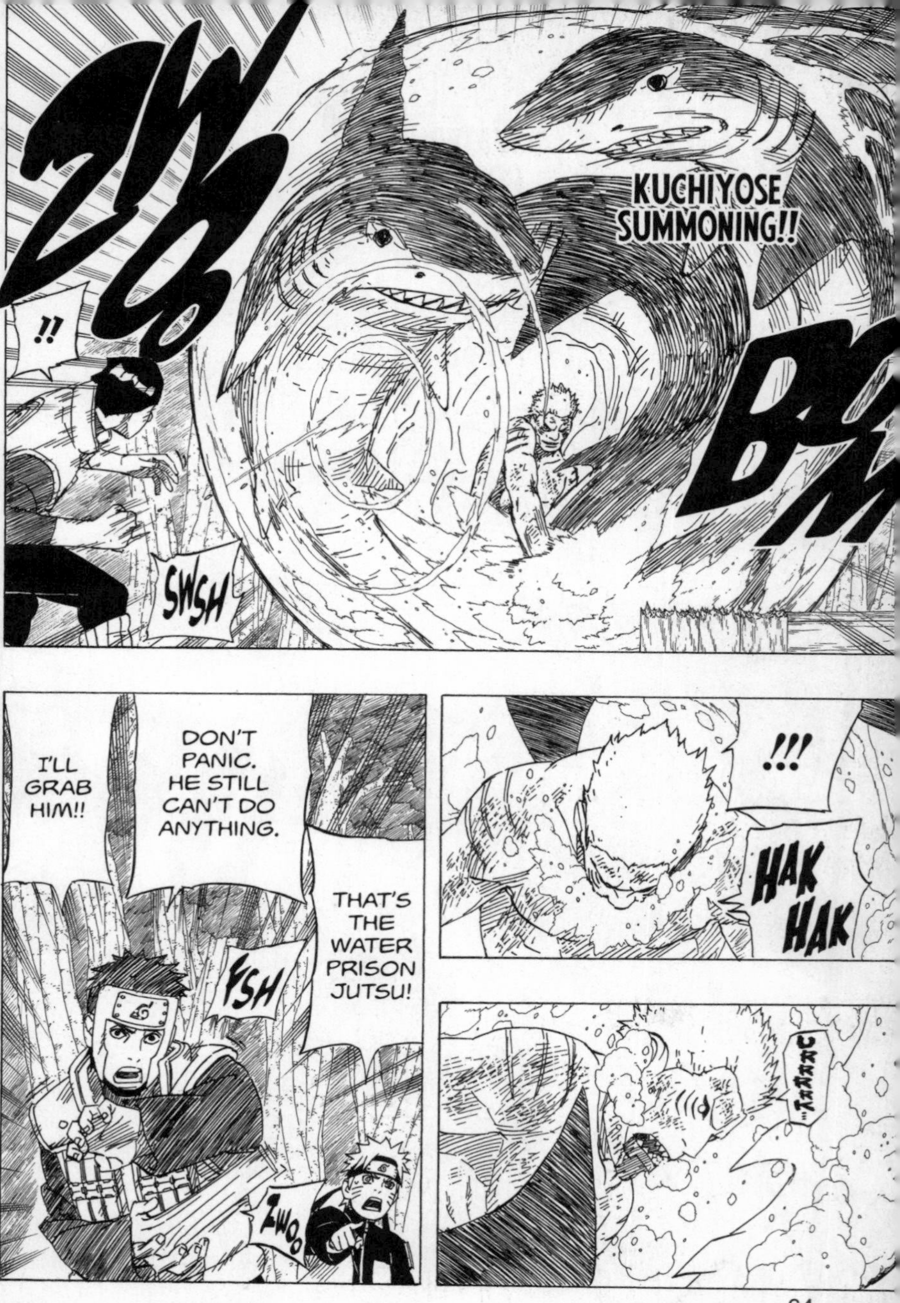
KUCHIYOSE SUMMONING!!
ZWOO
!!
SWSH
!!!
HAK HAK
URRRRK...
DON'T PANIC. HE STILL CAN'T DO ANYTHING.
I'LL GRAB HIM!!
THAT'S THE WATER PRISON JUTSU!
FSH
ZWOO

READ THIS WAY

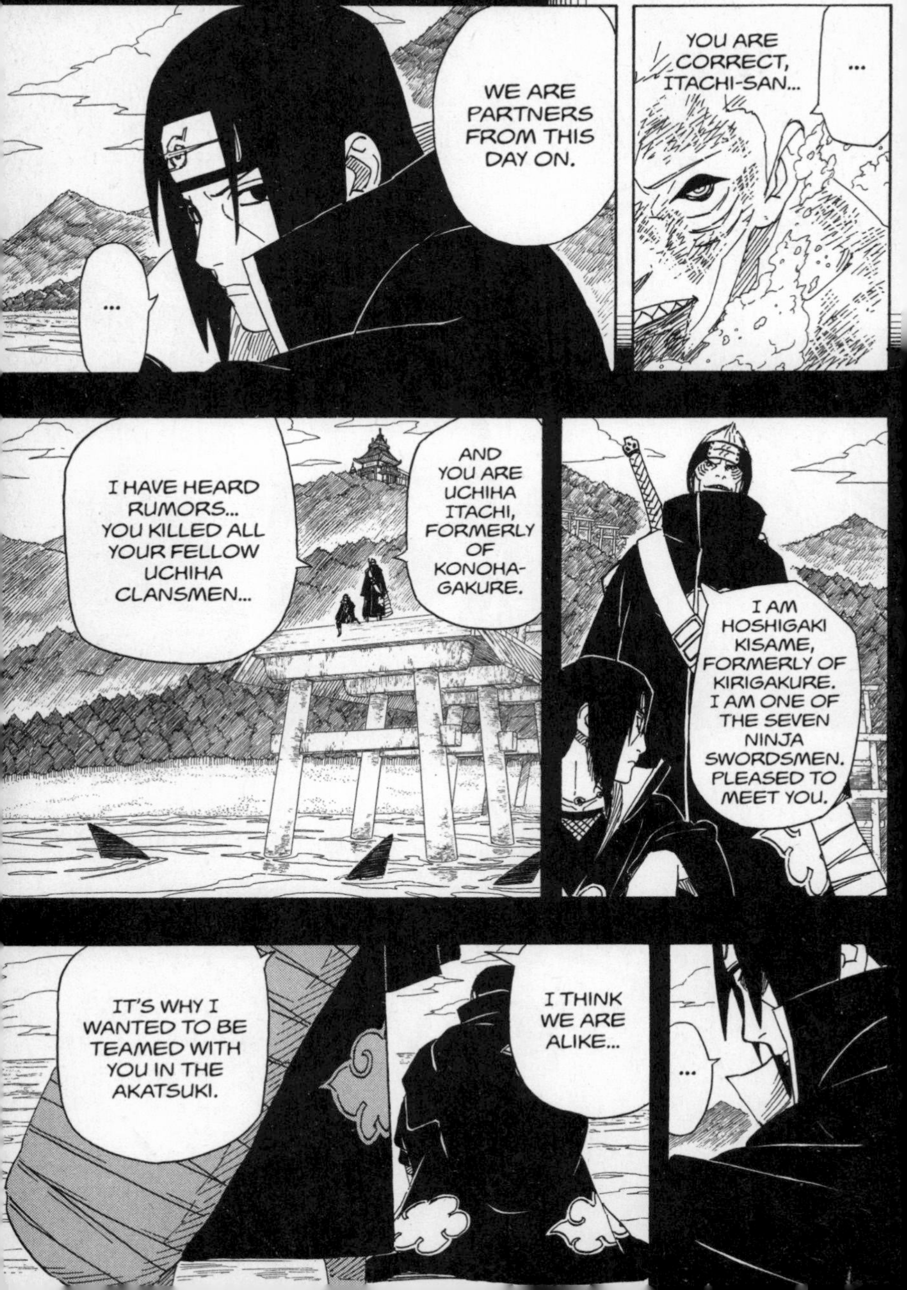
...
YOU ARE CORRECT, ITACHI-SAN...
WE ARE PARTNERS FROM THIS DAY ON.
...
I AM HOSHIGAKI KISAME, FORMERLY OF KIRIGAKURE. I AM ONE OF THE SEVEN NINJA SWORDSMEN. PLEASED TO MEET YOU.
AND YOU ARE UCHIHA ITACHI, FORMERLY OF KONOHA-GAKURE.
I HAVE HEARD RUMORS... YOU KILLED ALL YOUR FELLOW UCHIHA CLANSMEN...
...
I THINK WE ARE ALIKE...
IT'S WHY I WANTED TO BE TEAMED WITH YOU IN THE AKATSUKI.

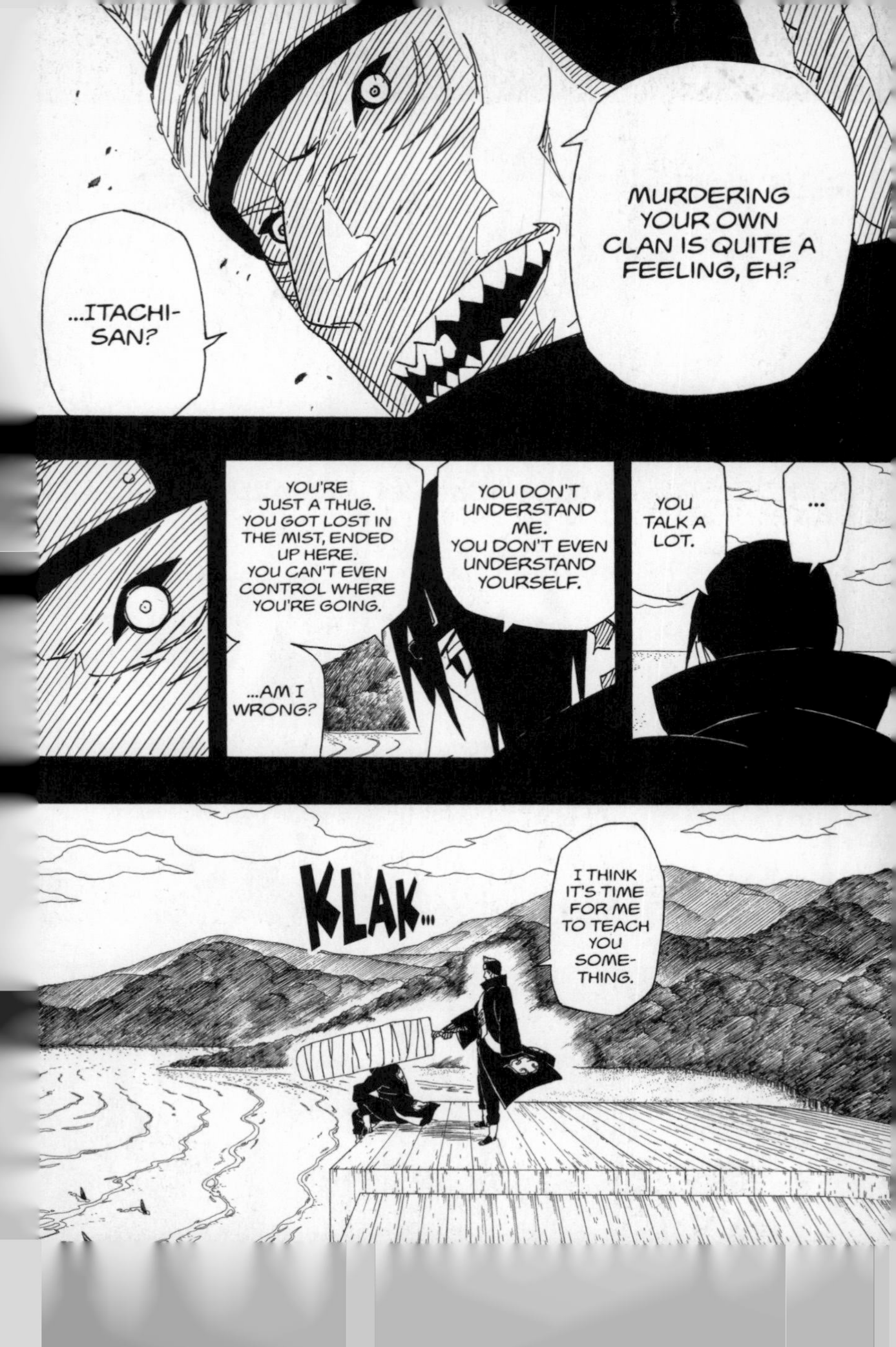

MURDERING YOUR OWN CLAN IS QUITE A FEELING, EH?
...ITACHI-SAN?
...
YOU TALK A LOT.
YOU DON'T UNDERSTAND ME. YOU DON'T EVEN UNDERSTAND YOURSELF.
YOU'RE JUST A THUG. YOU GOT LOST IN THE MIST, ENDED UP HERE. YOU CAN'T EVEN CONTROL WHERE YOU'RE GOING.
...AM I WRONG?
I THINK IT'S TIME FOR ME TO TEACH YOU SOME-THING.
KLAK...

READ THIS WAY

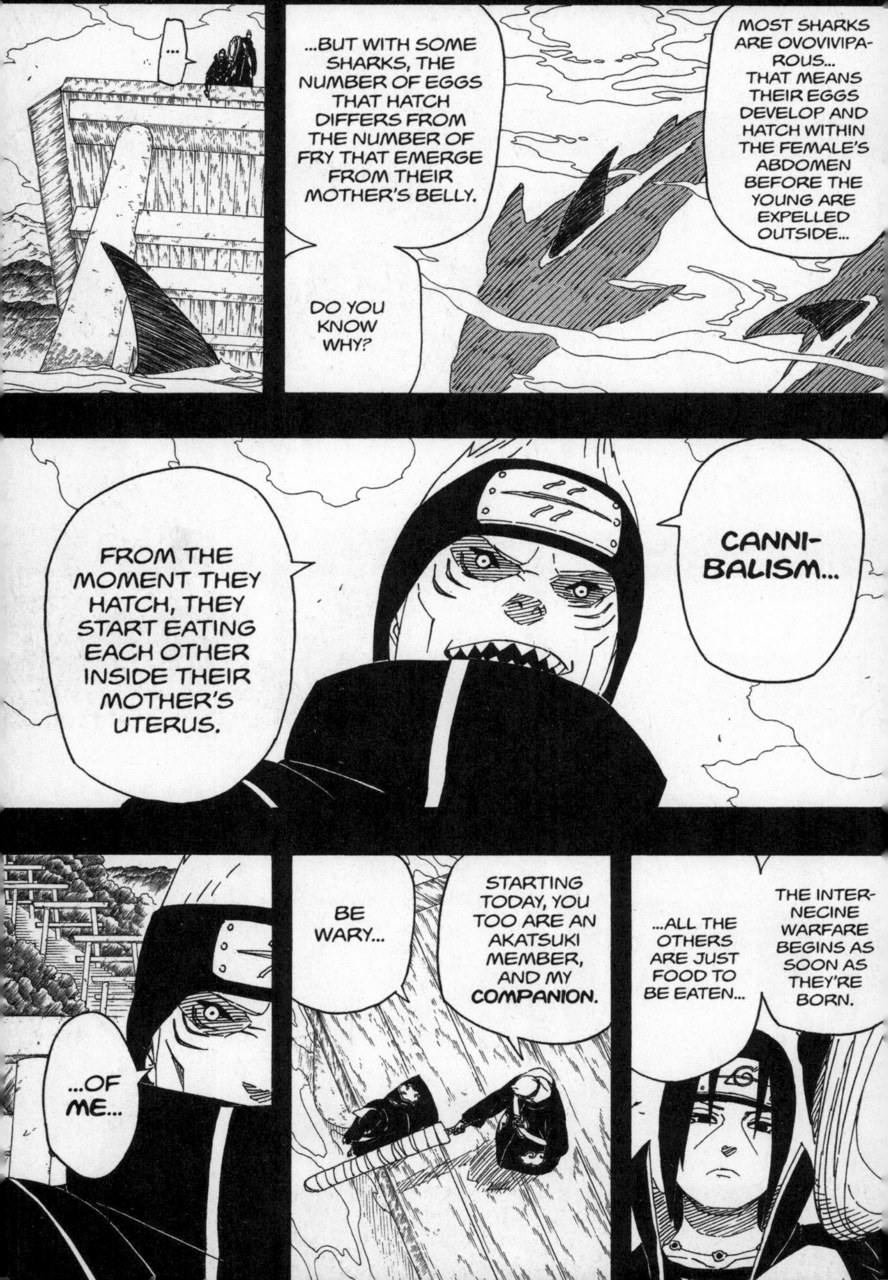
MOST SHARKS ARE OVOVIVIPAROUS... THAT MEANS THEIR EGGS DEVELOP AND HATCH WITHIN THE FEMALE'S ABDOMEN BEFORE THE YOUNG ARE EXPELLED OUTSIDE...
...BUT WITH SOME SHARKS, THE NUMBER OF EGGS THAT HATCH DIFFERS FROM THE NUMBER OF FRY THAT EMERGE FROM THEIR MOTHER'S BELLY.
DO YOU KNOW WHY?
...
CANNIBALISM...
FROM THE MOMENT THEY HATCH, THEY START EATING EACH OTHER INSIDE THEIR MOTHER'S UTERUS.
THE INTERNECINE WARFARE BEGINS AS SOON AS THEY'RE BORN.
...ALL THE OTHERS ARE JUST FOOD TO BE EATEN...
STARTING TODAY, YOU TOO ARE AN AKATSUKI MEMBER, AND MY **COMPANION**.
BE WARY...
...OF ME...

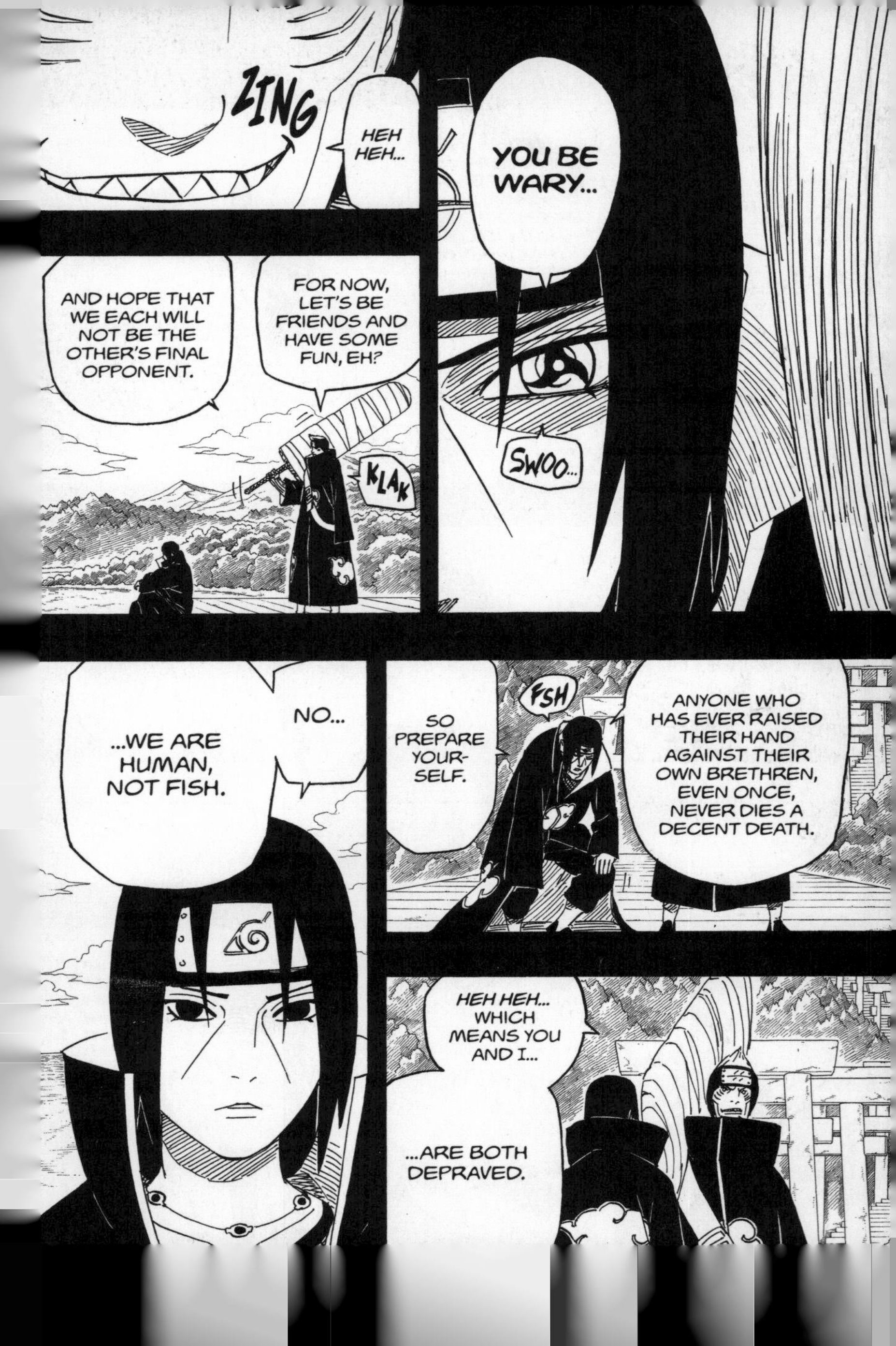
YOU BE WARY...
SWOO...
ZING
HEH HEH...
FOR NOW, LET'S BE FRIENDS AND HAVE SOME FUN, EH?
AND HOPE THAT WE EACH WILL NOT BE THE OTHER'S FINAL OPPONENT.
KLAK
ANYONE WHO HAS EVER RAISED THEIR HAND AGAINST THEIR OWN BRETHREN, EVEN ONCE, NEVER DIES A DECENT DEATH.
FSH
SO PREPARE YOURSELF.
HEH HEH... WHICH MEANS YOU AND I...
...ARE BOTH DEPRAVED.
NO...
...WE ARE HUMAN, NOT FISH.

READ THIS WAY

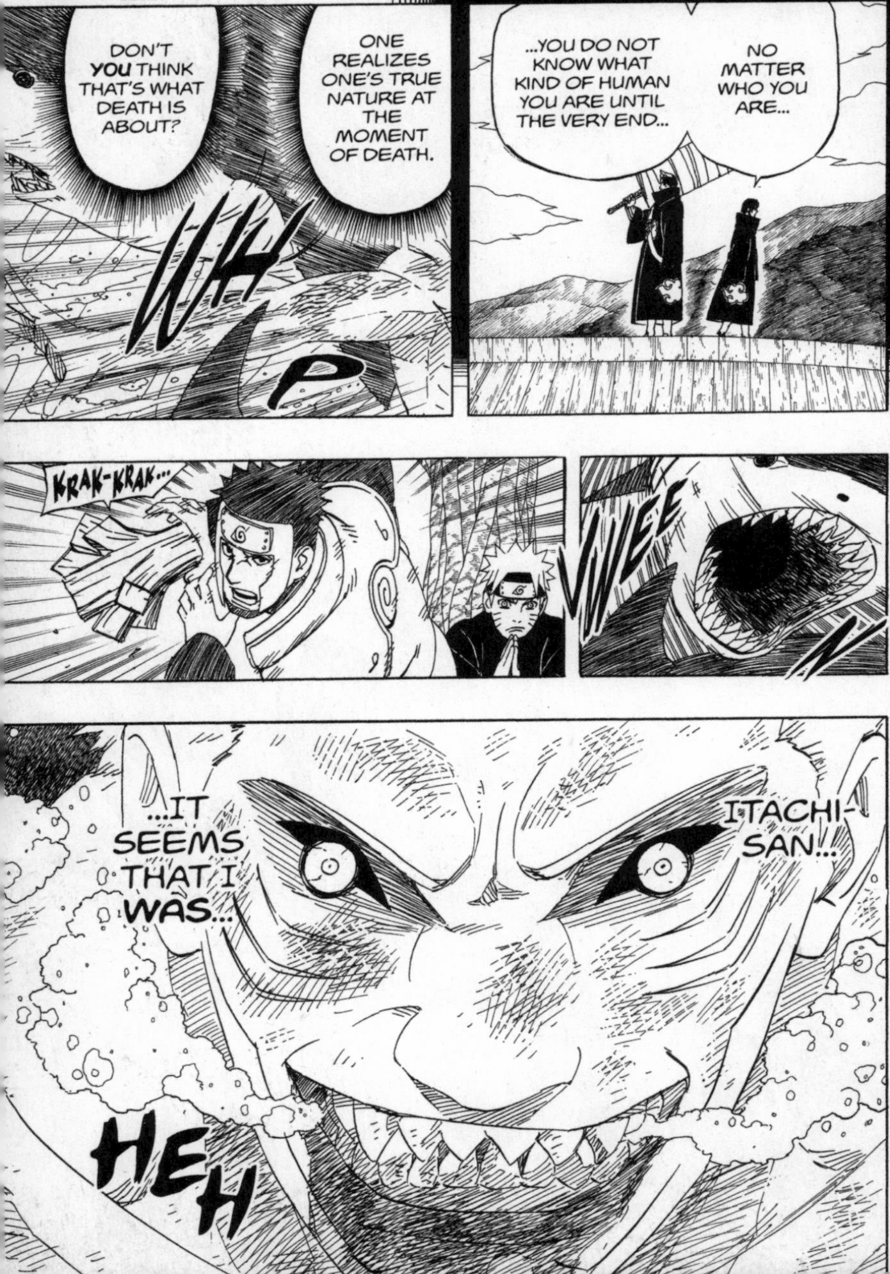

NO MATTER WHO YOU ARE...
...YOU DO NOT KNOW WHAT KIND OF HUMAN YOU ARE UNTIL THE VERY END...
ONE REALIZES ONE'S TRUE NATURE AT THE MOMENT OF DEATH.
DON'T YOU THINK THAT'S WHAT DEATH IS ABOUT?
WHP
VWEEN
KRAK-KRAK...
ITACHI-SAN...
...IT SEEMS THAT I WAS...
HEH

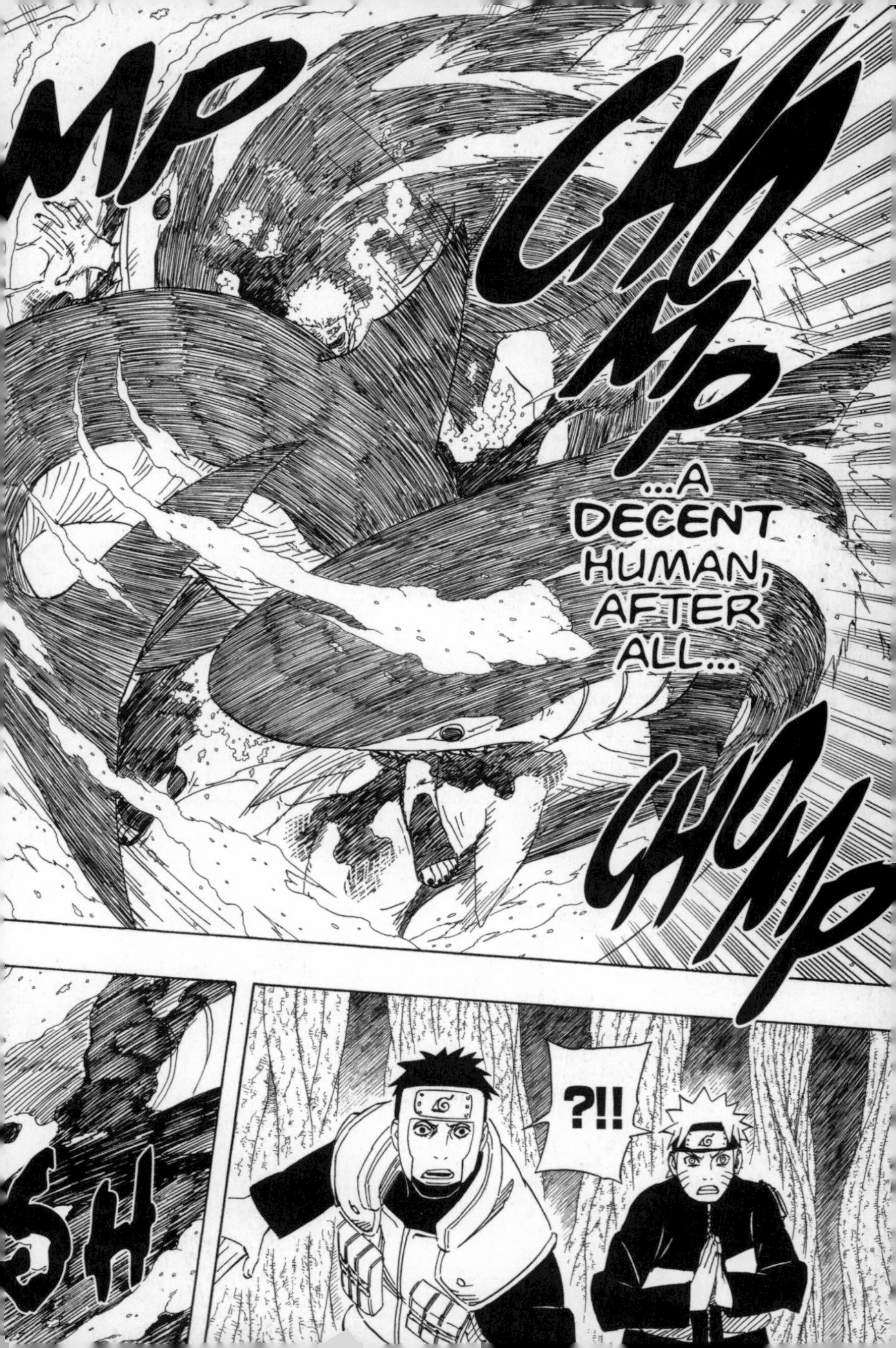
CHOMP
MP
...A DECENT HUMAN, AFTER ALL...
CHOMP
?!!
SH

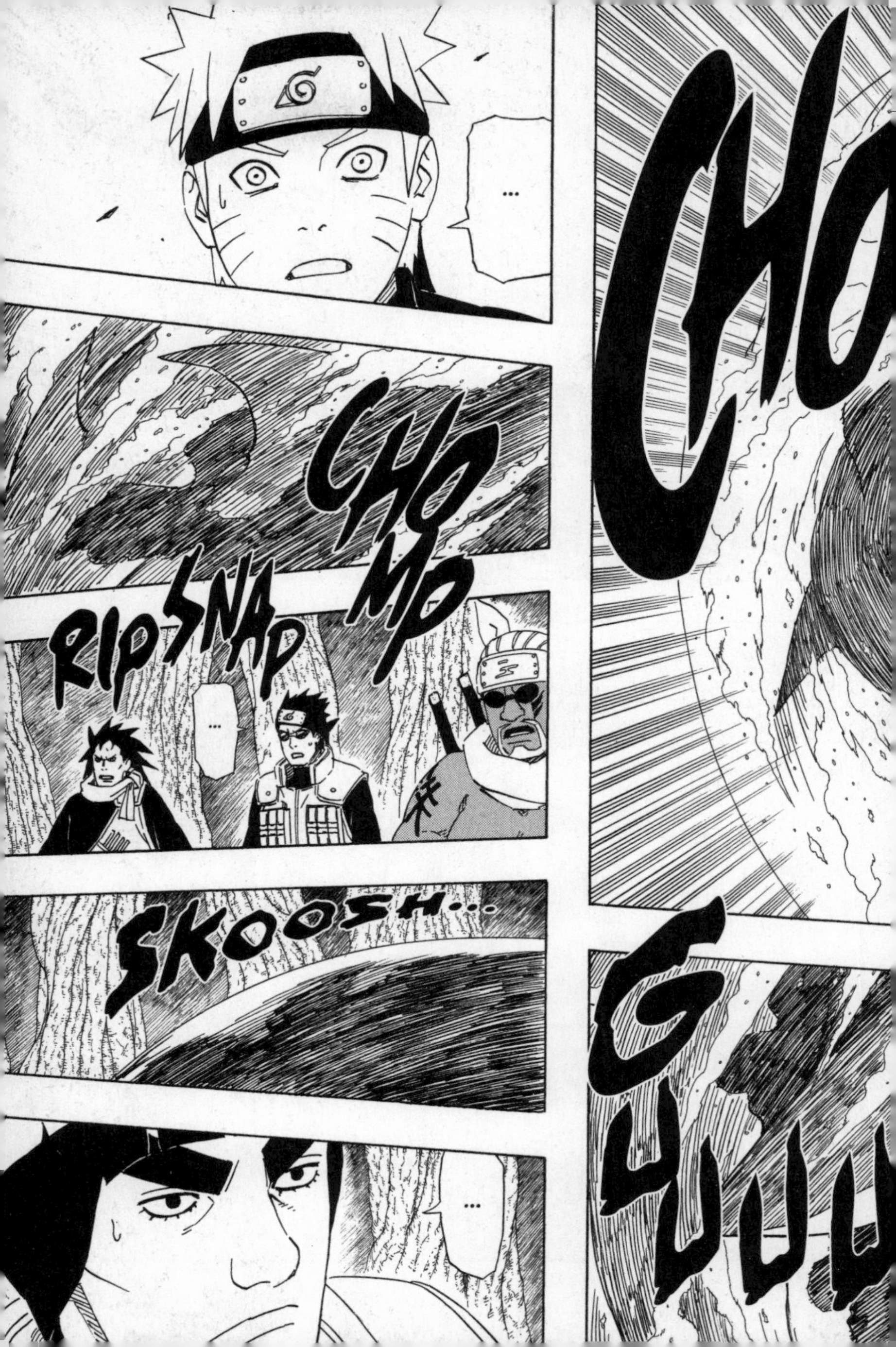
CHO
GYUU
...
CHOMP
RIPSNAP
...
SKOOSH...
...

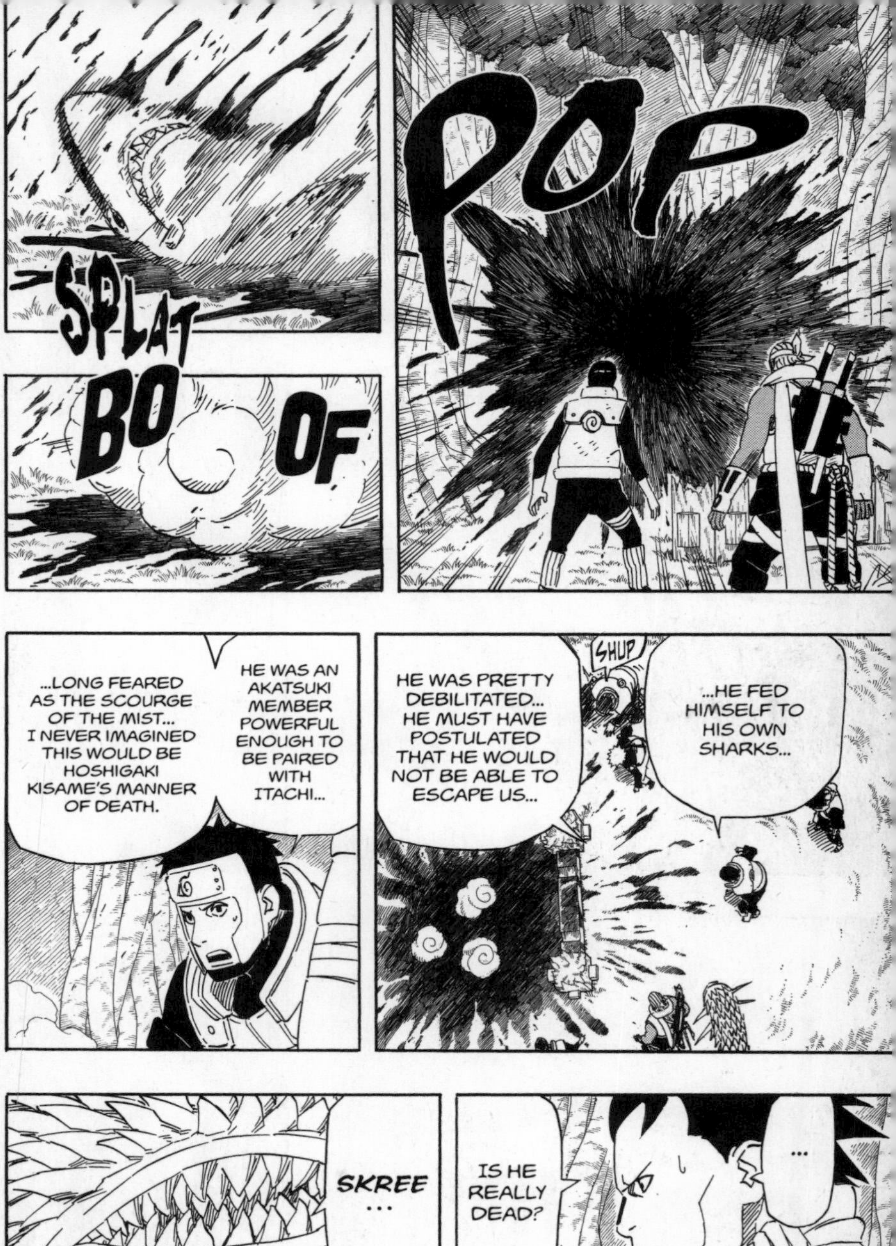
POP
SPLAT
BOOF
SHUP
...HE FED HIMSELF TO HIS OWN SHARKS...
HE WAS PRETTY DEBILITATED... HE MUST HAVE POSTULATED THAT HE WOULD NOT BE ABLE TO ESCAPE US...
HE WAS AN AKATSUKI MEMBER POWERFUL ENOUGH TO BE PAIRED WITH ITACHI...
...LONG FEARED AS THE SCOURGE OF THE MIST... I NEVER IMAGINED THIS WOULD BE HOSHIGAKI KISAME'S MANNER OF DEATH.
...
IS HE REALLY DEAD?
SKREE
...

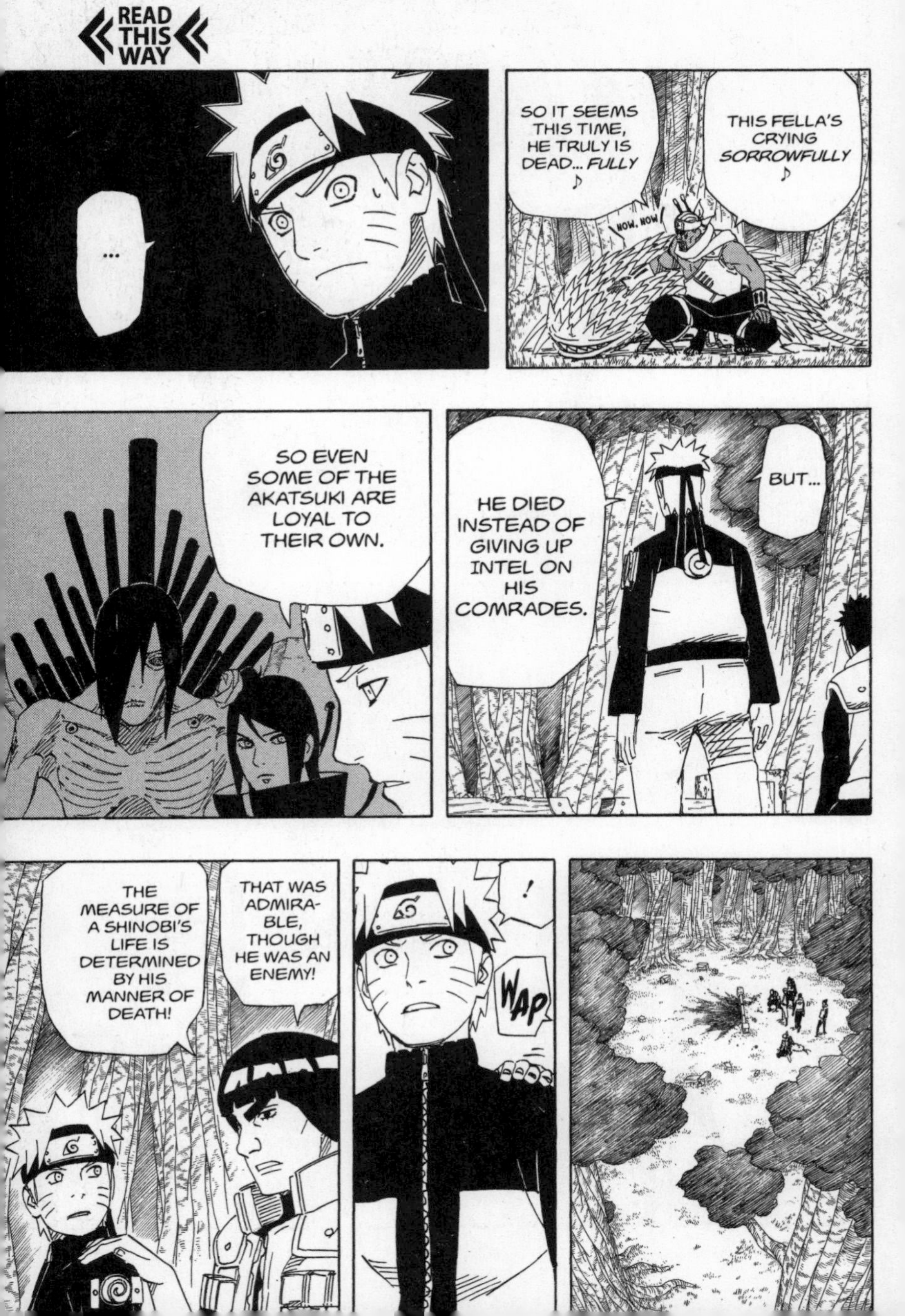
READ THIS WAY
THIS FELLA'S CRYING *SORROWFULLY* ♪
SO IT SEEMS THIS TIME, HE TRULY IS DEAD... *FULLY* ♪
NOW, NOW
...
BUT...
HE DIED INSTEAD OF GIVING UP INTEL ON HIS COMRADES.
SO EVEN SOME OF THE AKATSUKI ARE LOYAL TO THEIR OWN.
!
WAP
THAT WAS ADMIRA-BLE, THOUGH HE WAS AN ENEMY!
THE MEASURE OF A SHINOBI'S LIFE IS DETERMINED BY HIS MANNER OF DEATH!

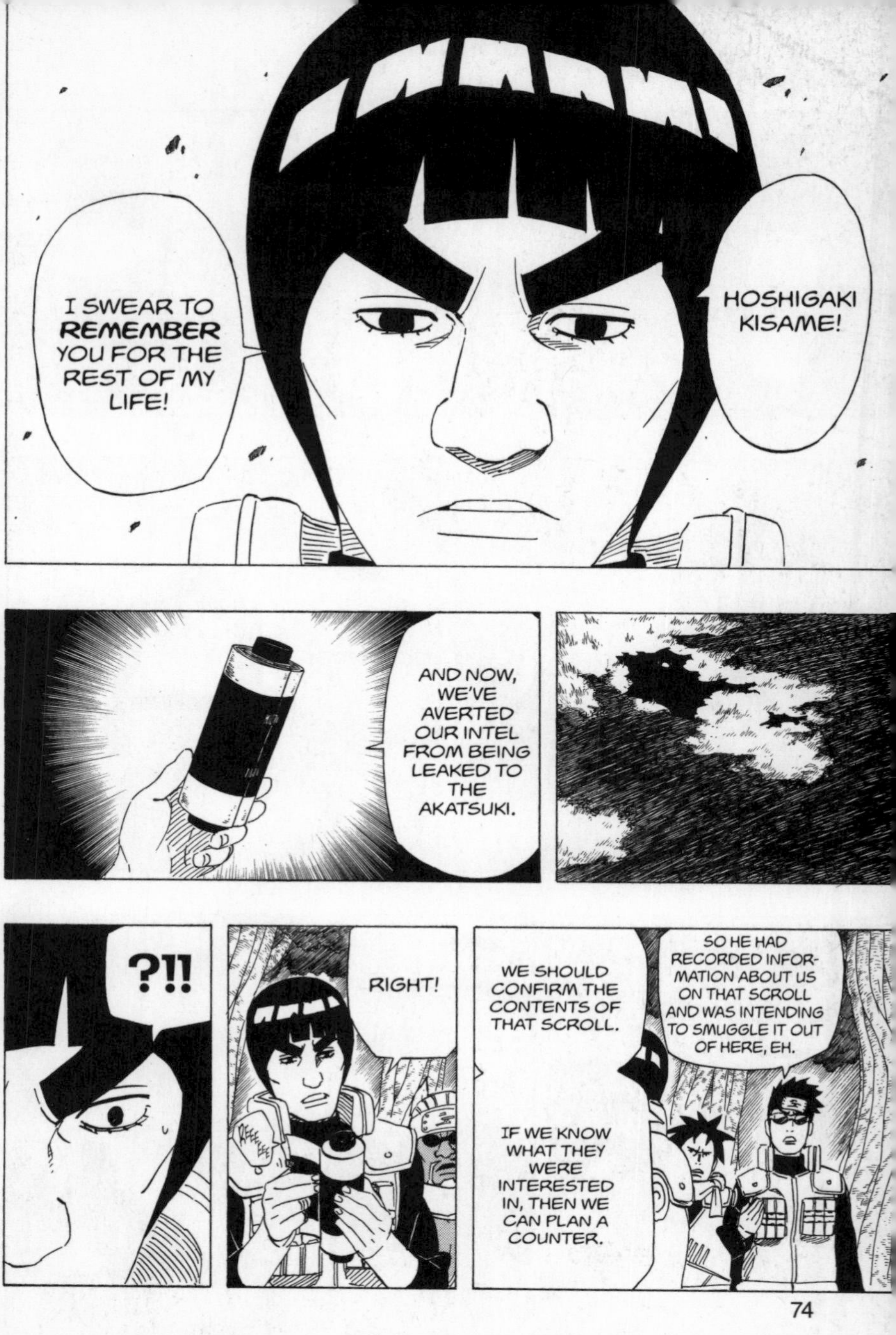
HOSHIGAKI KISAME!
I SWEAR TO REMEMBER YOU FOR THE REST OF MY LIFE!
AND NOW, WE'VE AVERTED OUR INTEL FROM BEING LEAKED TO THE AKATSUKI.
SO HE HAD RECORDED INFOR-MATION ABOUT US ON THAT SCROLL AND WAS INTENDING TO SMUGGLE IT OUT OF HERE, EH.
WE SHOULD CONFIRM THE CONTENTS OF THAT SCROLL.
IF WE KNOW WHAT THEY WERE INTERESTED IN, THEN WE CAN PLAN A COUNTER.
RIGHT!
?!!

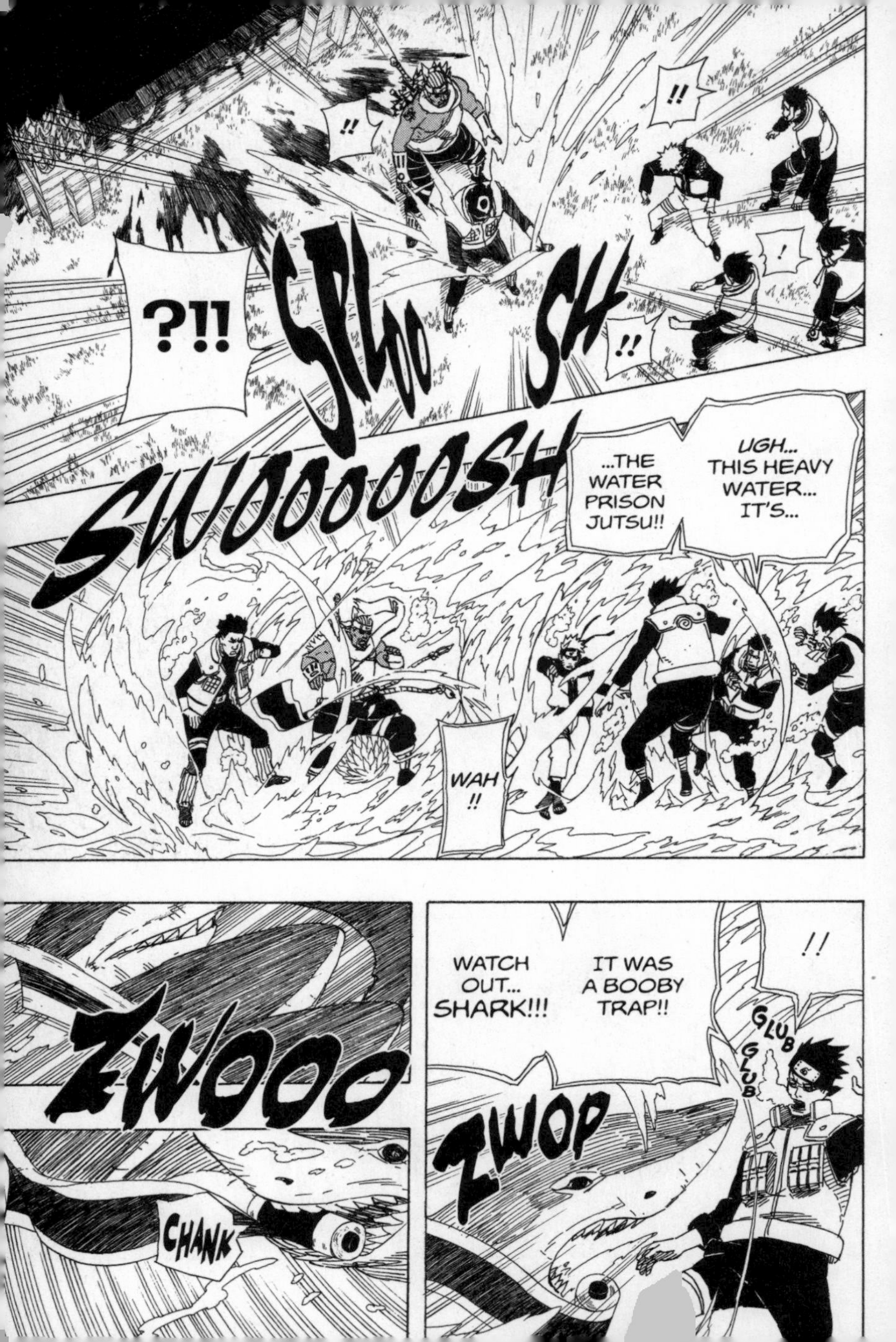
!!
!
!!
!!
?!!
SPLOOSH
UGH... THIS HEAVY WATER... IT'S...
...THE WATER PRISON JUTSU!!
SWOOOOOSH
WAH!!
!!
IT WAS A BOOBY TRAP!!
WATCH OUT... SHARK!!!
GLUB GLUB
ZWOP
ZWOOO
CHANK

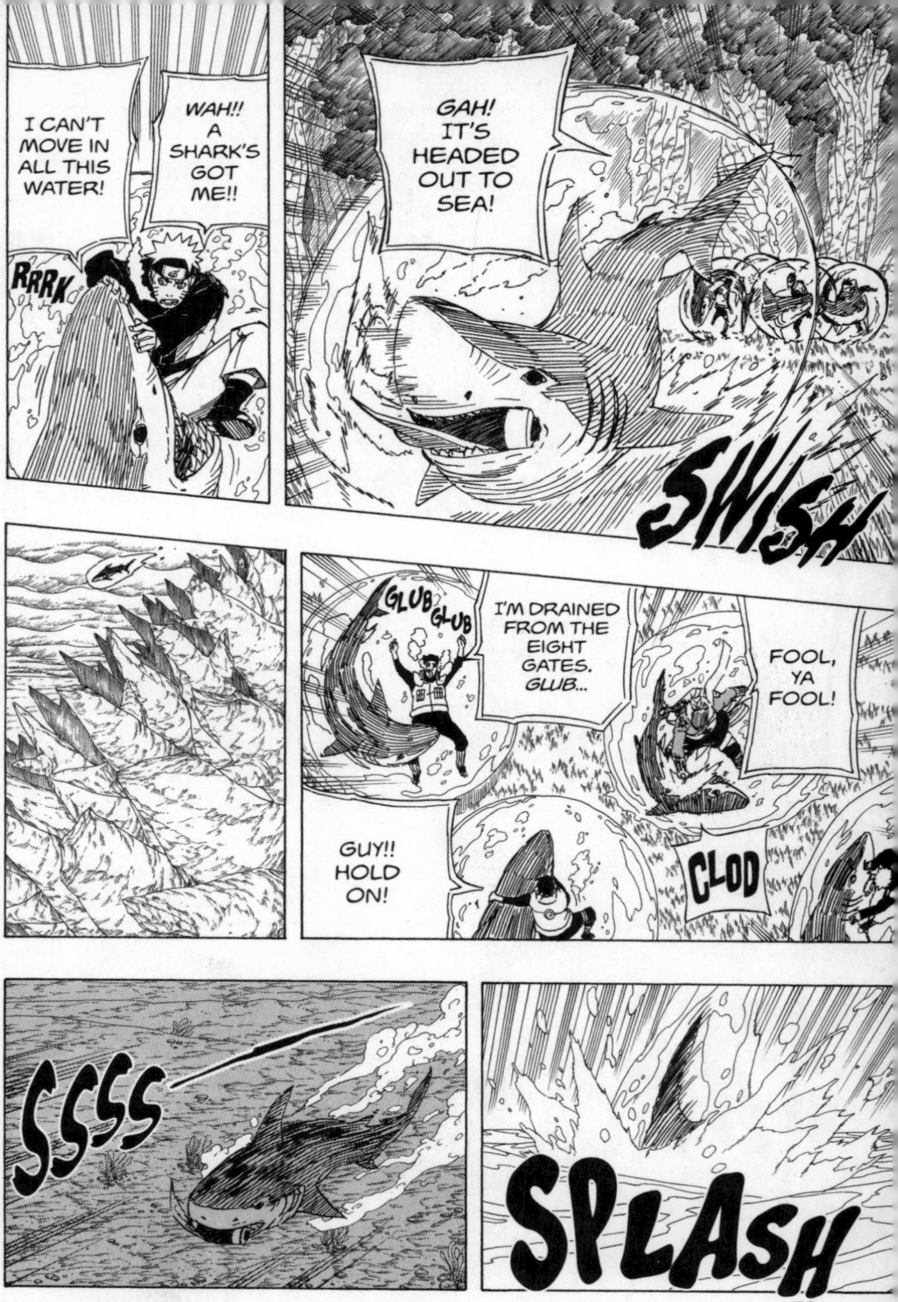
GAH! IT'S HEADED OUT TO SEA!
SWISH
WAH!! A SHARK'S GOT ME!!
I CAN'T MOVE IN ALL THIS WATER!
RRRK
FOOL, YA FOOL!
I'M DRAINED FROM THE EIGHT GATES. GLUB...
GLUB GLUB
CLOD
GUY!! HOLD ON!
SPLASH
SSSS

READ THIS WAY

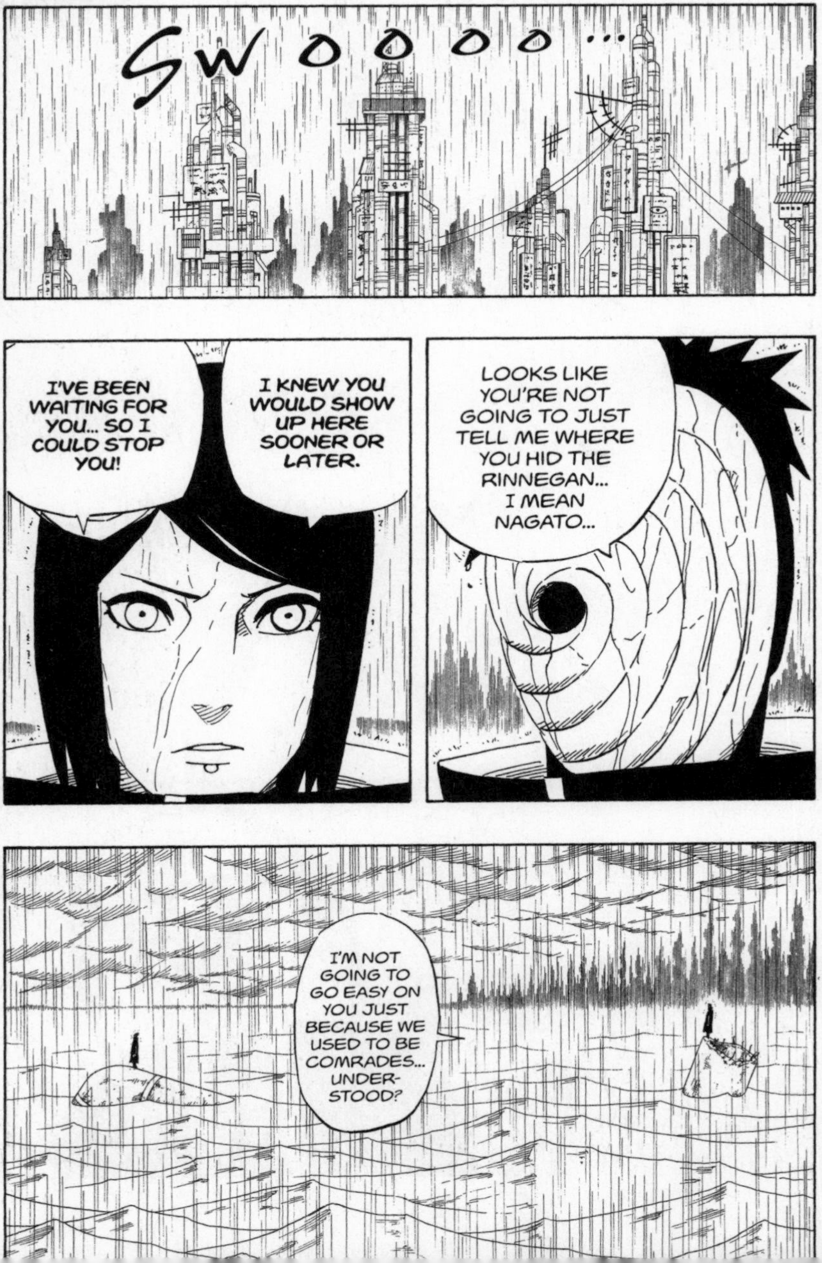
SWOOOO...
LOOKS LIKE YOU'RE NOT GOING TO JUST TELL ME WHERE YOU HID THE RINNEGAN... I MEAN NAGATO...
I KNEW YOU WOULD SHOW UP HERE SOONER OR LATER.
I'VE BEEN WAITING FOR YOU... SO I COULD STOP YOU!
I'M NOT GOING TO GO EASY ON YOU JUST BECAUSE WE USED TO BE COMRADES... UNDER-STOOD?

Number 509: Peace Viaduct

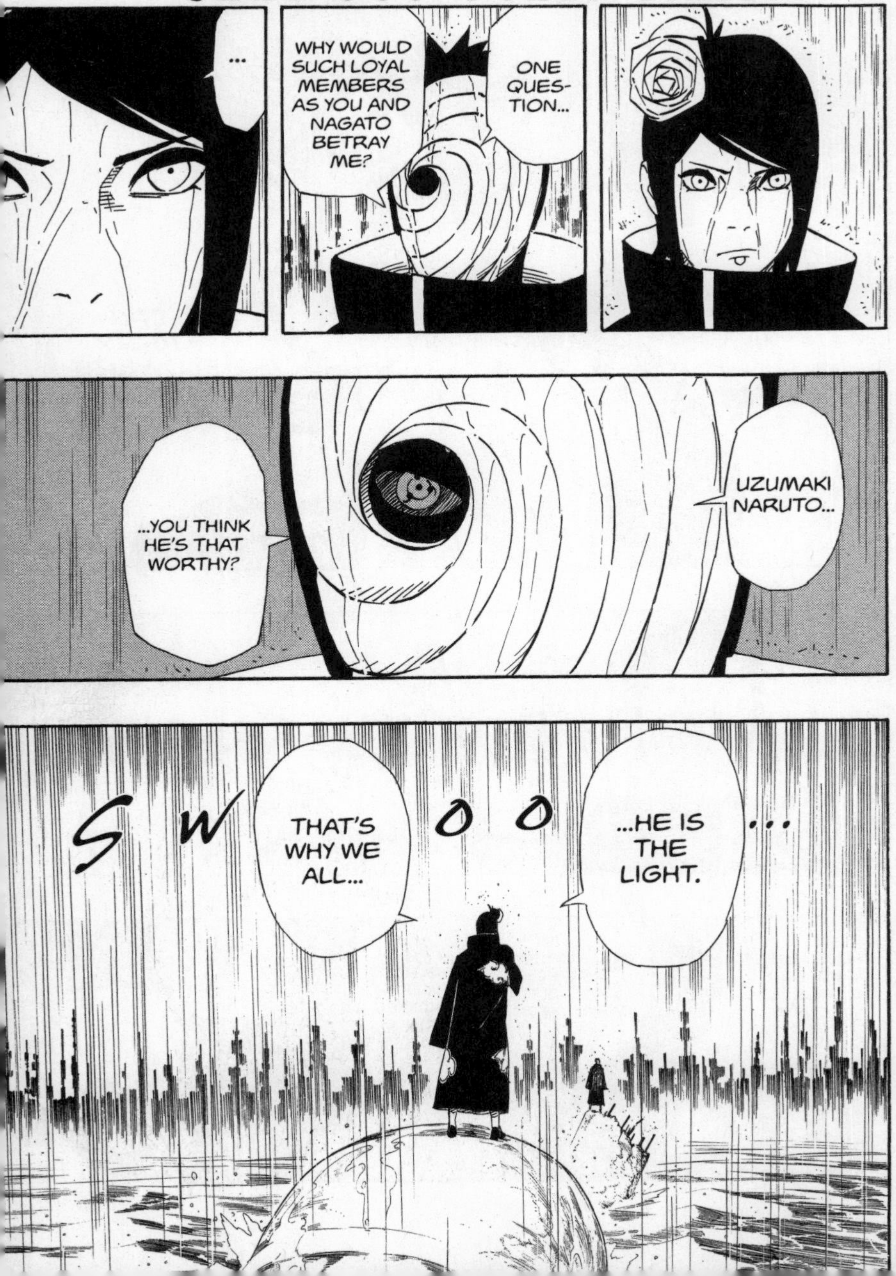
ONE QUES-TION...
WHY WOULD SUCH LOYAL MEMBERS AS YOU AND NAGATO BETRAY ME?
...
UZUMAKI NARUTO...
...YOU THINK HE'S THAT WORTHY?
...HE IS THE LIGHT.
SWOO...
THAT'S WHY WE ALL...

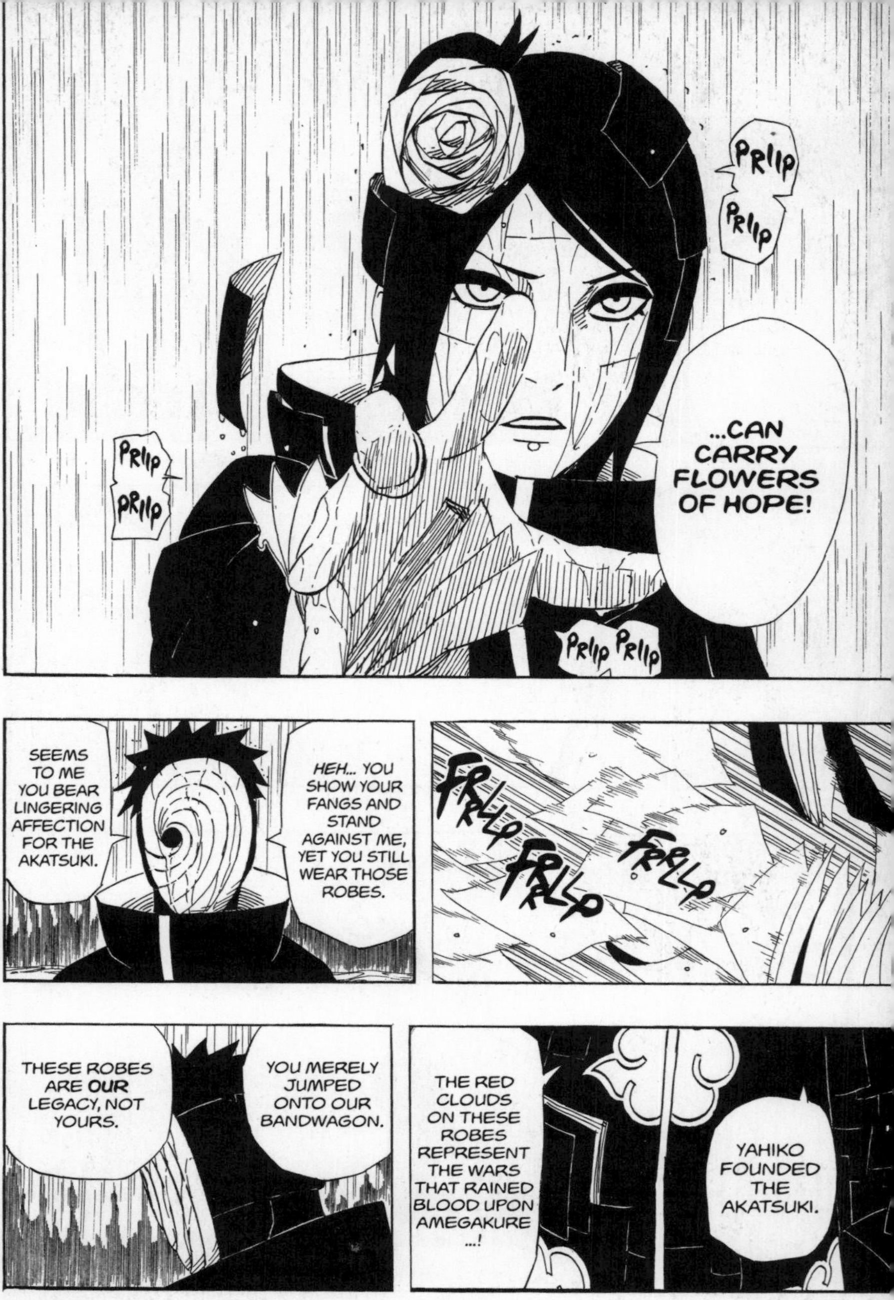
PRIIP PRIIP
...CAN CARRY FLOWERS OF HOPE!
PRIIP PRIIP
PRIIP PRIIP
FRRLLP FRRLLP FRRLLP
HEH... YOU SHOW YOUR FANGS AND STAND AGAINST ME, YET YOU STILL WEAR THOSE ROBES.
SEEMS TO ME YOU BEAR LINGERING AFFECTION FOR THE AKATSUKI.
YAHIKO FOUNDED THE AKATSUKI.
THE RED CLOUDS ON THESE ROBES REPRESENT THE WARS THAT RAINED BLOOD UPON AMEGAKURE ...!
YOU MERELY JUMPED ONTO OUR BANDWAGON.
THESE ROBES ARE **OUR** LEGACY, NOT YOURS.

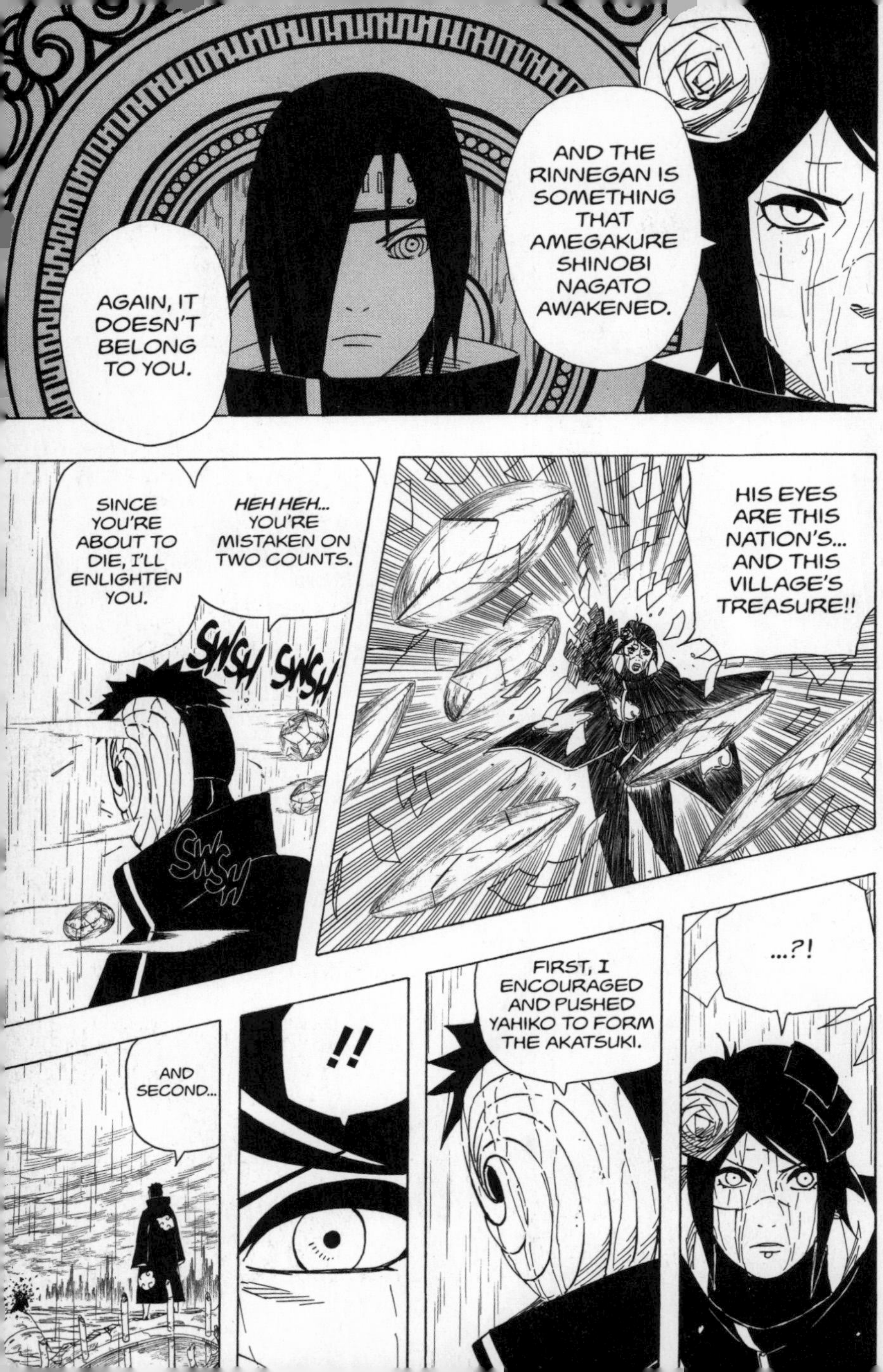
AND THE RINNEGAN IS SOMETHING THAT AMEGAKURE SHINOBI NAGATO AWAKENED.
AGAIN, IT DOESN'T BELONG TO YOU.
HIS EYES ARE THIS NATION'S... AND THIS VILLAGE'S TREASURE!!
HEH HEH... YOU'RE MISTAKEN ON TWO COUNTS.
SINCE YOU'RE ABOUT TO DIE, I'LL ENLIGHTEN YOU.
SWSH SWSH
SWSH SWSH
...?!
FIRST, I ENCOURAGED AND PUSHED YAHIKO TO FORM THE AKATSUKI.
!!
AND SECOND...

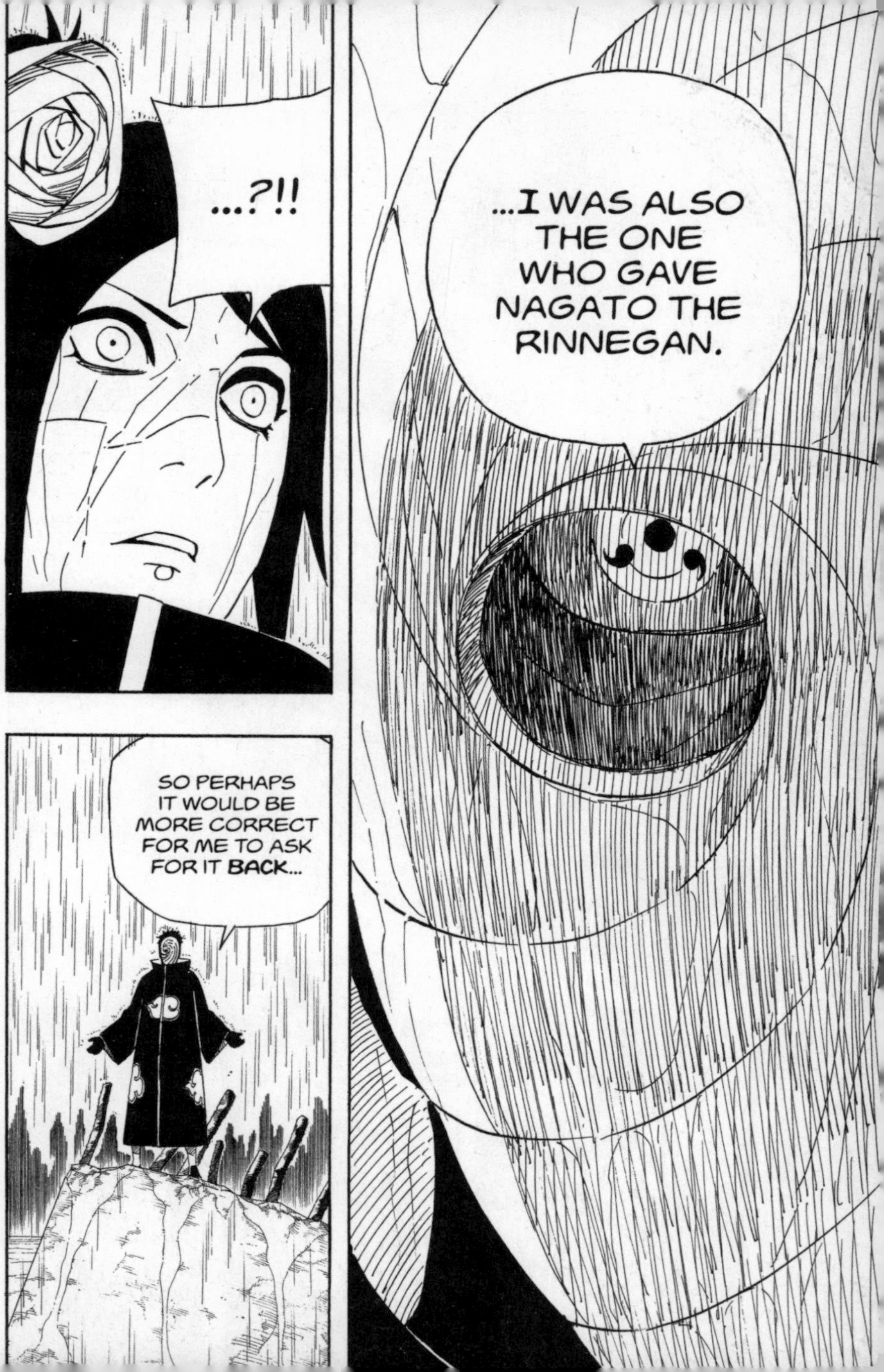
...I WAS ALSO THE ONE WHO GAVE NAGATO THE RINNEGAN.
...?!!
SO PERHAPS IT WOULD BE MORE CORRECT FOR ME TO ASK FOR IT **BACK**...

READ THIS WAY

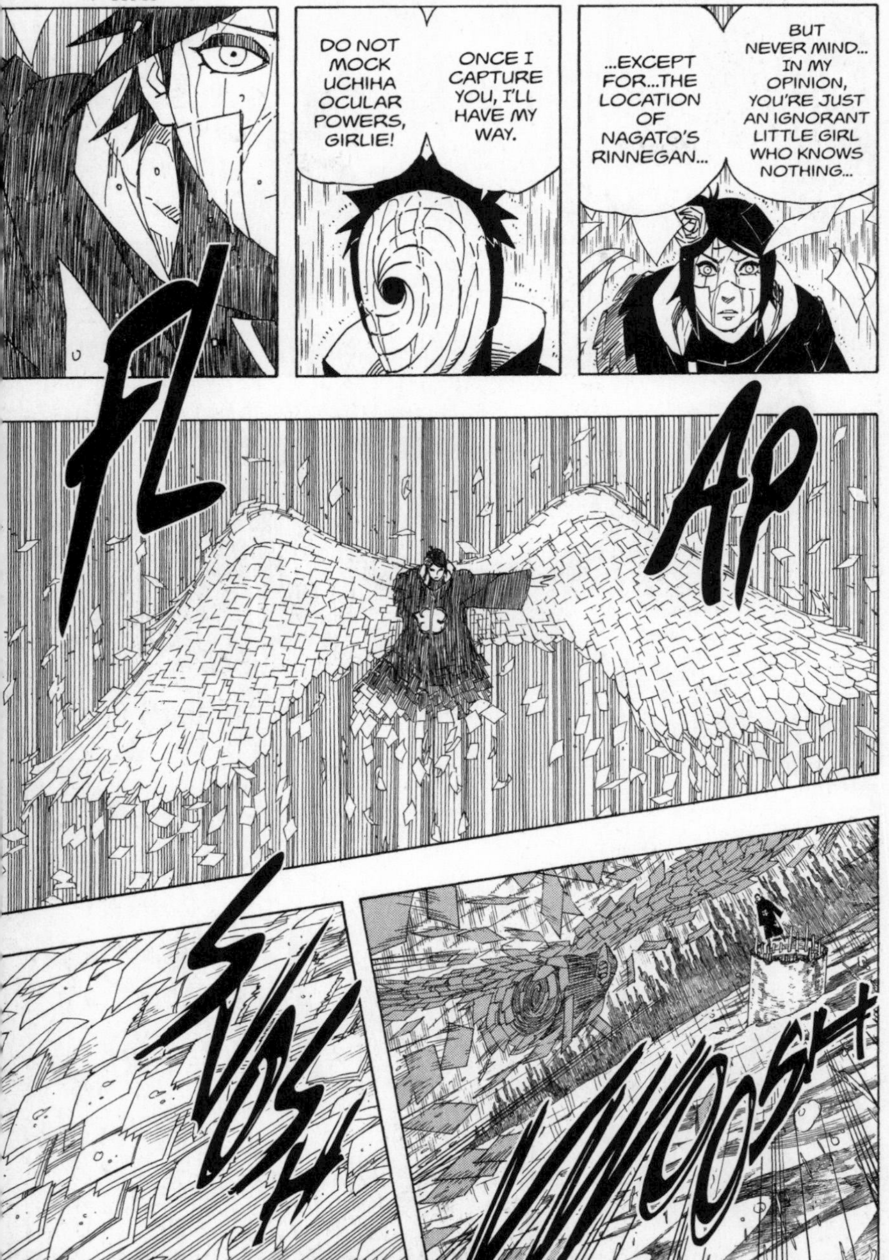
BUT NEVER MIND... IN MY OPINION, YOU'RE JUST AN IGNORANT LITTLE GIRL WHO KNOWS NOTHING...
...EXCEPT FOR...THE LOCATION OF NAGATO'S RINNEGAN...
ONCE I CAPTURE YOU, I'LL HAVE MY WAY.
DO NOT MOCK UCHIHA OCULAR POWERS, GIRLIE!
FLAP
VWOOSH

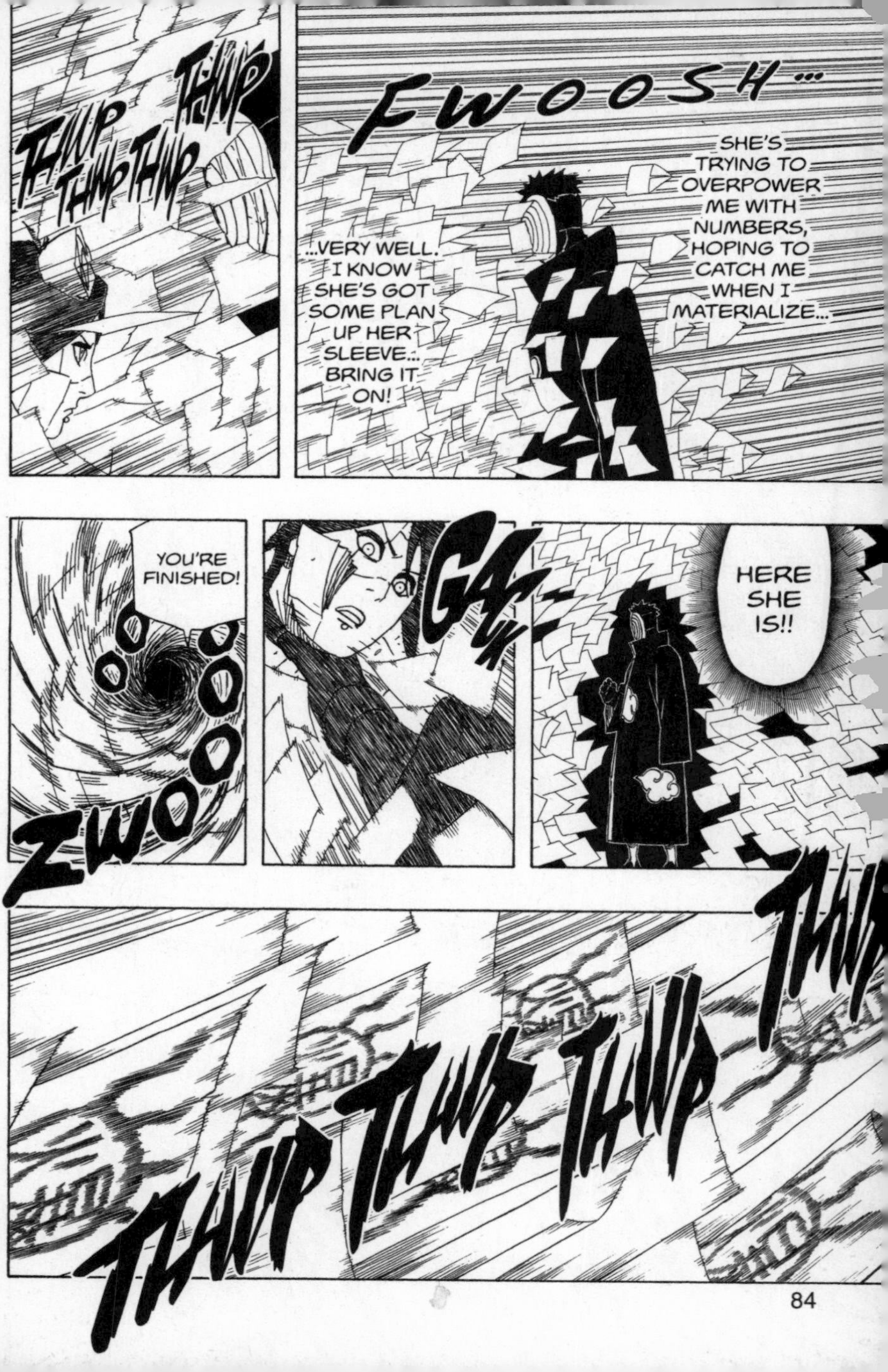
FWOOSH...
SHE'S TRYING TO OVERPOWER ME WITH NUMBERS, HOPING TO CATCH ME WHEN I MATERIALIZE...
...VERY WELL. I KNOW SHE'S GOT SOME PLAN UP HER SLEEVE... BRING IT ON!
THWP THWP THWP THWP
HERE SHE IS!!
GA
YOU'RE FINISHED!
ZWOO
THWP THWP THWP THWP

READ THIS WAY

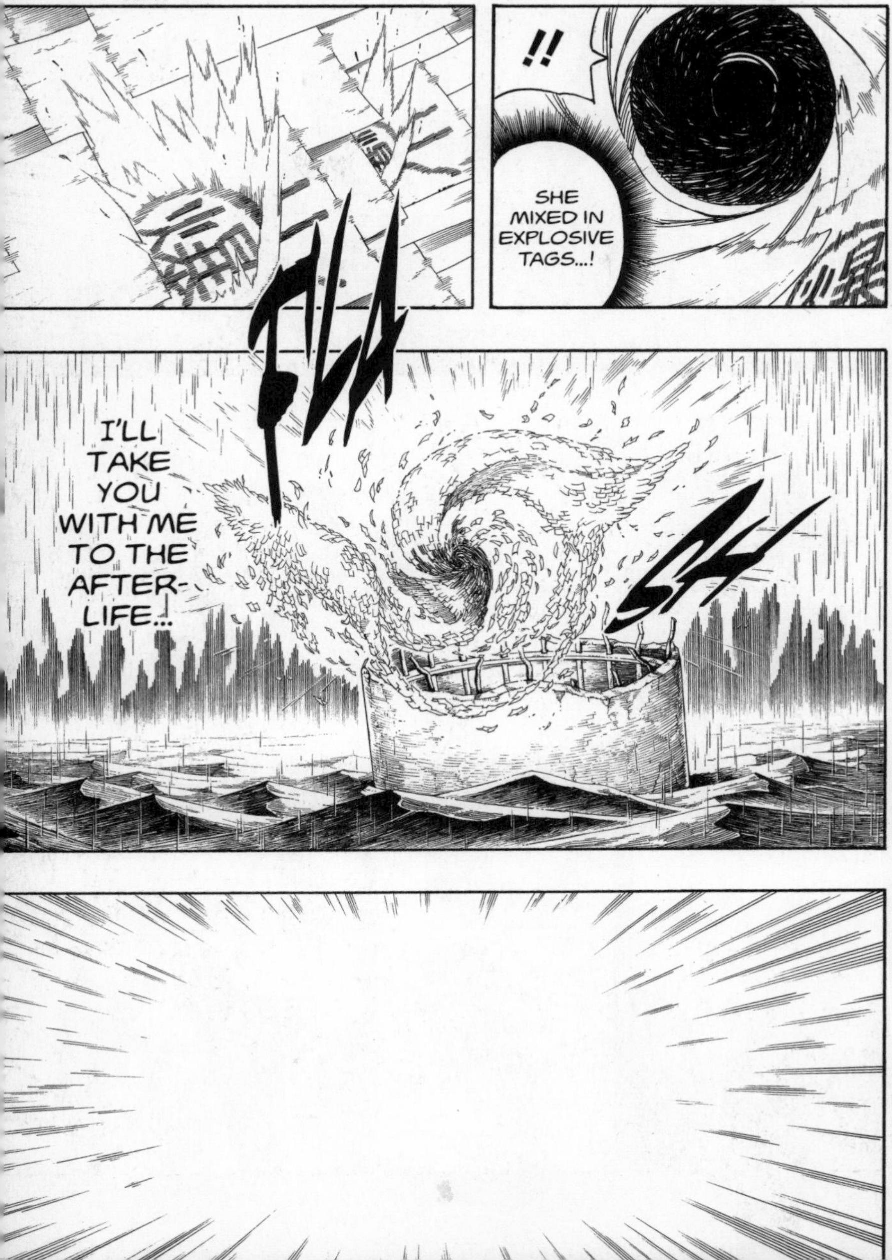
!!
SHE MIXED IN EXPLOSIVE TAGS...!
FLA
I'LL TAKE YOU WITH ME TO THE AFTER-LIFE...
SH

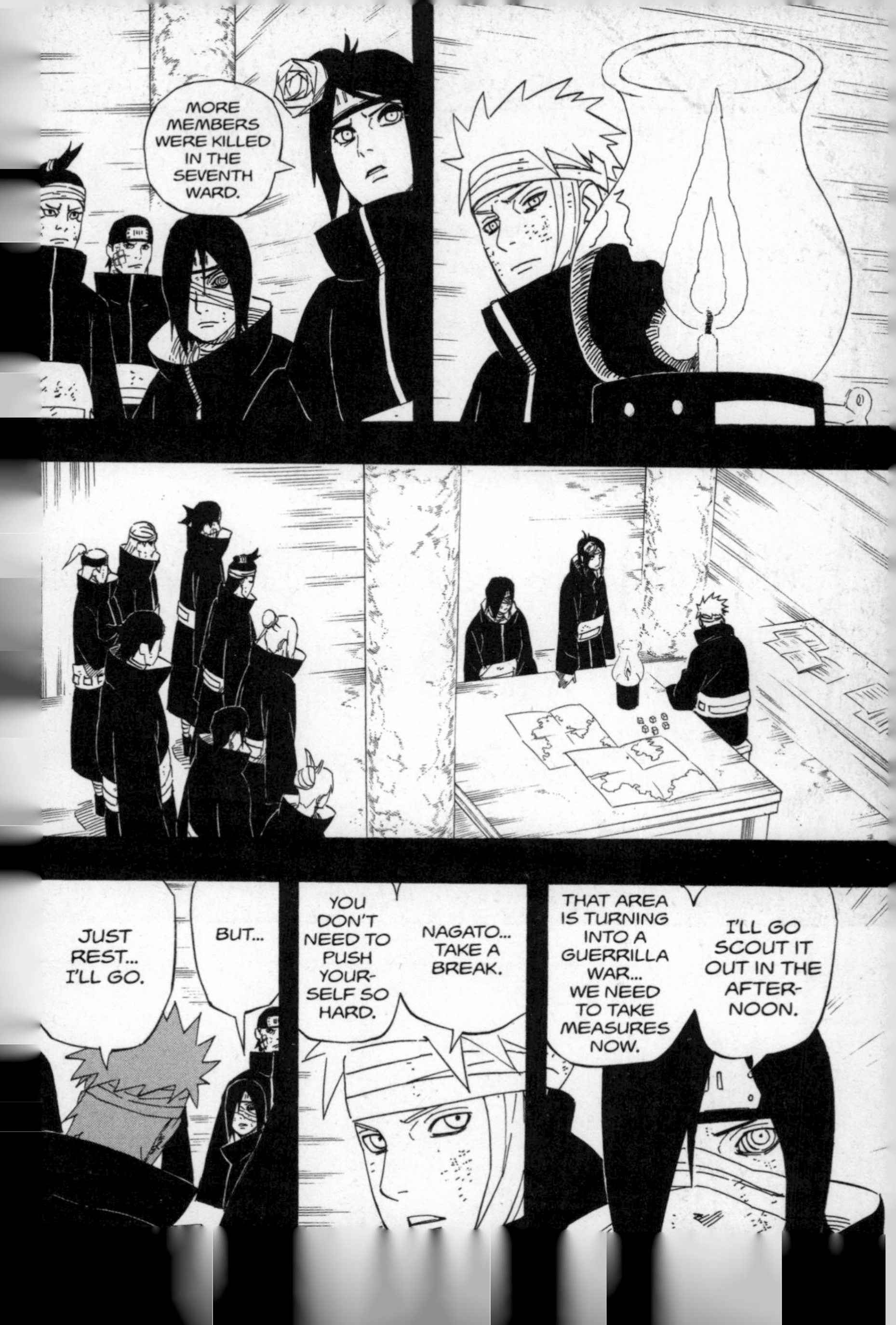
MORE MEMBERS WERE KILLED IN THE SEVENTH WARD.
THAT AREA IS TURNING INTO A GUERRILLA WAR... WE NEED TO TAKE MEASURES NOW.
I'LL GO SCOUT IT OUT IN THE AFTER-NOON.
NAGATO... TAKE A BREAK.
YOU DON'T NEED TO PUSH YOUR-SELF SO HARD.
BUT...
JUST REST... I'LL GO.

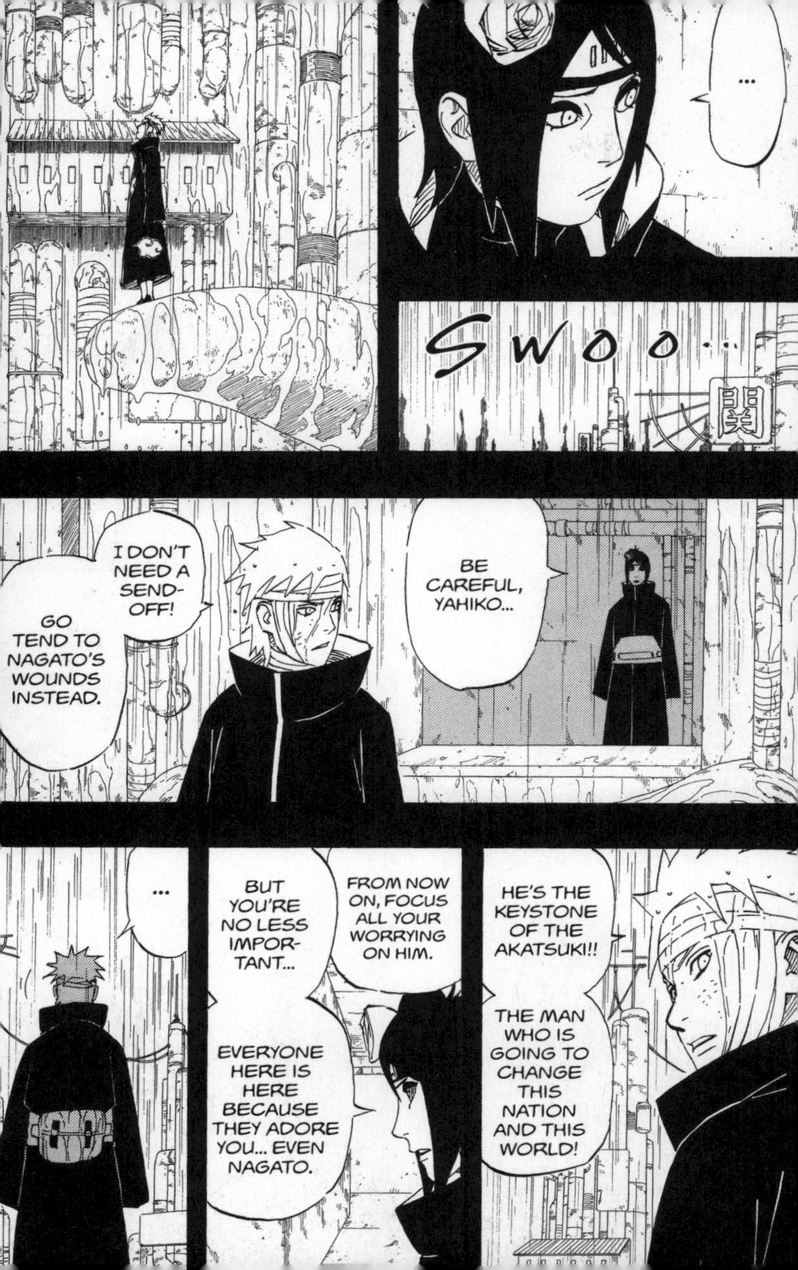
...
SWOO...
BE CAREFUL, YAHIKO...
I DON'T NEED A SEND-OFF!
GO TEND TO NAGATO'S WOUNDS INSTEAD.
HE'S THE KEYSTONE OF THE AKATSUKI!!
THE MAN WHO IS GOING TO CHANGE THIS NATION AND THIS WORLD!
FROM NOW ON, FOCUS ALL YOUR WORRYING ON HIM.
BUT YOU'RE NO LESS IMPORTANT...
EVERYONE HERE IS HERE BECAUSE THEY ADORE YOU... EVEN NAGATO.
...

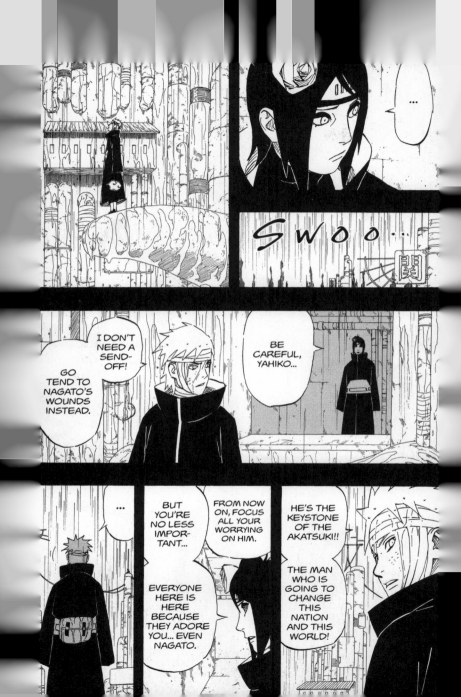

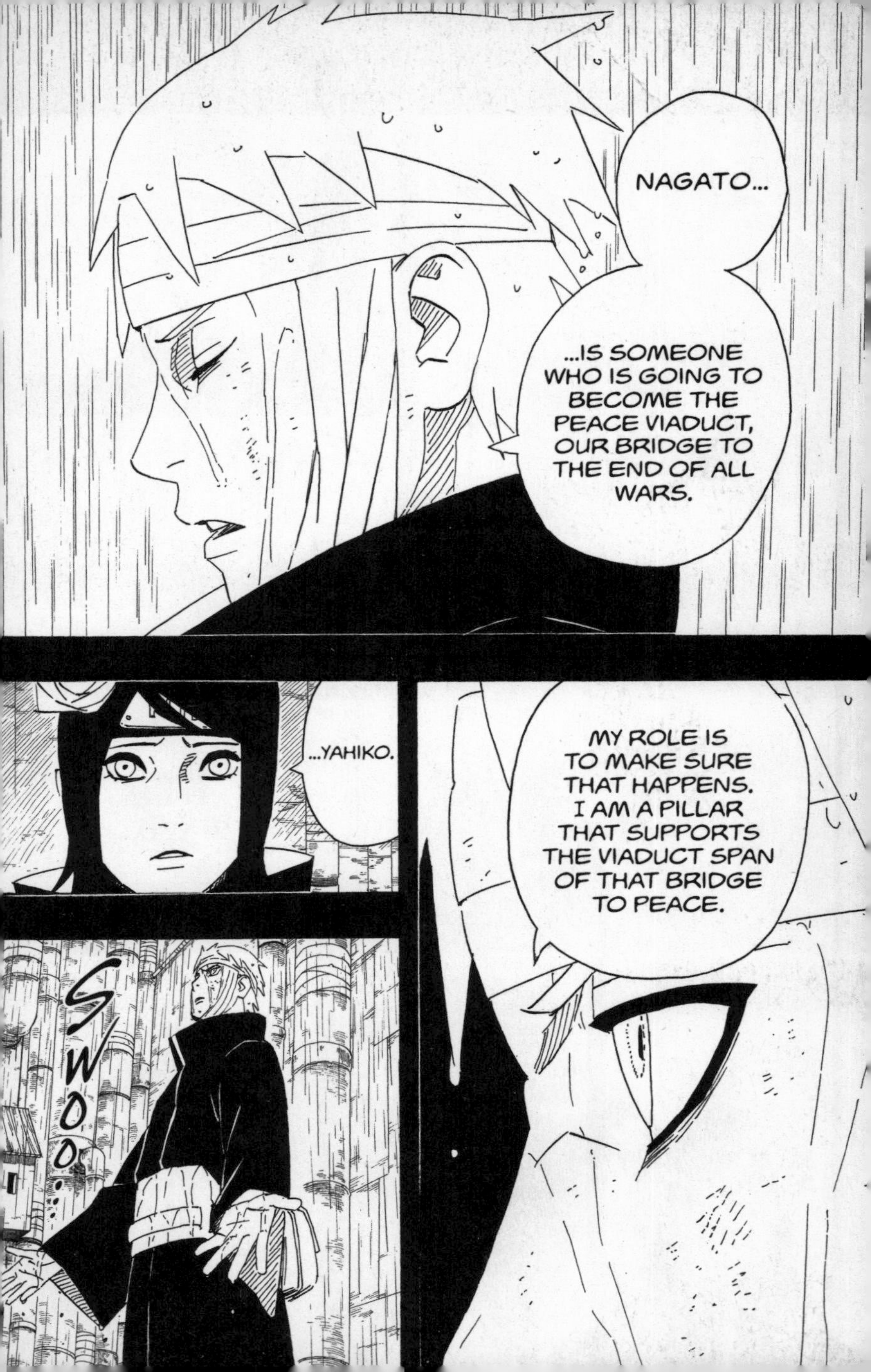
NAGATO...
...IS SOMEONE WHO IS GOING TO BECOME THE PEACE VIADUCT, OUR BRIDGE TO THE END OF ALL WARS.
MY ROLE IS TO MAKE SURE THAT HAPPENS. I AM A PILLAR THAT SUPPORTS THE VIADUCT SPAN OF THAT BRIDGE TO PEACE.
...YAHIKO.
SWOO...

READ THIS WAY

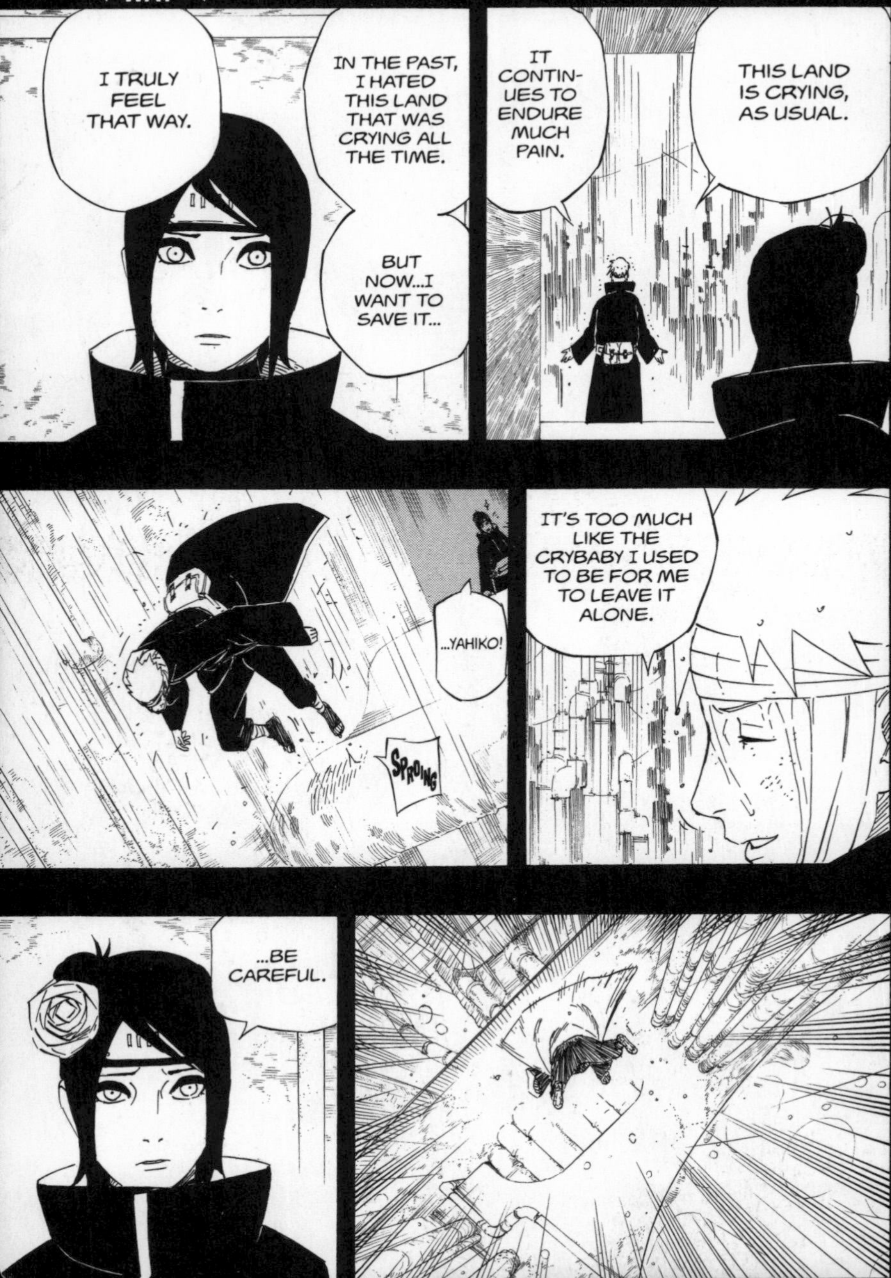
THIS LAND IS CRYING, AS USUAL.
IT CONTINUES TO ENDURE MUCH PAIN.
IN THE PAST, I HATED THIS LAND THAT WAS CRYING ALL THE TIME.
BUT NOW...I WANT TO SAVE IT...
I TRULY FEEL THAT WAY.
IT'S TOO MUCH LIKE THE CRYBABY I USED TO BE FOR ME TO LEAVE IT ALONE.
...YAHIKO!
SPROING
...BE CAREFUL.

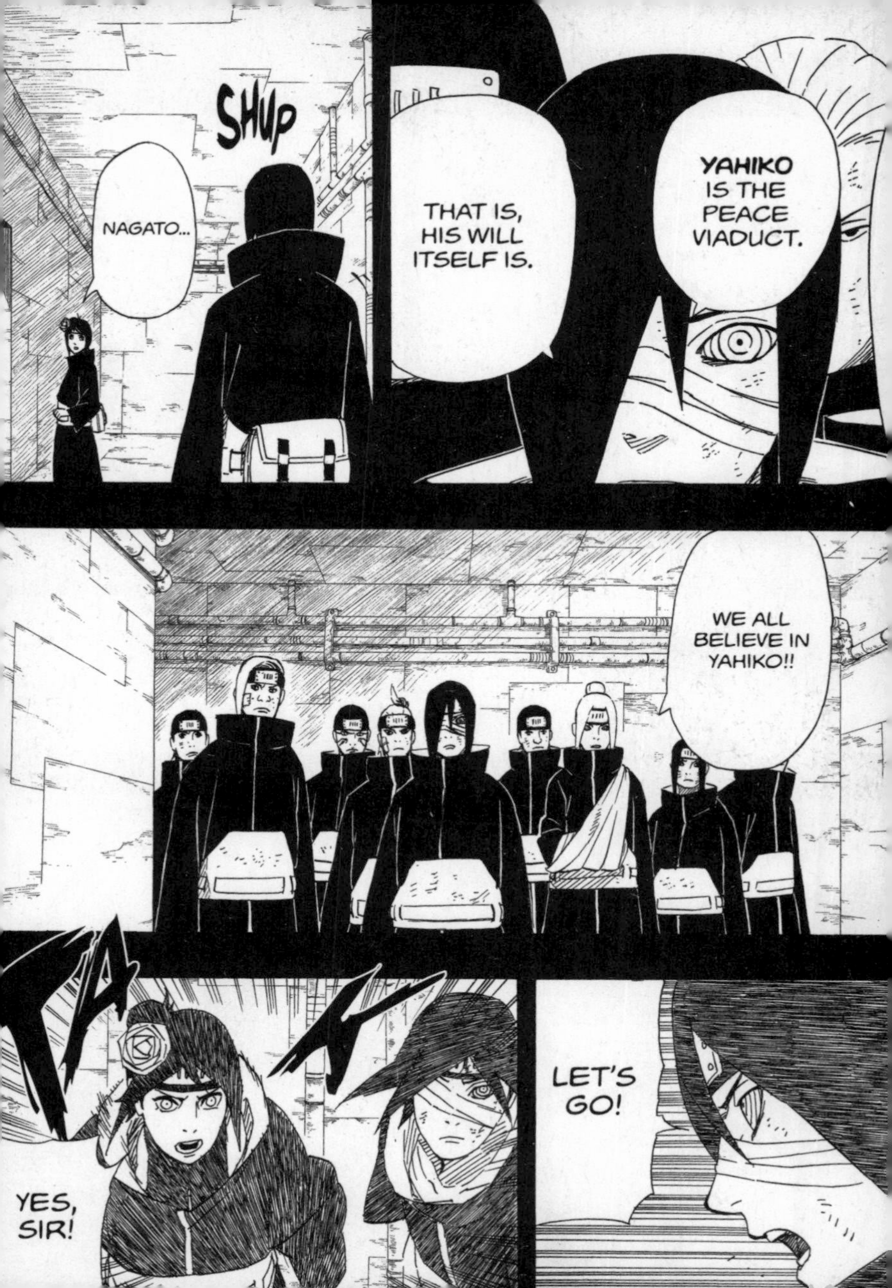
YAHIKO IS THE PEACE VIADUCT.
THAT IS, HIS WILL ITSELF IS.
SHUP
NAGATO...
WE ALL BELIEVE IN YAHIKO!!
LET'S GO!
YES, SIR!

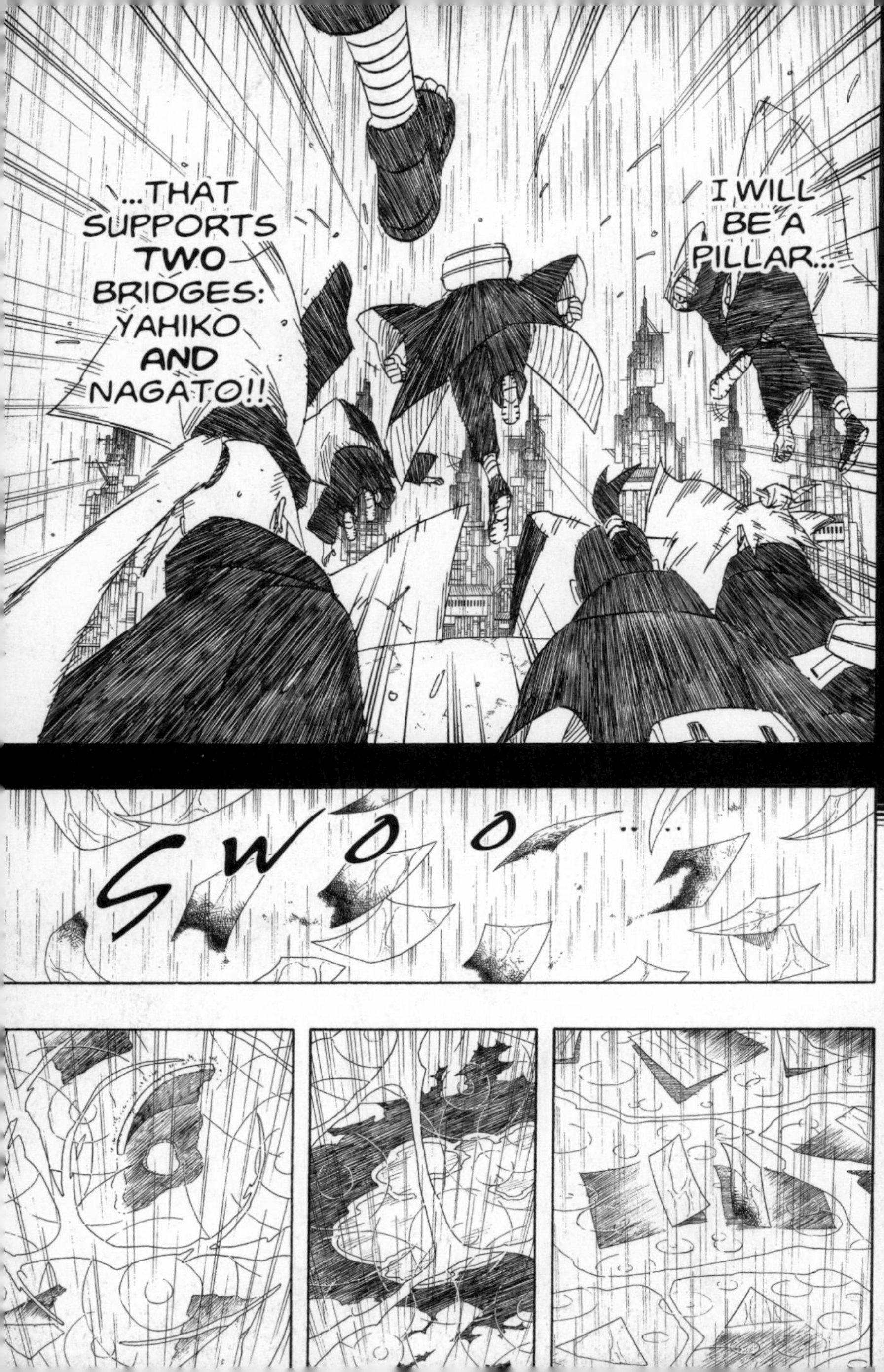
I WILL BE A PILLAR...
...THAT SUPPORTS TWO BRIDGES: YAHIKO AND NAGATO!!
SWOO...

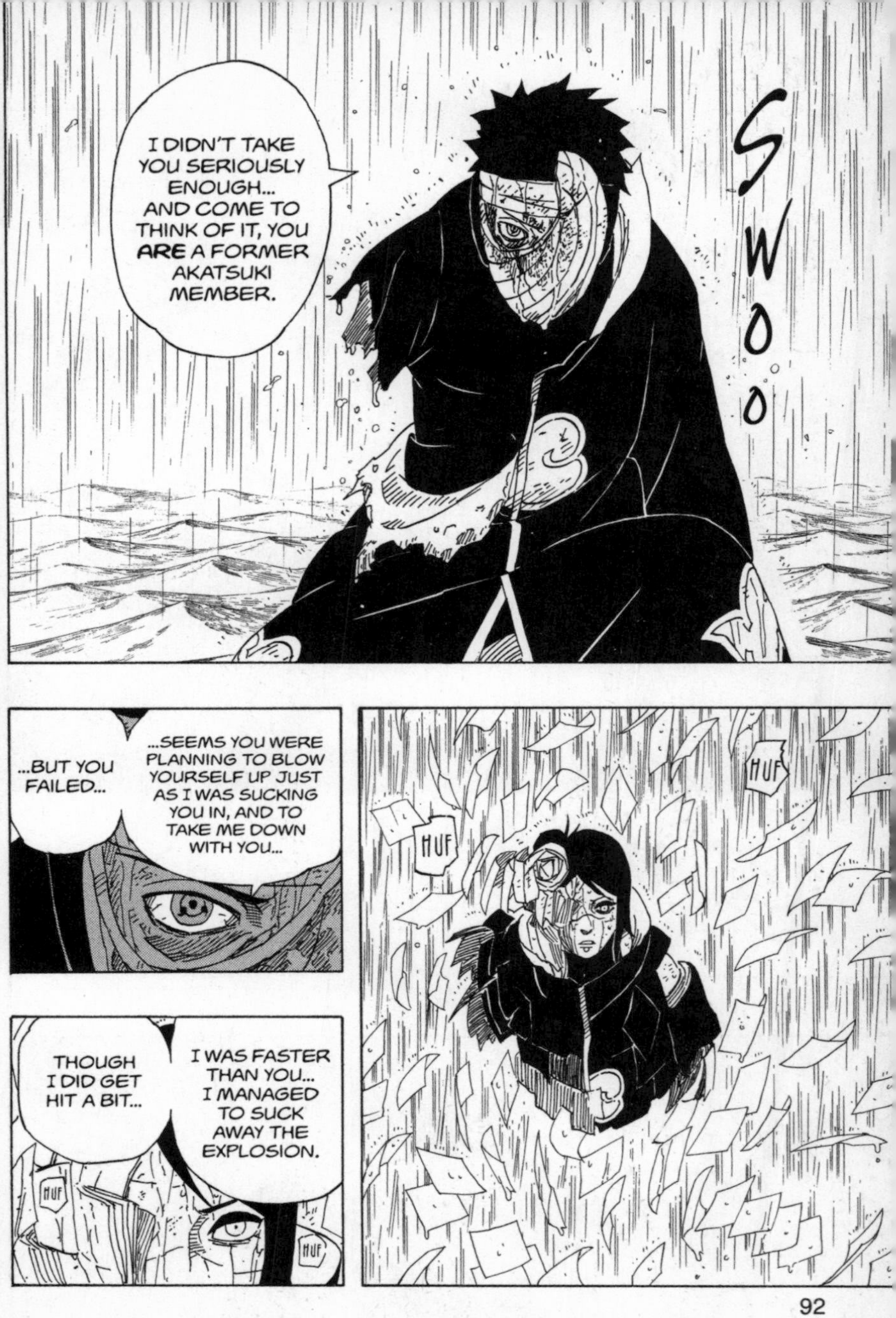
SWOOO
I DIDN'T TAKE YOU SERIOUSLY ENOUGH... AND COME TO THINK OF IT, YOU **ARE** A FORMER AKATSUKI MEMBER.
HUF
HUF
...SEEMS YOU WERE PLANNING TO BLOW YOURSELF UP JUST AS I WAS SUCKING YOU IN, AND TO TAKE ME DOWN WITH YOU...
...BUT YOU FAILED...
I WAS FASTER THAN YOU... I MANAGED TO SUCK AWAY THE EXPLOSION.
THOUGH I DID GET HIT A BIT...
HUF
HUF

READ THIS WAY

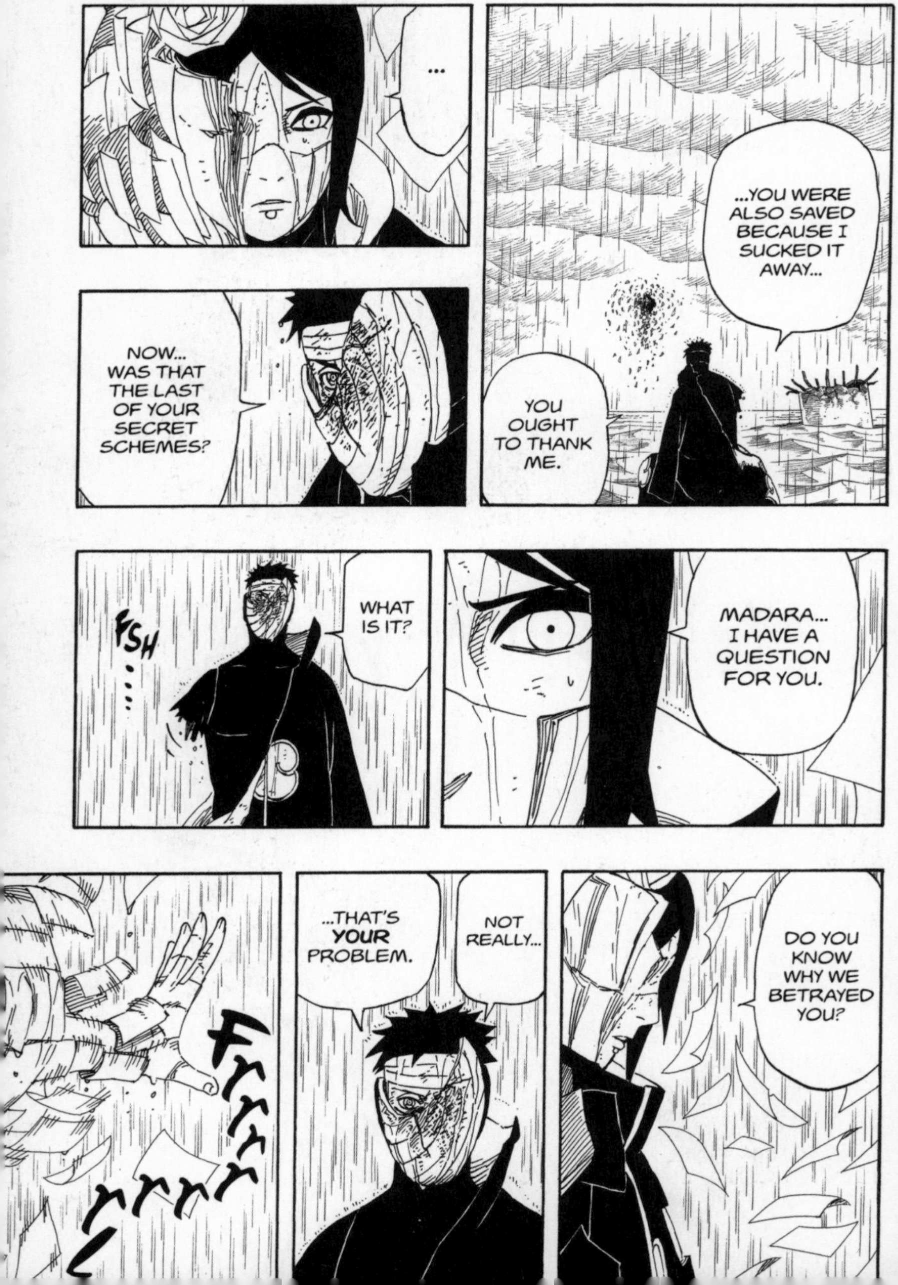
...YOU WERE ALSO SAVED BECAUSE I SUCKED IT AWAY...
YOU OUGHT TO THANK ME.
...
NOW... WAS THAT THE LAST OF YOUR SECRET SCHEMES?
MADARA... I HAVE A QUESTION FOR YOU.
WHAT IS IT?
FSH
DO YOU KNOW WHY WE BETRAYED YOU?
NOT REALLY...
...THAT'S YOUR PROBLEM.
Frrrrrrrrrl

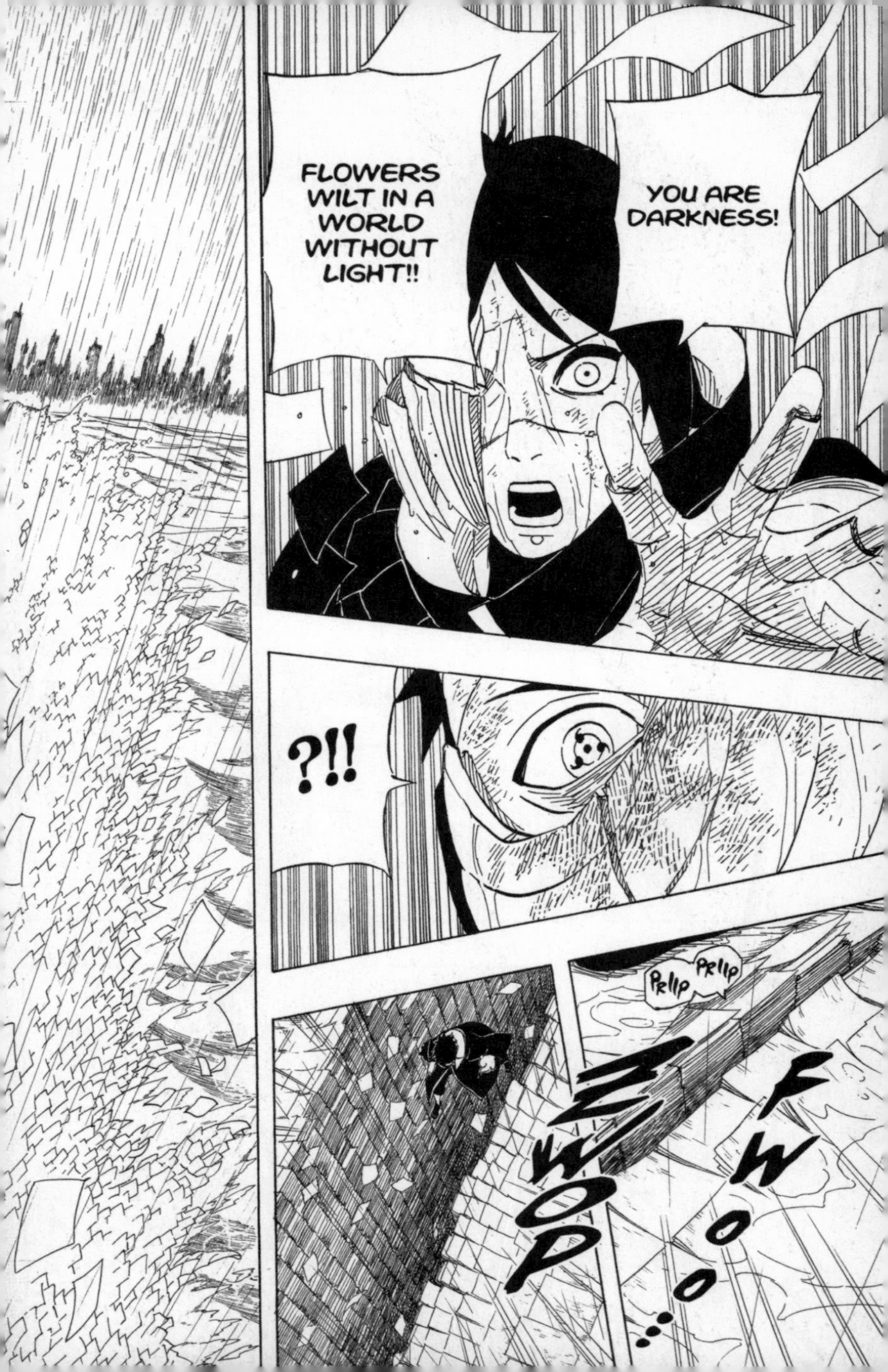
YOU ARE DARKNESS!
FLOWERS WILT IN A WORLD WITHOUT LIGHT!!
?!!
PRIIP PRIIP
FWOOO...
FWOOP

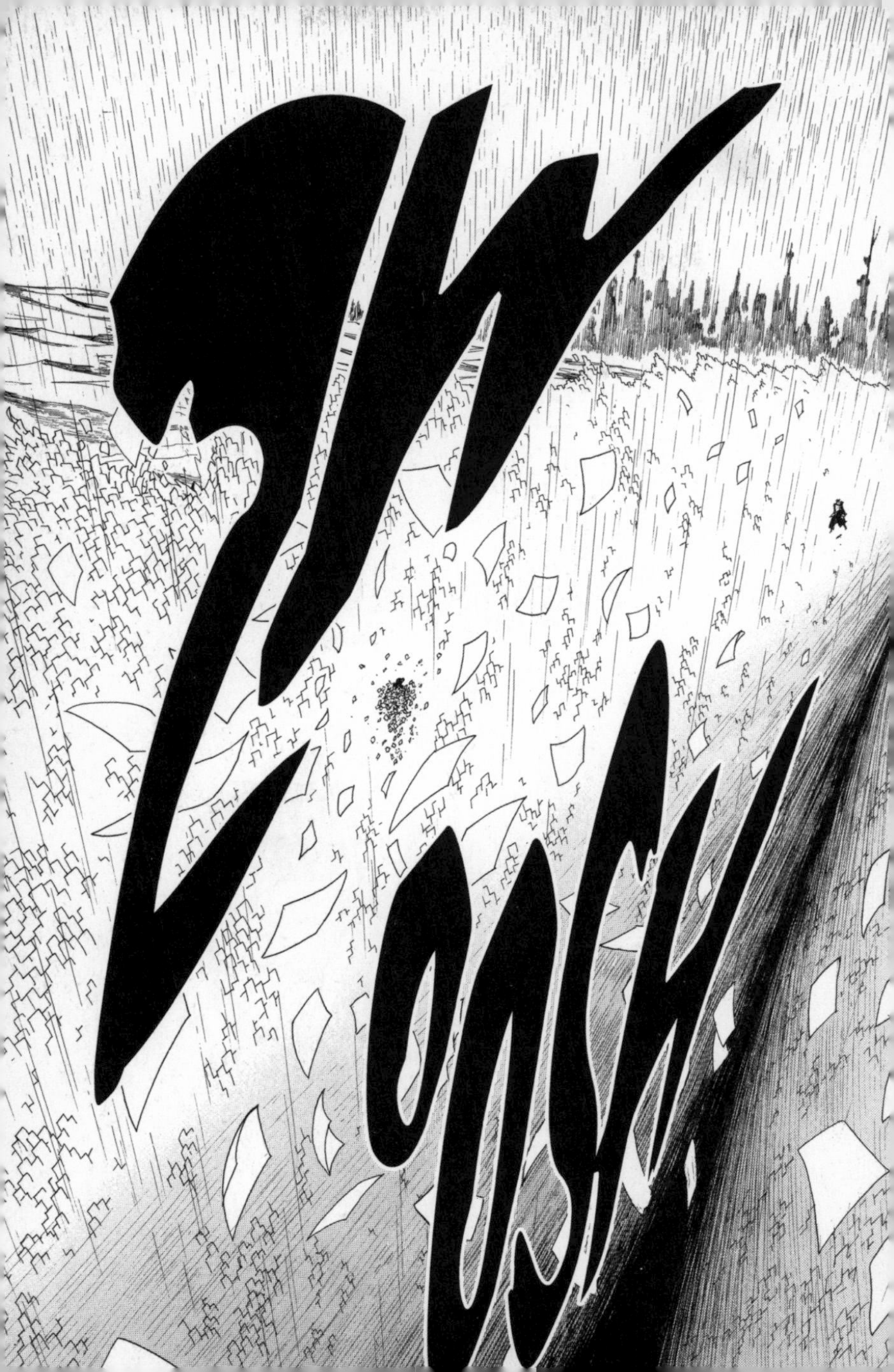
Zwash!

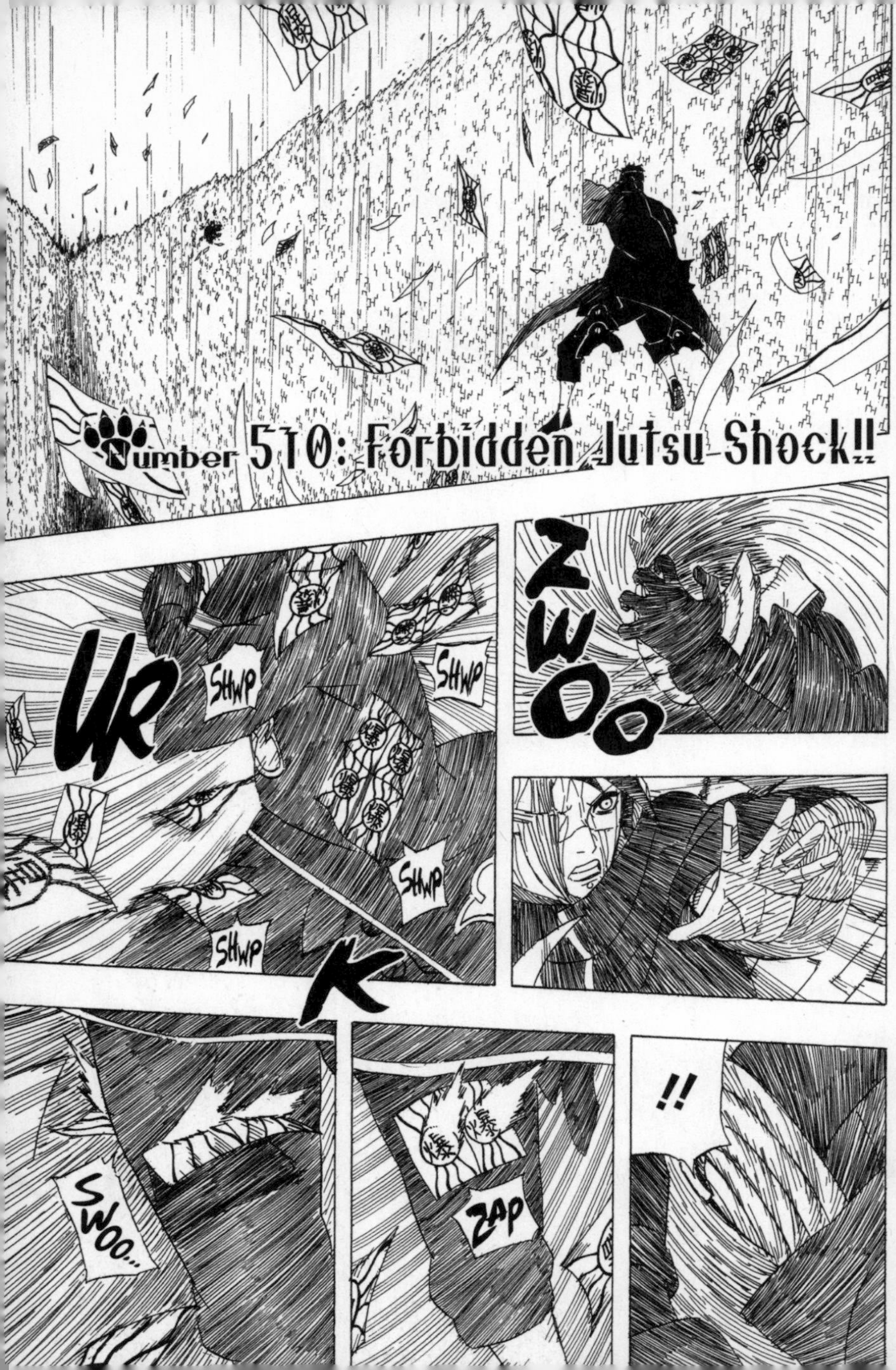
Number 510: Forbidden Jutsu Shock!!
ZWOO
SHWP
SHWP
URK
SHWP
SHWP
!!
ZAP
SWOO...

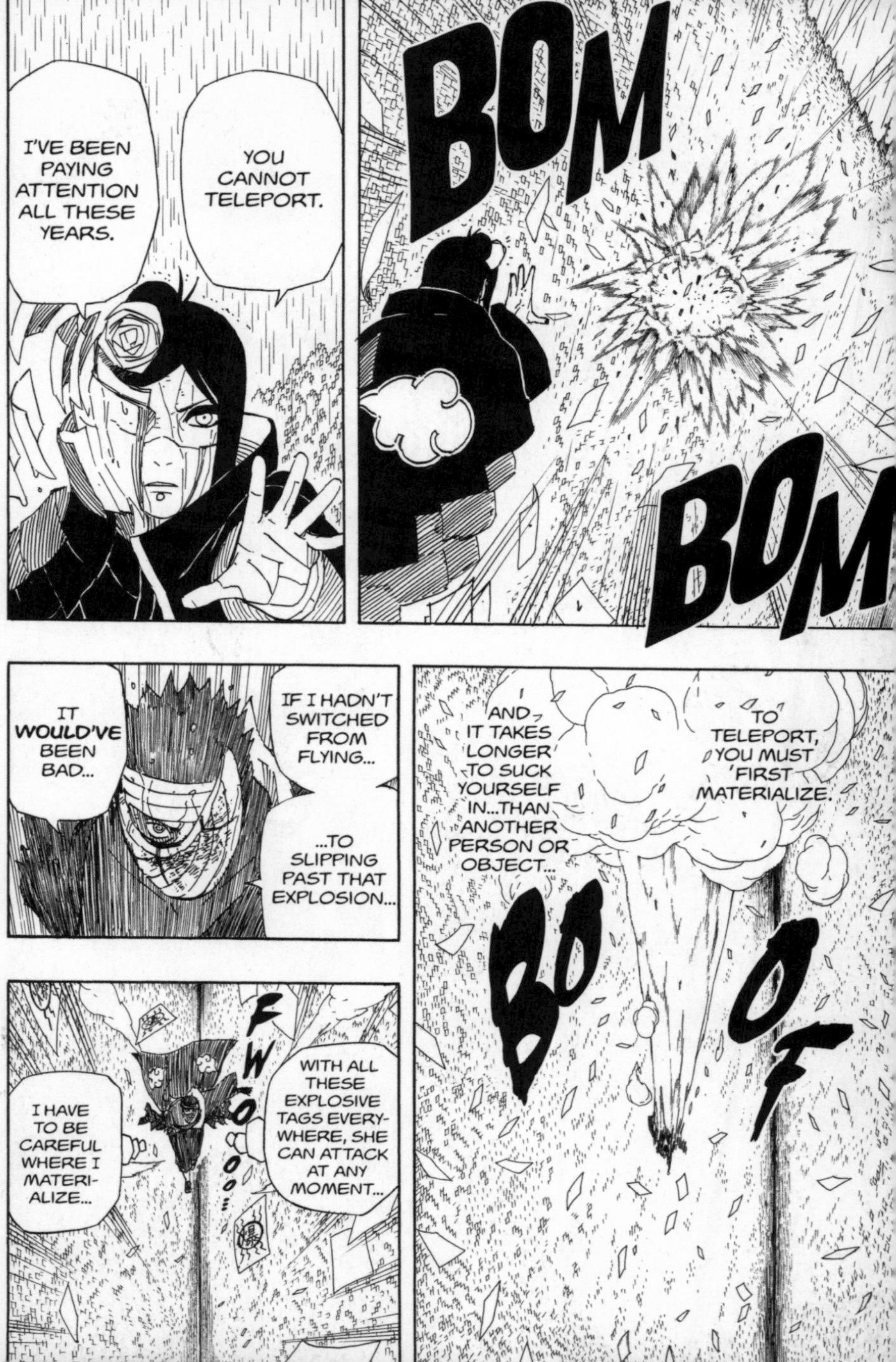
BOM
BOM
YOU CANNOT TELEPORT.
I'VE BEEN PAYING ATTENTION ALL THESE YEARS.
TO TELEPORT, YOU MUST FIRST MATERIALIZE.
AND IT TAKES LONGER TO SUCK YOURSELF IN...THAN ANOTHER PERSON OR OBJECT...
BOOF
IF I HADN'T SWITCHED FROM FLYING...
...TO SLIPPING PAST THAT EXPLOSION...
IT **WOULD'VE** BEEN BAD...
FWOOO...
WITH ALL THESE EXPLOSIVE TAGS EVERY-WHERE, SHE CAN ATTACK AT ANY MOMENT...
I HAVE TO BE CAREFUL WHERE I MATERI-ALIZE...

READ THIS WAY

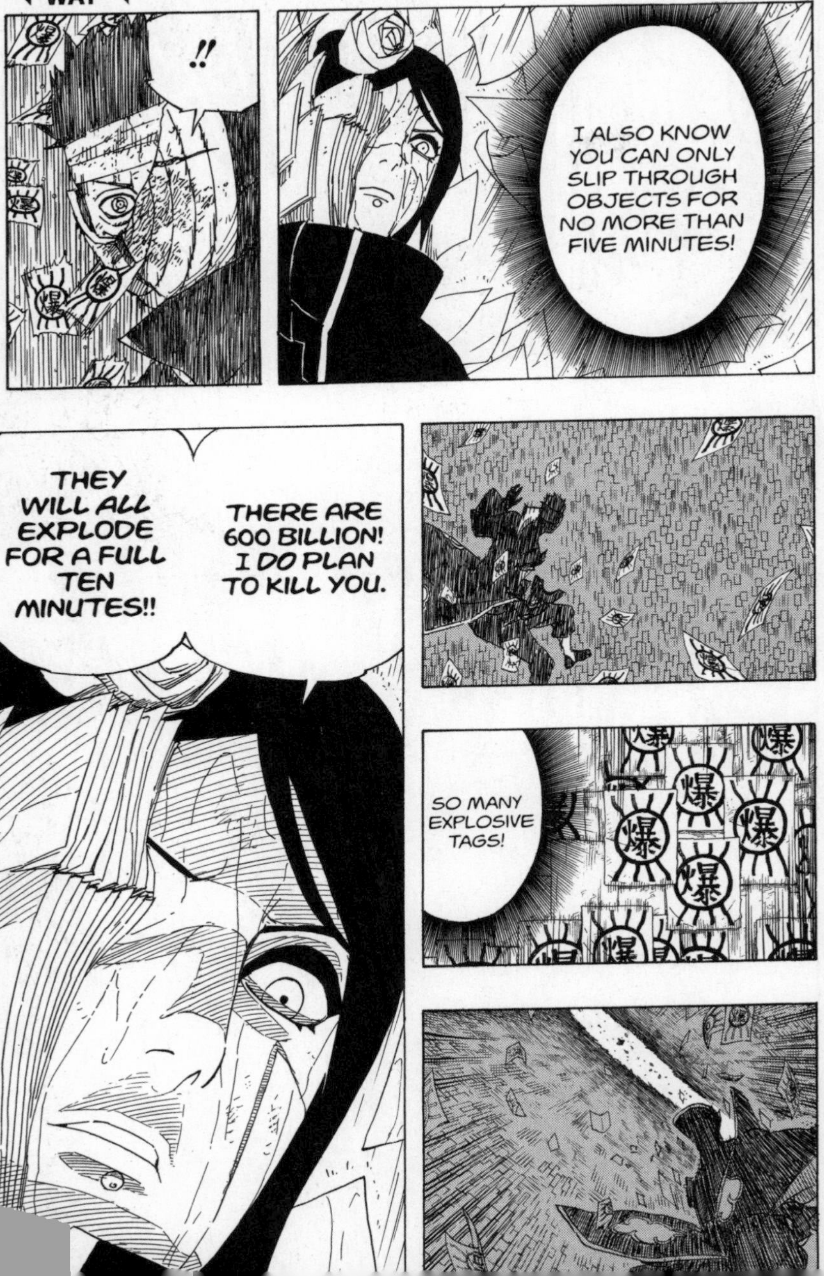
I ALSO KNOW YOU CAN ONLY SLIP THROUGH OBJECTS FOR NO MORE THAN FIVE MINUTES!
!!
SO MANY EXPLOSIVE TAGS!
THERE ARE 600 BILLION! I DO PLAN TO KILL YOU.
THEY WILL ALL EXPLODE FOR A FULL TEN MINUTES!!

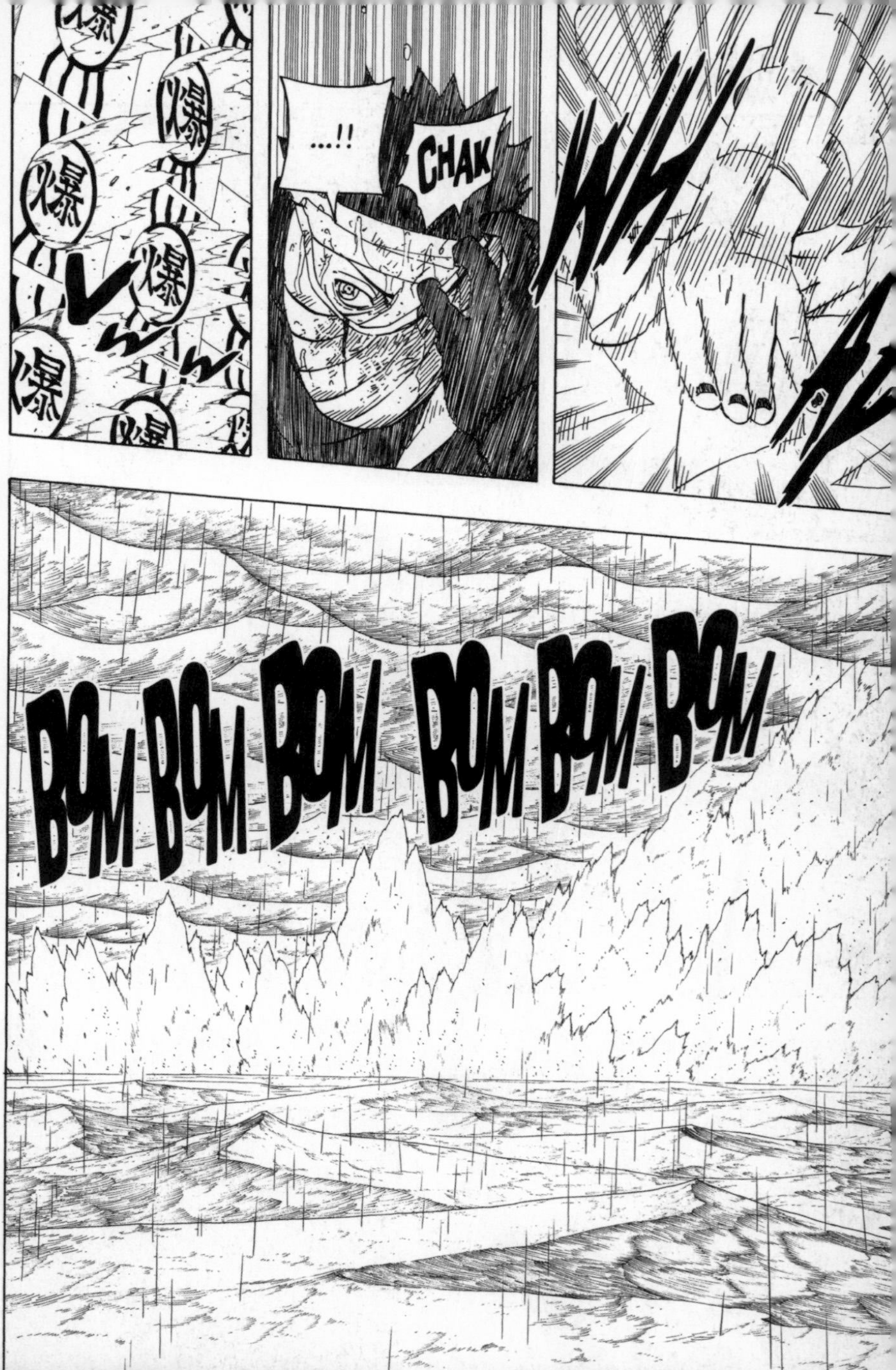
...!!
CHAK
BOM BOM BOM BOM BOM BOM

READ THIS WAY

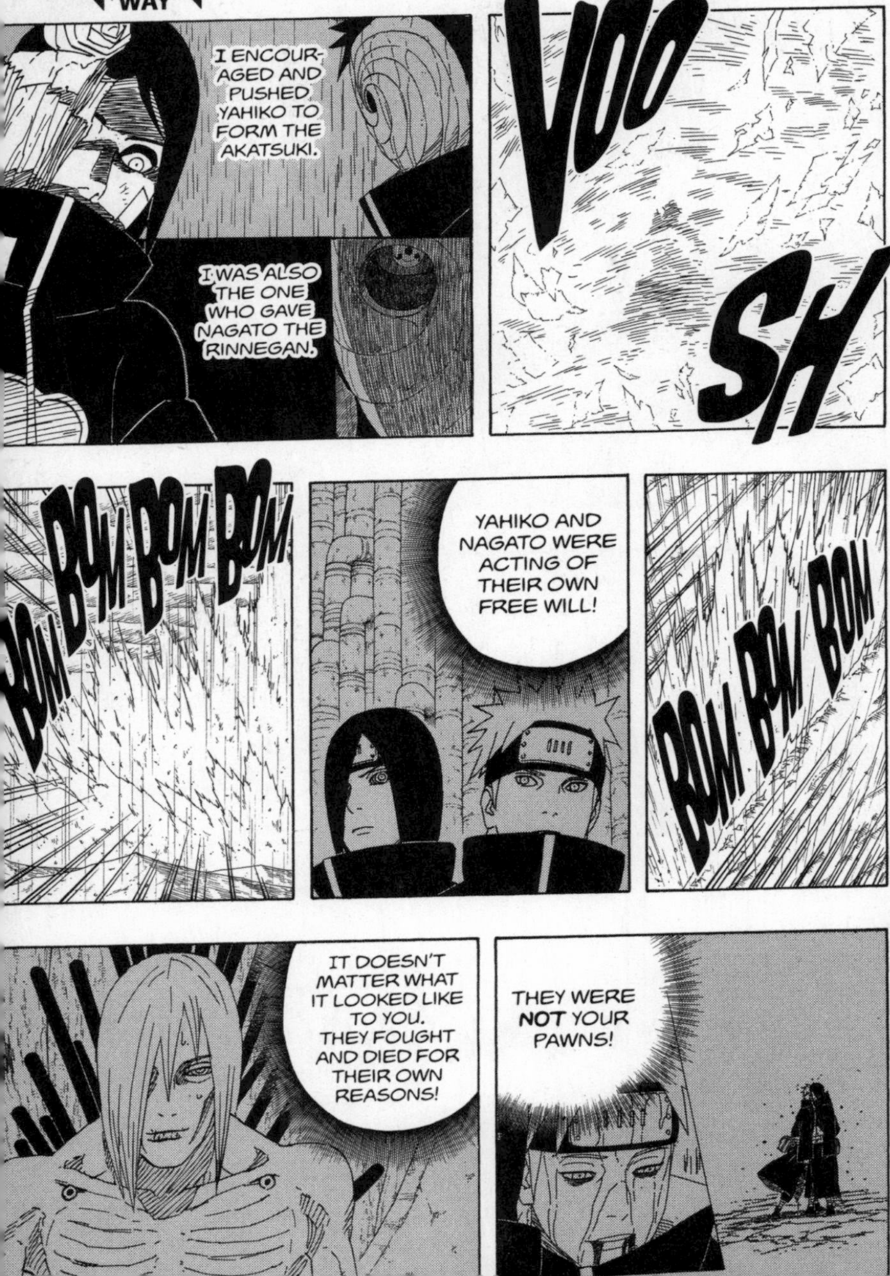
VOO
SH
I ENCOURAGED AND PUSHED YAHIKO TO FORM THE AKATSUKI.
I WAS ALSO THE ONE WHO GAVE NAGATO THE RINNEGAN.
BOM BOM BOM
YAHIKO AND NAGATO WERE ACTING OF THEIR OWN FREE WILL!
BOM BOM BOM BOM
THEY WERE **NOT** YOUR PAWNS!
IT DOESN'T MATTER WHAT IT LOOKED LIKE TO YOU. THEY FOUGHT AND DIED FOR THEIR OWN REASONS!

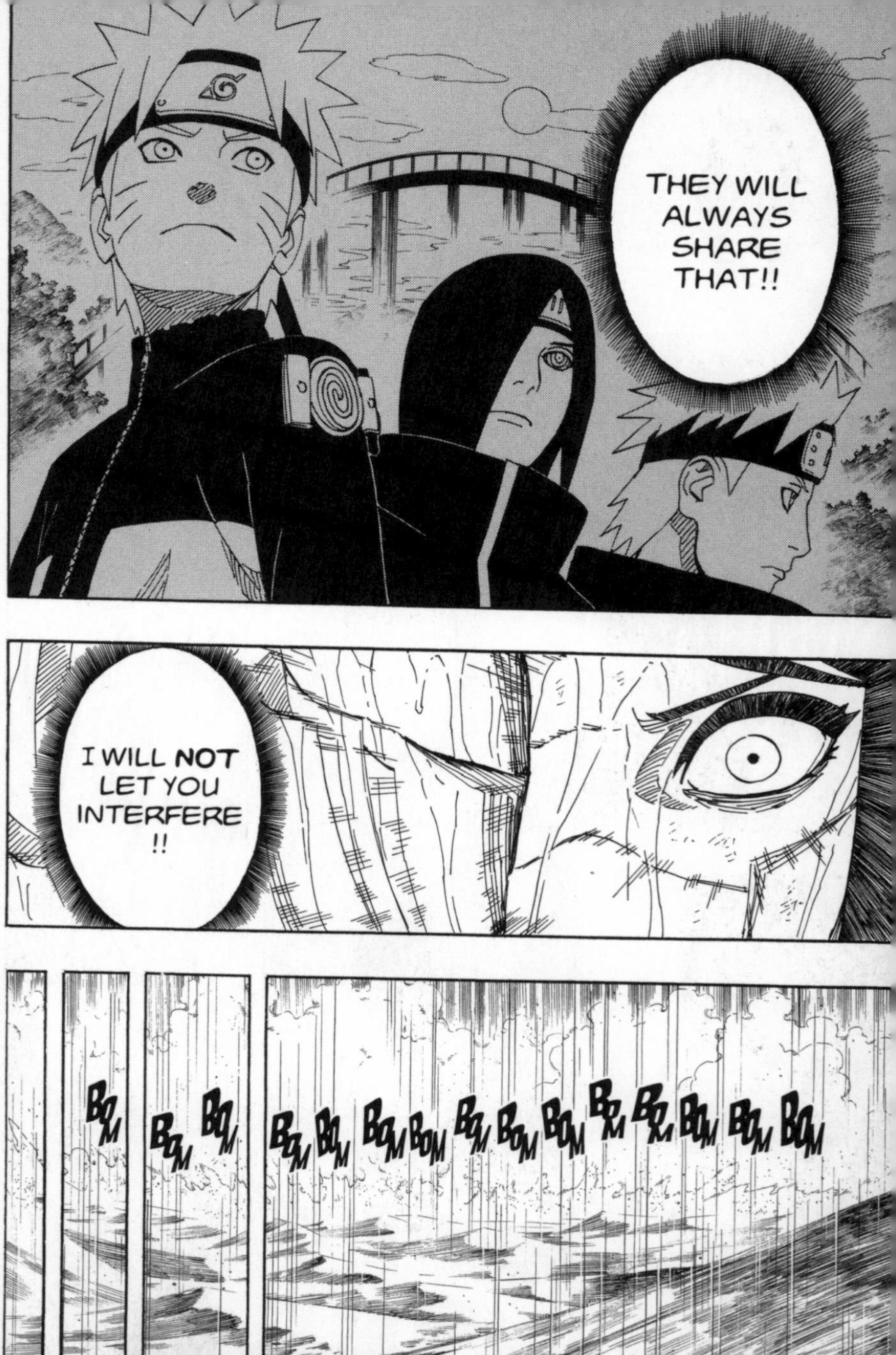
THEY WILL ALWAYS SHARE THAT!!
I WILL NOT LET YOU INTERFERE !!
BOM BOM BOM BOM BOM BOM BOM BOM BOM BOM BOM BOM
BOM BOM
BOM

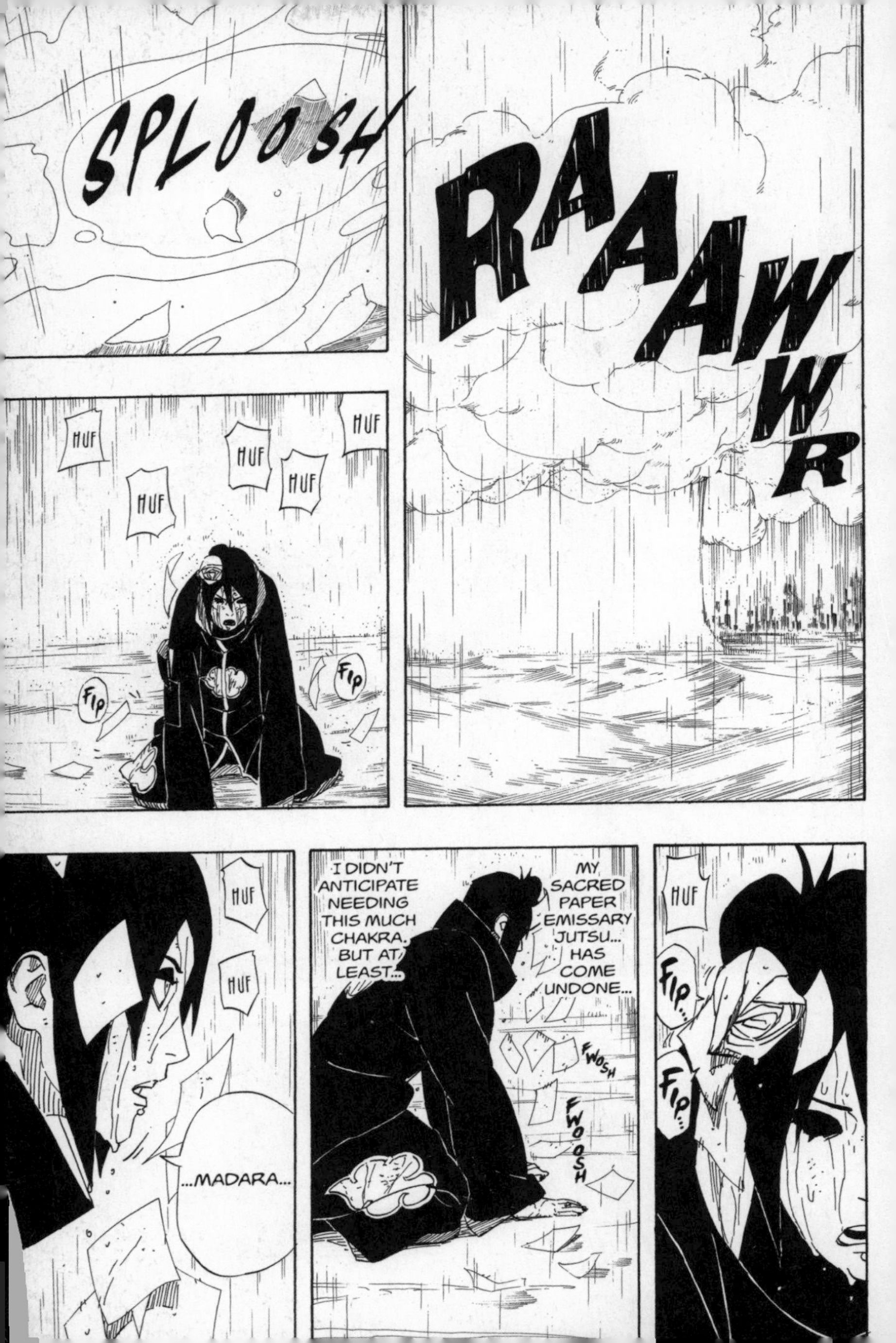
RAAAWWR
SPLOOSH
HUF
HUF
HUF
HUF
HUF
FLIP
FLIP
HUF
FLIP...
FLIP...
MY SACRED PAPER EMISSARY JUTSU... HAS COME UNDONE...
I DIDN'T ANTICIPATE NEEDING THIS MUCH CHAKRA. BUT AT LEAST...
FWOSH
FWOOSH
HUF
HUF
...MADARA...

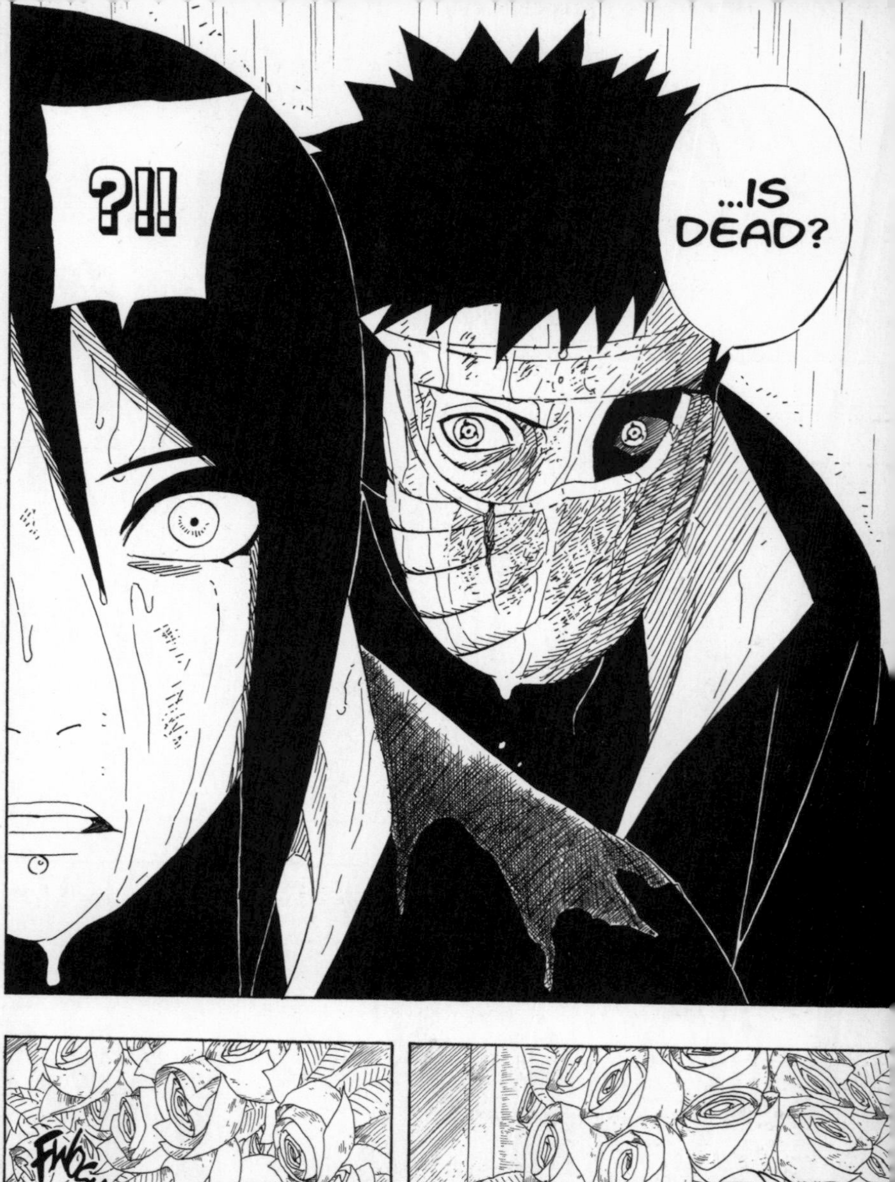
...IS DEAD?
?!!
FWOSH FWOSH FWOSH

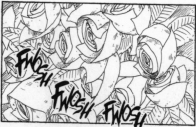

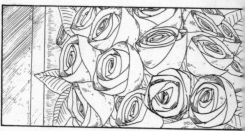

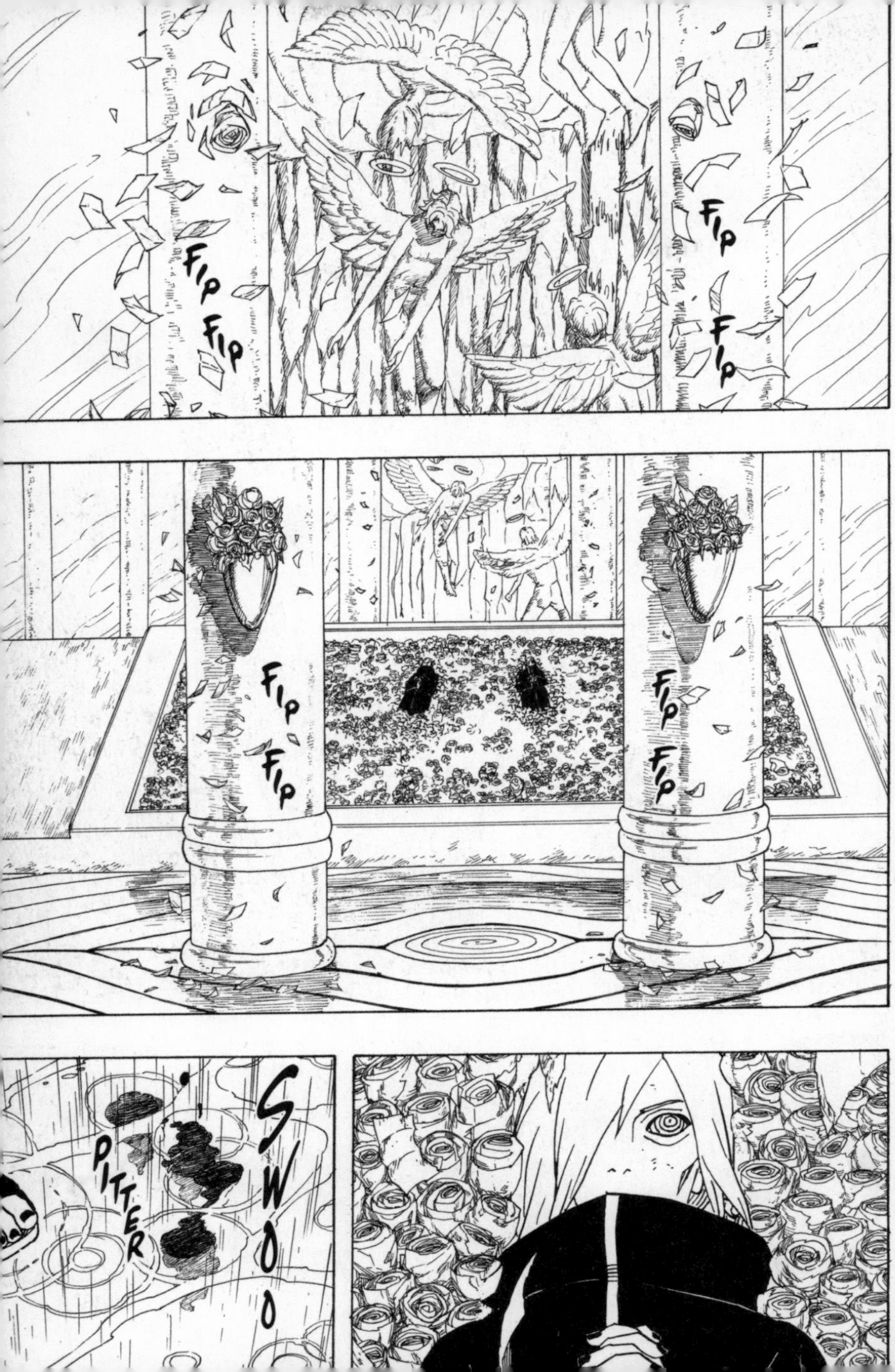
FIP
FIP
FIP
FIP
FIP
FIP
FIP
FIP
SWOOO
PITTER

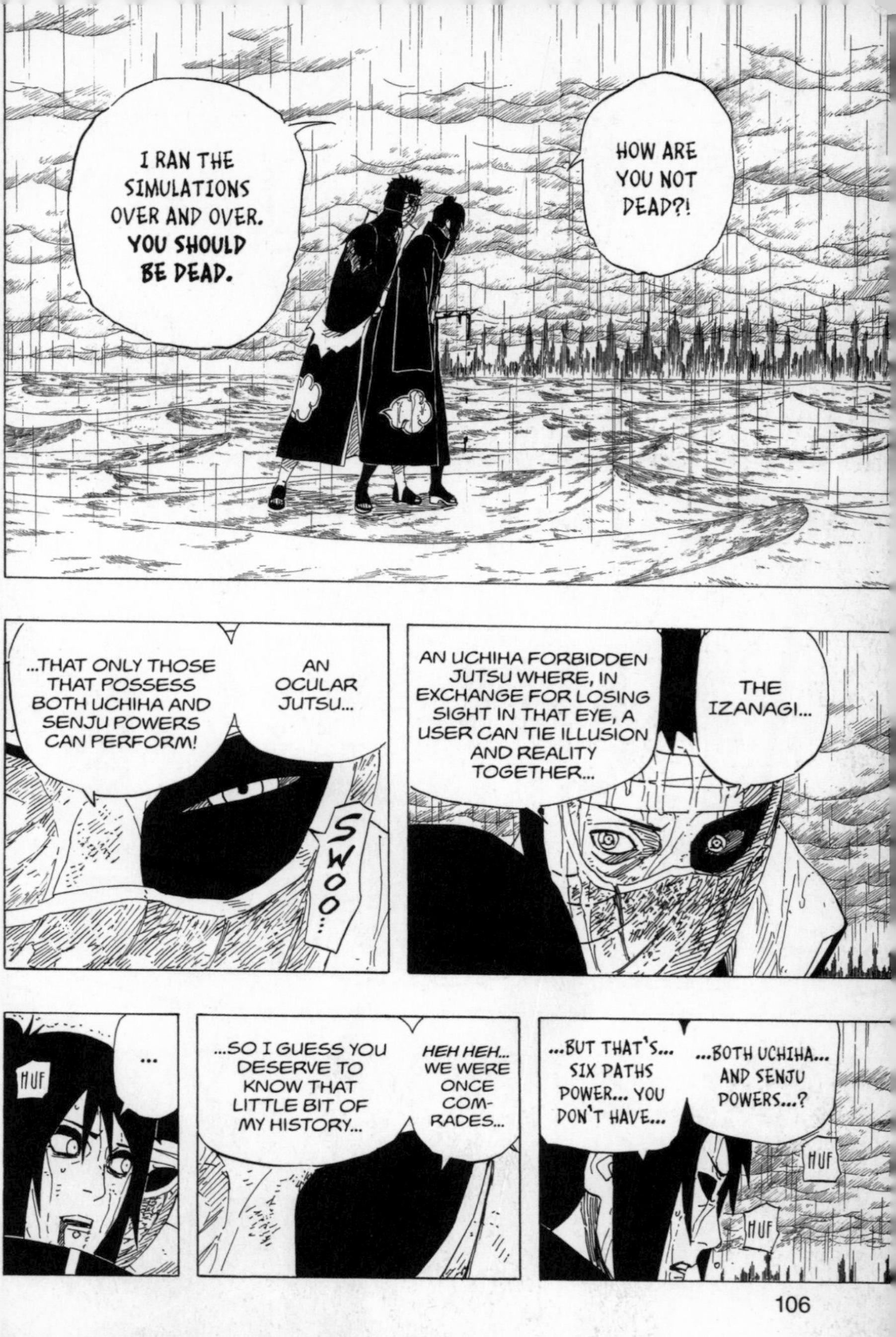
HOW ARE YOU NOT DEAD?!
I RAN THE SIMULATIONS OVER AND OVER. YOU SHOULD BE DEAD.
THE IZANAGI...
AN UCHIHA FORBIDDEN JUTSU WHERE, IN EXCHANGE FOR LOSING SIGHT IN THAT EYE, A USER CAN TIE ILLUSION AND REALITY TOGETHER...
AN OCULAR JUTSU...
...THAT ONLY THOSE THAT POSSESS BOTH UCHIHA AND SENJU POWERS CAN PERFORM!
SWOO...
...BOTH UCHIHA... AND SENJU POWERS...?
...BUT THAT'S... SIX PATHS POWER... YOU DON'T HAVE...
HUF
HUF
HEH HEH... WE WERE ONCE COM-RADES...
...SO I GUESS YOU DESERVE TO KNOW THAT LITTLE BIT OF MY HISTORY...
...
HUF

READ THIS WAY

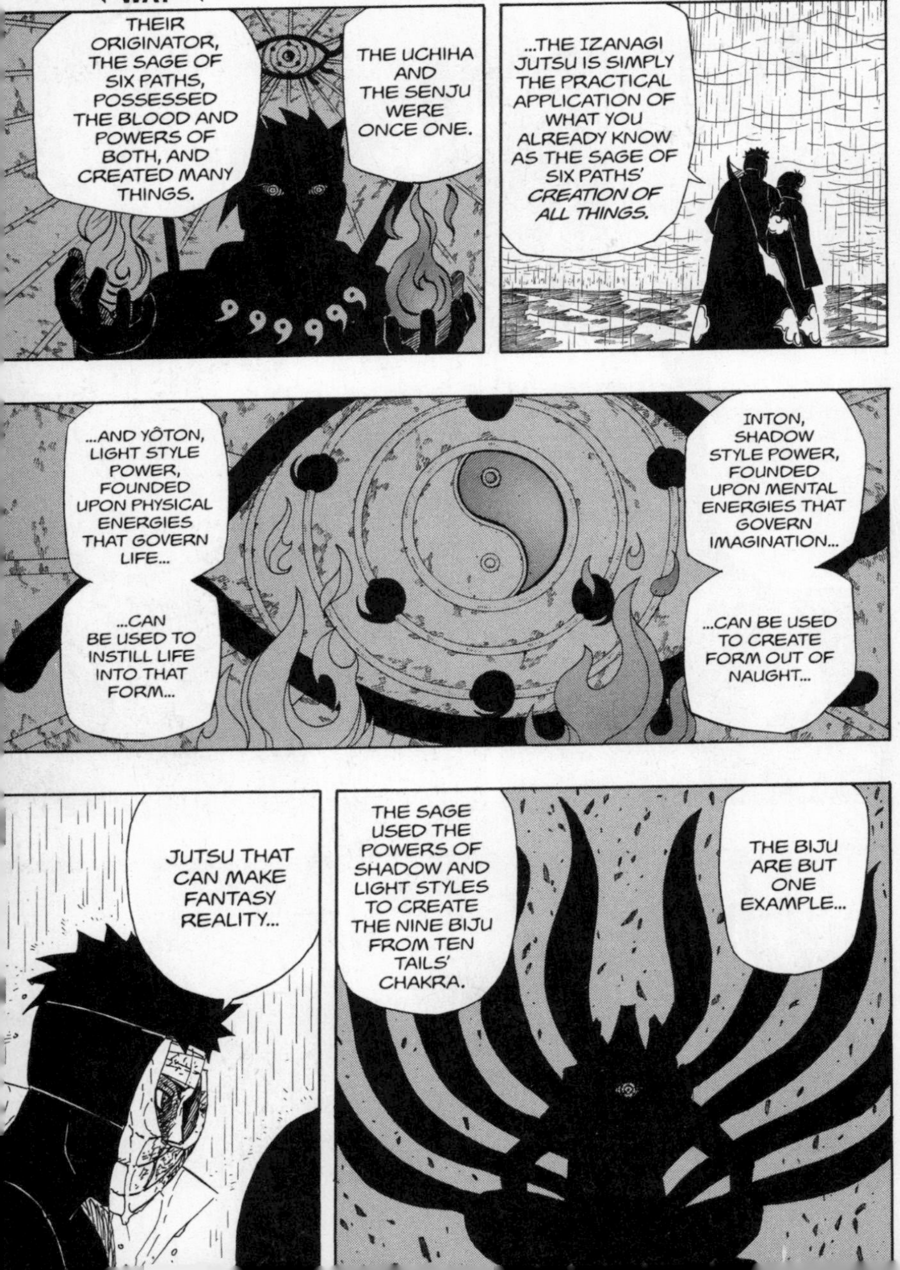
...THE IZANAGI JUTSU IS SIMPLY THE PRACTICAL APPLICATION OF WHAT YOU ALREADY KNOW AS THE SAGE OF SIX PATHS' *CREATION OF ALL THINGS.*
THE UCHIHA AND THE SENJU WERE ONCE ONE.
THEIR ORIGINATOR, THE SAGE OF SIX PATHS, POSSESSED THE BLOOD AND POWERS OF BOTH, AND CREATED MANY THINGS.
INTON, SHADOW STYLE POWER, FOUNDED UPON MENTAL ENERGIES THAT GOVERN IMAGINATION...
...CAN BE USED TO CREATE FORM OUT OF NAUGHT...
...AND YÔTON, LIGHT STYLE POWER, FOUNDED UPON PHYSICAL ENERGIES THAT GOVERN LIFE...
...CAN BE USED TO INSTILL LIFE INTO THAT FORM...
THE BIJU ARE BUT ONE EXAMPLE...
THE SAGE USED THE POWERS OF SHADOW AND LIGHT STYLES TO CREATE THE NINE BIJU FROM TEN TAILS' CHAKRA.
JUTSU THAT CAN MAKE FANTASY REALITY...

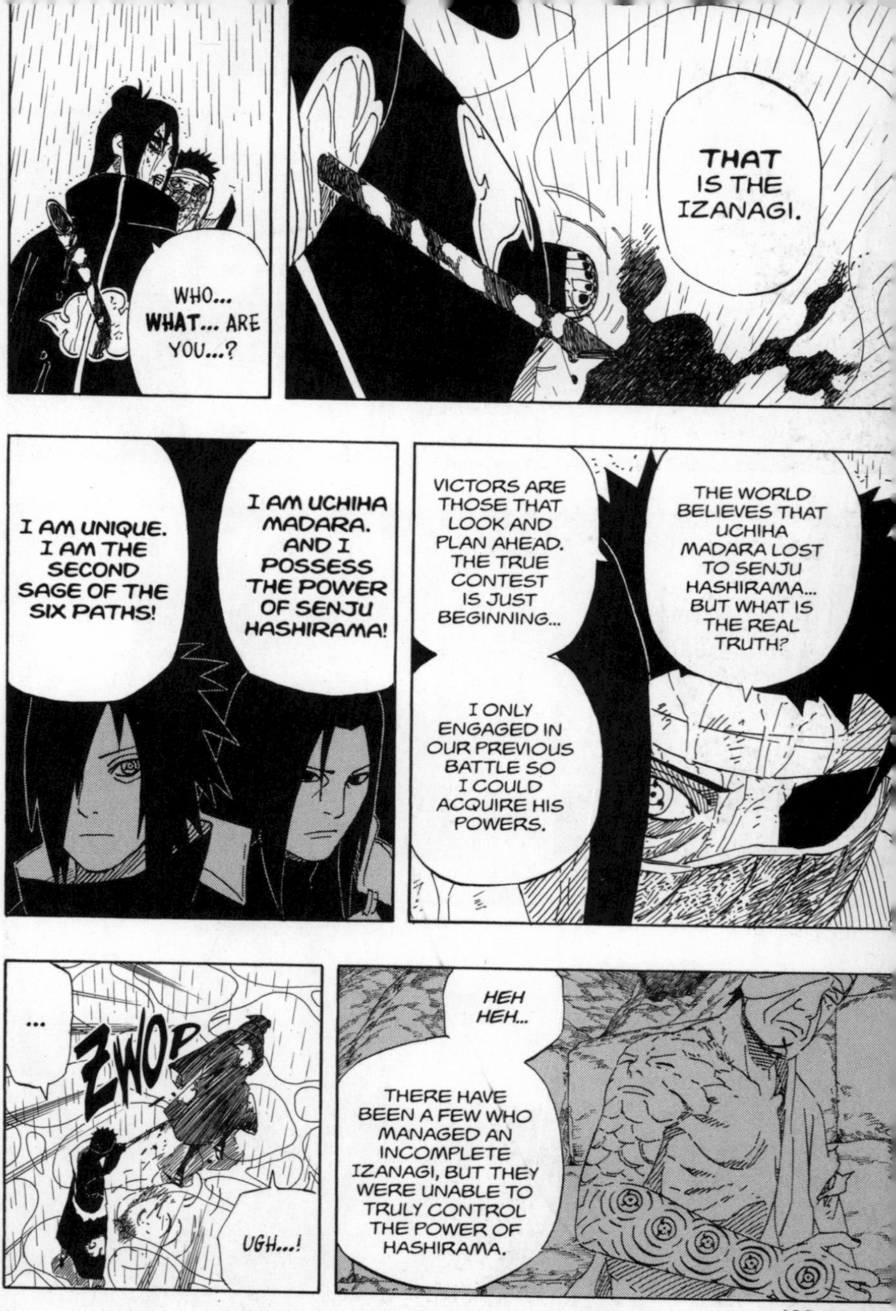
THAT IS THE IZANAGI.
WHO... WHAT... ARE YOU...?
THE WORLD BELIEVES THAT UCHIHA MADARA LOST TO SENJU HASHIRAMA... BUT WHAT IS THE REAL TRUTH?
VICTORS ARE THOSE THAT LOOK AND PLAN AHEAD. THE TRUE CONTEST IS JUST BEGINNING...
I ONLY ENGAGED IN OUR PREVIOUS BATTLE SO I COULD ACQUIRE HIS POWERS.
I AM UCHIHA MADARA. AND I POSSESS THE POWER OF SENJU HASHIRAMA!
I AM UNIQUE. I AM THE SECOND SAGE OF THE SIX PATHS!
HEH HEH...
THERE HAVE BEEN A FEW WHO MANAGED AN INCOMPLETE IZANAGI, BUT THEY WERE UNABLE TO TRULY CONTROL THE POWER OF HASHIRAMA.
...
ZWOP
UGH...!

READ THIS WAY

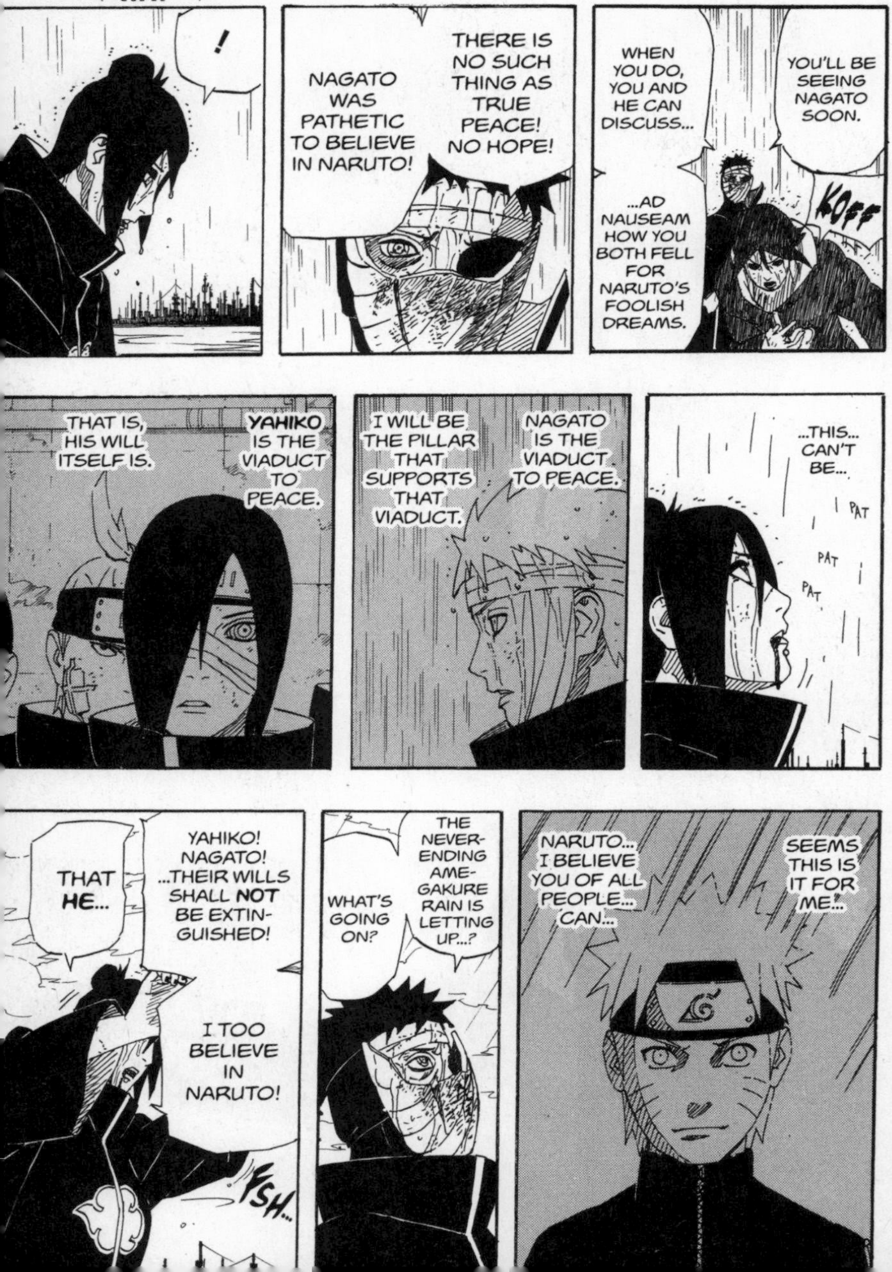
YOU'LL BE SEEING NAGATO SOON.
WHEN YOU DO, YOU AND HE CAN DISCUSS...
...AD NAUSEAM HOW YOU BOTH FELL FOR NARUTO'S FOOLISH DREAMS.
KOFF
THERE IS NO SUCH THING AS TRUE PEACE! NO HOPE!
NAGATO WAS PATHETIC TO BELIEVE IN NARUTO!
!
...THIS... CAN'T BE...
PAT
PAT
PAT
NAGATO IS THE VIADUCT TO PEACE.
I WILL BE THE PILLAR THAT SUPPORTS THAT VIADUCT.
YAHIKO IS THE VIADUCT TO PEACE.
THAT IS, HIS WILL ITSELF IS.
SEEMS THIS IS IT FOR ME...
NARUTO... I BELIEVE YOU OF ALL PEOPLE... CAN...
THE NEVER-ENDING AME-GAKURE RAIN IS LETTING UP...?
WHAT'S GOING ON?
YAHIKO! NAGATO! ...THEIR WILLS SHALL NOT BE EXTIN-GUISHED!
THAT HE...
I TOO BELIEVE IN NARUTO!
FSH...

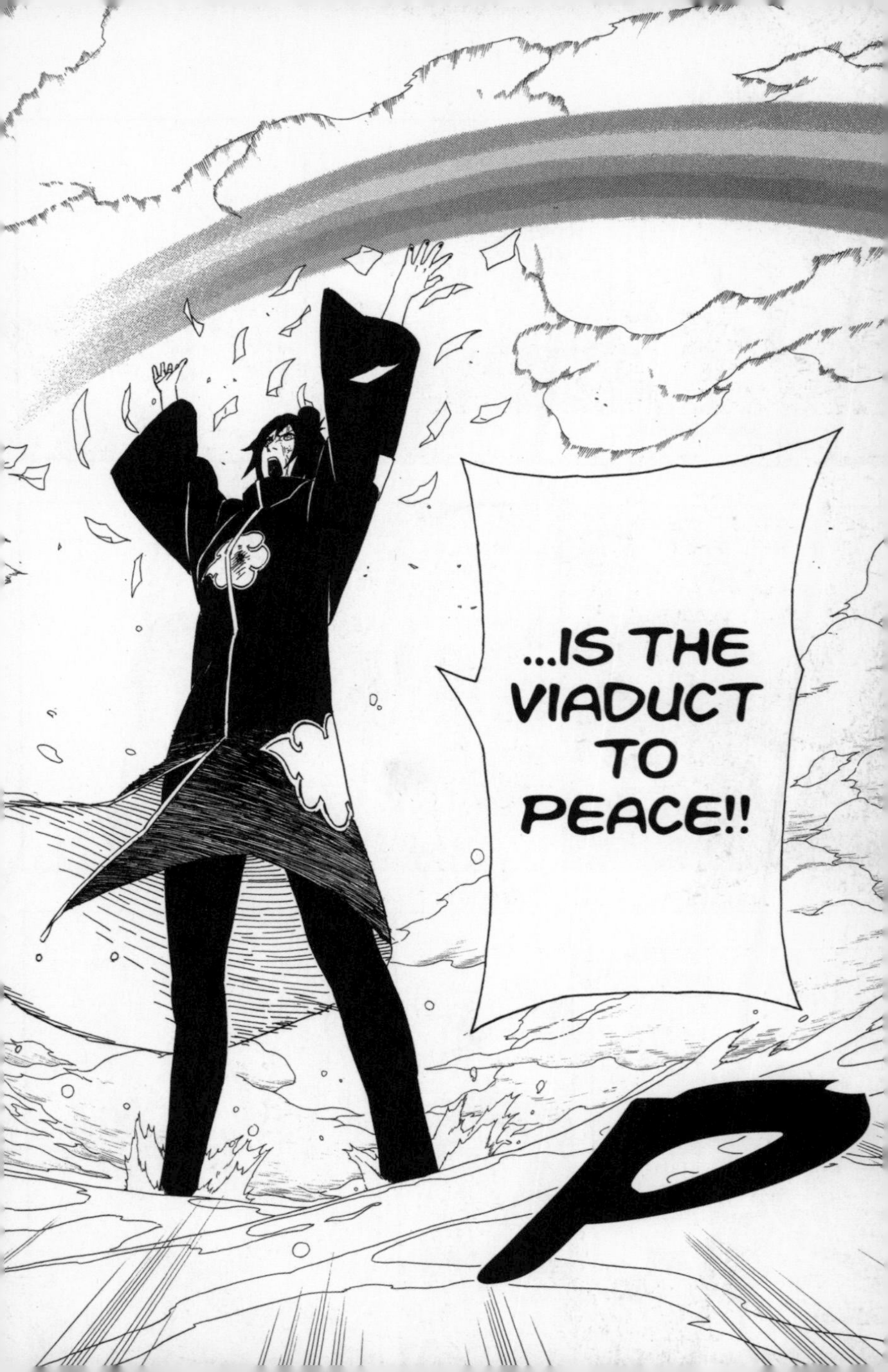
...IS THE VIADUCT TO PEACE!!

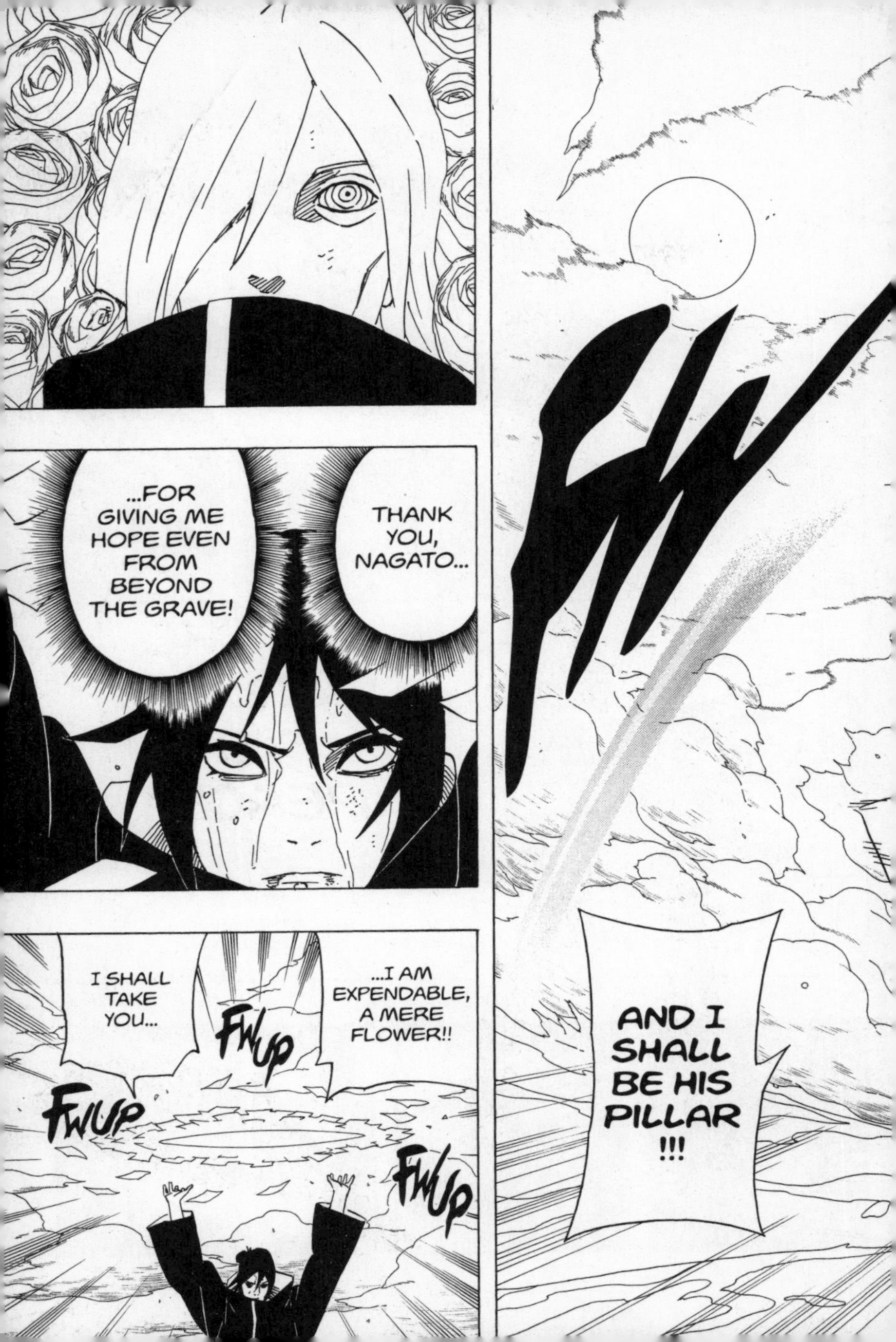
THANK YOU, NAGATO...
...FOR GIVING ME HOPE EVEN FROM BEYOND THE GRAVE!
...I AM EXPENDABLE, A MERE FLOWER!!
FWUP
I SHALL TAKE YOU...
FWUP
FWUP
FWH
AND I SHALL BE HIS PILLAR!!!

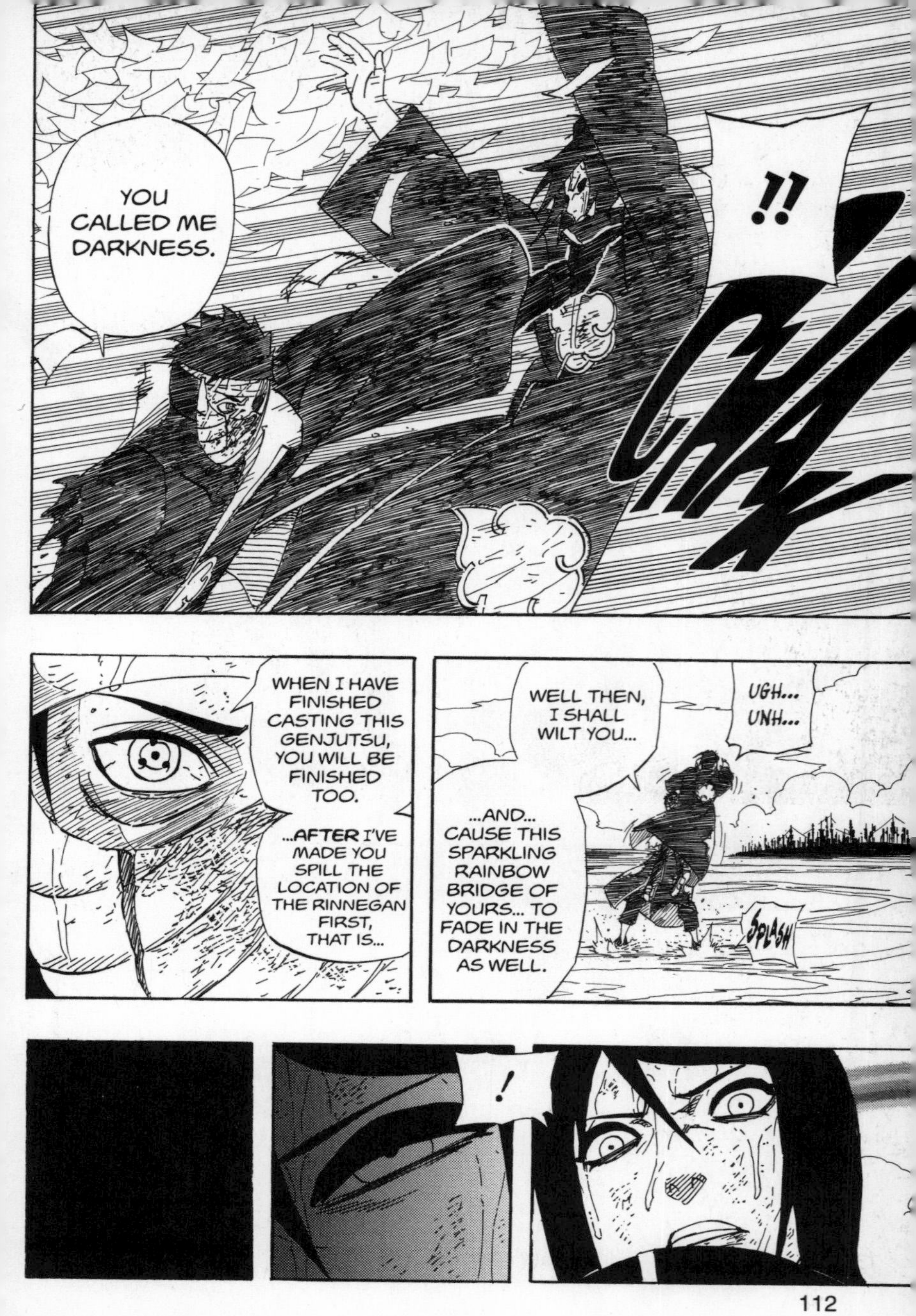
YOU CALLED ME DARKNESS.
!!
CHAK
UGH... UNH...
WELL THEN, I SHALL WILT YOU...
...AND... CAUSE THIS SPARKLING RAINBOW BRIDGE OF YOURS... TO FADE IN THE DARKNESS AS WELL.
SPLASH
WHEN I HAVE FINISHED CASTING THIS GENJUTSU, YOU WILL BE FINISHED TOO.
...AFTER I'VE MADE YOU SPILL THE LOCATION OF THE RINNEGAN FIRST, THAT IS...
!

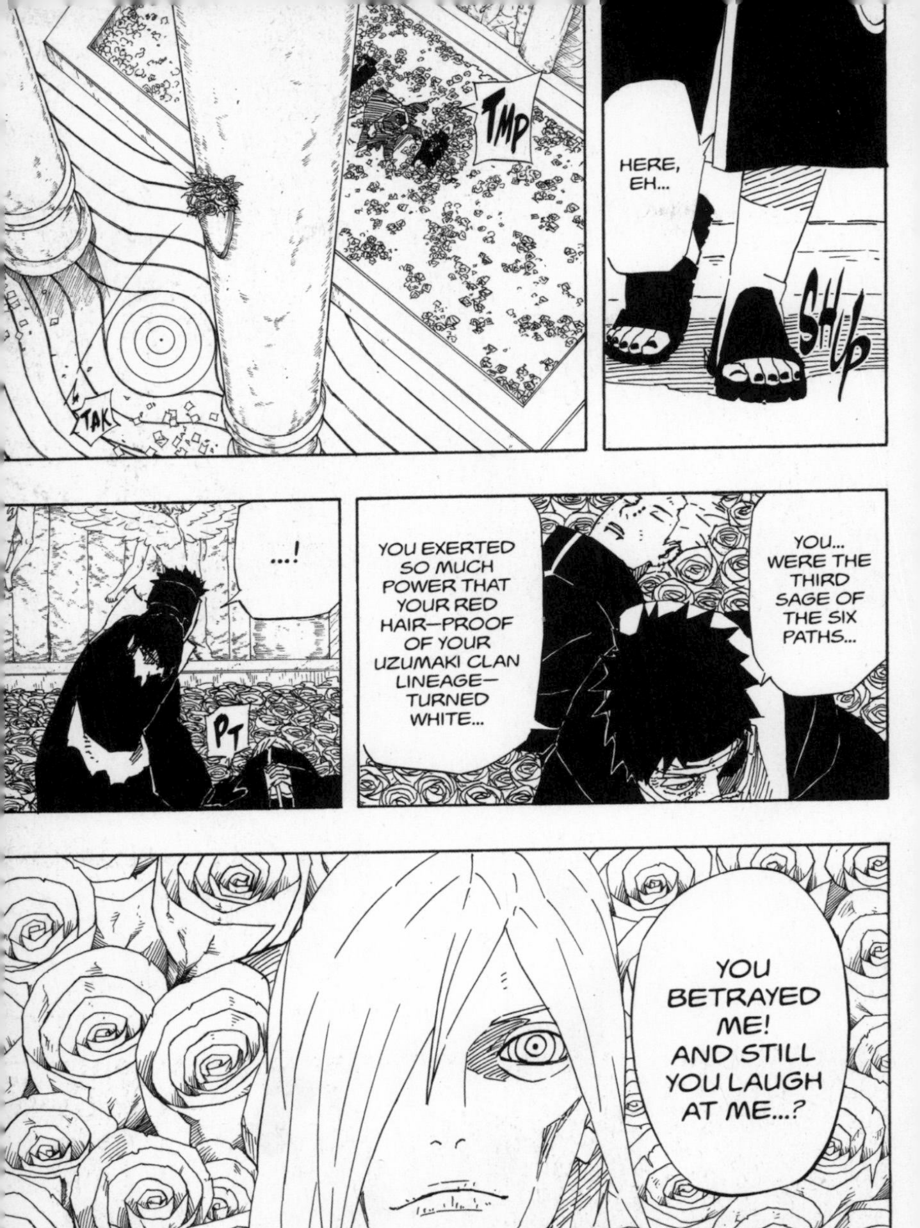
HERE, EH...
SHUP
TMP
TAK
YOU... WERE THE THIRD SAGE OF THE SIX PATHS...
YOU EXERTED SO MUCH POWER THAT YOUR RED HAIR—PROOF OF YOUR UZUMAKI CLAN LINEAGE—TURNED WHITE...
...!
PT
YOU BETRAYED ME! AND STILL YOU LAUGH AT ME...?

NARUTO

Number 511: We Shall Return

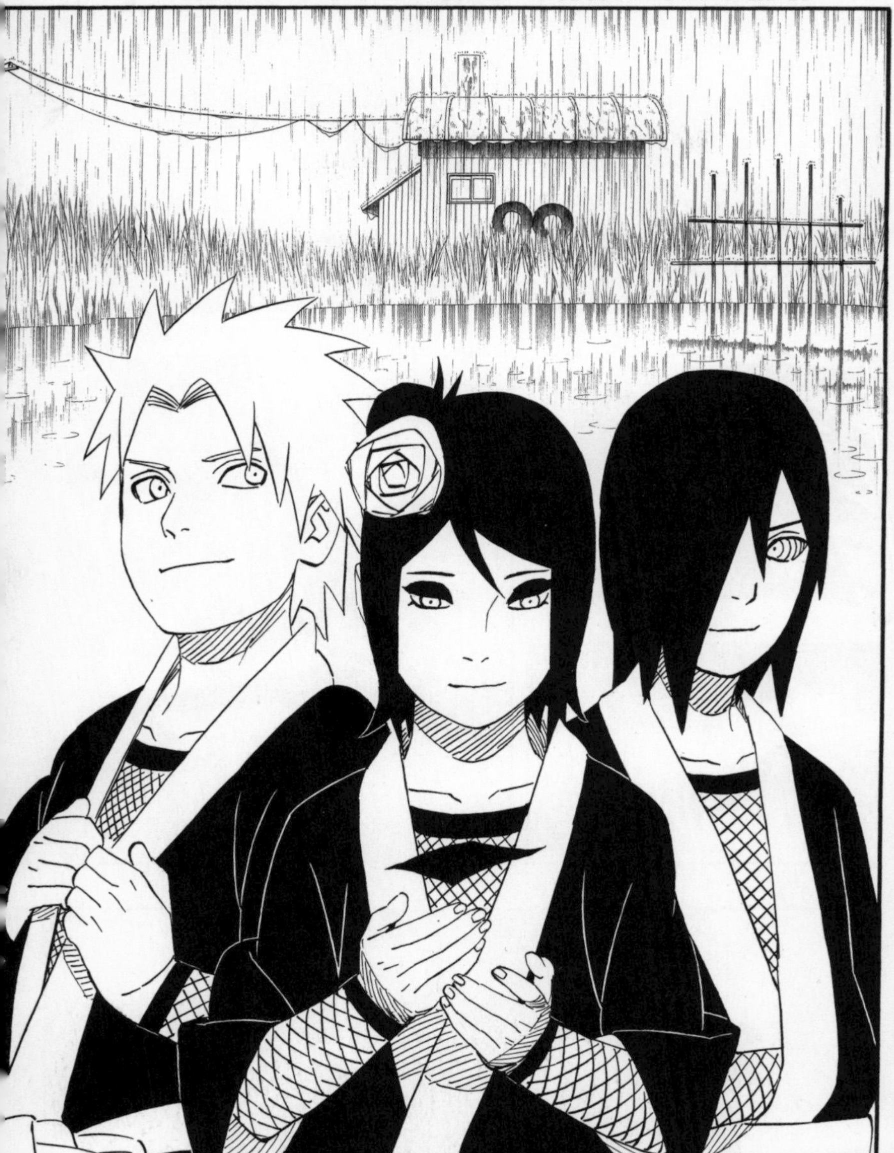

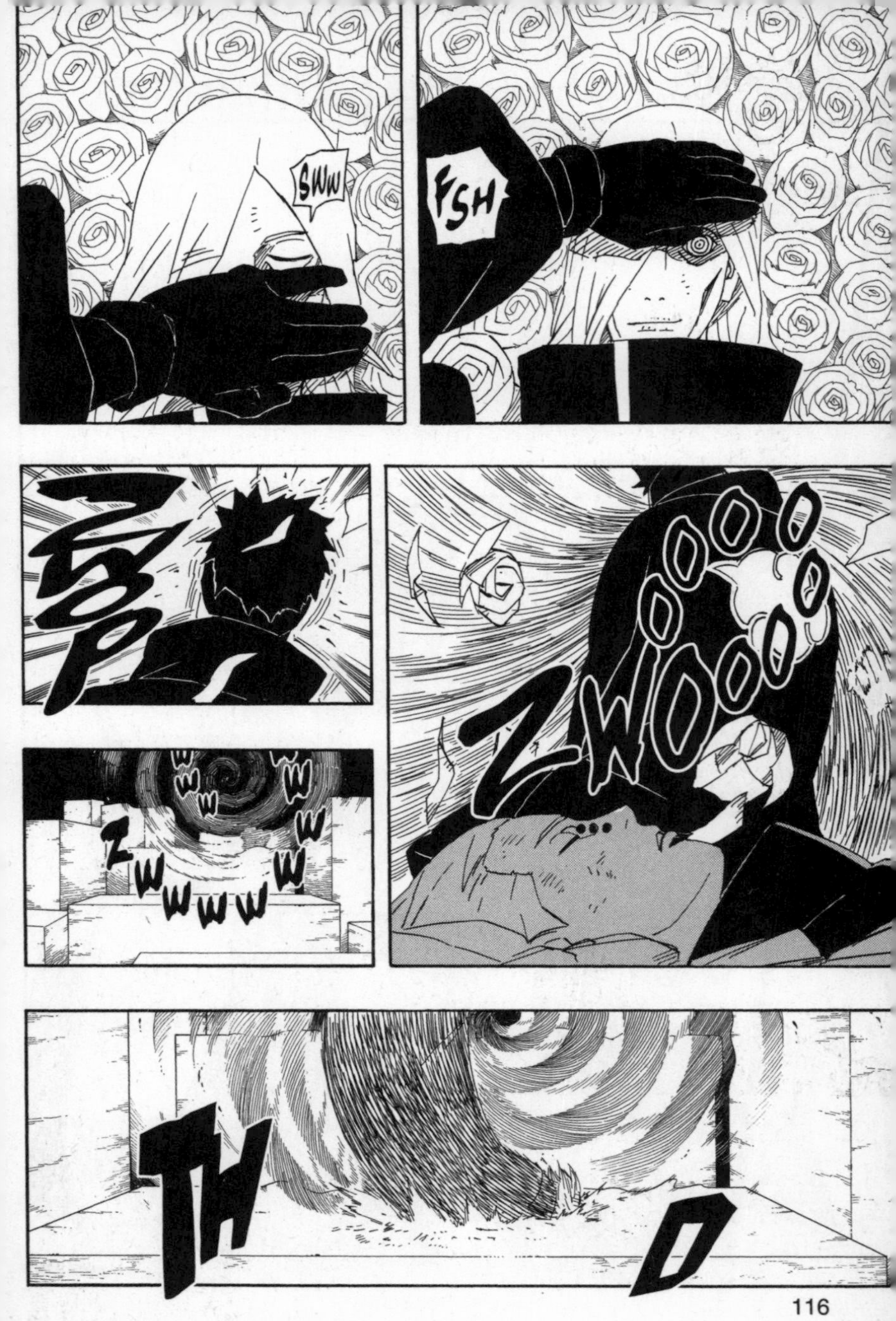
FSH
SWW
ZWOOOOOOOOOOO
ZOOP
ZWWWWWWWWWWW
THD

READ THIS WAY

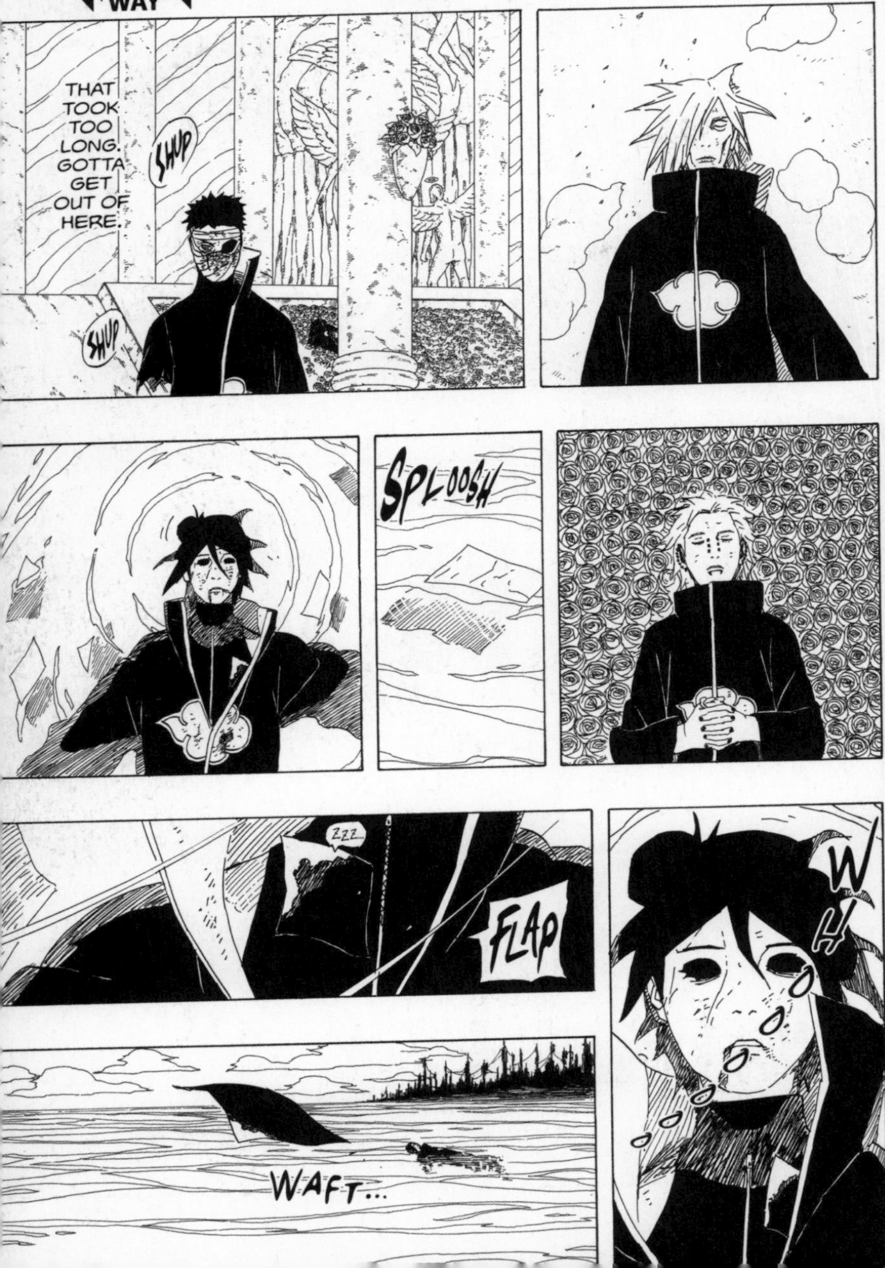
SHUP
SHUP
THAT TOOK TOO LONG. GOTTA GET OUT OF HERE.
SPLOOSH
WHOOOOOO
ZZZ...
FLAP
WAFT...

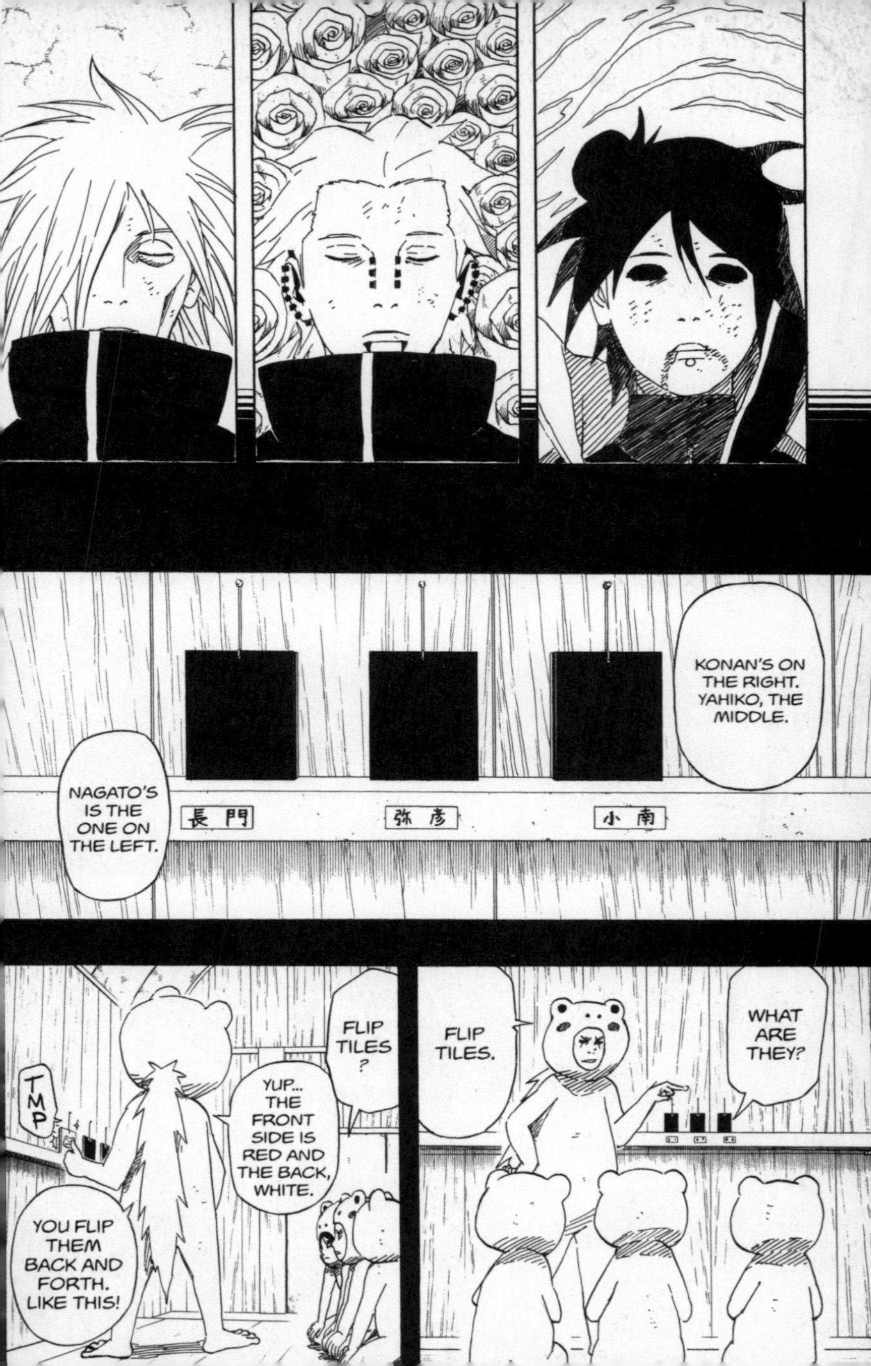
KONAN'S ON THE RIGHT. YAHIKO, THE MIDDLE.
NAGATO'S IS THE ONE ON THE LEFT.
小南
弥彦
長門
WHAT ARE THEY?
FLIP TILES.
FLIP TILES?
YUP... THE FRONT SIDE IS RED AND THE BACK, WHITE.
TMP
YOU FLIP THEM BACK AND FORTH. LIKE THIS!

READ THIS WAY

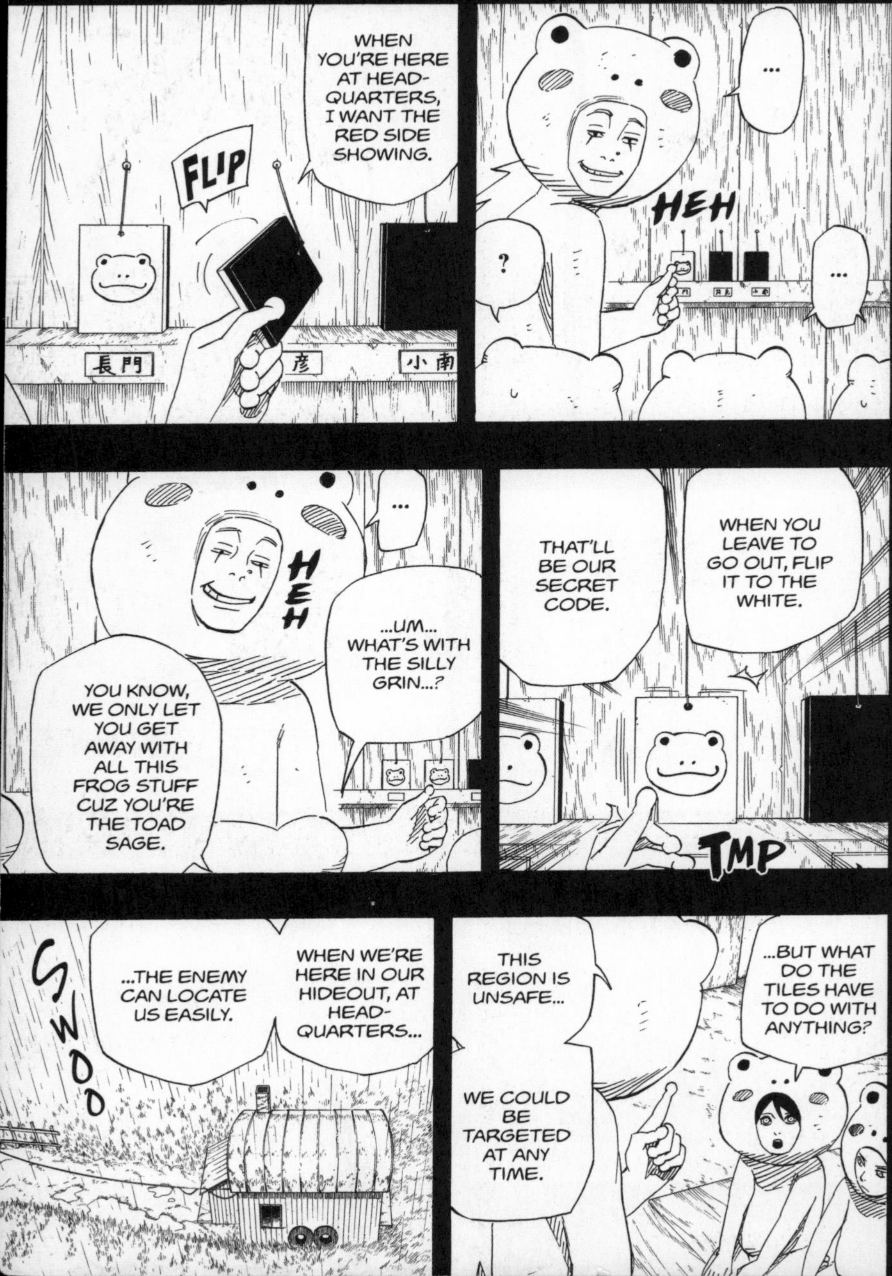
...
HEH
?
...
WHEN YOU'RE HERE AT HEAD-QUARTERS, I WANT THE RED SIDE SHOWING.
FLIP
長門
彦
小南
WHEN YOU LEAVE TO GO OUT, FLIP IT TO THE WHITE.
THAT'LL BE OUR SECRET CODE.
TMP
...
HEH
...UM... WHAT'S WITH THE SILLY GRIN...?
YOU KNOW, WE ONLY LET YOU GET AWAY WITH ALL THIS FROG STUFF CUZ YOU'RE THE TOAD SAGE.
...BUT WHAT DO THE TILES HAVE TO DO WITH ANYTHING?
THIS REGION IS UNSAFE...
WE COULD BE TARGETED AT ANY TIME.
WHEN WE'RE HERE IN OUR HIDEOUT, AT HEAD-QUARTERS...
...THE ENEMY CAN LOCATE US EASILY.
SWOO

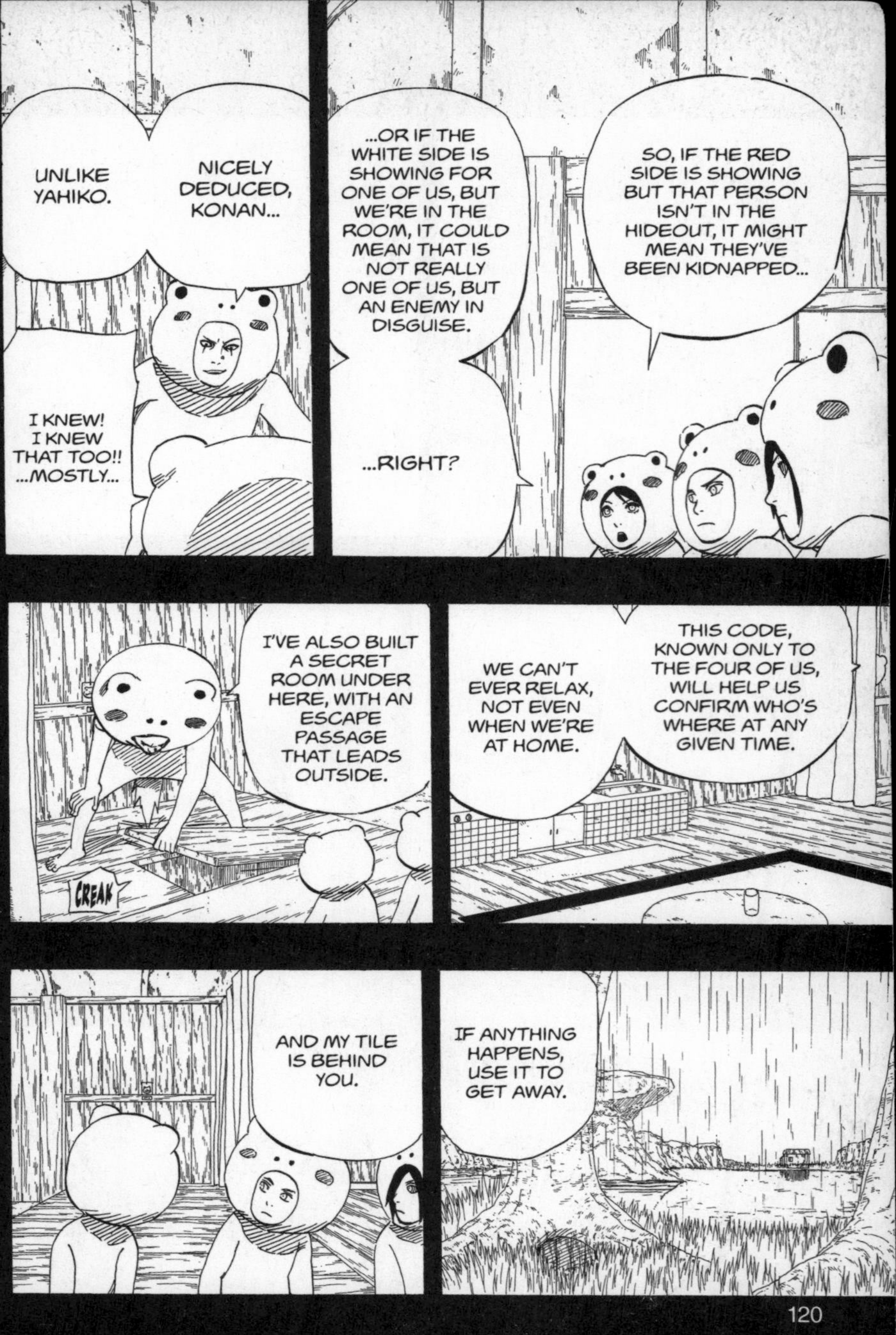
SO, IF THE RED SIDE IS SHOWING BUT THAT PERSON ISN'T IN THE HIDEOUT, IT MIGHT MEAN THEY'VE BEEN KIDNAPPED...
...OR IF THE WHITE SIDE IS SHOWING FOR ONE OF US, BUT WE'RE IN THE ROOM, IT COULD MEAN THAT IS NOT REALLY ONE OF US, BUT AN ENEMY IN DISGUISE.
...RIGHT?
NICELY DEDUCED, KONAN...
UNLIKE YAHIKO.
I KNEW! I KNEW THAT TOO!! ...MOSTLY...
THIS CODE, KNOWN ONLY TO THE FOUR OF US, WILL HELP US CONFIRM WHO'S WHERE AT ANY GIVEN TIME.
WE CAN'T EVER RELAX, NOT EVEN WHEN WE'RE AT HOME.
I'VE ALSO BUILT A SECRET ROOM UNDER HERE, WITH AN ESCAPE PASSAGE THAT LEADS OUTSIDE.
CREAK
IF ANYTHING HAPPENS, USE IT TO GET AWAY.
AND MY TILE IS BEHIND YOU.

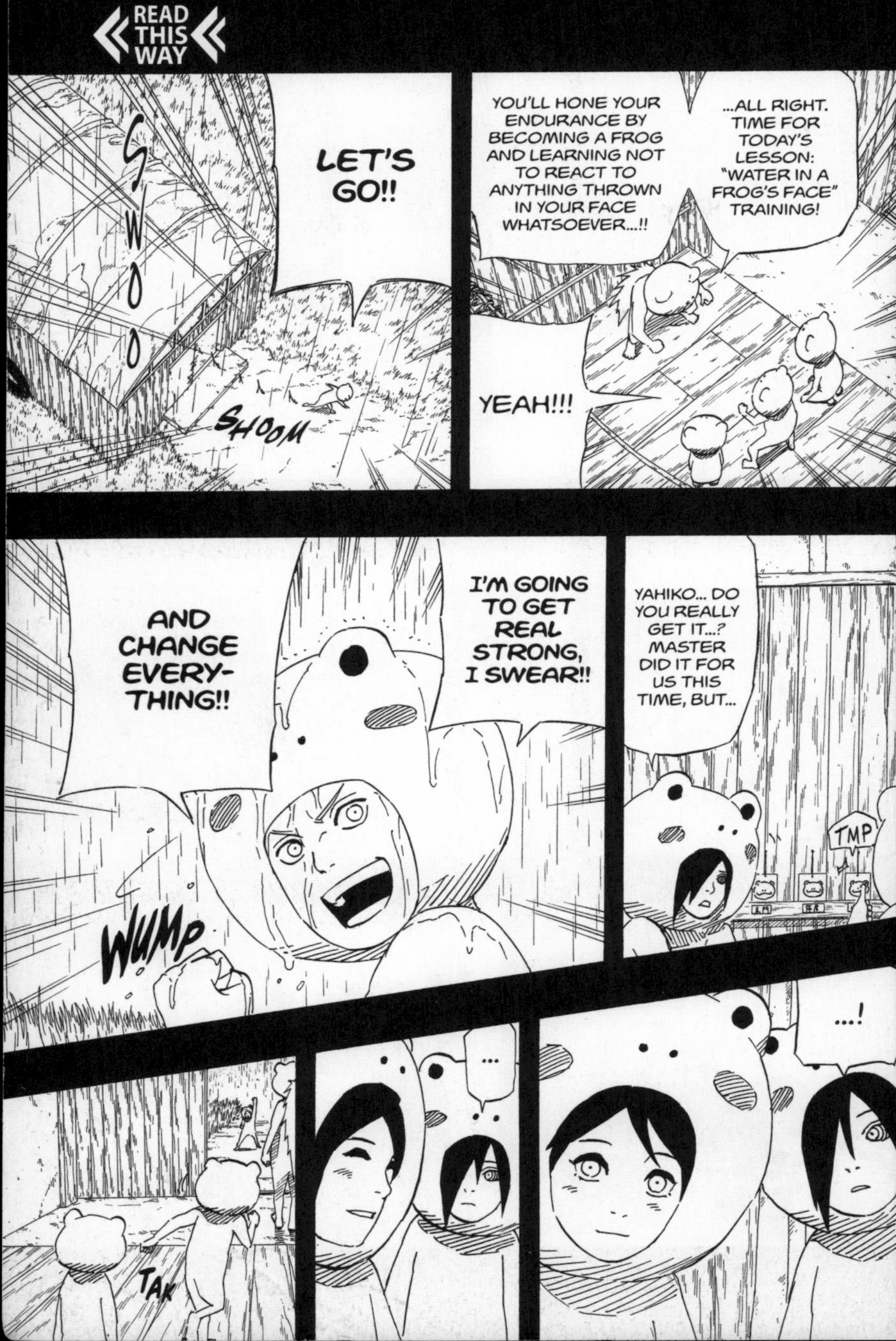
READ THIS WAY
...ALL RIGHT. TIME FOR TODAY'S LESSON: "WATER IN A FROG'S FACE" TRAINING!
YOU'LL HONE YOUR ENDURANCE BY BECOMING A FROG AND LEARNING NOT TO REACT TO ANYTHING THROWN IN YOUR FACE WHATSOEVER...!!
YEAH!!!
LET'S GO!!
SWOO
SHOOM
YAHIKO... DO YOU REALLY GET IT...? MASTER DID IT FOR US THIS TIME, BUT...
TMP
I'M GOING TO GET REAL STRONG, I SWEAR!!
AND CHANGE EVERY-THING!!
WUMP
...!
...
TAK

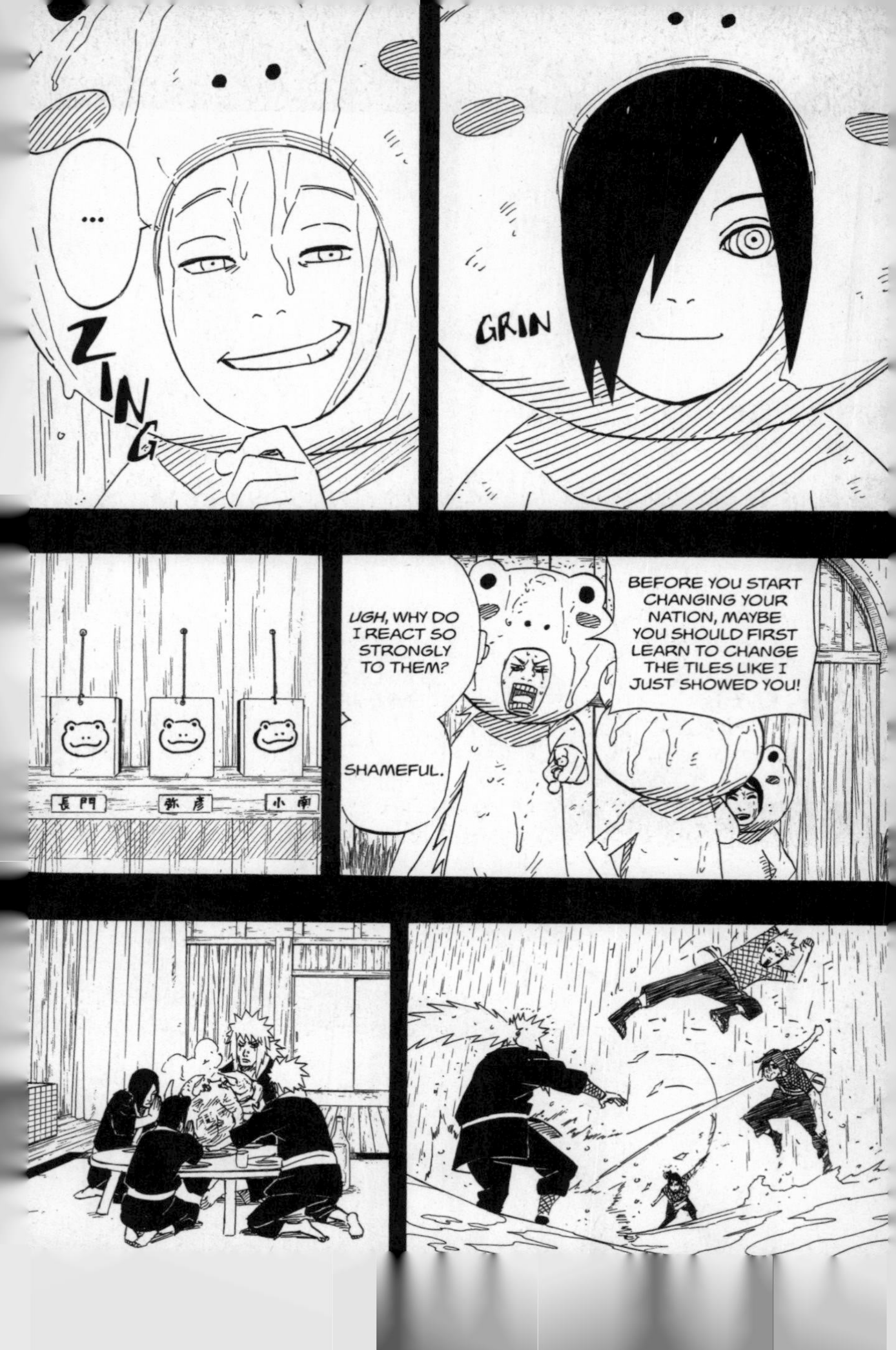
GRIN
...
ZING
BEFORE YOU START CHANGING YOUR NATION, MAYBE YOU SHOULD FIRST LEARN TO CHANGE THE TILES LIKE I JUST SHOWED YOU!
UGH, WHY DO I REACT SO STRONGLY TO THEM?
SHAMEFUL.
長門
弥彦
小南

READ THIS WAY

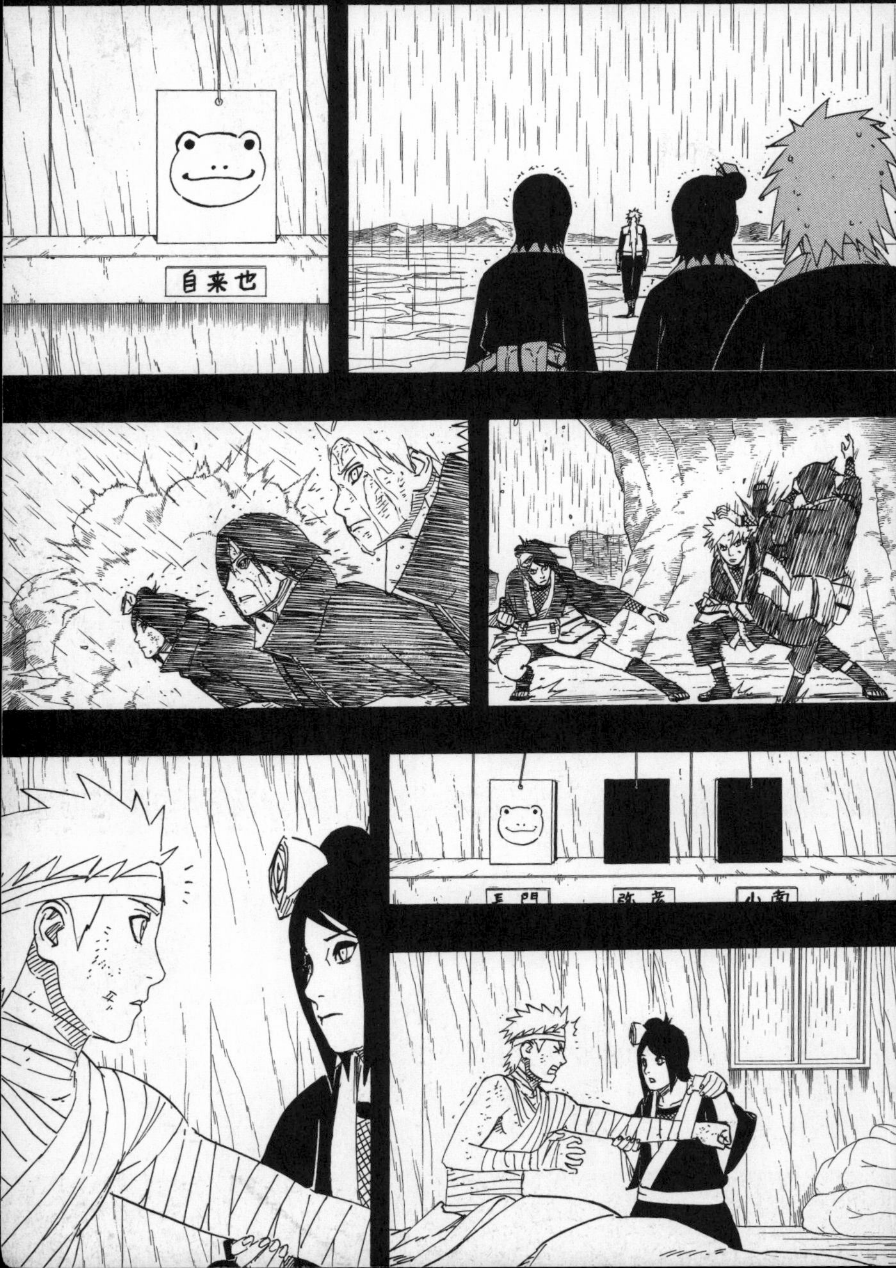
自来也

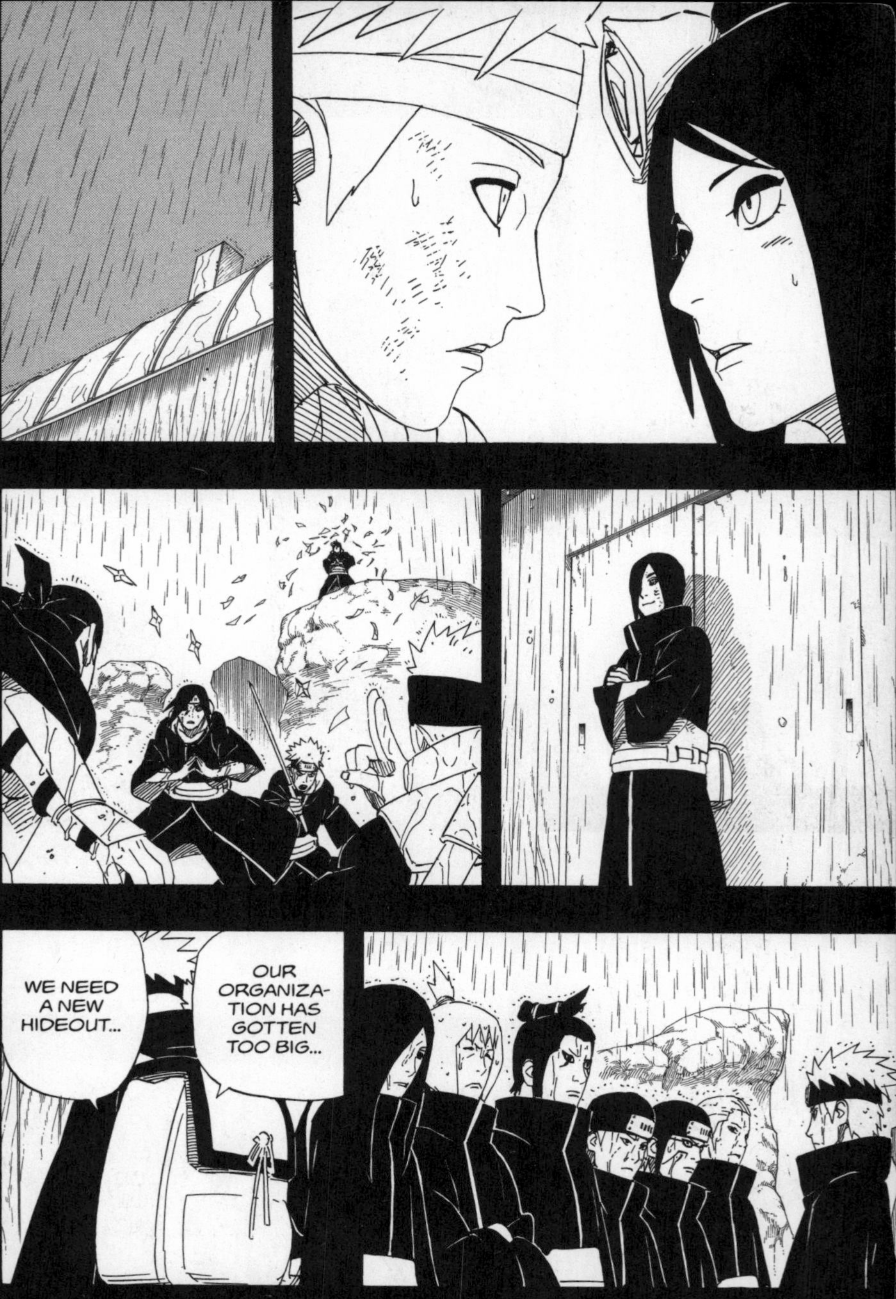
OUR ORGANIZATION HAS GOTTEN TOO BIG...
WE NEED A NEW HIDEOUT...

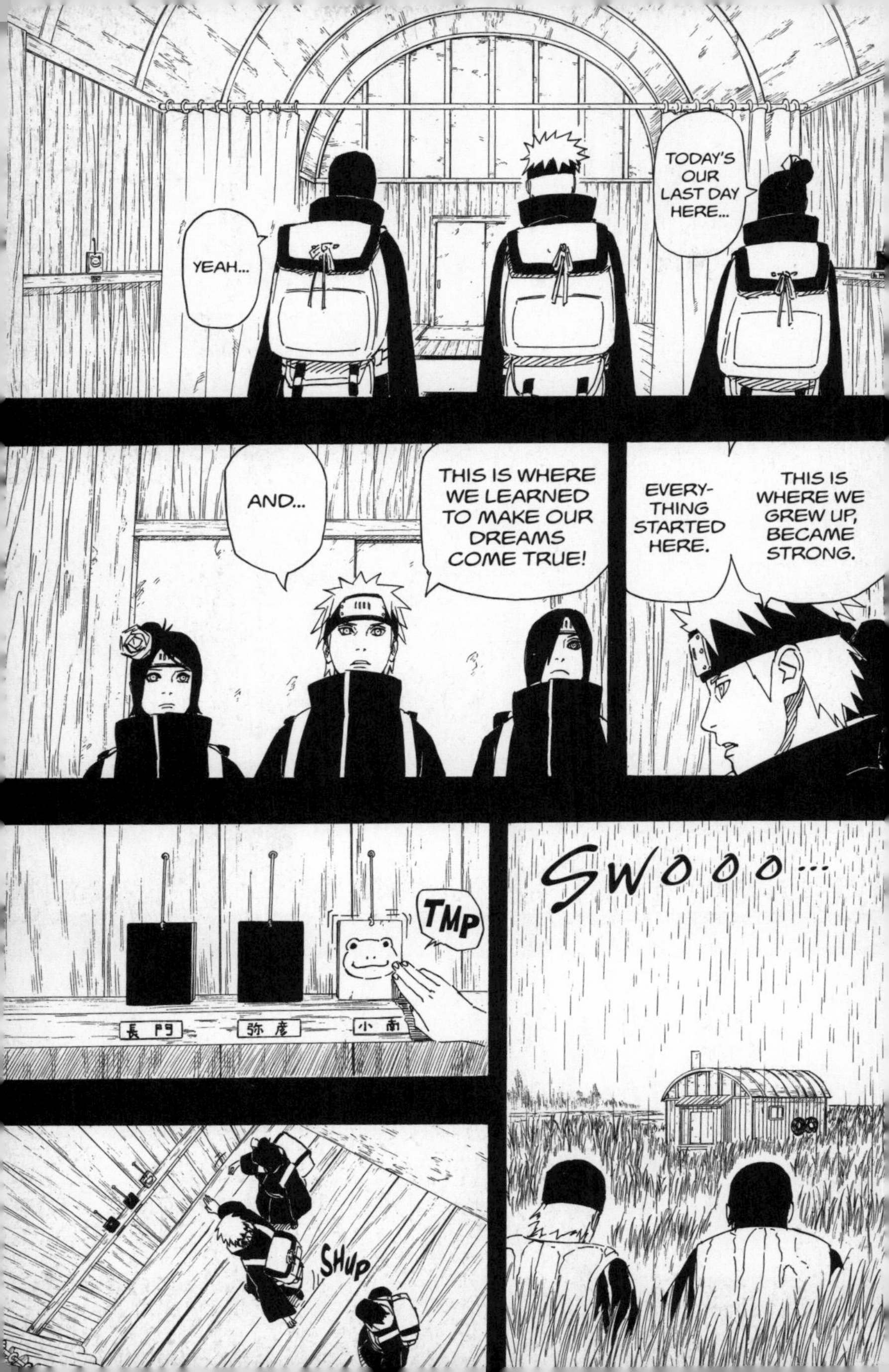
TODAY'S OUR LAST DAY HERE...
YEAH...
THIS IS WHERE WE GREW UP, BECAME STRONG.
EVERY-THING STARTED HERE.
THIS IS WHERE WE LEARNED TO MAKE OUR DREAMS COME TRUE!
AND...
SWOOO...
TMP
小南
弥彦
長門
SHUP

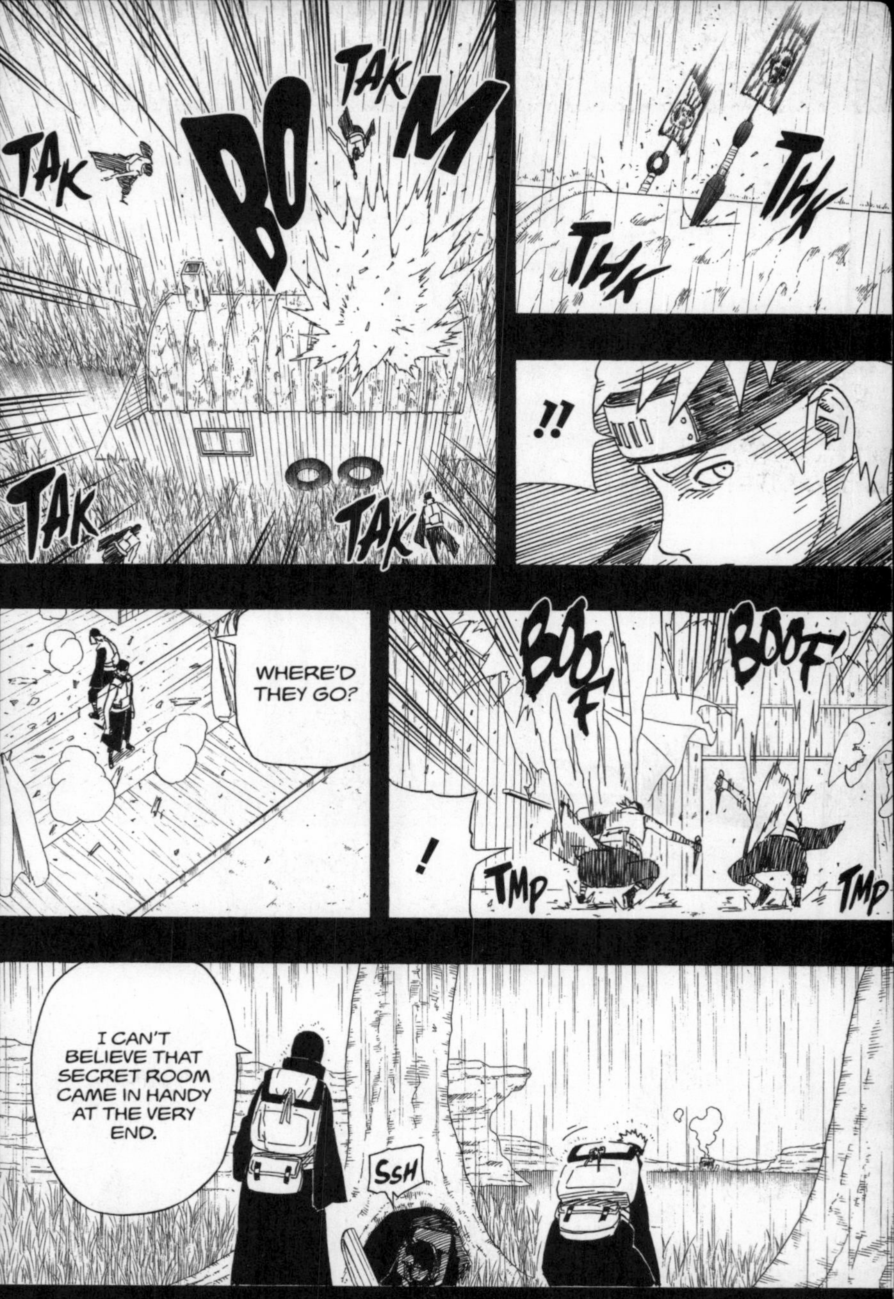
THK
THK
!!
TAK
BOOM
TAK
TAK
TAK
BOOF
BOOF
!
TMP
TMP
WHERE'D THEY GO?
I CAN'T BELIEVE THAT SECRET ROOM CAME IN HANDY AT THE VERY END.
SSH

READ THIS WAY

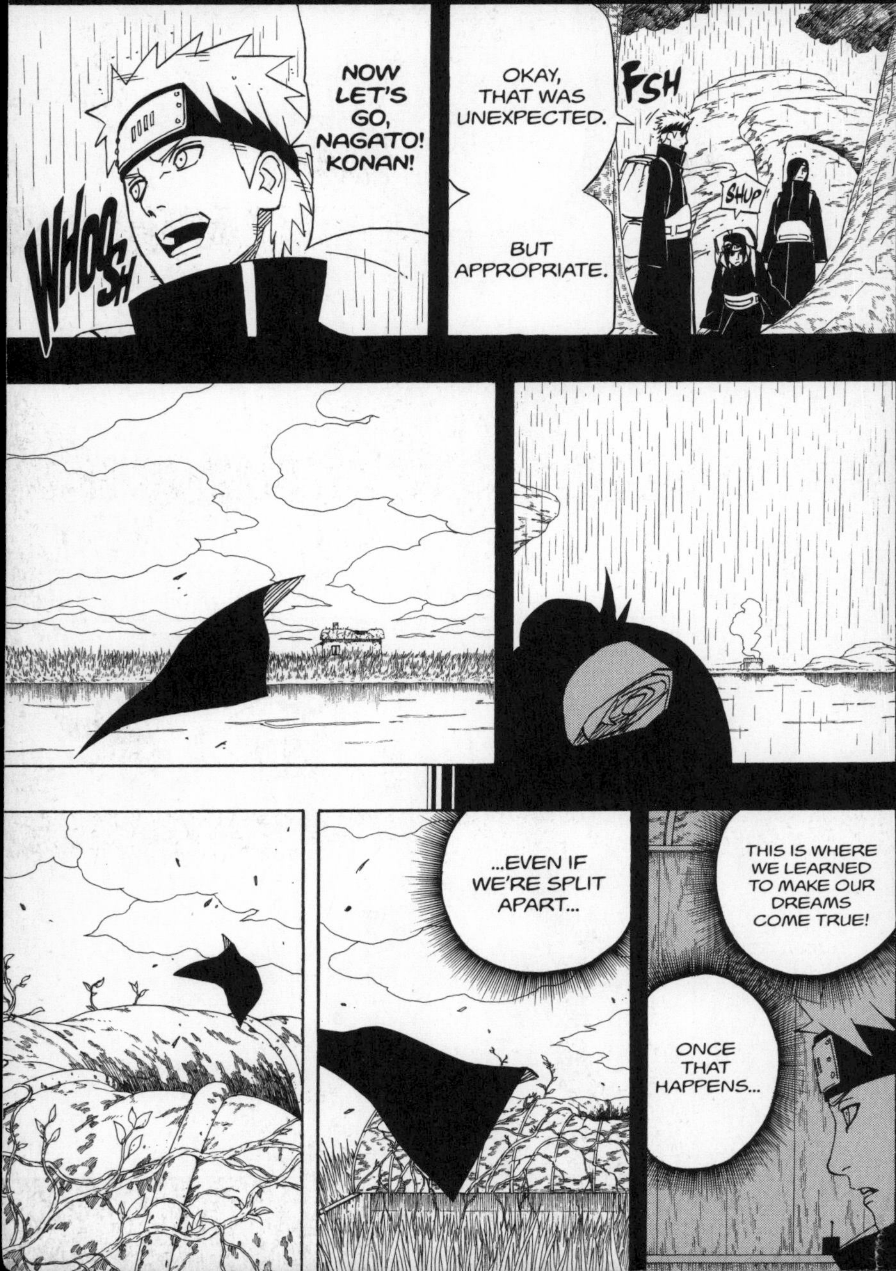
OKAY, THAT WAS UNEXPECTED.
FSH
SHUP
BUT APPROPRIATE.
NOW LET'S GO, NAGATO! KONAN!
WHOOSH
THIS IS WHERE WE LEARNED TO MAKE OUR DREAMS COME TRUE!
ONCE THAT HAPPENS...
...EVEN IF WE'RE SPLIT APART...

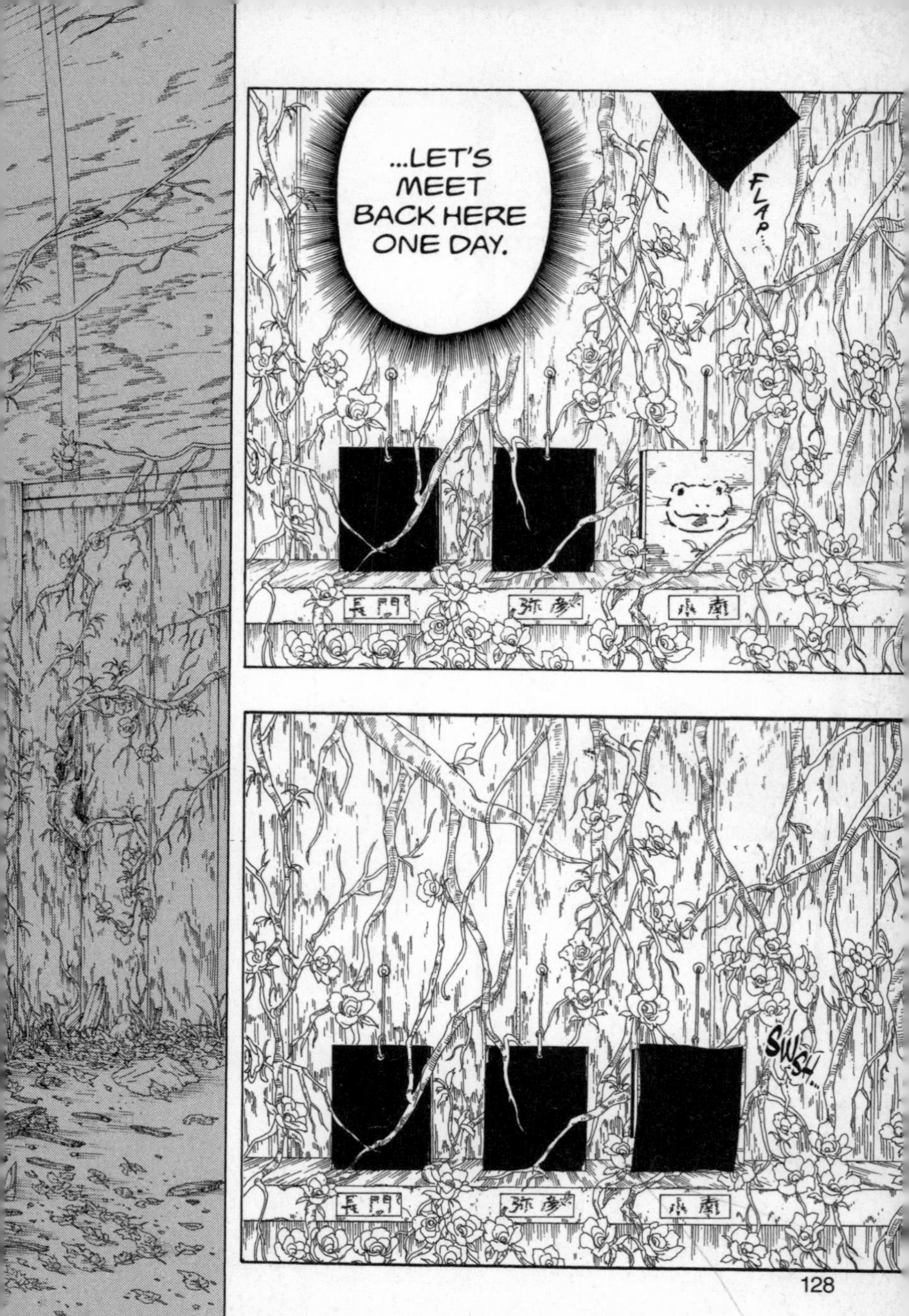
...LET'S MEET BACK HERE ONE DAY.
FLAP...
長門
弥彦
小南
SWSH...
長門
弥彦
小南

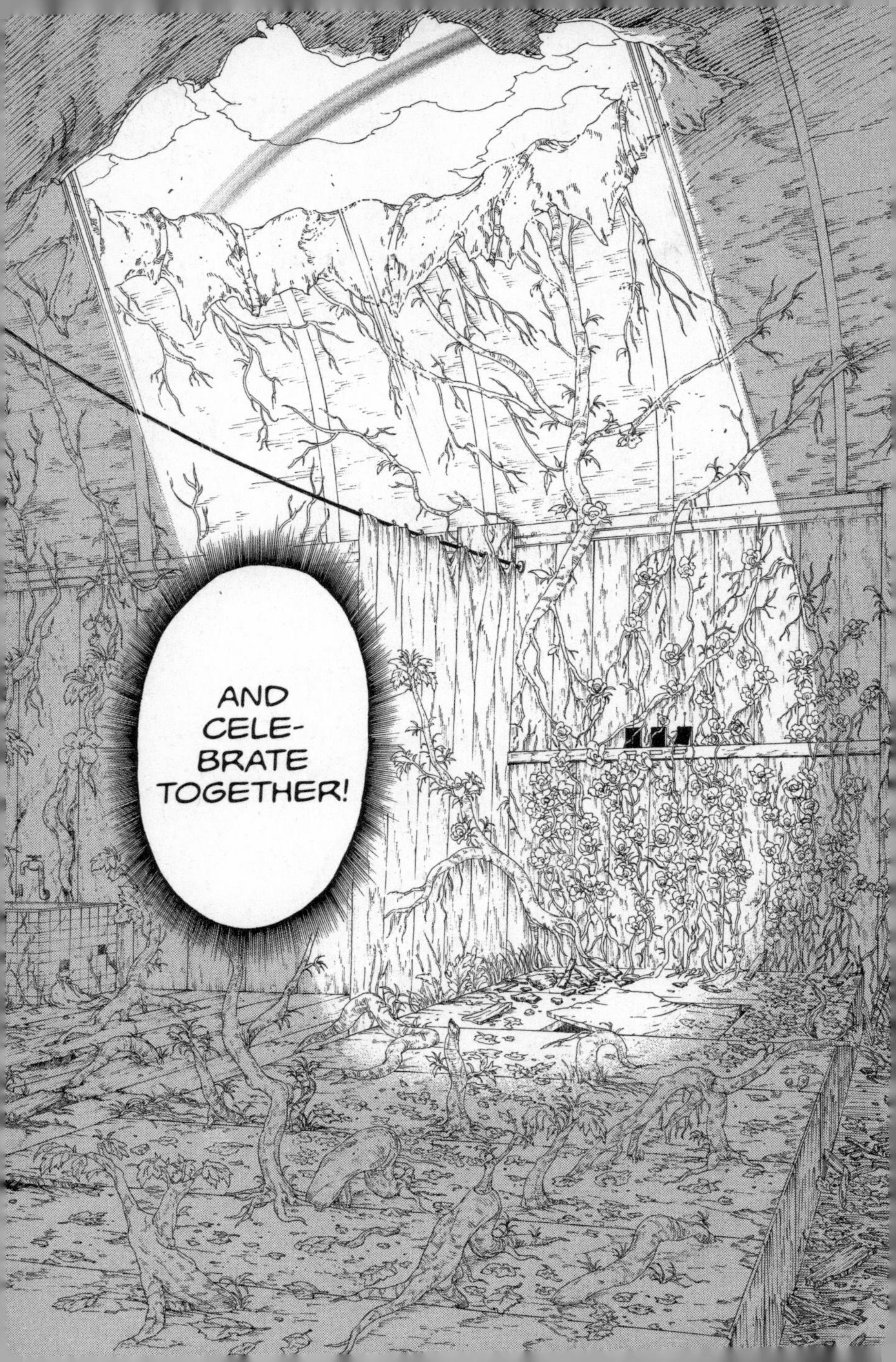
AND CELE-BRATE TOGETHER!

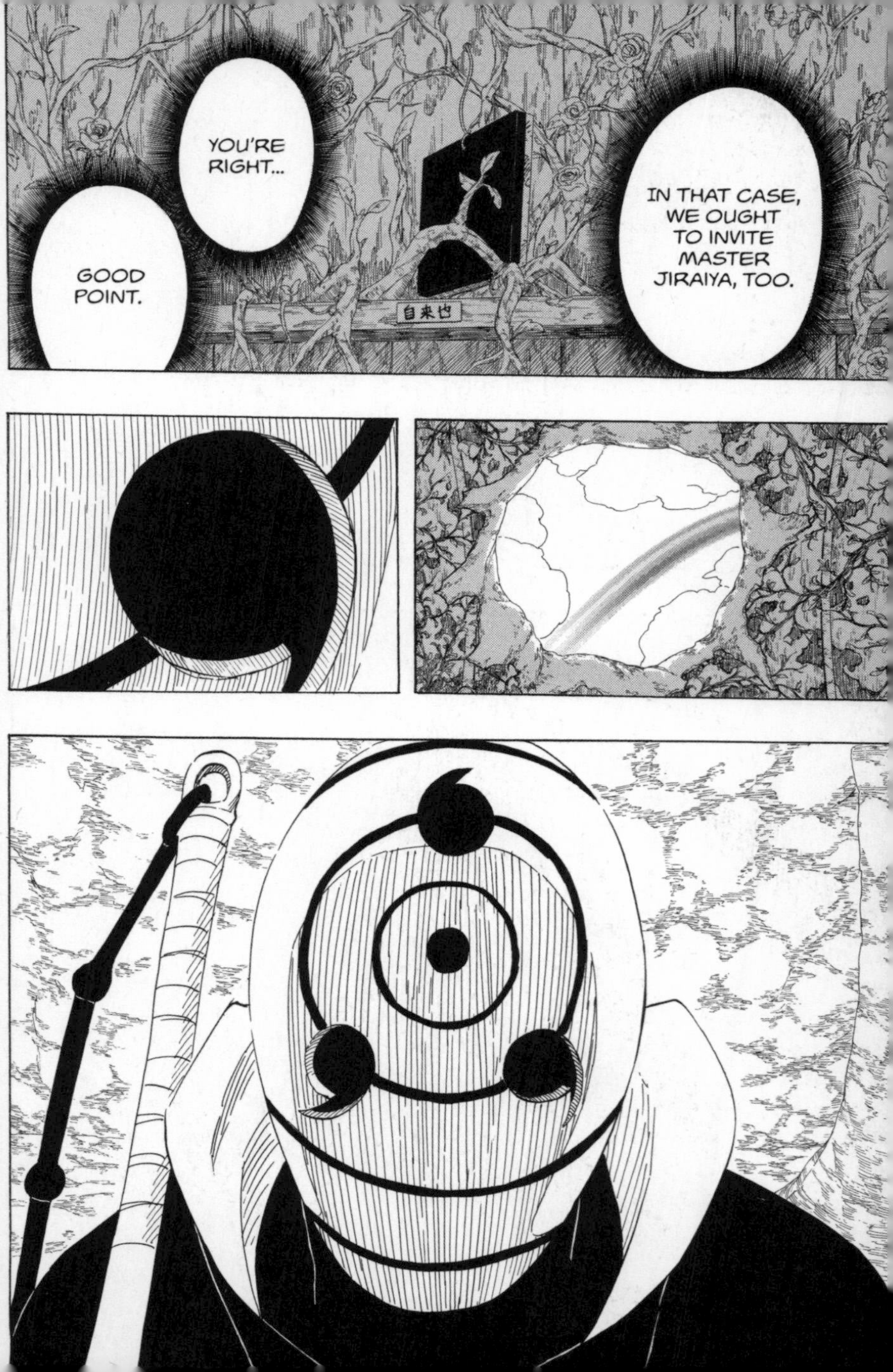
IN THAT CASE, WE OUGHT TO INVITE MASTER JIRAIYA, TOO.
YOU'RE RIGHT...
GOOD POINT.
自来也

READ THIS WAY

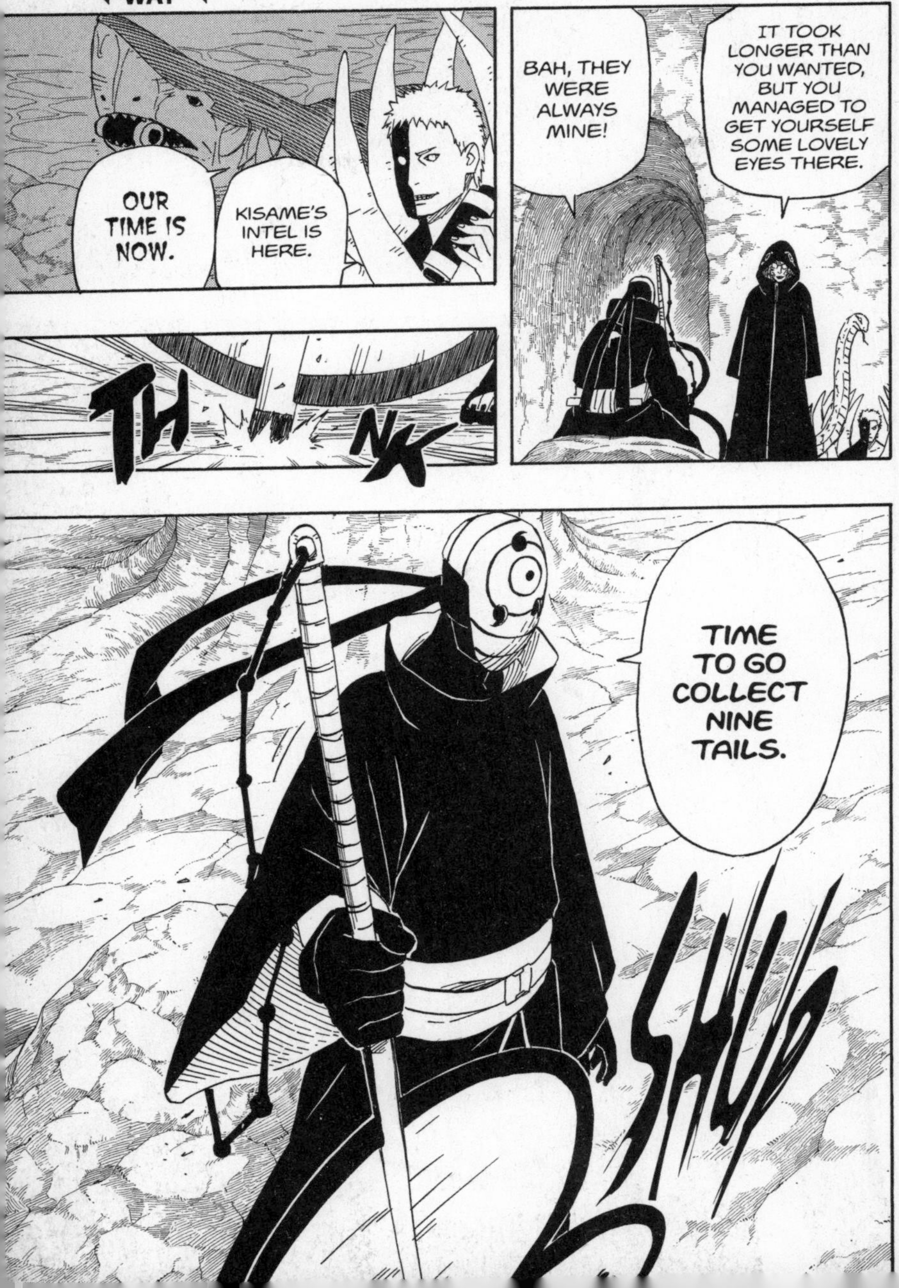
IT TOOK LONGER THAN YOU WANTED, BUT YOU MANAGED TO GET YOURSELF SOME LOVELY EYES THERE.
BAH, THEY WERE ALWAYS MINE!
KISAME'S INTEL IS HERE.
OUR TIME IS NOW.
THNK
TIME TO GO COLLECT NINE TAILS.
SHUP

SWSH...
長門
弥彦
小南

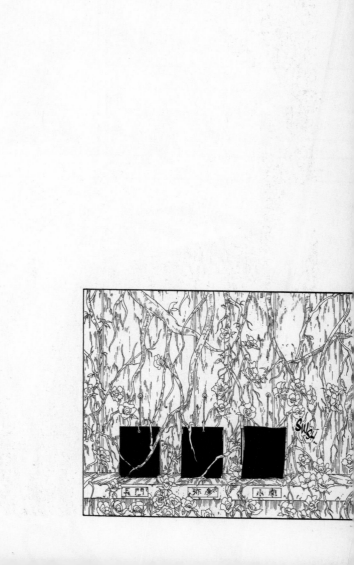

Number 512: The Truth About Zetsu!!

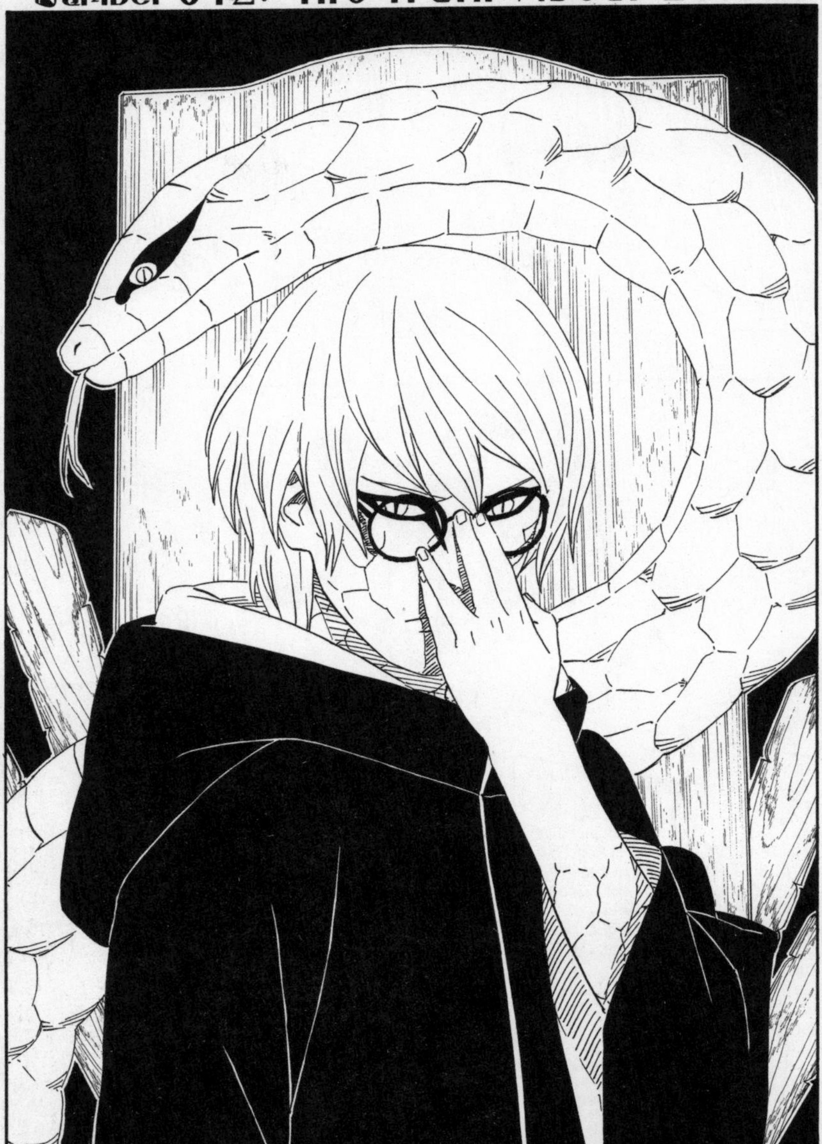

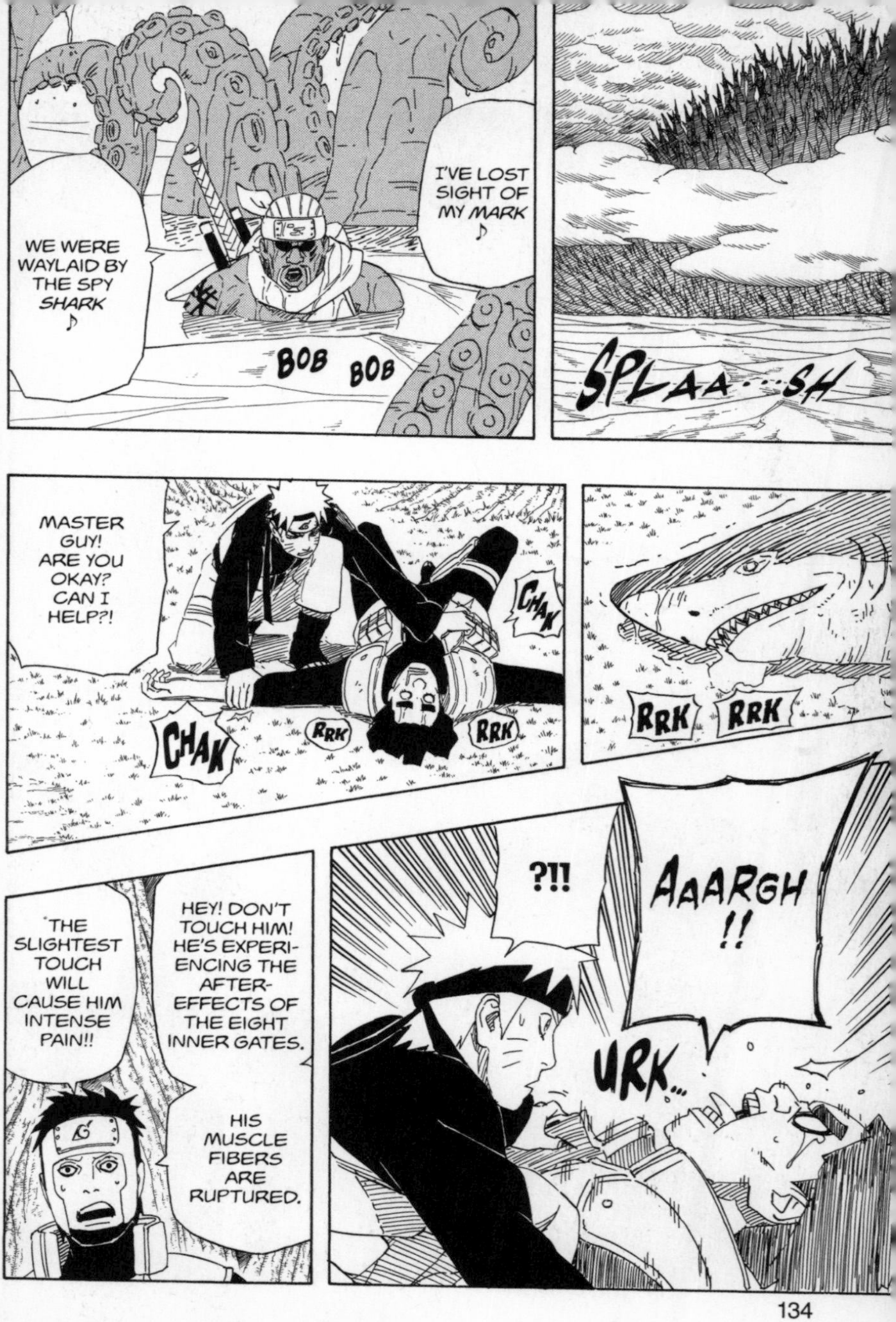
SPLAA...SH
I'VE LOST SIGHT OF MY MARK ♪
WE WERE WAYLAID BY THE SPY SHARK ♪
BOB
BOB
RRK
RRK
MASTER GUY! ARE YOU OKAY? CAN I HELP?!
CHAK
CHAK
RRK
RRK
AAARGH!!
?!!
URK...
HEY! DON'T TOUCH HIM! HE'S EXPERIENCING THE AFTER-EFFECTS OF THE EIGHT INNER GATES.
THE SLIGHTEST TOUCH WILL CAUSE HIM INTENSE PAIN!!
HIS MUSCLE FIBERS ARE RUPTURED.

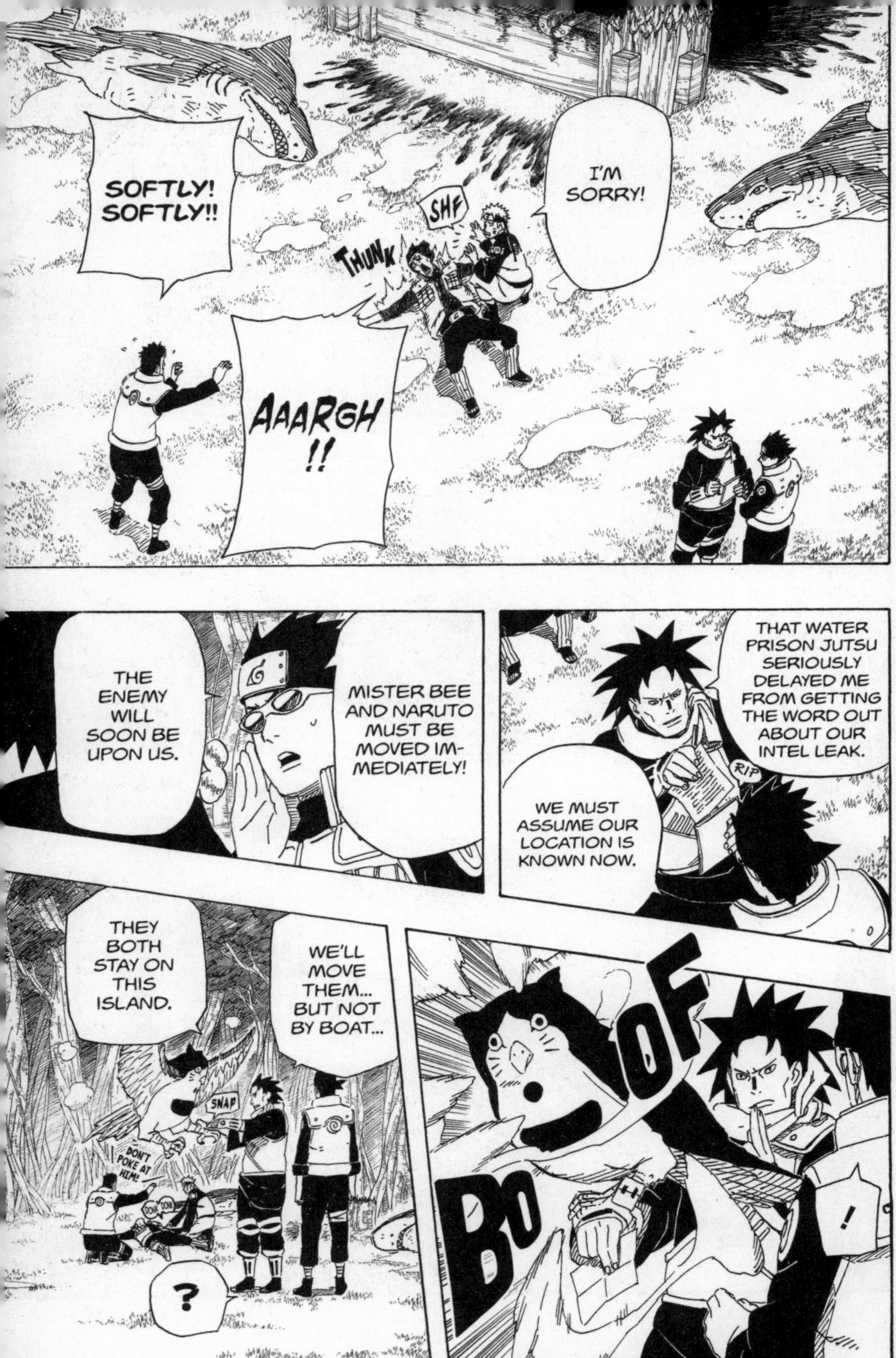
I'M SORRY!
SHF
THUNK
SOFTLY! SOFTLY!!
AAARGH!!
THAT WATER PRISON JUTSU SERIOUSLY DELAYED ME FROM GETTING THE WORD OUT ABOUT OUR INTEL LEAK.
RIP
WE MUST ASSUME OUR LOCATION IS KNOWN NOW.
MISTER BEE AND NARUTO MUST BE MOVED IM-MEDIATELY!
THE ENEMY WILL SOON BE UPON US.
BOOF
!
WE'LL MOVE THEM... BUT NOT BY BOAT...
THEY BOTH STAY ON THIS ISLAND.
SNAP
DON'T POKE AT HIM!
?

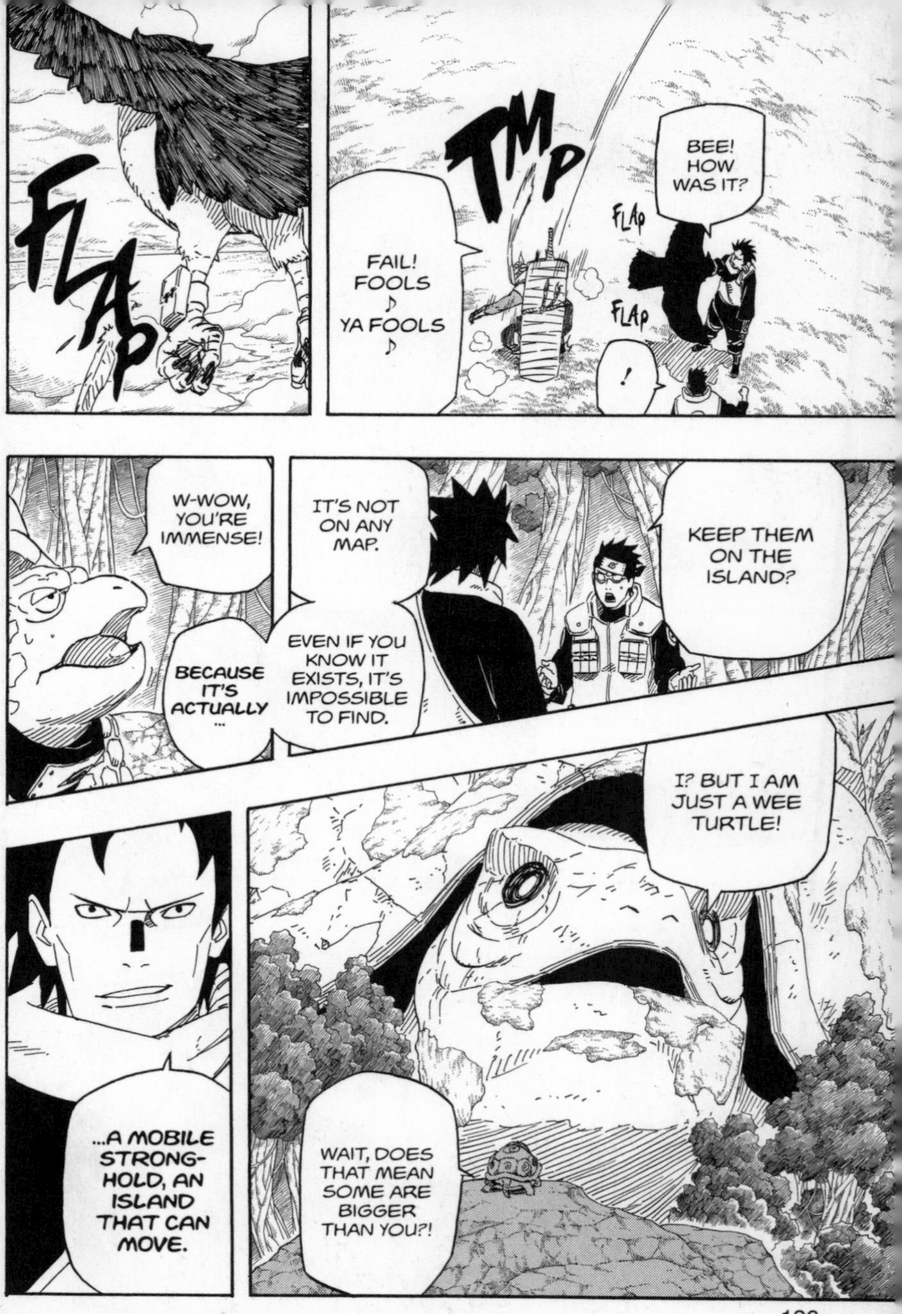

BEE! HOW WAS IT?
FLAP
FLAP
TMP
FAIL! FOOLS ♪ YA FOOLS ♪
!
FLAP
KEEP THEM ON THE ISLAND?
IT'S NOT ON ANY MAP.
EVEN IF YOU KNOW IT EXISTS, IT'S IMPOSSIBLE TO FIND.
BECAUSE IT'S ACTUALLY...
...A MOBILE STRONG-HOLD, AN ISLAND THAT CAN MOVE.
W-WOW, YOU'RE IMMENSE!
I? BUT I AM JUST A WEE TURTLE!
WAIT, DOES THAT MEAN SOME ARE BIGGER THAN YOU?!

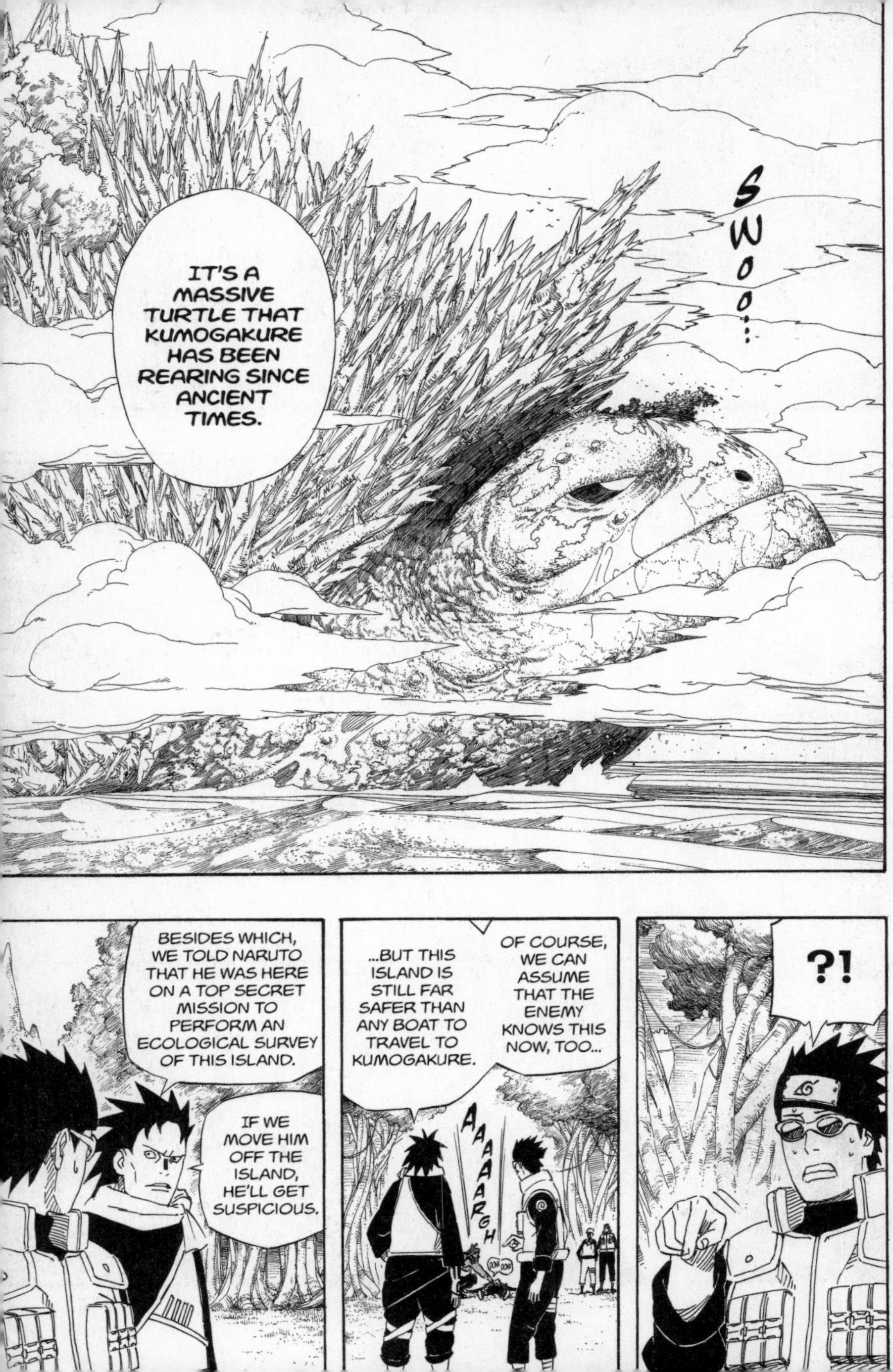

SWOO...
IT'S A MASSIVE TURTLE THAT KUMOGAKURE HAS BEEN REARING SINCE ANCIENT TIMES.
?!
OF COURSE, WE CAN ASSUME THAT THE ENEMY KNOWS THIS NOW, TOO...
...BUT THIS ISLAND IS STILL FAR SAFER THAN ANY BOAT TO TRAVEL TO KUMOGAKURE.
AAAAARGH
BESIDES WHICH, WE TOLD NARUTO THAT HE WAS HERE ON A TOP SECRET MISSION TO PERFORM AN ECOLOGICAL SURVEY OF THIS ISLAND.
IF WE MOVE HIM OFF THE ISLAND, HE'LL GET SUSPICIOUS.

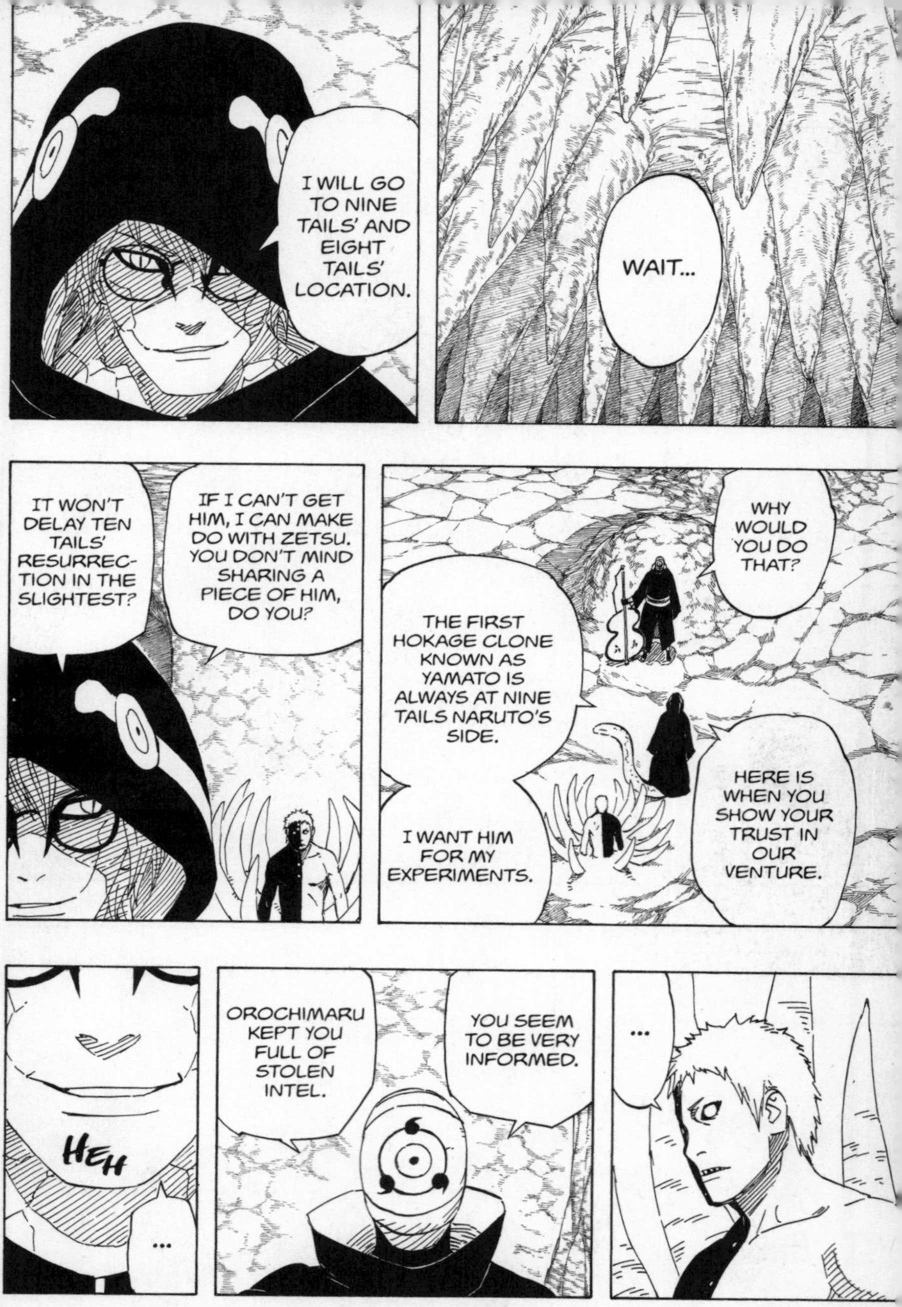
WAIT...
I WILL GO TO NINE TAILS' AND EIGHT TAILS' LOCATION.
WHY WOULD YOU DO THAT?
THE FIRST HOKAGE CLONE KNOWN AS YAMATO IS ALWAYS AT NINE TAILS NARUTO'S SIDE.
I WANT HIM FOR MY EXPERIMENTS.
HERE IS WHEN YOU SHOW YOUR TRUST IN OUR VENTURE.
IF I CAN'T GET HIM, I CAN MAKE DO WITH ZETSU. YOU DON'T MIND SHARING A PIECE OF HIM, DO YOU?
IT WON'T DELAY TEN TAILS' RESURREC-TION IN THE SLIGHTEST?
...
YOU SEEM TO BE VERY INFORMED.
OROCHIMARU KEPT YOU FULL OF STOLEN INTEL.
HEH
...

READ THIS WAY

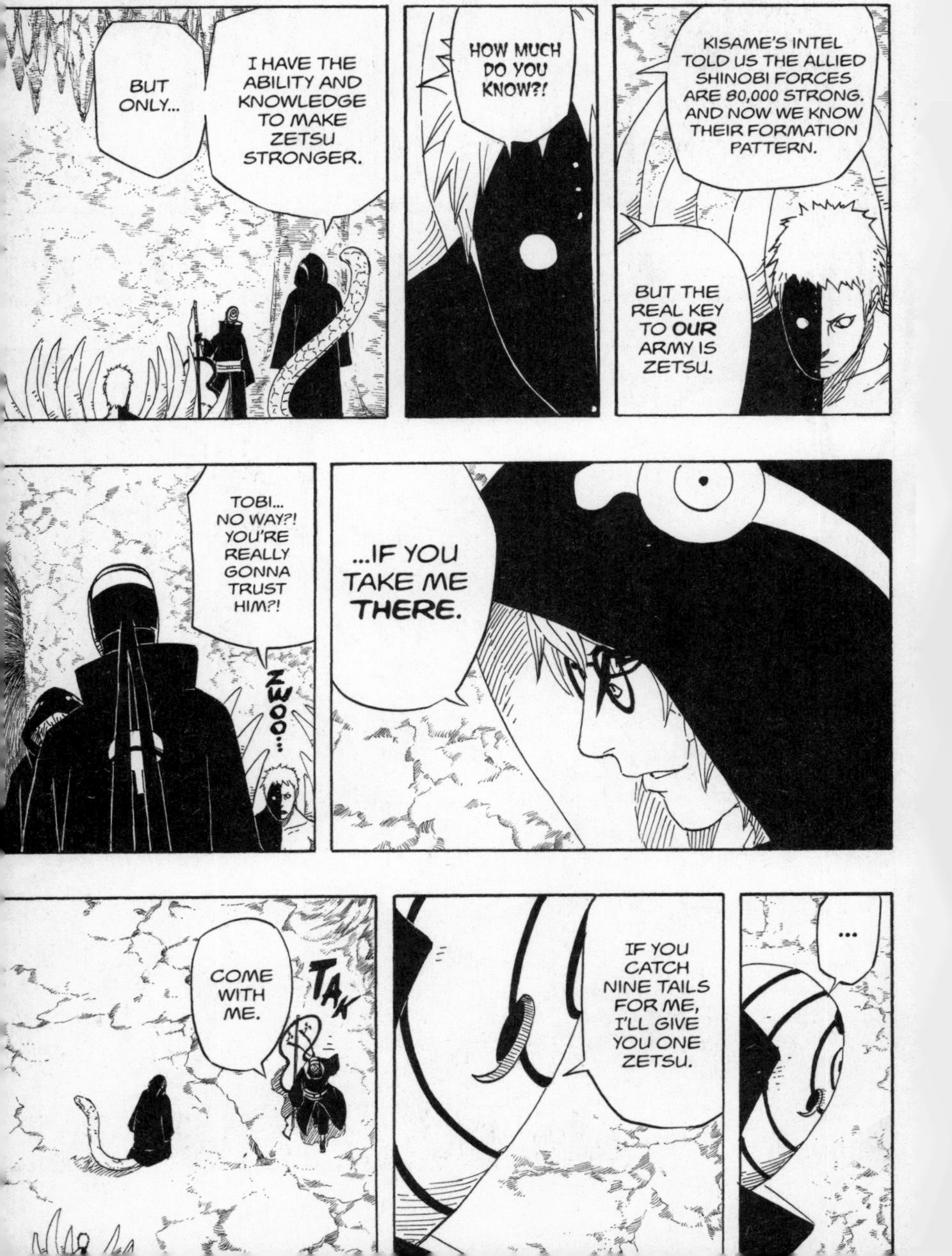
KISAME'S INTEL TOLD US THE ALLIED SHINOBI FORCES ARE 80,000 STRONG. AND NOW WE KNOW THEIR FORMATION PATTERN.
BUT THE REAL KEY TO **OUR** ARMY IS ZETSU.
HOW MUCH DO YOU KNOW?!
I HAVE THE ABILITY AND KNOWLEDGE TO MAKE ZETSU STRONGER.
BUT ONLY...
...IF YOU TAKE ME **THERE.**
TOBI... NO WAY?! YOU'RE REALLY GONNA TRUST HIM?!
ZWOO...
...
IF YOU CATCH NINE TAILS FOR ME, I'LL GIVE YOU ONE ZETSU.
COME WITH ME.
TAK

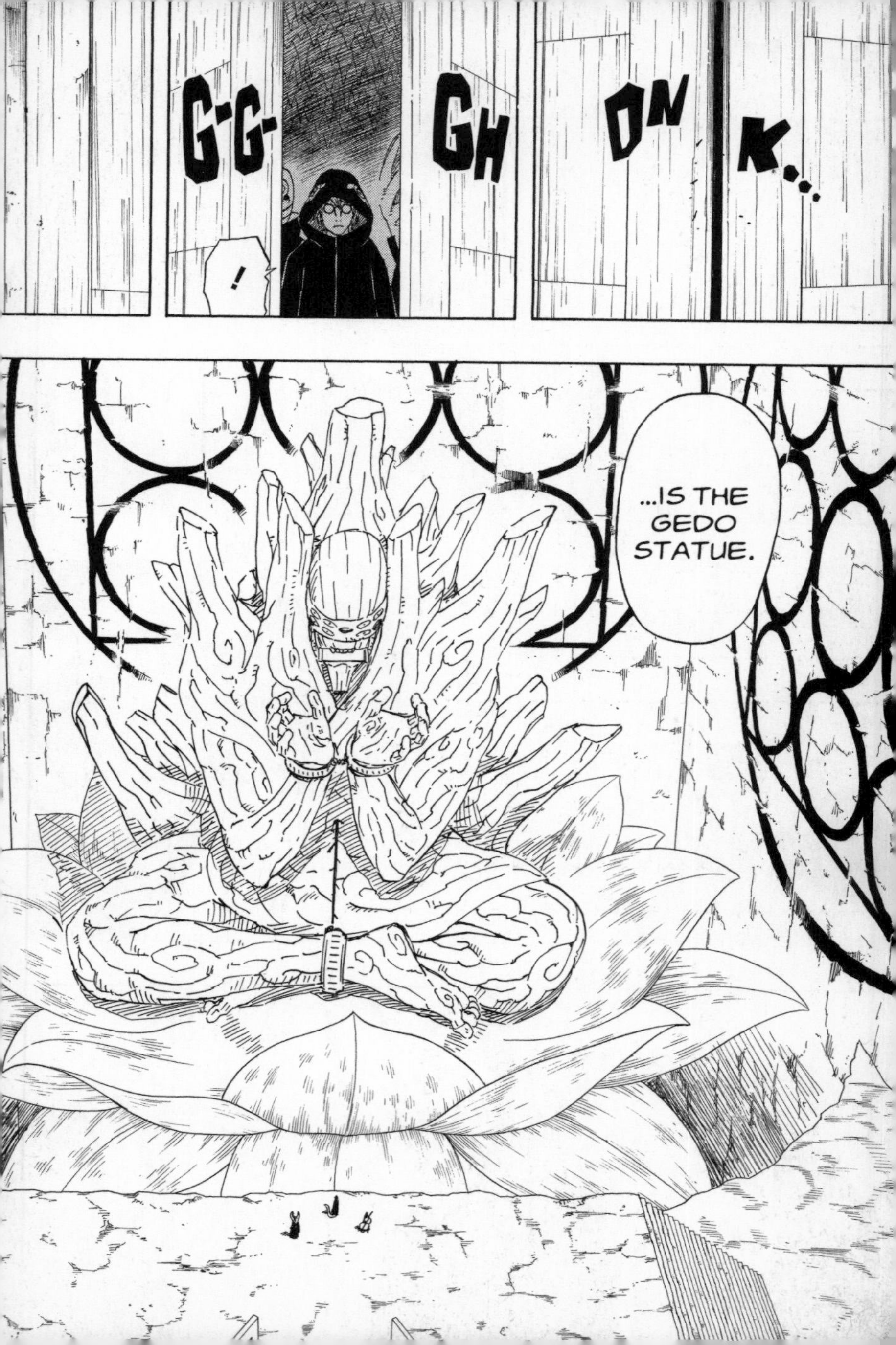
G-G-GH ON K...
!
...IS THE GEDO STATUE.

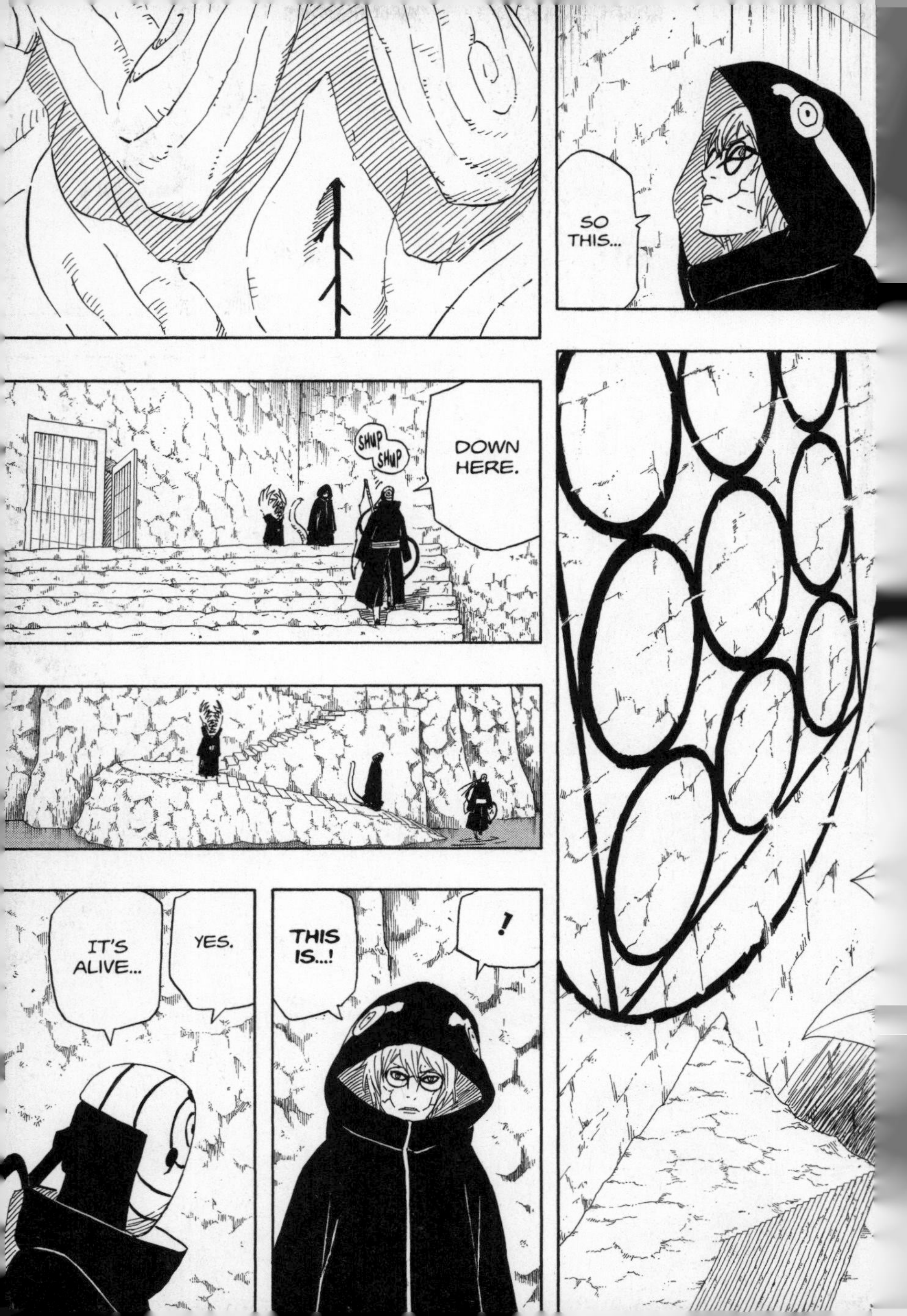
SO THIS...
DOWN HERE.
SHUP SHUP
!
THIS IS...!
YES.
IT'S ALIVE...

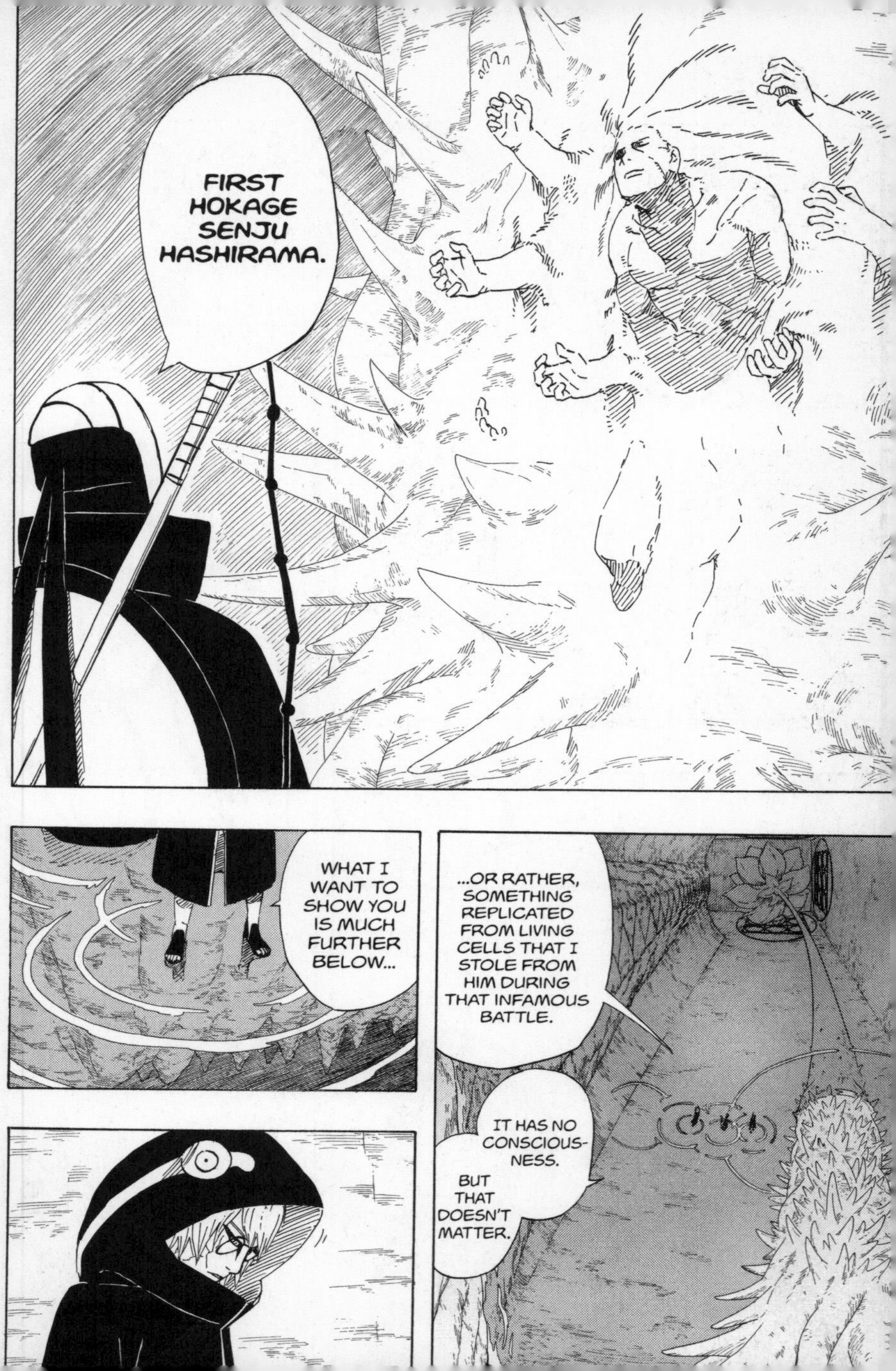
FIRST HOKAGE SENJU HASHIRAMA.
...OR RATHER, SOMETHING REPLICATED FROM LIVING CELLS THAT I STOLE FROM HIM DURING THAT INFAMOUS BATTLE.
IT HAS NO CONSCIOUS-NESS.
BUT THAT DOESN'T MATTER.
WHAT I WANT TO SHOW YOU IS MUCH FURTHER BELOW...

READ THIS WAY

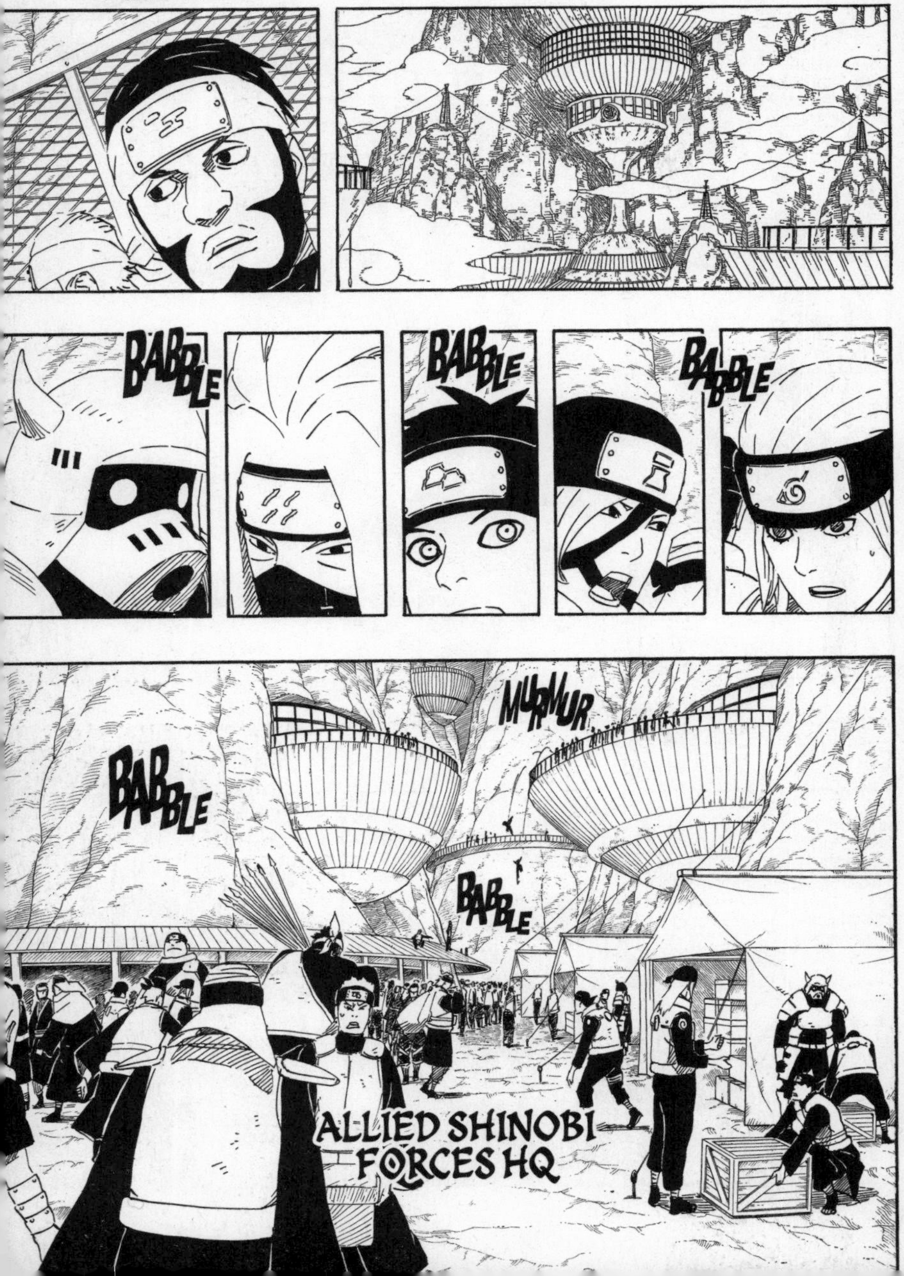
BABBLE
BABBLE
BABBLE
MURMUR
BABBLE
BABBLE
ALLIED SHINOBI FORCES HQ

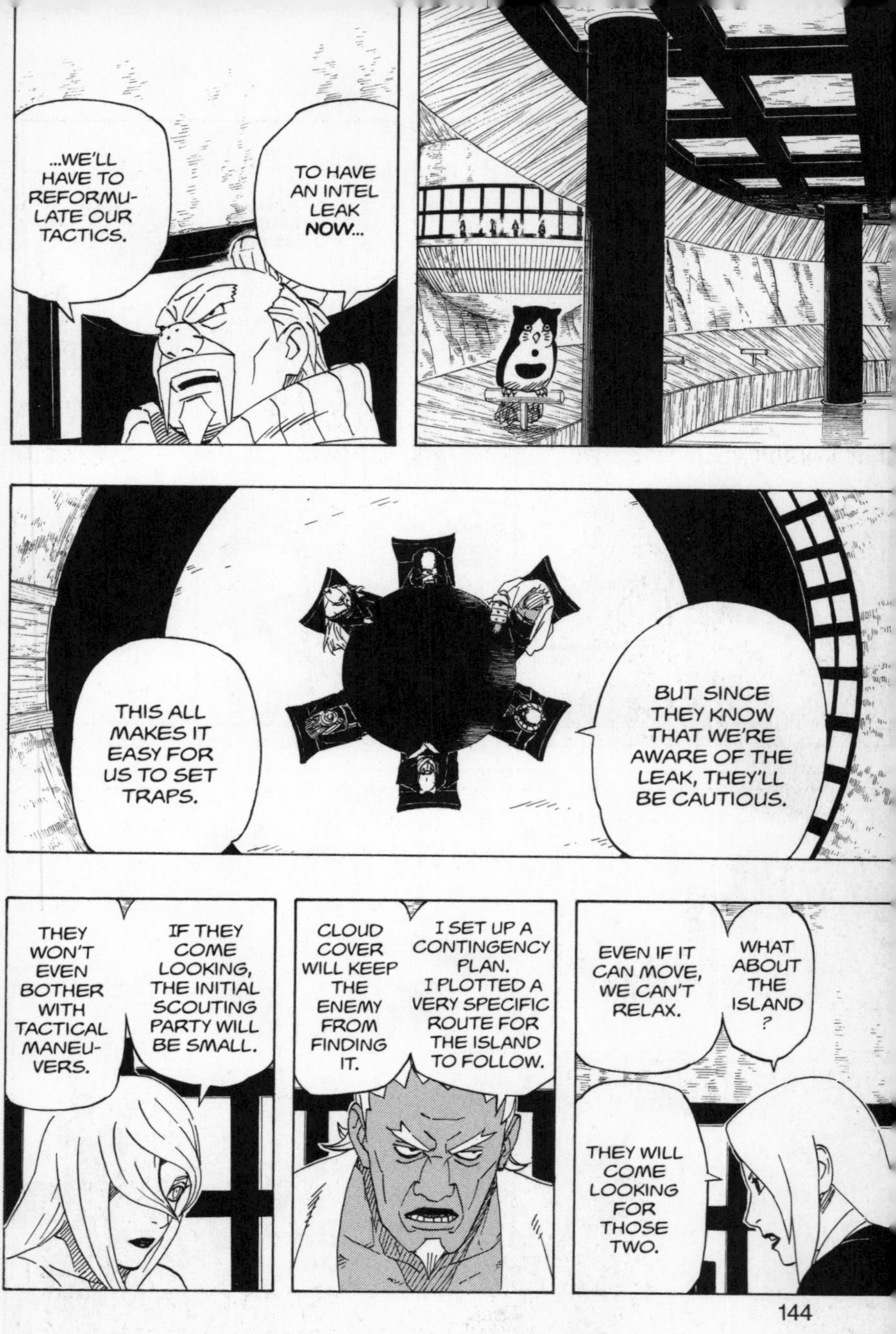
TO HAVE AN INTEL LEAK NOW...
...WE'LL HAVE TO REFORMULATE OUR TACTICS.
BUT SINCE THEY KNOW THAT WE'RE AWARE OF THE LEAK, THEY'LL BE CAUTIOUS.
THIS ALL MAKES IT EASY FOR US TO SET TRAPS.
WHAT ABOUT THE ISLAND?
EVEN IF IT CAN MOVE, WE CAN'T RELAX.
THEY WILL COME LOOKING FOR THOSE TWO.
I SET UP A CONTINGENCY PLAN. I PLOTTED A VERY SPECIFIC ROUTE FOR THE ISLAND TO FOLLOW.
CLOUD COVER WILL KEEP THE ENEMY FROM FINDING IT.
IF THEY COME LOOKING, THE INITIAL SCOUTING PARTY WILL BE SMALL.
THEY WON'T EVEN BOTHER WITH TACTICAL MANEUVERS.

READ THIS WAY

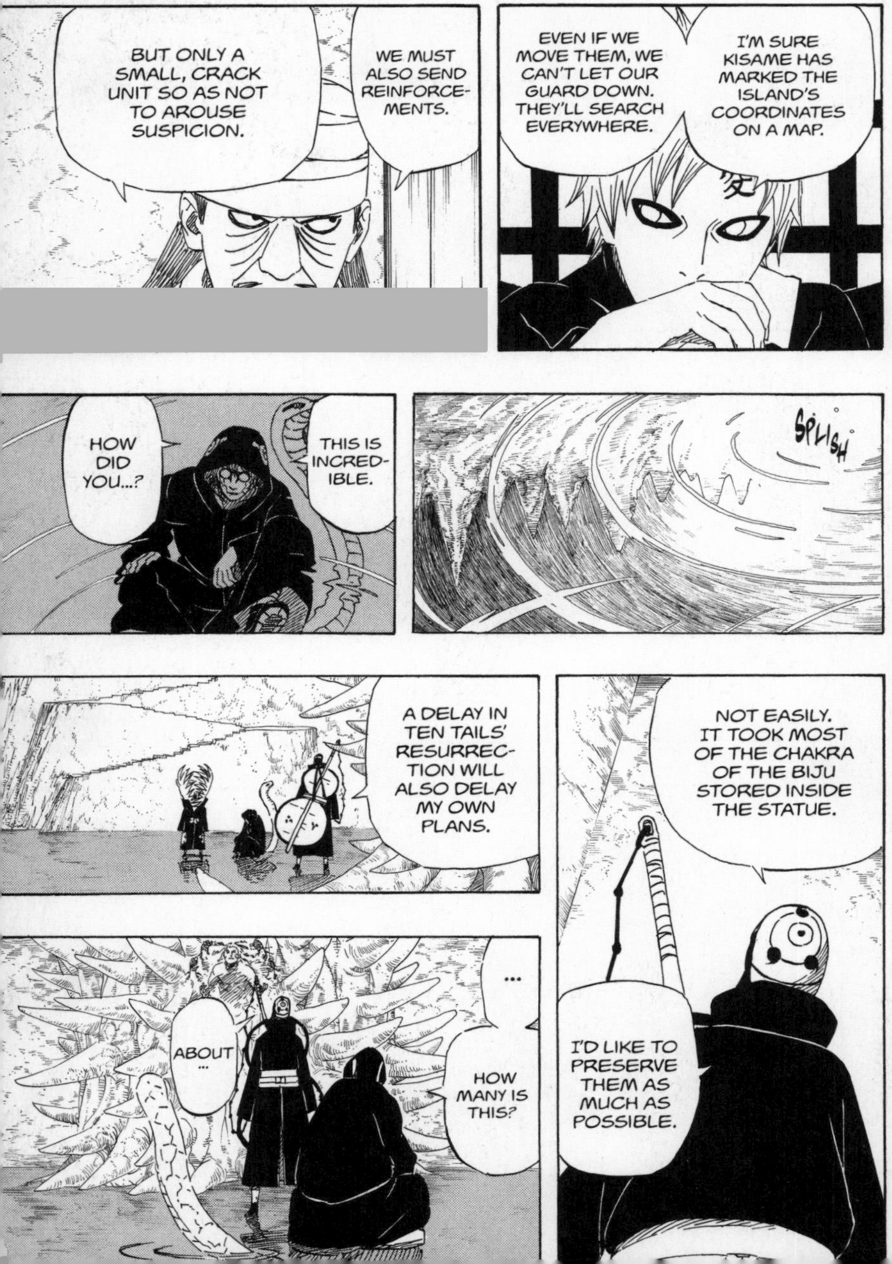
I'M SURE KISAME HAS MARKED THE ISLAND'S COORDINATES ON A MAP.
EVEN IF WE MOVE THEM, WE CAN'T LET OUR GUARD DOWN. THEY'LL SEARCH EVERYWHERE.
WE MUST ALSO SEND REINFORCE-MENTS.
BUT ONLY A SMALL, CRACK UNIT SO AS NOT TO AROUSE SUSPICION.
SPLISH
THIS IS INCRED-IBLE.
HOW DID YOU...?
NOT EASILY. IT TOOK MOST OF THE CHAKRA OF THE BIJU STORED INSIDE THE STATUE.
I'D LIKE TO PRESERVE THEM AS MUCH AS POSSIBLE.
A DELAY IN TEN TAILS' RESURREC-TION WILL ALSO DELAY MY OWN PLANS.
...
HOW MANY IS THIS?
ABOUT ...

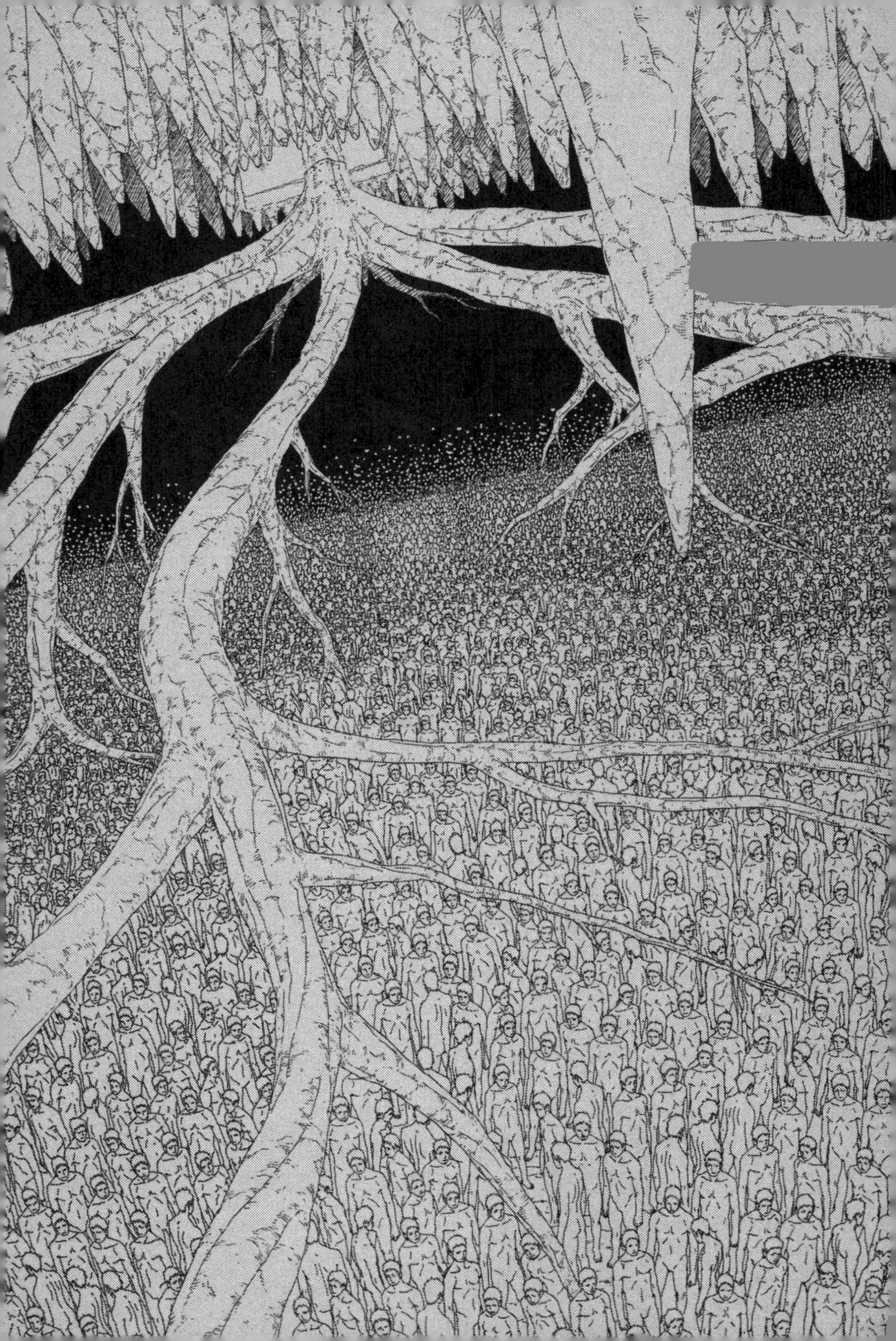

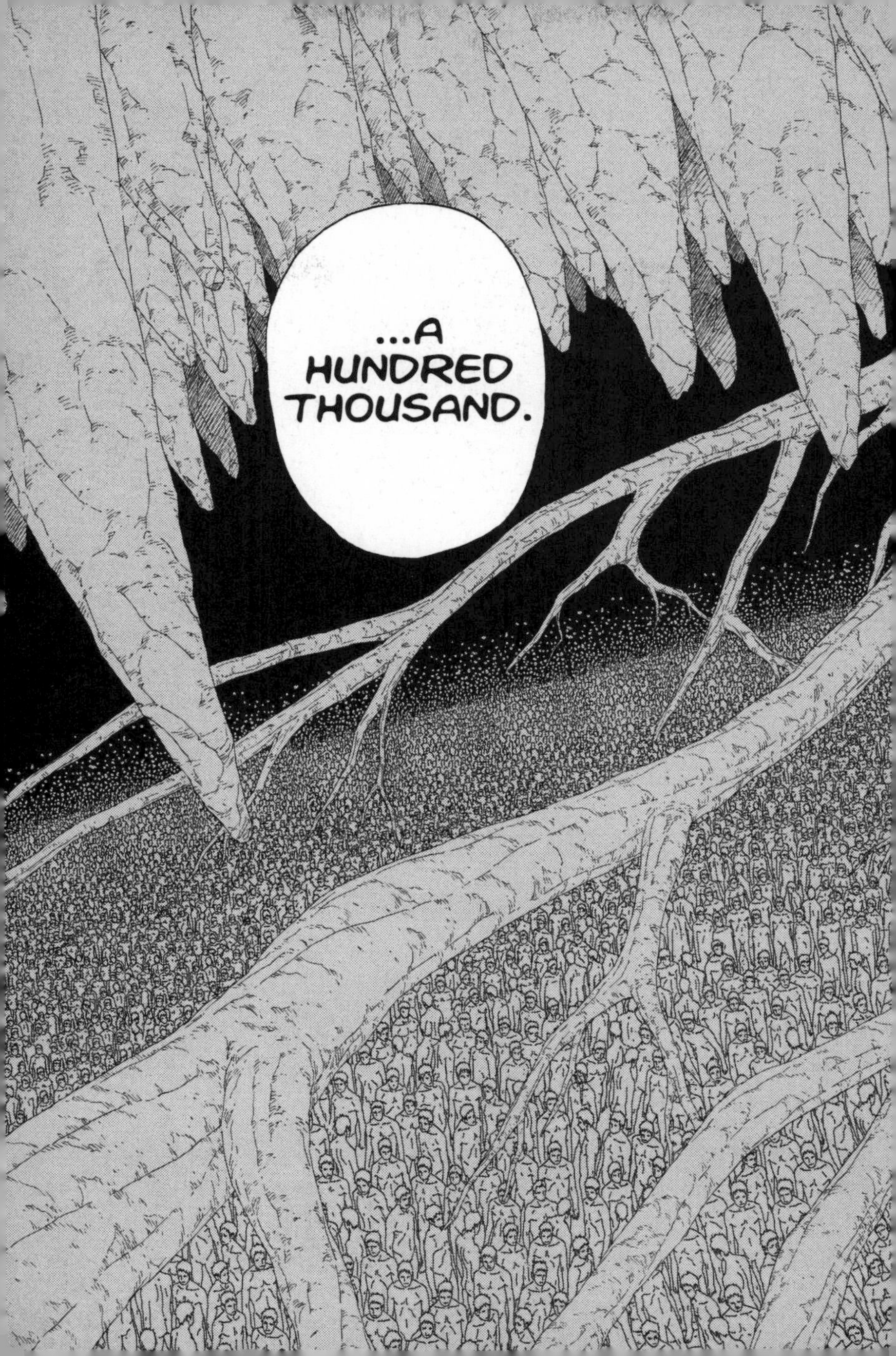
...A HUNDRED THOUSAND.

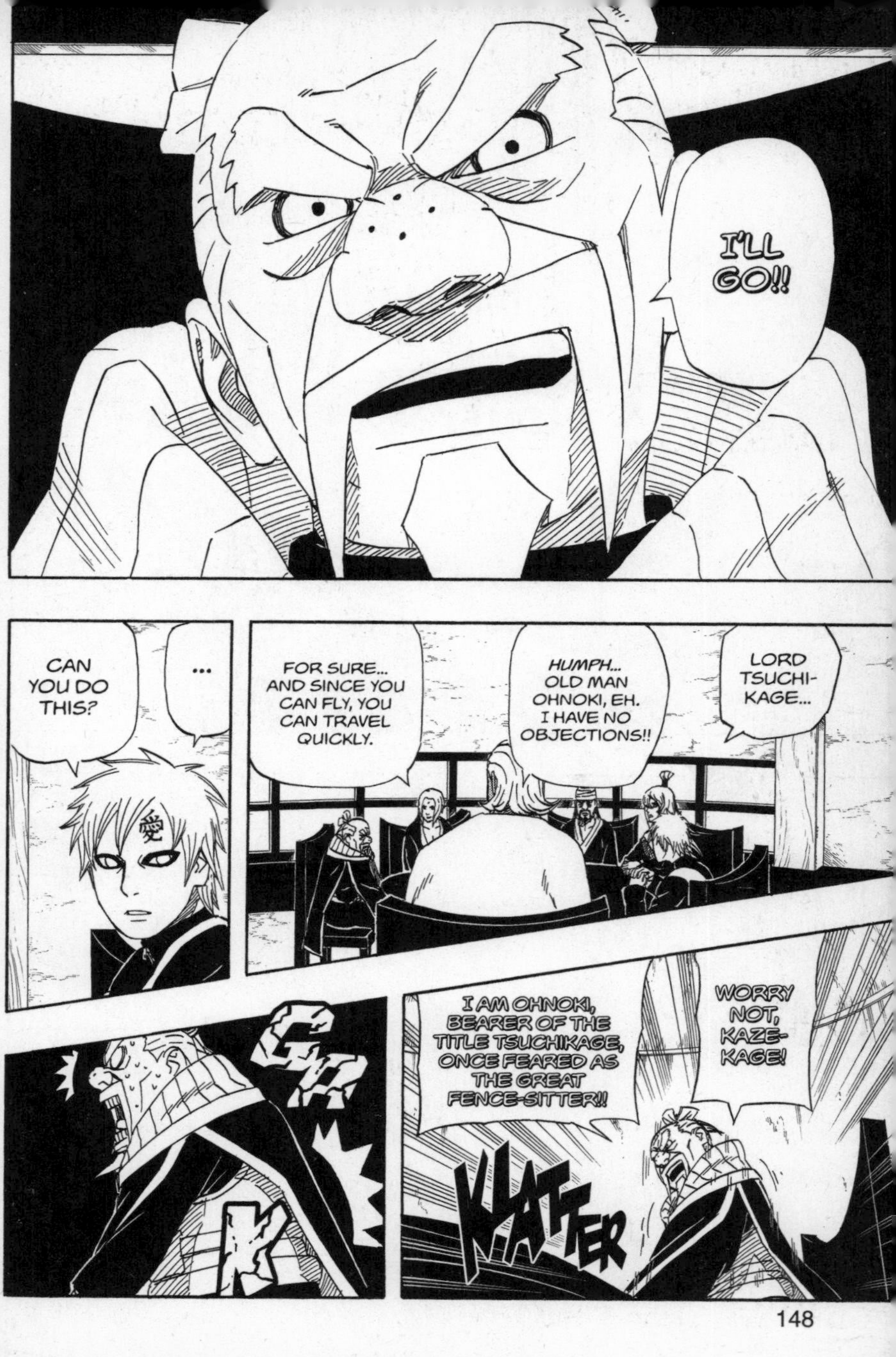
I'LL GO!!
LORD TSUCHI-KAGE...
HUMPH... OLD MAN OHNOKI, EH. I HAVE NO OBJECTIONS!!
FOR SURE... AND SINCE YOU CAN FLY, YOU CAN TRAVEL QUICKLY.
...
CAN YOU DO THIS?
WORRY NOT, KAZE-KAGE!
I AM OHNOKI, BEARER OF THE TITLE TSUCHIKAGE, ONCE FEARED AS THE GREAT FENCE-SITTER!!
KLATTER

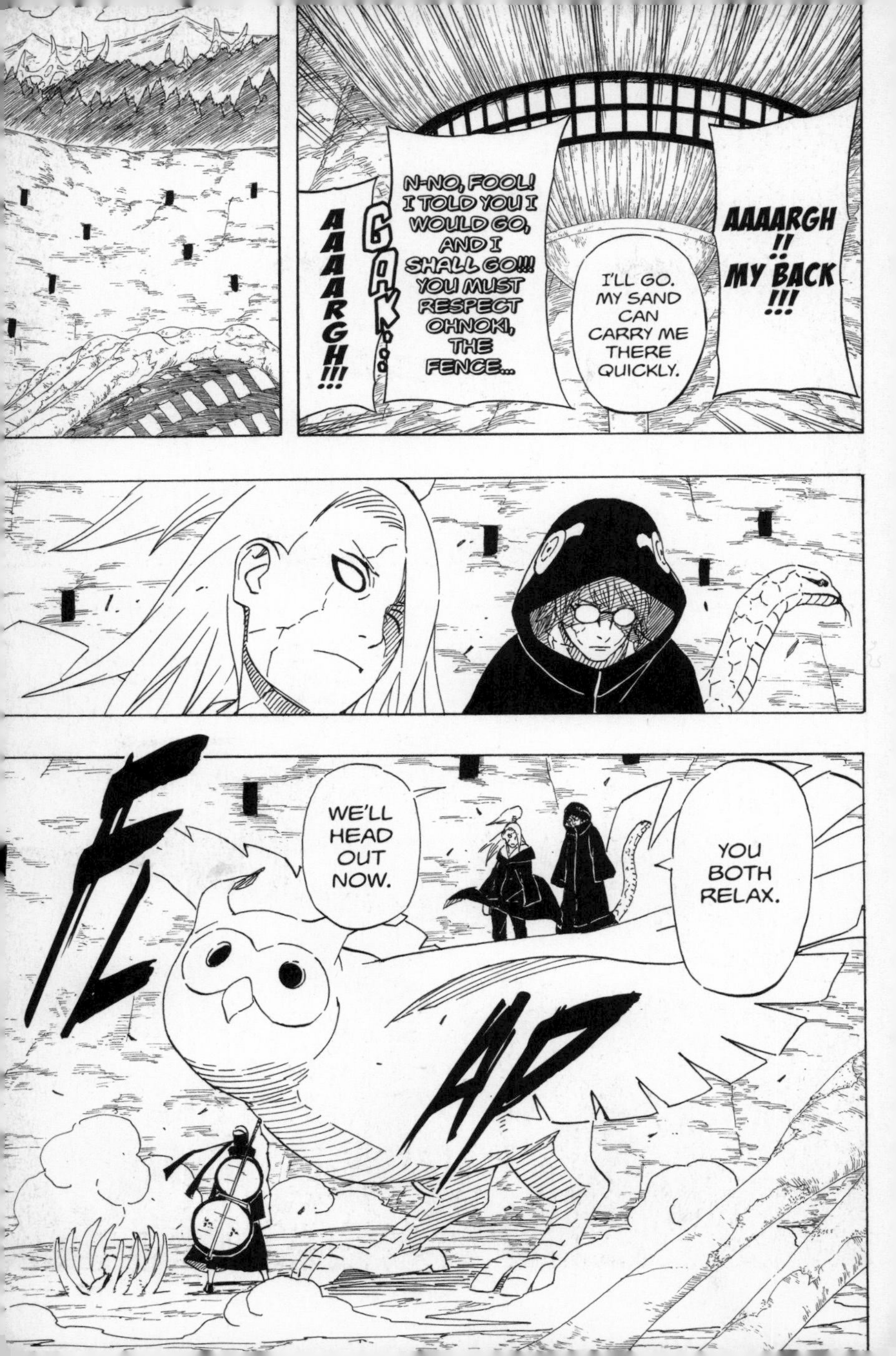
AAAARGH!! MY BACK!!!
I'LL GO. MY SAND CAN CARRY ME THERE QUICKLY.
N-NO, FOOL! I TOLD YOU I WOULD GO, AND I SHALL GO!!! YOU MUST RESPECT OHNOKI, THE FENCE...
GAK...
AAAARGH!!!
YOU BOTH RELAX.
WE'LL HEAD OUT NOW.
FLAP

NARUTO

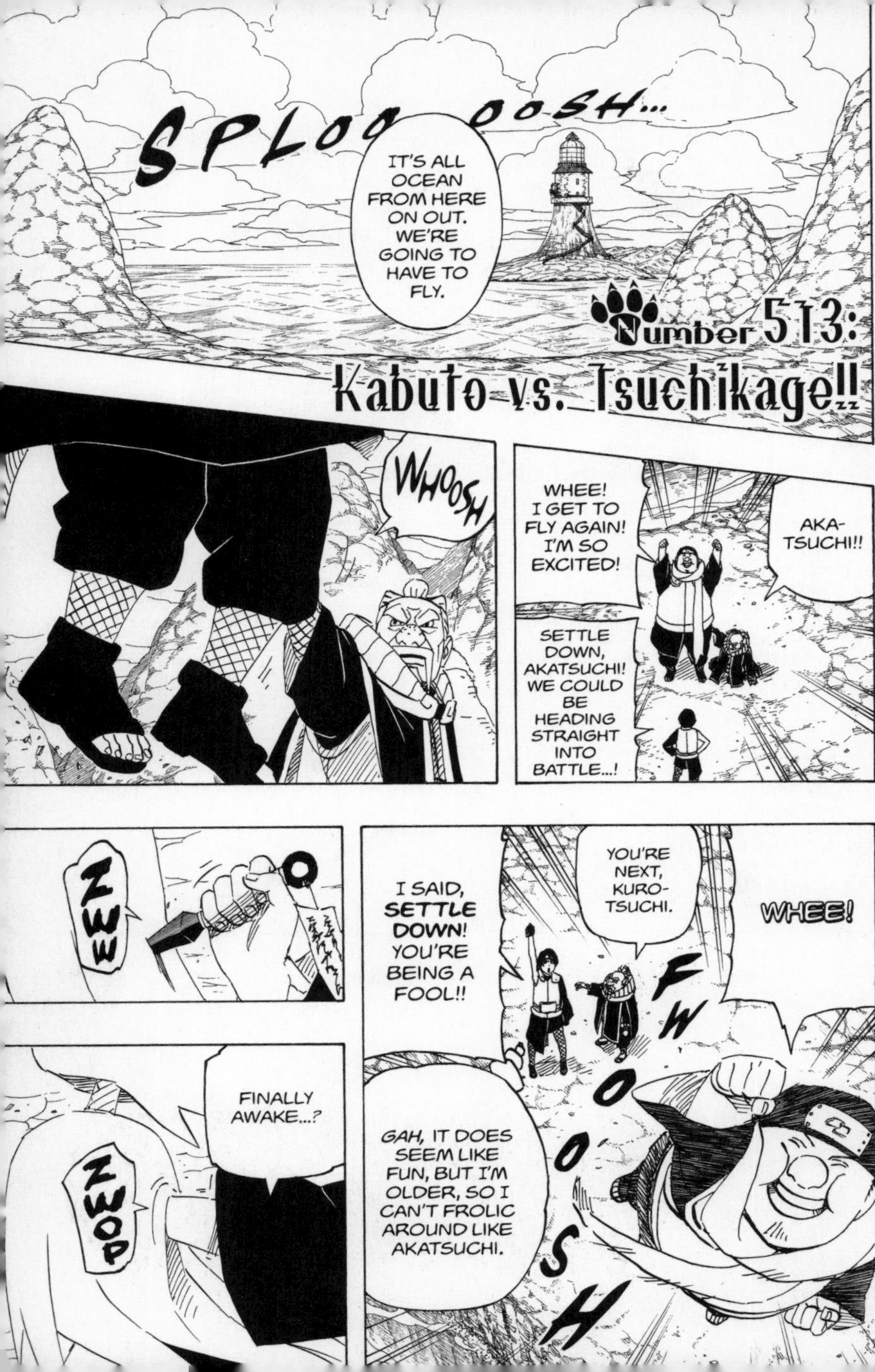

SPLOO OOSH...
IT'S ALL OCEAN FROM HERE ON OUT. WE'RE GOING TO HAVE TO FLY.
Number 513: Kabuto vs. Tsuchikage!!
AKA-TSUCHI!!
WHEE! I GET TO FLY AGAIN! I'M SO EXCITED!
SETTLE DOWN, AKATSUCHI! WE COULD BE HEADING STRAIGHT INTO BATTLE...!
WHOOSH
WHEE!
YOU'RE NEXT, KURO-TSUCHI.
I SAID, **SETTLE DOWN**! YOU'RE BEING A FOOL!!
FWOOOSH
GAH, IT DOES SEEM LIKE FUN, BUT I'M OLDER, SO I CAN'T FROLIC AROUND LIKE AKATSUCHI.
ZWW
FINALLY AWAKE...?
ZWOP

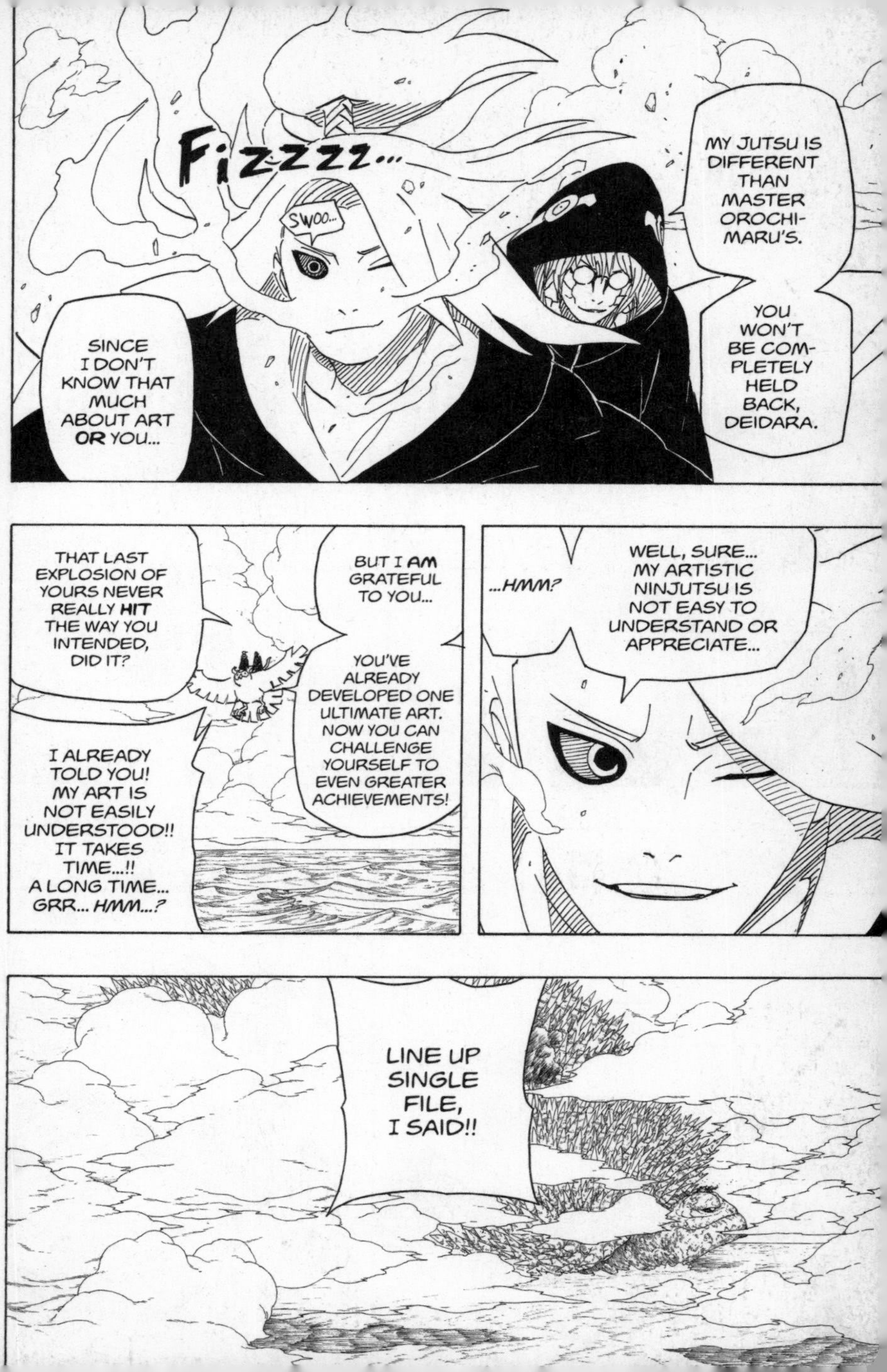
MY JUTSU IS DIFFERENT THAN MASTER OROCHI-MARU'S.
YOU WON'T BE COM-PLETELY HELD BACK, DEIDARA.
Fizzzzz...
SWOO...
SINCE I DON'T KNOW THAT MUCH ABOUT ART **OR** YOU...
WELL, SURE... MY ARTISTIC NINJUTSU IS NOT EASY TO UNDERSTAND OR APPRECIATE...
...*HMM?*
BUT I **AM** GRATEFUL TO YOU...
YOU'VE ALREADY DEVELOPED ONE ULTIMATE ART. NOW YOU CAN CHALLENGE YOURSELF TO EVEN GREATER ACHIEVEMENTS!
THAT LAST EXPLOSION OF YOURS NEVER REALLY **HIT** THE WAY YOU INTENDED, DID IT?
I ALREADY TOLD YOU! MY ART IS NOT EASILY UNDERSTOOD!! IT TAKES TIME...!! A LONG TIME... GRR... *HMM...?*
LINE UP SINGLE FILE, I SAID!!

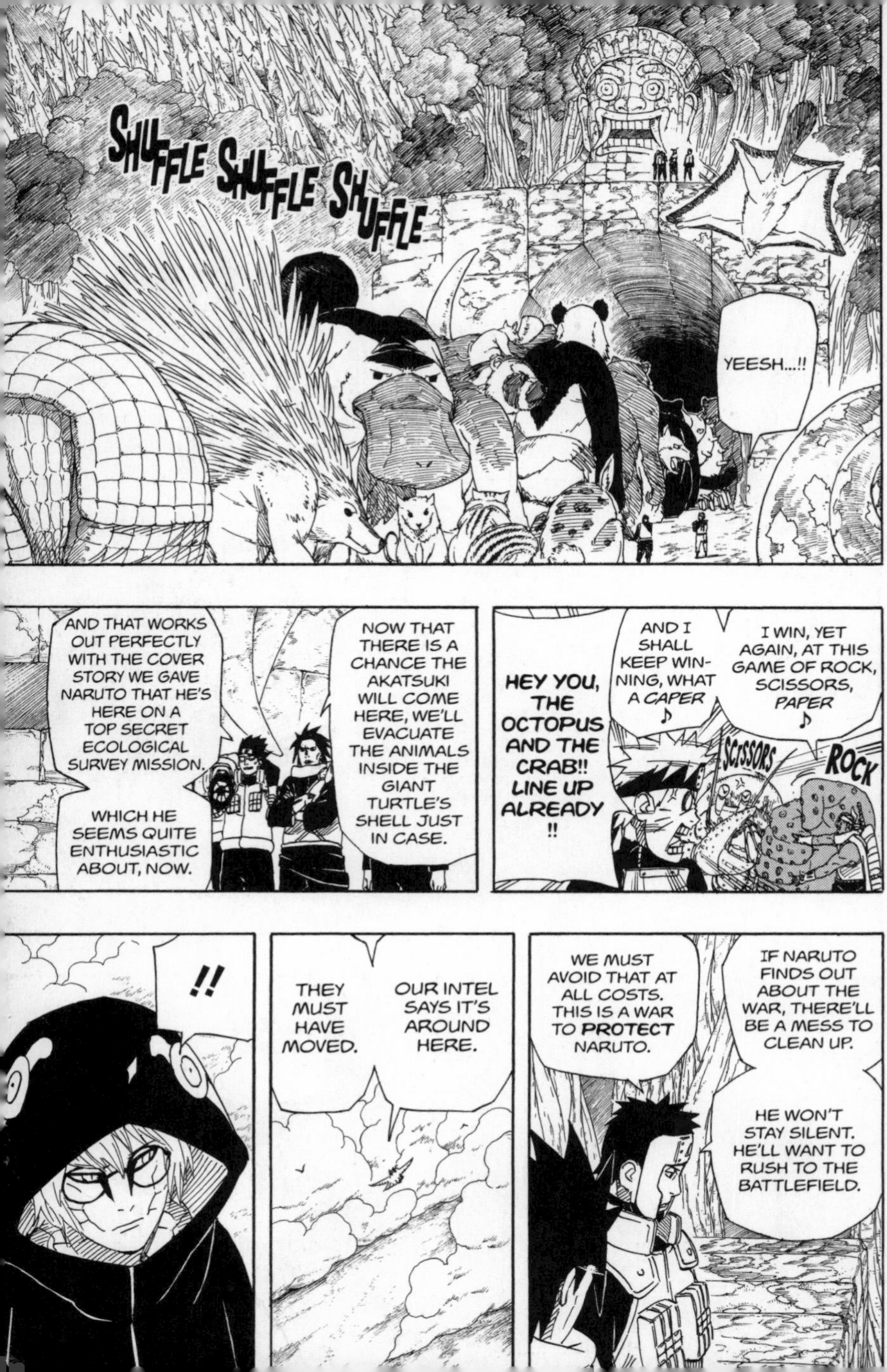
SHUFFLE SHUFFLE SHUFFLE
YEESH...!!
I WIN, YET AGAIN, AT THIS GAME OF ROCK, SCISSORS, *PAPER* ♪
AND I SHALL KEEP WINNING, WHAT A *CAPER* ♪
ROCK
SCISSORS
HEY YOU, THE OCTOPUS AND THE CRAB!! LINE UP ALREADY!!
NOW THAT THERE IS A CHANCE THE AKATSUKI WILL COME HERE, WE'LL EVACUATE THE ANIMALS INSIDE THE GIANT TURTLE'S SHELL JUST IN CASE.
AND THAT WORKS OUT PERFECTLY WITH THE COVER STORY WE GAVE NARUTO THAT HE'S HERE ON A TOP SECRET ECOLOGICAL SURVEY MISSION.
WHICH HE SEEMS QUITE ENTHUSIASTIC ABOUT, NOW.
IF NARUTO FINDS OUT ABOUT THE WAR, THERE'LL BE A MESS TO CLEAN UP.
HE WON'T STAY SILENT. HE'LL WANT TO RUSH TO THE BATTLEFIELD.
WE MUST AVOID THAT AT ALL COSTS. THIS IS A WAR TO **PROTECT** NARUTO.
OUR INTEL SAYS IT'S AROUND HERE.
THEY MUST HAVE MOVED.
!!

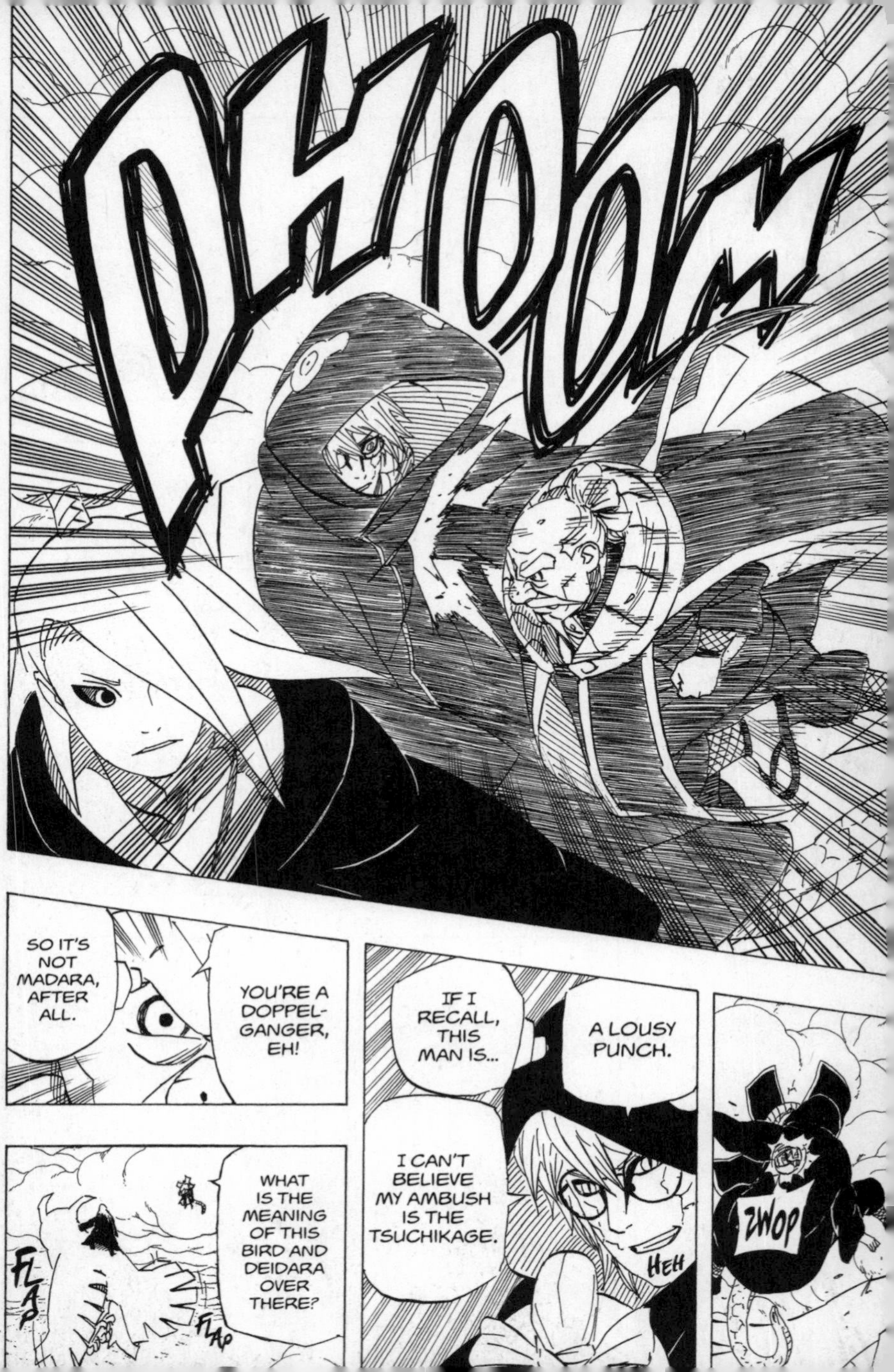
DHOOOM
ZWOP
A LOUSY PUNCH.
IF I RECALL, THIS MAN IS...
I CAN'T BELIEVE MY AMBUSH IS THE TSUCHIKAGE.
HEH
YOU'RE A DOPPEL-GANGER, EH!
SO IT'S NOT MADARA, AFTER ALL.
WHAT IS THE MEANING OF THIS BIRD AND DEIDARA OVER THERE?
FLAP
FLAP

READ THIS WAY

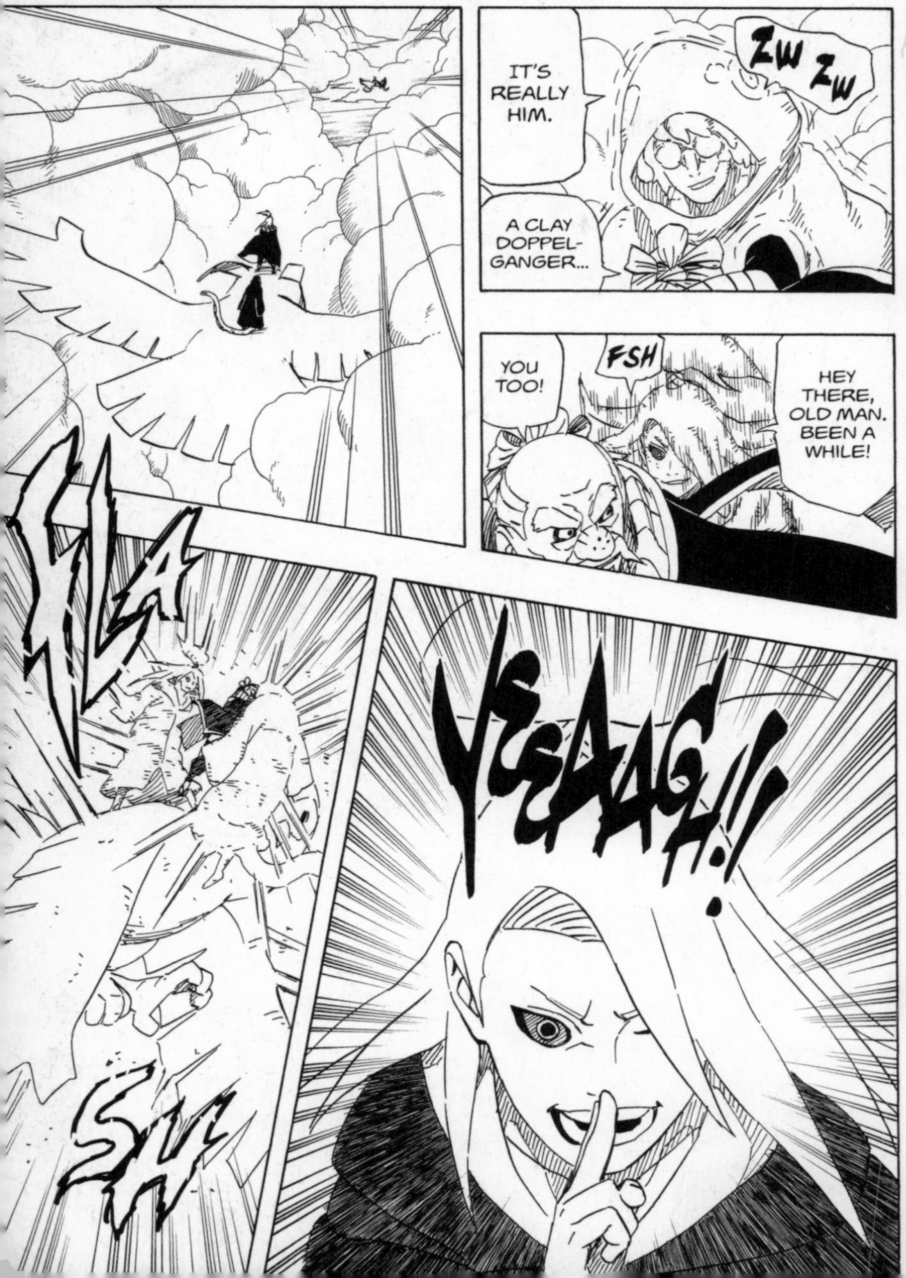
ZW ZW
IT'S REALLY HIM.
A CLAY DOPPEL-GANGER...
HEY THERE, OLD MAN. BEEN A WHILE!
FSH
YOU TOO!
YEEAAGH!!

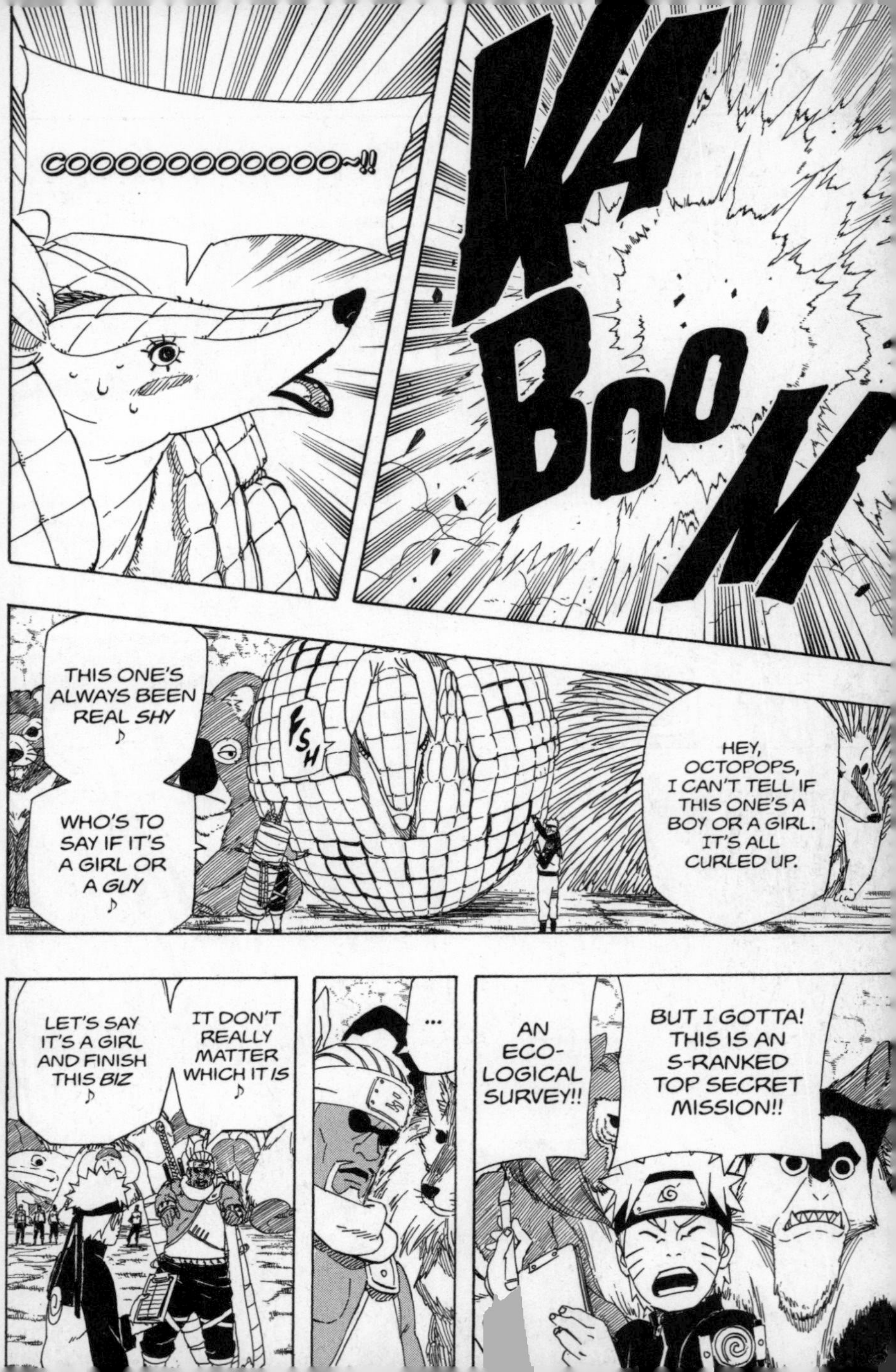
KA BOOM
COOOOOOOOOOOO~!!
HEY, OCTOPOPS, I CAN'T TELL IF THIS ONE'S A BOY OR A GIRL. IT'S ALL CURLED UP.
FSH
THIS ONE'S ALWAYS BEEN REAL *SHY* ♪
WHO'S TO SAY IF IT'S A GIRL OR A *GUY* ♪
BUT I GOTTA! THIS IS AN S-RANKED TOP SECRET MISSION!!
AN ECO-LOGICAL SURVEY!!
...
IT DON'T REALLY MATTER WHICH IT *IS* ♪
LET'S SAY IT'S A GIRL AND FINISH THIS *BIZ* ♪

READ THIS WAY

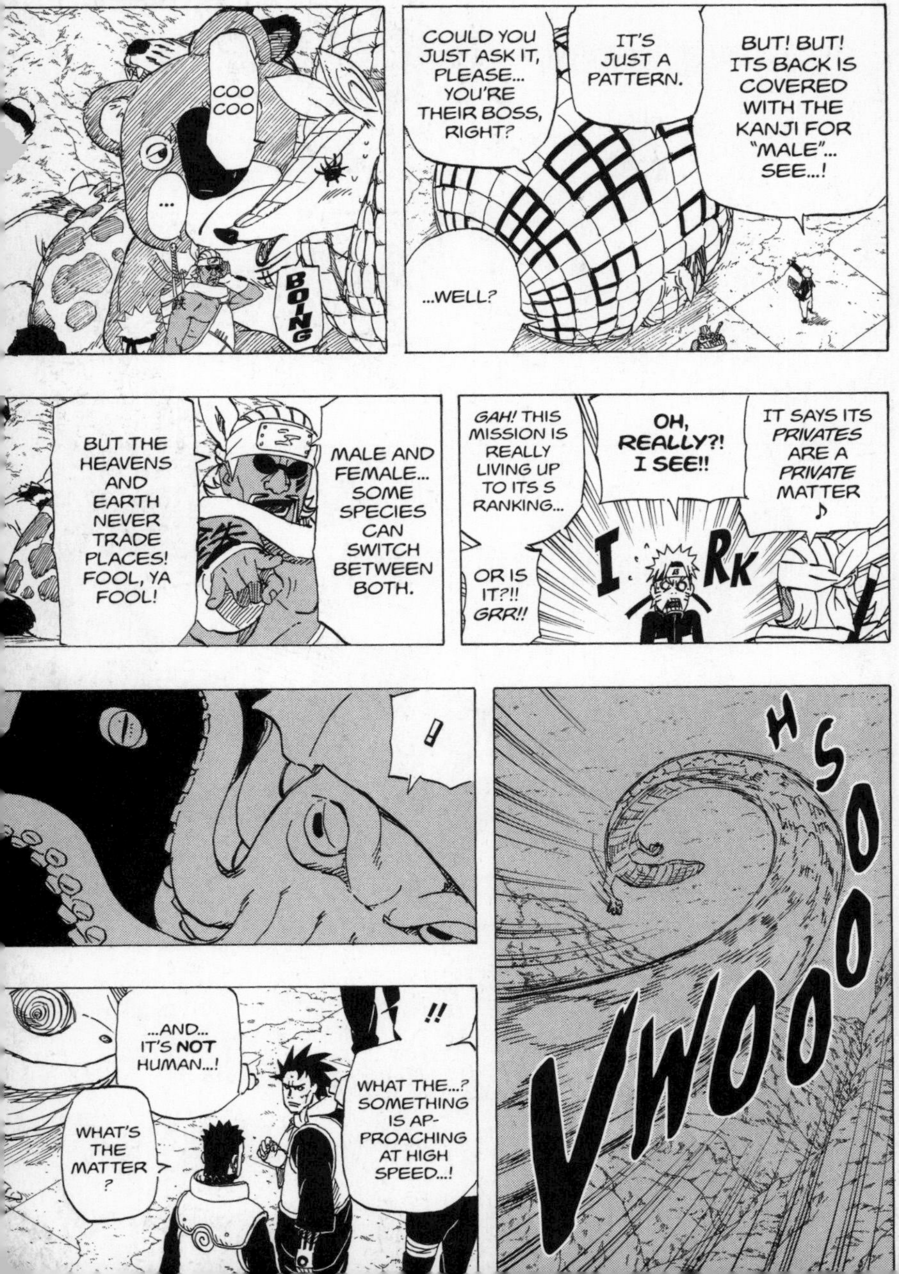
BUT! BUT! ITS BACK IS COVERED WITH THE KANJI FOR "MALE"... SEE...!
IT'S JUST A PATTERN.
COULD YOU JUST ASK IT, PLEASE... YOU'RE THEIR BOSS, RIGHT?
...WELL?
COO COO
...
BOING
IT SAYS ITS *PRIVATES* ARE A *PRIVATE* MATTER ♪
OH, *REALLY*?! I SEE!!
GAH! THIS MISSION IS REALLY LIVING UP TO ITS S RANKING...
IRK
OR IS IT?!! *GRR!!*
MALE AND FEMALE... SOME SPECIES CAN SWITCH BETWEEN BOTH.
BUT THE HEAVENS AND EARTH NEVER TRADE PLACES! FOOL, YA FOOL!
VWOOOOSH
!
!!
WHAT THE...? SOMETHING IS AP-PROACHING AT HIGH SPEED...!
...AND... IT'S **NOT** HUMAN...!
WHAT'S THE MATTER?

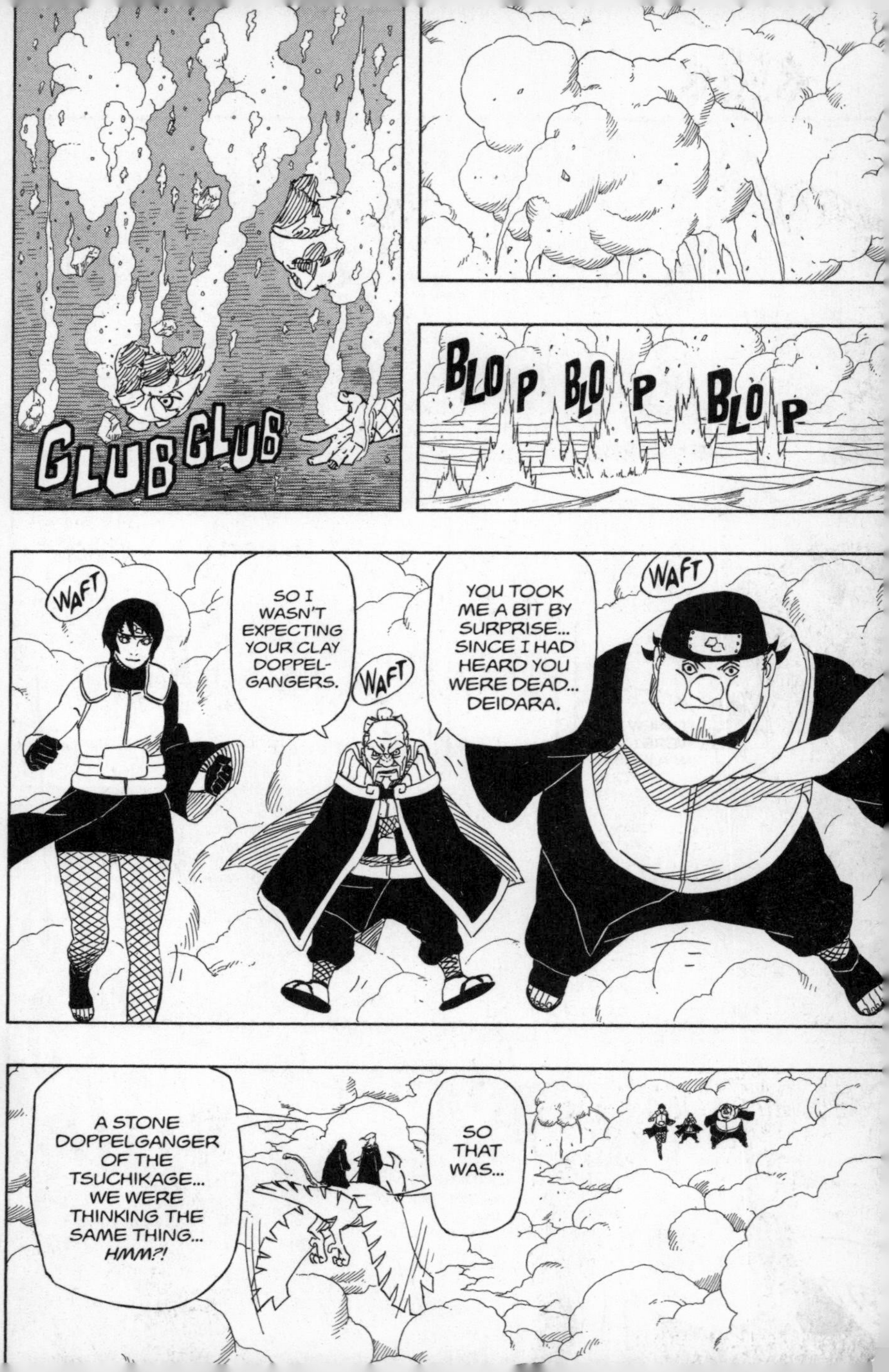
BLOP BLOP BLOP
CLUB CLUB
WAFT
YOU TOOK ME A BIT BY SURPRISE... SINCE I HAD HEARD YOU WERE DEAD... DEIDARA.
SO I WASN'T EXPECTING YOUR CLAY DOPPEL-GANGERS.
WAFT
WAFT
SO THAT WAS...
A STONE DOPPELGANGER OF THE TSUCHIKAGE... WE WERE THINKING THE SAME THING... *HMM?!*

READ THIS WAY

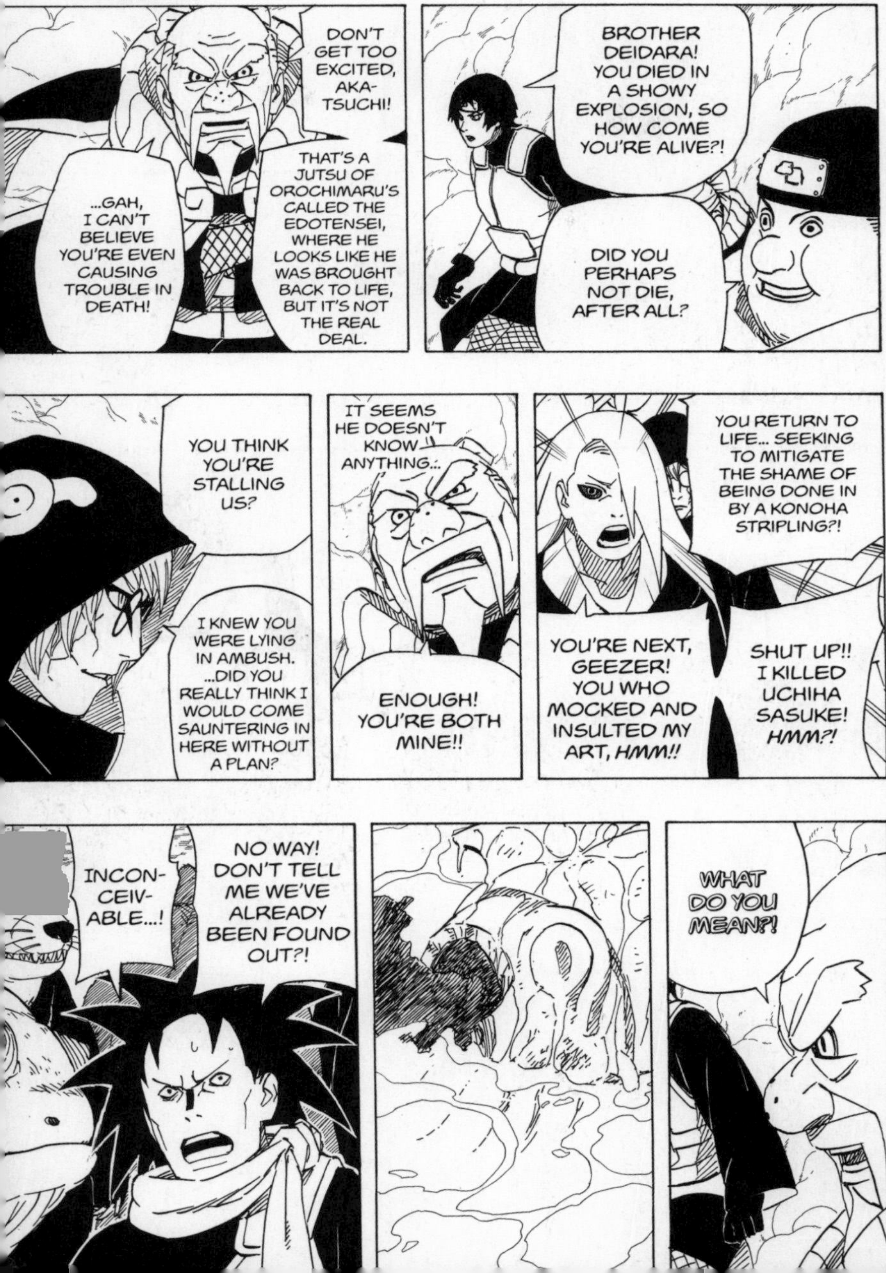

BROTHER DEIDARA! YOU DIED IN A SHOWY EXPLOSION, SO HOW COME YOU'RE ALIVE?!
DID YOU PERHAPS NOT DIE, AFTER ALL?
DON'T GET TOO EXCITED, AKA-TSUCHI!
THAT'S A JUTSU OF OROCHIMARU'S CALLED THE EDOTENSEI, WHERE HE LOOKS LIKE HE WAS BROUGHT BACK TO LIFE, BUT IT'S NOT THE REAL DEAL.
...GAH, I CAN'T BELIEVE YOU'RE EVEN CAUSING TROUBLE IN DEATH!
YOU RETURN TO LIFE... SEEKING TO MITIGATE THE SHAME OF BEING DONE IN BY A KONOHA STRIPLING?!
SHUT UP!! I KILLED UCHIHA SASUKE! HMM?!
YOU'RE NEXT, GEEZER! YOU WHO MOCKED AND INSULTED MY ART, HMM!!
IT SEEMS HE DOESN'T KNOW ANYTHING...
ENOUGH! YOU'RE BOTH MINE!!
YOU THINK YOU'RE STALLING US?
I KNEW YOU WERE LYING IN AMBUSH. ...DID YOU REALLY THINK I WOULD COME SAUNTERING IN HERE WITHOUT A PLAN?
WHAT DO YOU MEAN?!
NO WAY! DON'T TELL ME WE'VE ALREADY BEEN FOUND OUT?!
INCON-CEIV-ABLE...!

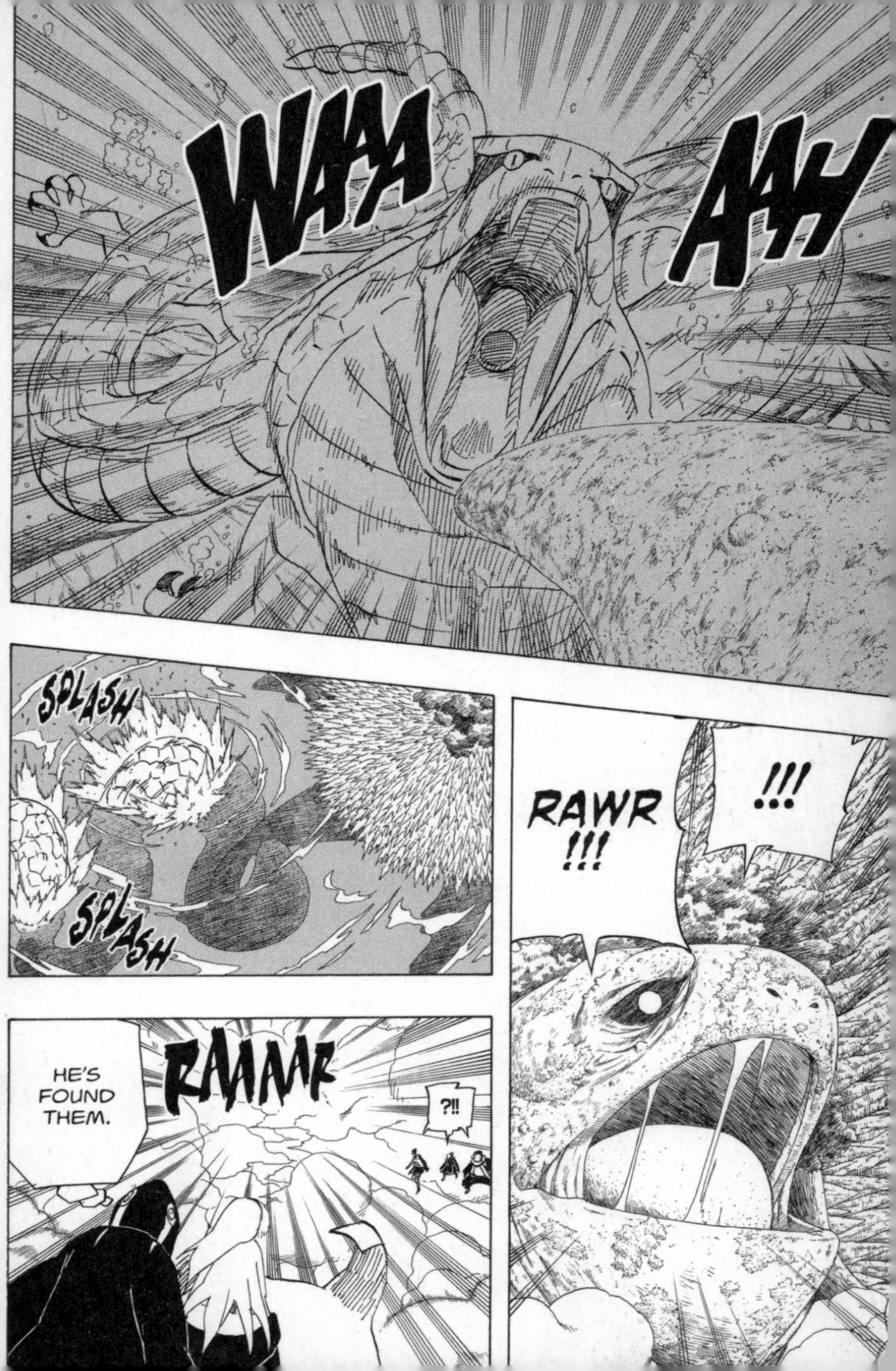
WAAA
AAH
!!!
RAWR
!!!
SPLASH
SPLASH
RAAAAR
?!!
HE'S
FOUND
THEM.

READ THIS WAY

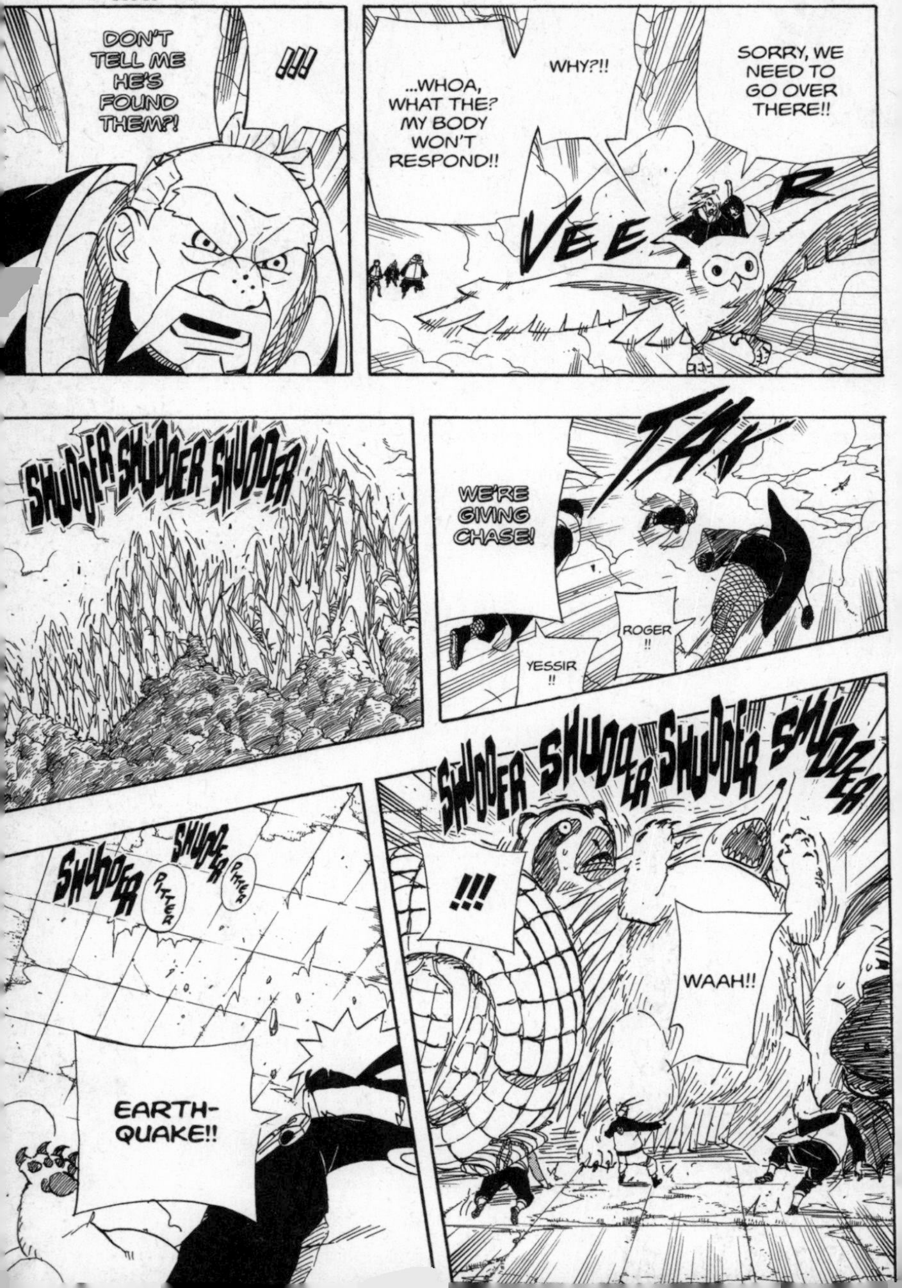
SORRY, WE NEED TO GO OVER THERE!!
WHY?!!
...WHOA, WHAT THE? MY BODY WON'T RESPOND!!
VEEER
!!!
DON'T TELL ME HE'S FOUND THEM?!
TAK
WE'RE GIVING CHASE!
ROGER!!
YESSIR!!
SHUDDER SHUDDER SHUDDER
SHUDDER SHUDDER SHUDDER SHUDDER
!!!
WAAH!!
SHUDDER
PITTER
SHUDDER
PITTER
EARTHQUAKE!!

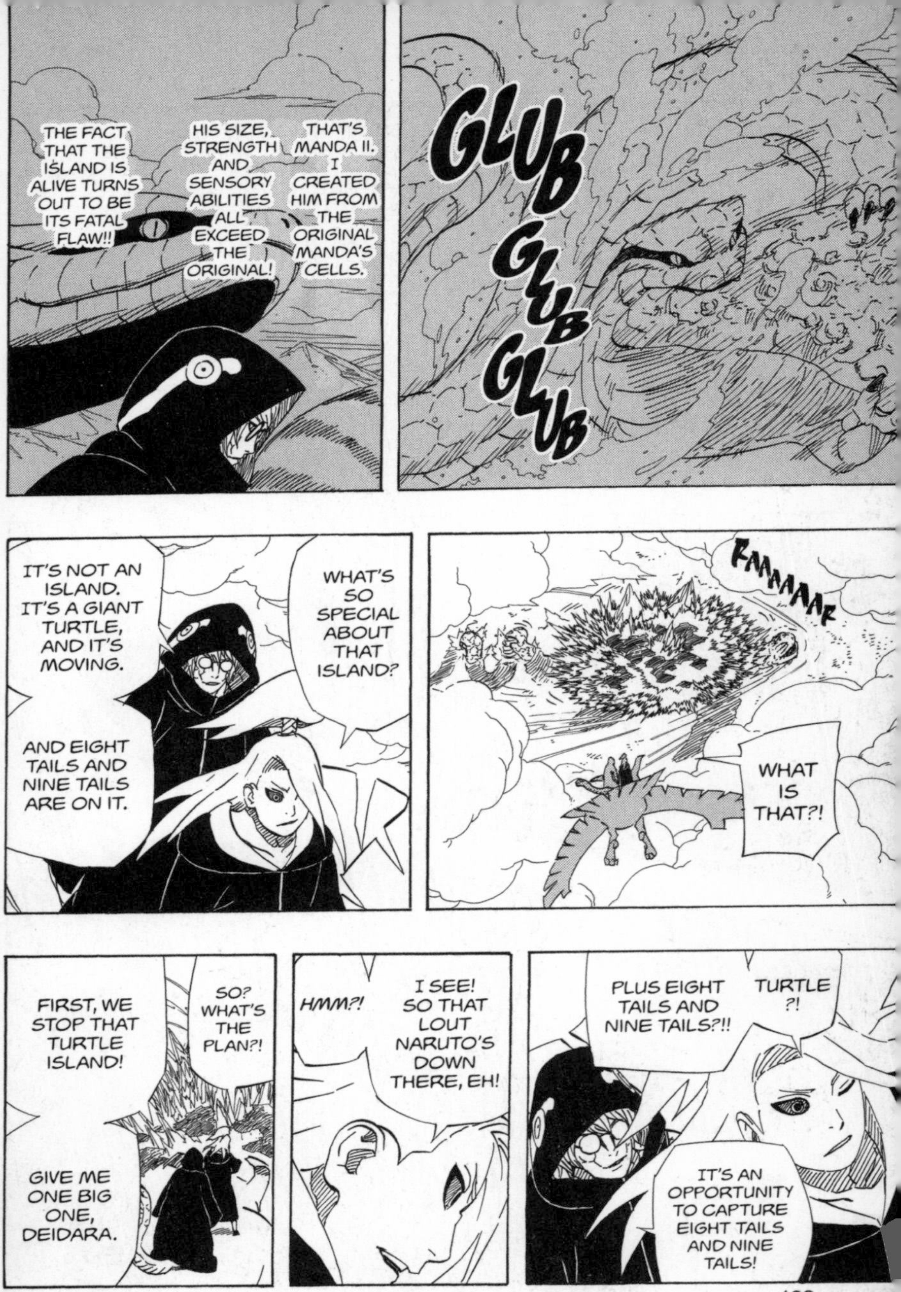
GLUB
GLUB
GLUB
THAT'S MANDA II. I CREATED HIM FROM THE ORIGINAL MANDA'S CELLS.
HIS SIZE, STRENGTH AND SENSORY ABILITIES ALL EXCEED THE ORIGINAL!
THE FACT THAT THE ISLAND IS ALIVE TURNS OUT TO BE ITS FATAL FLAW!!
RAAAAAAR
WHAT IS THAT?!
WHAT'S SO SPECIAL ABOUT THAT ISLAND?
IT'S NOT AN ISLAND. IT'S A GIANT TURTLE, AND IT'S MOVING.
AND EIGHT TAILS AND NINE TAILS ARE ON IT.
TURTLE ?!
PLUS EIGHT TAILS AND NINE TAILS?!!
IT'S AN OPPORTUNITY TO CAPTURE EIGHT TAILS AND NINE TAILS!
I SEE! SO THAT LOUT NARUTO'S DOWN THERE, EH!
HMM?!
SO? WHAT'S THE PLAN?!
FIRST, WE STOP THAT TURTLE ISLAND!
GIVE ME ONE BIG ONE, DEIDARA.

READ THIS WAY

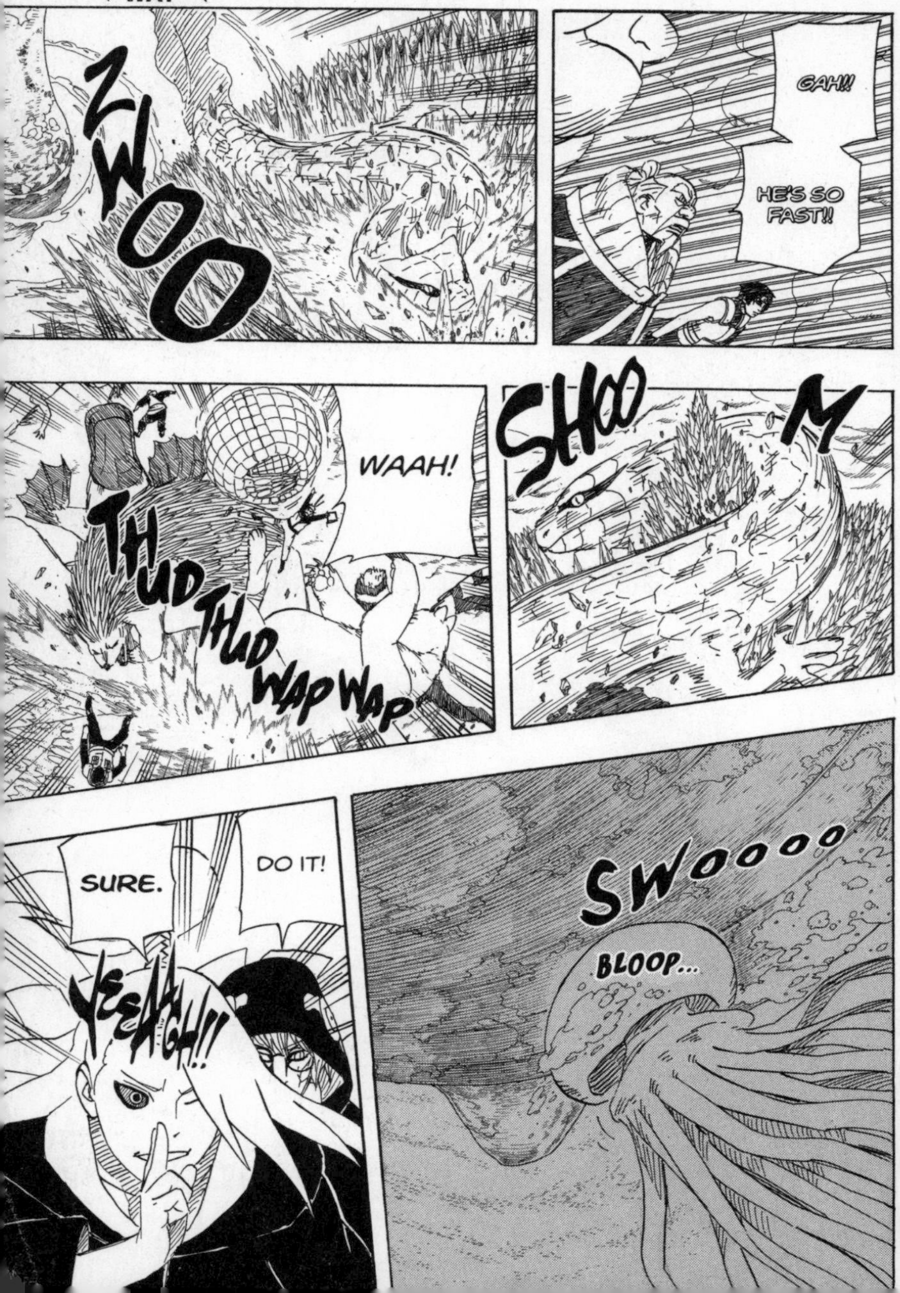
GAH!!
HE'S SO FAST!!
ZWOOO
SHOOM
WAAH!
THUD THUD WAP WAP
SWOOOO
BLOOP...
DO IT!
SURE.
YEEAAGH!!

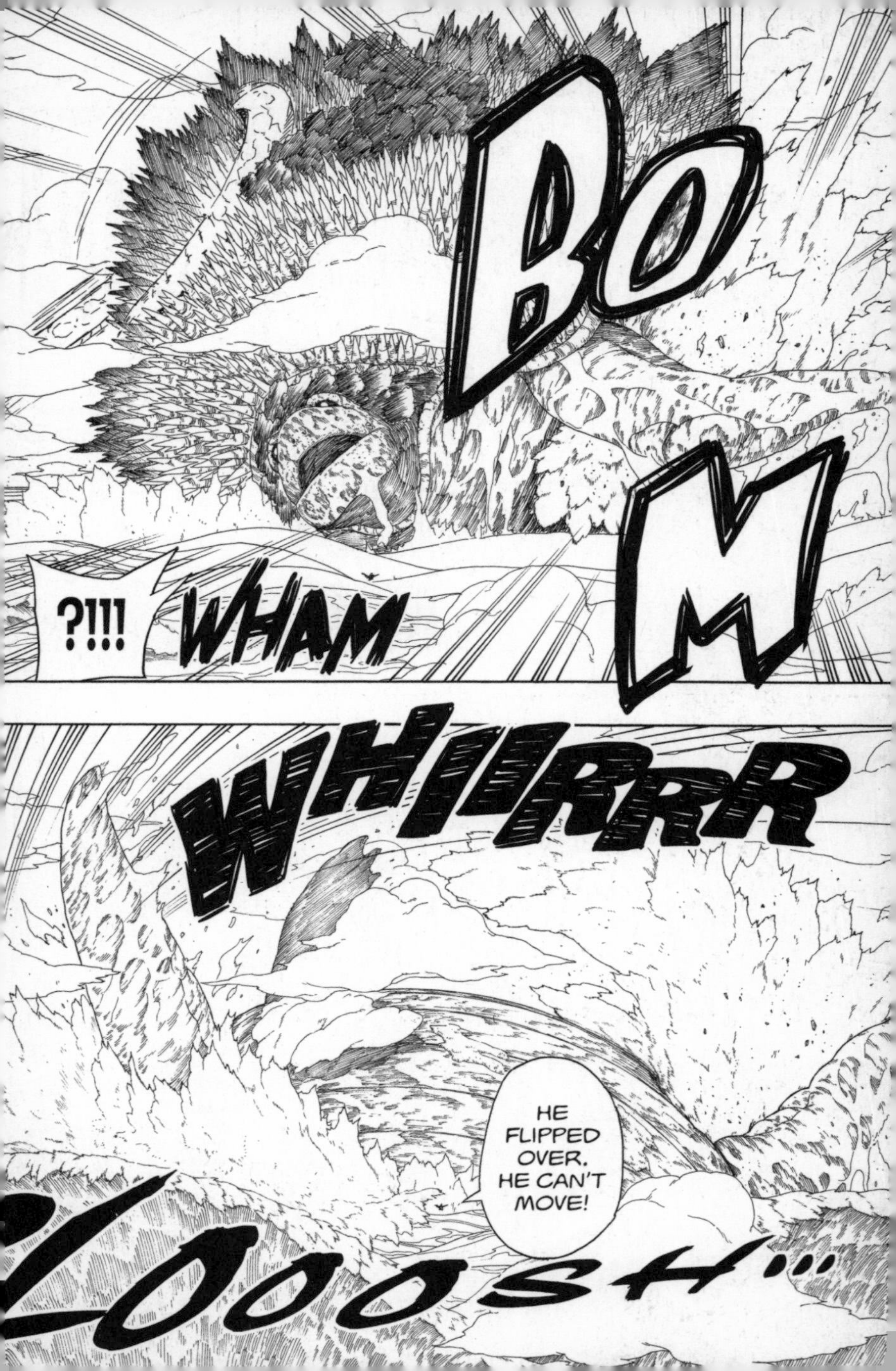
BOOM
WHAM
?!!!
WHIRRR
HE FLIPPED OVER. HE CAN'T MOVE!
OOOSH…

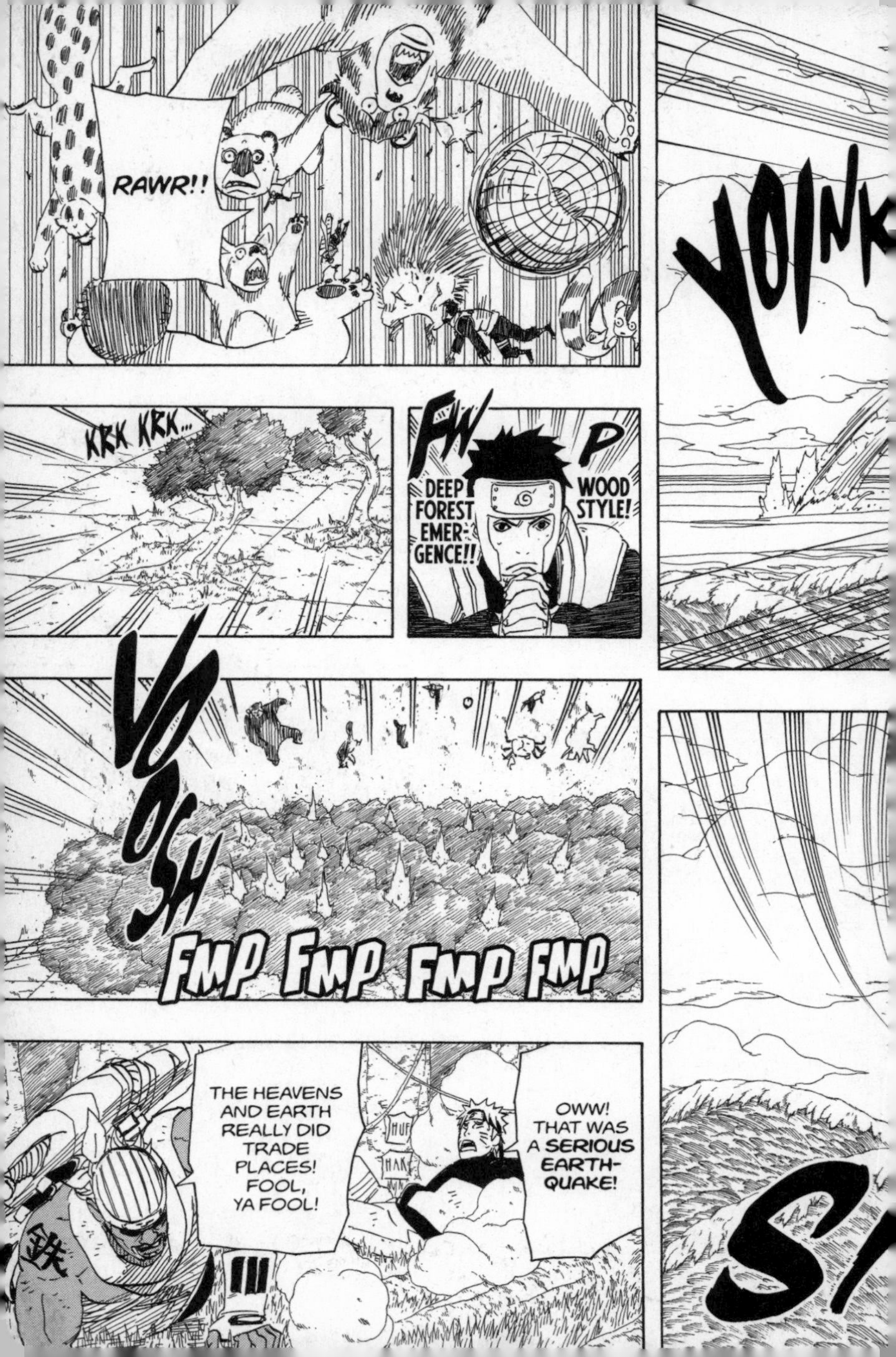
YOINK
RAWR!!
FWP
WOOD STYLE!
DEEP FOREST EMERGENCE!!
KRK KRK...
VOOSH
FMP FMP FMP FMP
OWW! THAT WAS A SERIOUS EARTHQUAKE!
HUF
HAK
THE HEAVENS AND EARTH REALLY DID TRADE PLACES! FOOL, YA FOOL!

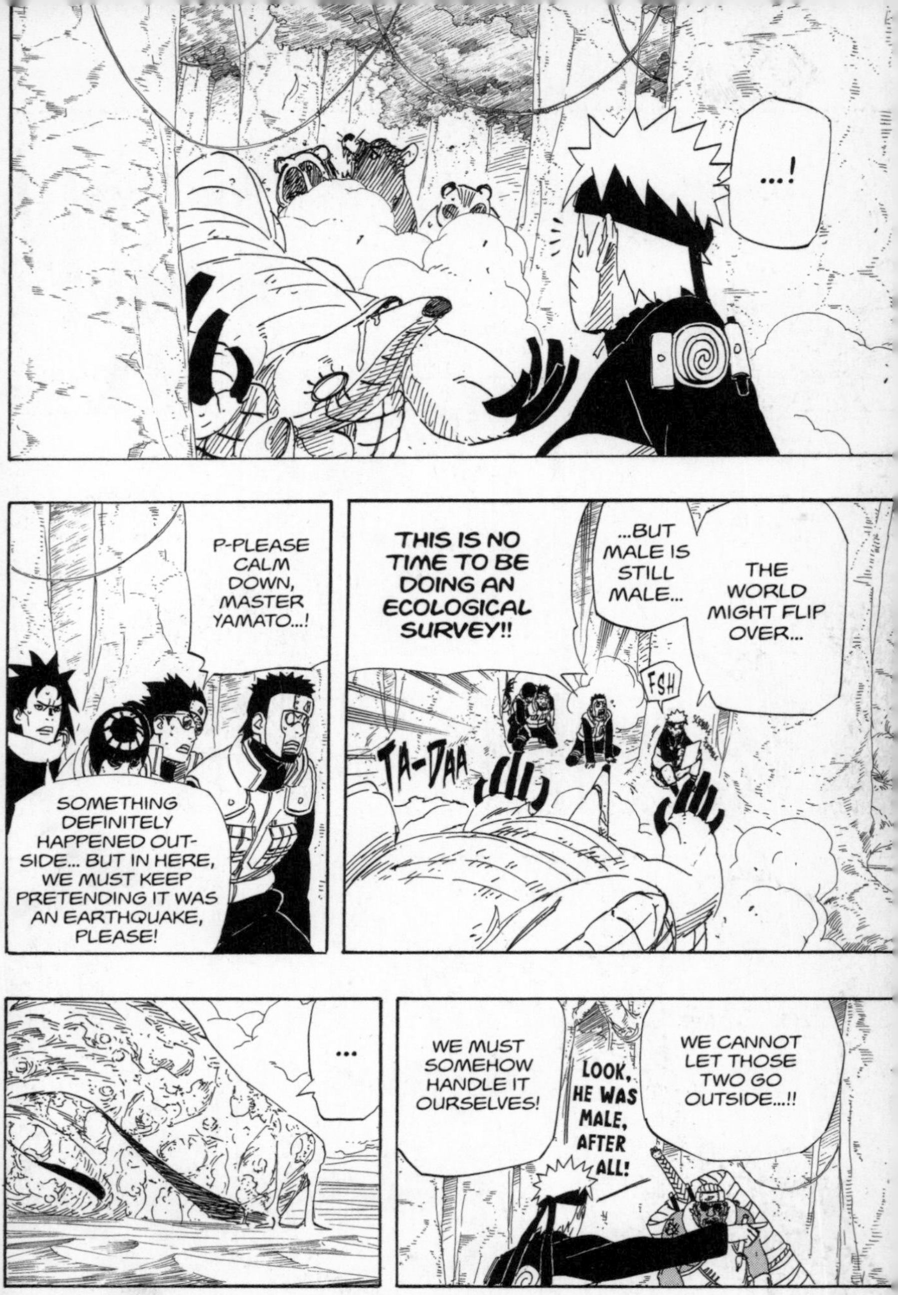

...!
THE WORLD MIGHT FLIP OVER...
...BUT MALE IS STILL MALE...
THIS IS NO TIME TO BE DOING AN ECOLOGICAL SURVEY!!
FSH
TA-DAA
P-PLEASE CALM DOWN, MASTER YAMATO...!
SOMETHING DEFINITELY HAPPENED OUT-SIDE... BUT IN HERE, WE MUST KEEP PRETENDING IT WAS AN EARTHQUAKE, PLEASE!
WE CANNOT LET THOSE TWO GO OUTSIDE...!!
WE MUST SOMEHOW HANDLE IT OURSELVES!
LOOK, HE WAS MALE, AFTER ALL!
...

READ THIS WAY

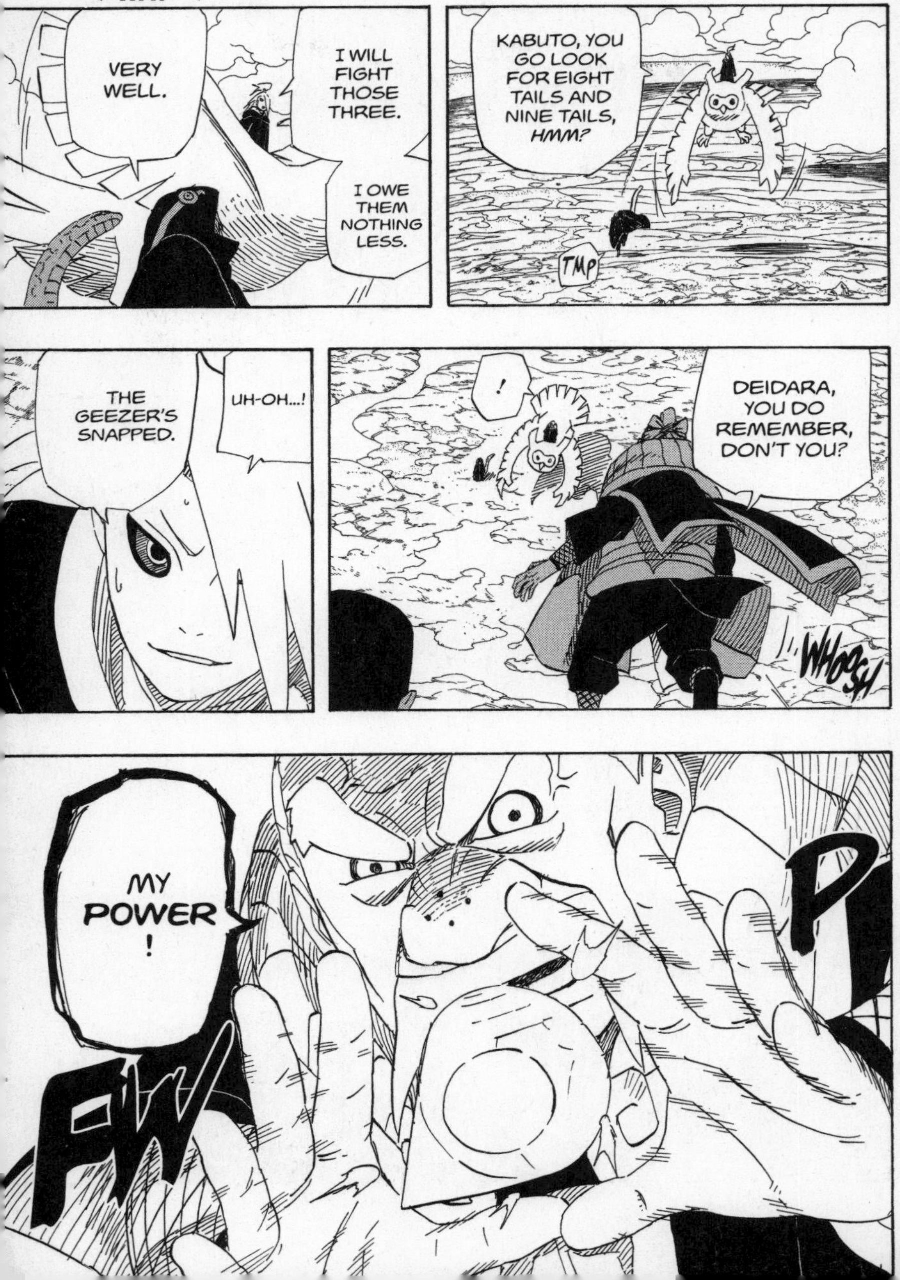
KABUTO, YOU GO LOOK FOR EIGHT TAILS AND NINE TAILS, *HMM?*
TMP
I WILL FIGHT THOSE THREE.
I OWE THEM NOTHING LESS.
VERY WELL.
DEIDARA, YOU DO REMEMBER, DON'T YOU?
!
WHOOSH
UH-OH...!
THE GEEZER'S SNAPPED.
P
MY **POWER** !
FW

NARUTO

Number 514: Kabuto's Plan!!

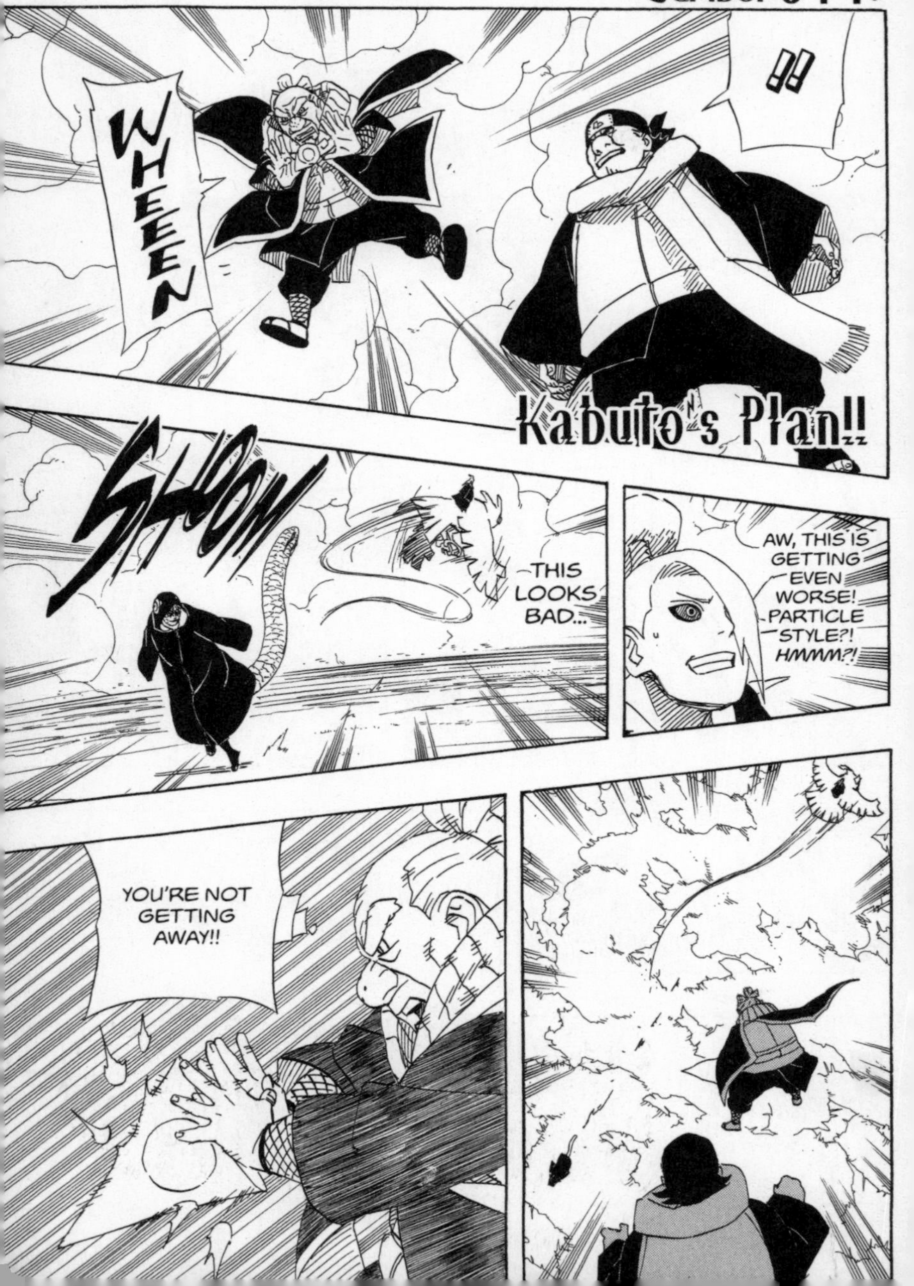
!!
WHEEEEN
AW, THIS IS GETTING EVEN WORSE! PARTICLE STYLE?! HMMM?!
SHOOM
THIS LOOKS BAD...
YOU'RE NOT GETTING AWAY!!

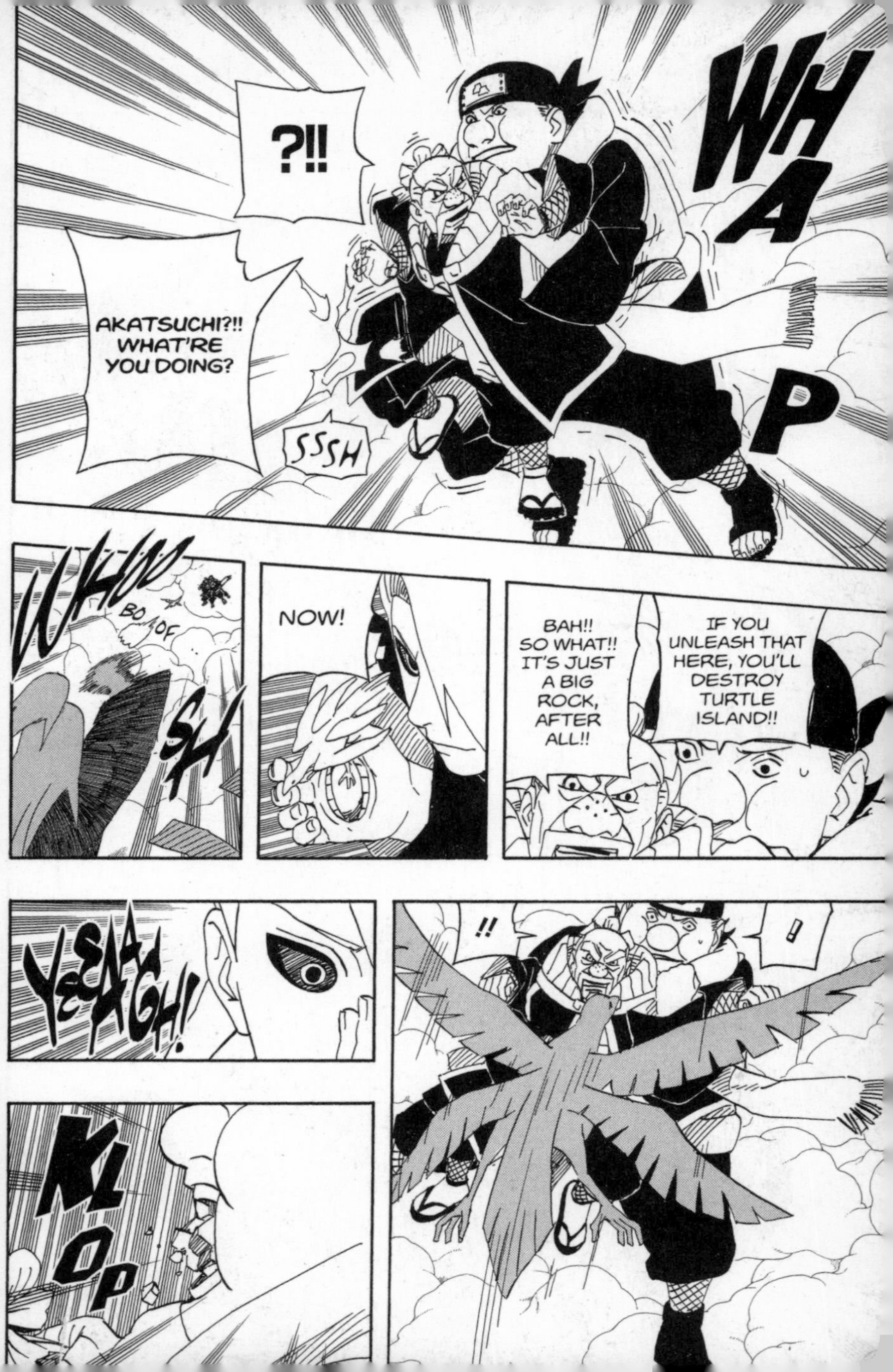
?!!
AKATSUCHI?!! WHAT'RE YOU DOING?
WHAP
SSSH
IF YOU UNLEASH THAT HERE, YOU'LL DESTROY TURTLE ISLAND!!
BAH!! SO WHAT!! IT'S JUST A BIG ROCK, AFTER ALL!!
NOW!
BOOF
SH
!
!!
YESAAAGH!
KLOP

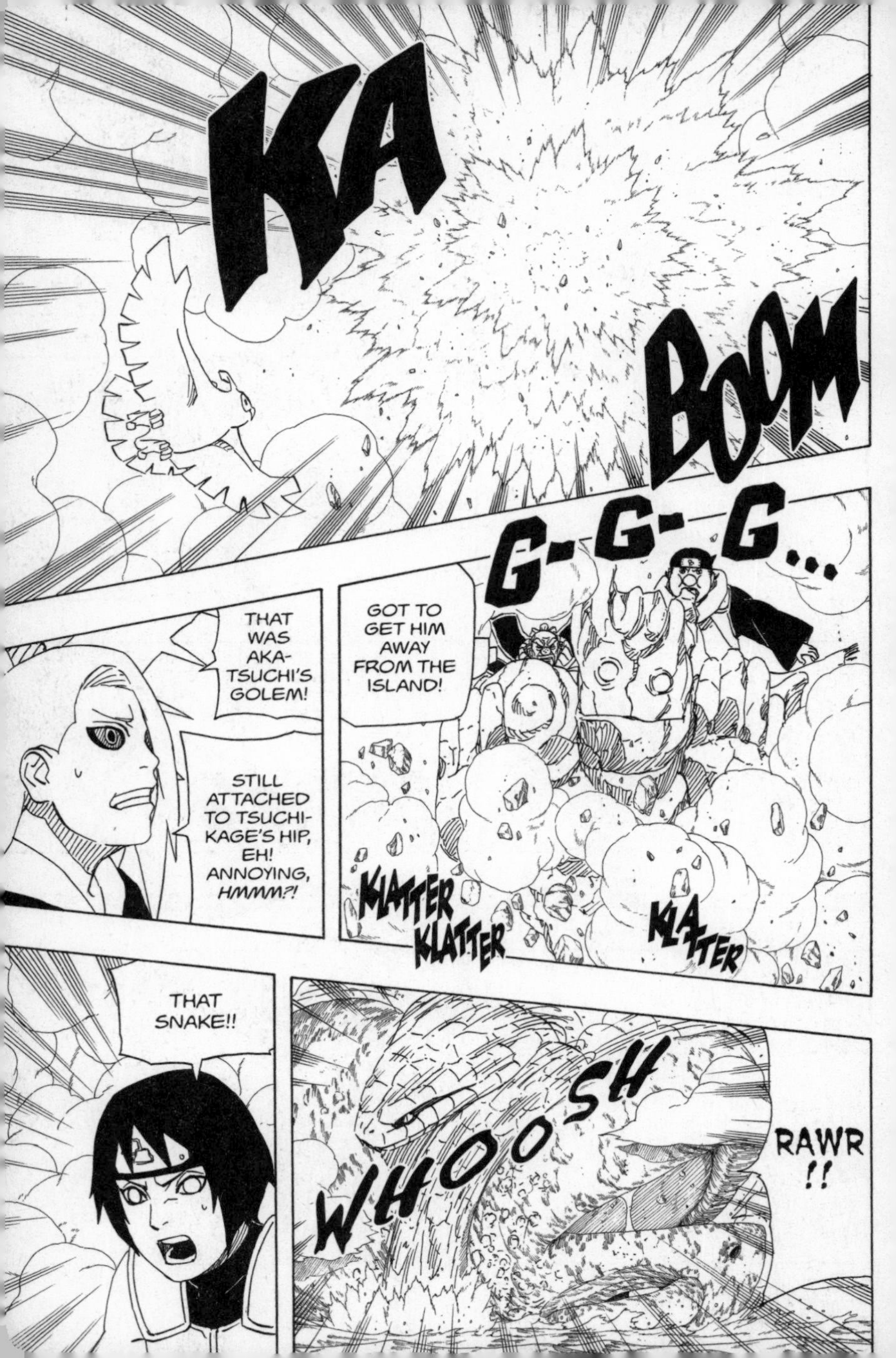
KA
BOOM
G-G-G...
GOT TO GET HIM AWAY FROM THE ISLAND!
KLATTER
KLATTER KLATTER
THAT WAS AKA-TSUCHI'S GOLEM!
STILL ATTACHED TO TSUCHI-KAGE'S HIP, EH! ANNOYING, *HMMM?!*
RAWR !!
WHOOOSH
THAT SNAKE!!

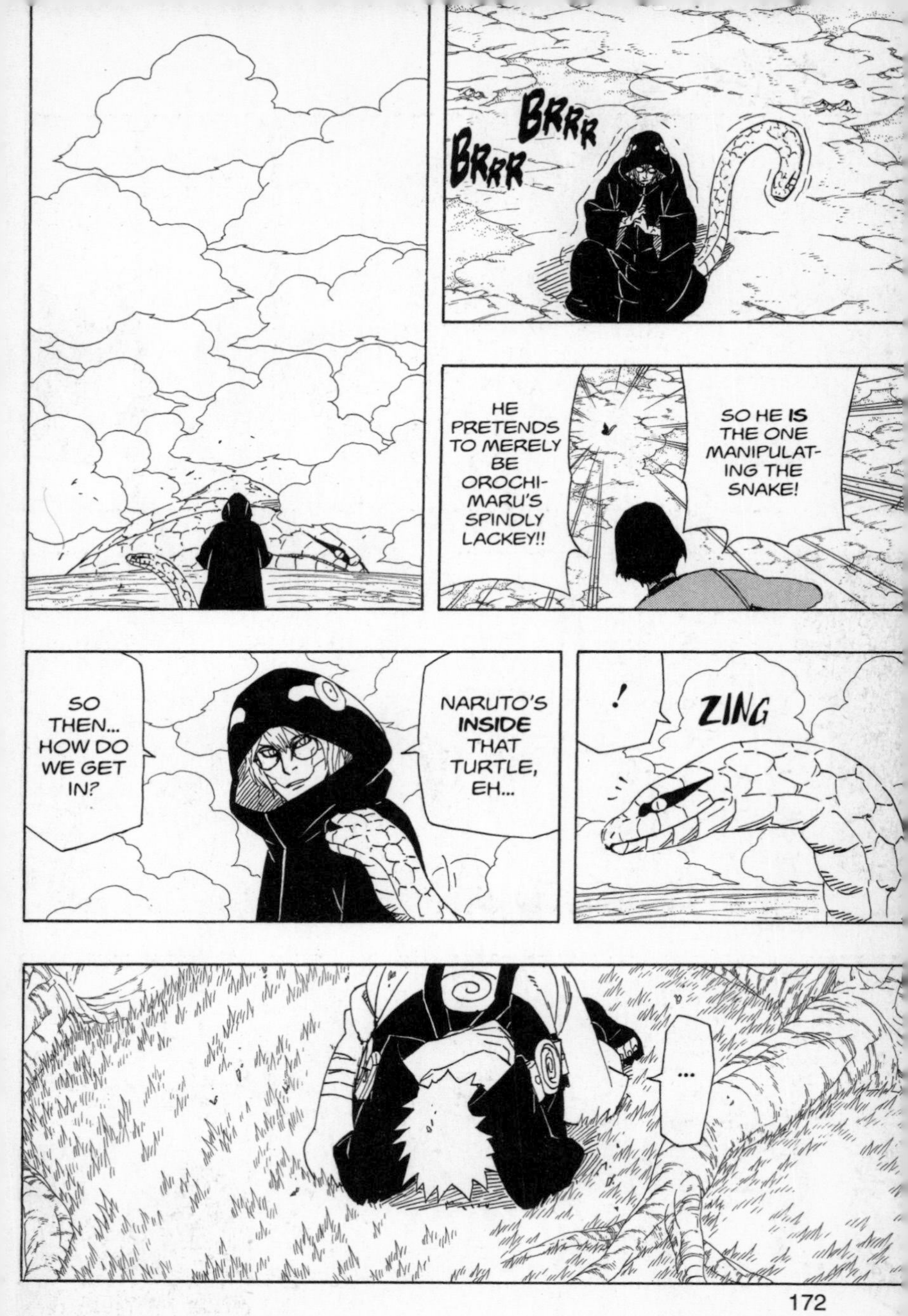
BRRR
BRRR
SO HE IS THE ONE MANIPULATING THE SNAKE!
HE PRETENDS TO MERELY BE OROCHIMARU'S SPINDLY LACKEY!!
ZING
!
NARUTO'S INSIDE THAT TURTLE, EH...
SO THEN... HOW DO WE GET IN?
...

READ THIS WAY

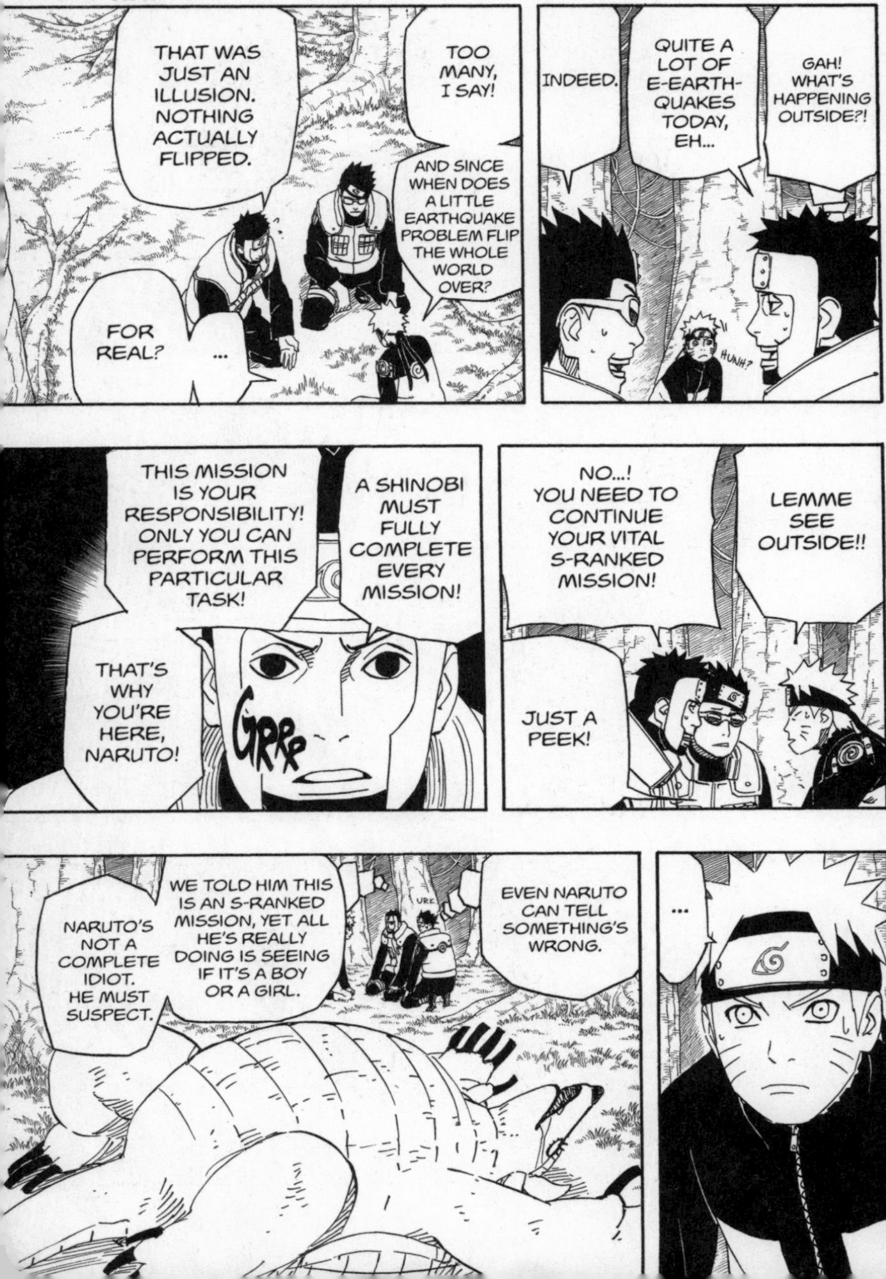
GAH! WHAT'S HAPPENING OUTSIDE?!
QUITE A LOT OF E-EARTH-QUAKES TODAY, EH...
INDEED.
HUNH?
TOO MANY, I SAY!
THAT WAS JUST AN ILLUSION. NOTHING ACTUALLY FLIPPED.
AND SINCE WHEN DOES A LITTLE EARTHQUAKE PROBLEM FLIP THE WHOLE WORLD OVER?
...
FOR REAL?
LEMME SEE OUTSIDE!!
NO...! YOU NEED TO CONTINUE YOUR VITAL S-RANKED MISSION!
JUST A PEEK!
A SHINOBI MUST FULLY COMPLETE EVERY MISSION!
THIS MISSION IS YOUR RESPONSIBILITY! ONLY YOU CAN PERFORM THIS PARTICULAR TASK!
GRRR
THAT'S WHY YOU'RE HERE, NARUTO!
...
EVEN NARUTO CAN TELL SOMETHING'S WRONG.
URK
WE TOLD HIM THIS IS AN S-RANKED MISSION, YET ALL HE'S REALLY DOING IS SEEING IF IT'S A BOY OR A GIRL.
NARUTO'S NOT A COMPLETE IDIOT. HE MUST SUSPECT.

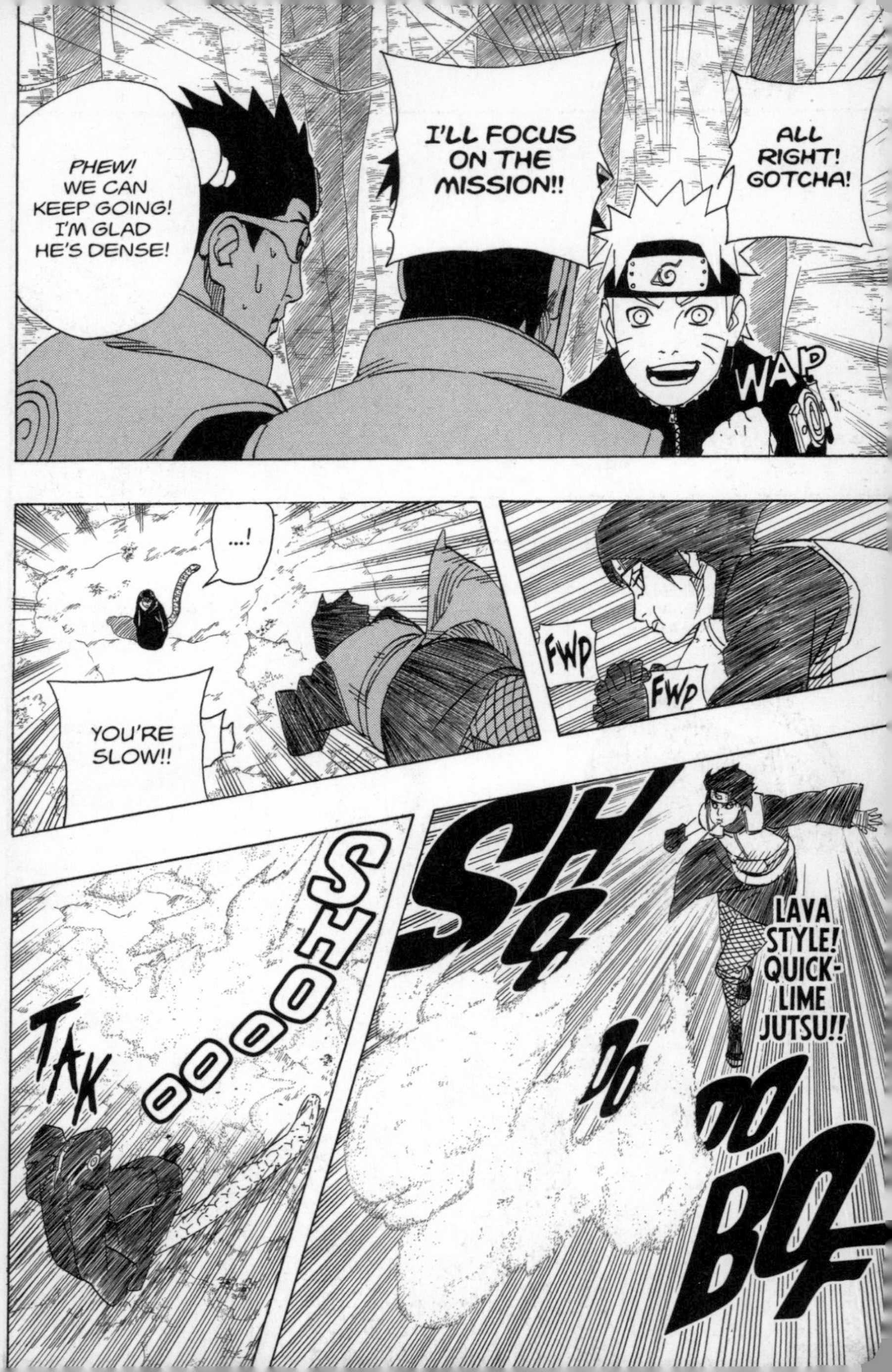
ALL RIGHT! GOTCHA!
WAP
I'LL FOCUS ON THE MISSION!!
PHEW! WE CAN KEEP GOING! I'M GLAD HE'S DENSE!
FWP
FWP
...!
YOU'RE SLOW!!
LAVA STYLE! QUICKLIME JUTSU!!
SHOOOOOO
TAK

READ THIS WAY

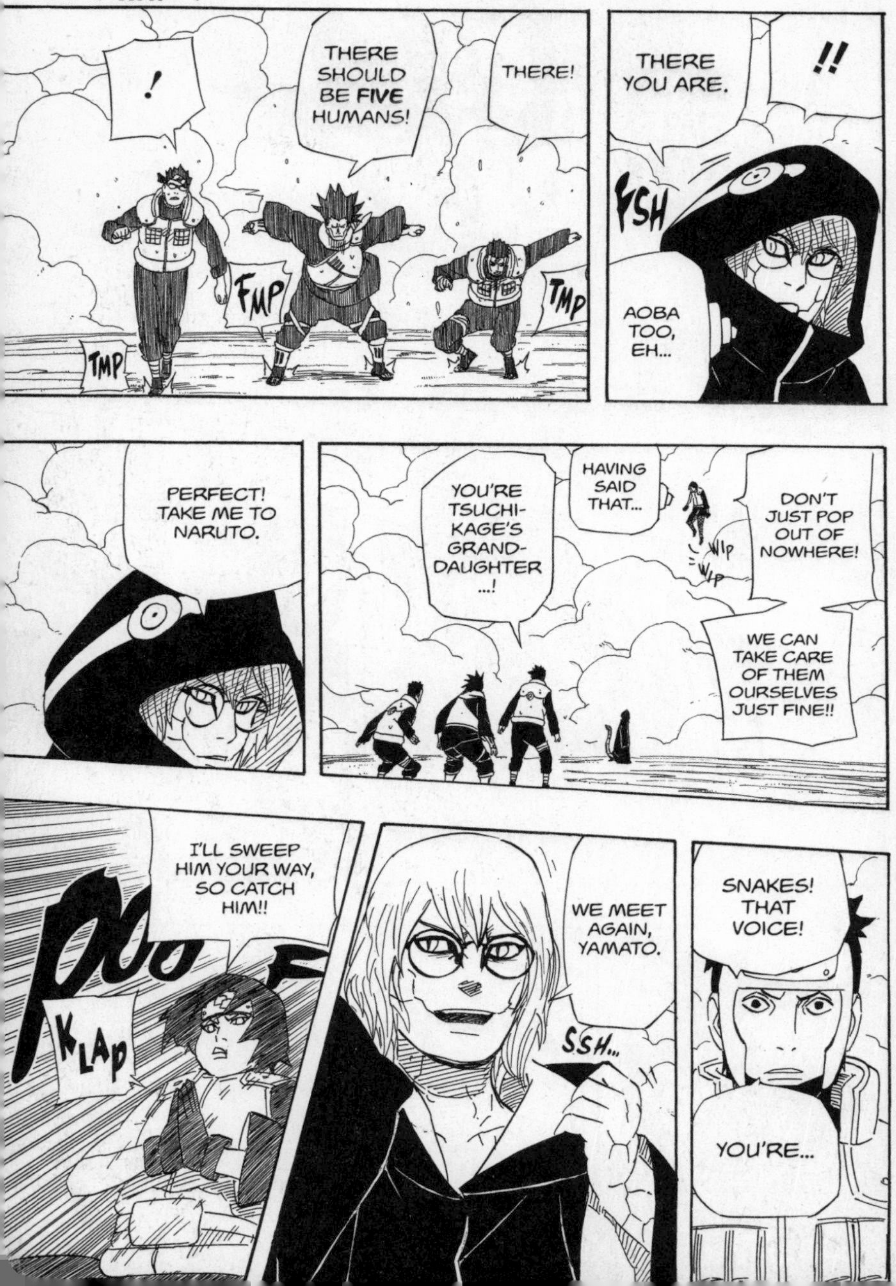
!!
THERE YOU ARE.
FSH
AOBA TOO, EH...
THERE!
THERE SHOULD BE FIVE HUMANS!
!
TMP
FMP
TMP
DON'T JUST POP OUT OF NOWHERE!
HAVING SAID THAT...
WIP
WIP
YOU'RE TSUCHI-KAGE'S GRAND-DAUGHTER...!
WE CAN TAKE CARE OF THEM OURSELVES JUST FINE!!
PERFECT! TAKE ME TO NARUTO.
SNAKES! THAT VOICE!
YOU'RE...
WE MEET AGAIN, YAMATO.
SSH...
I'LL SWEEP HIM YOUR WAY, SO CATCH HIM!!
POOF
KLAP

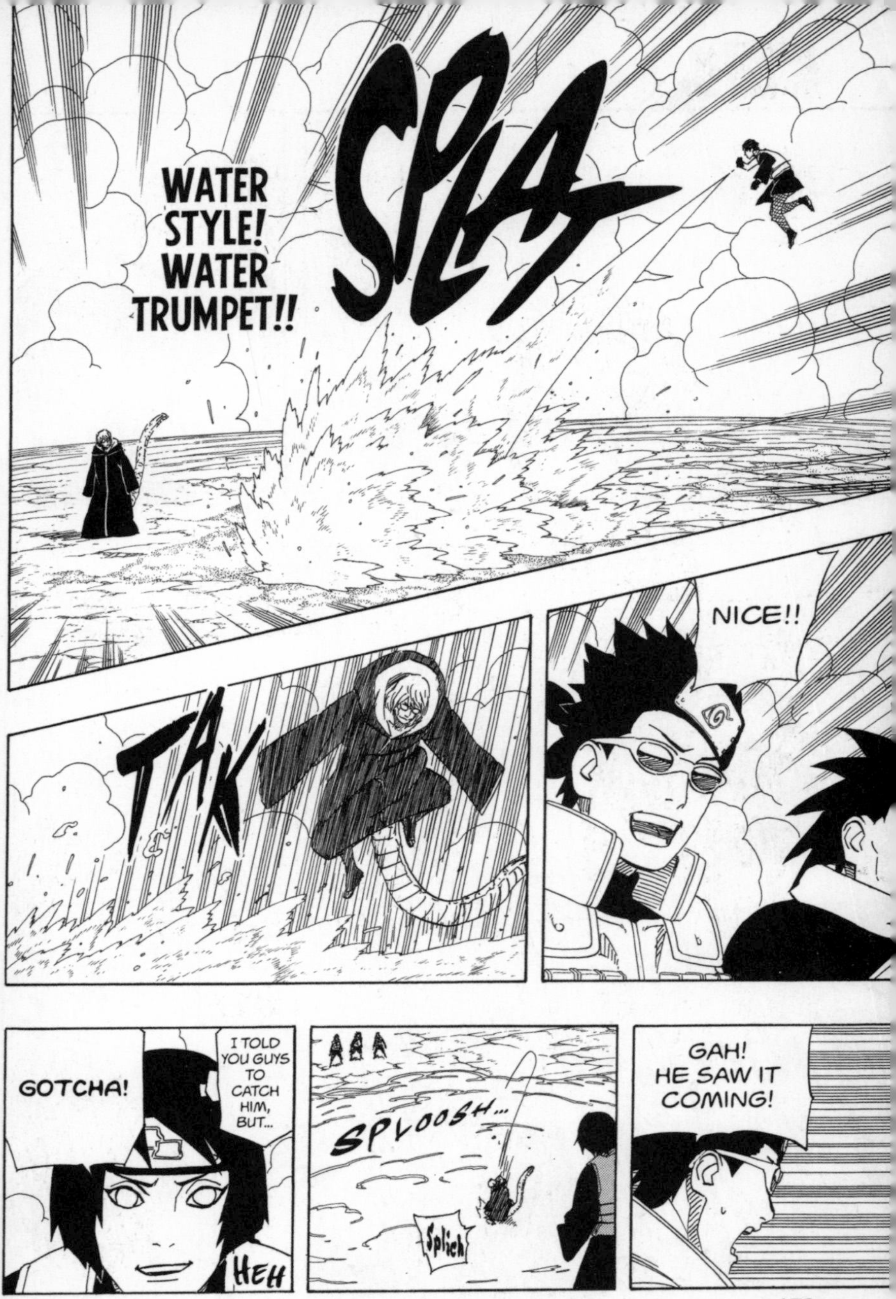
WATER STYLE! WATER TRUMPET!!
SPLA
NICE!!
TAK
GAH! HE SAW IT COMING!
SPLOOSH...
Splich
I TOLD YOU GUYS TO CATCH HIM, BUT...
GOTCHA!
HEH

READ THIS WAY

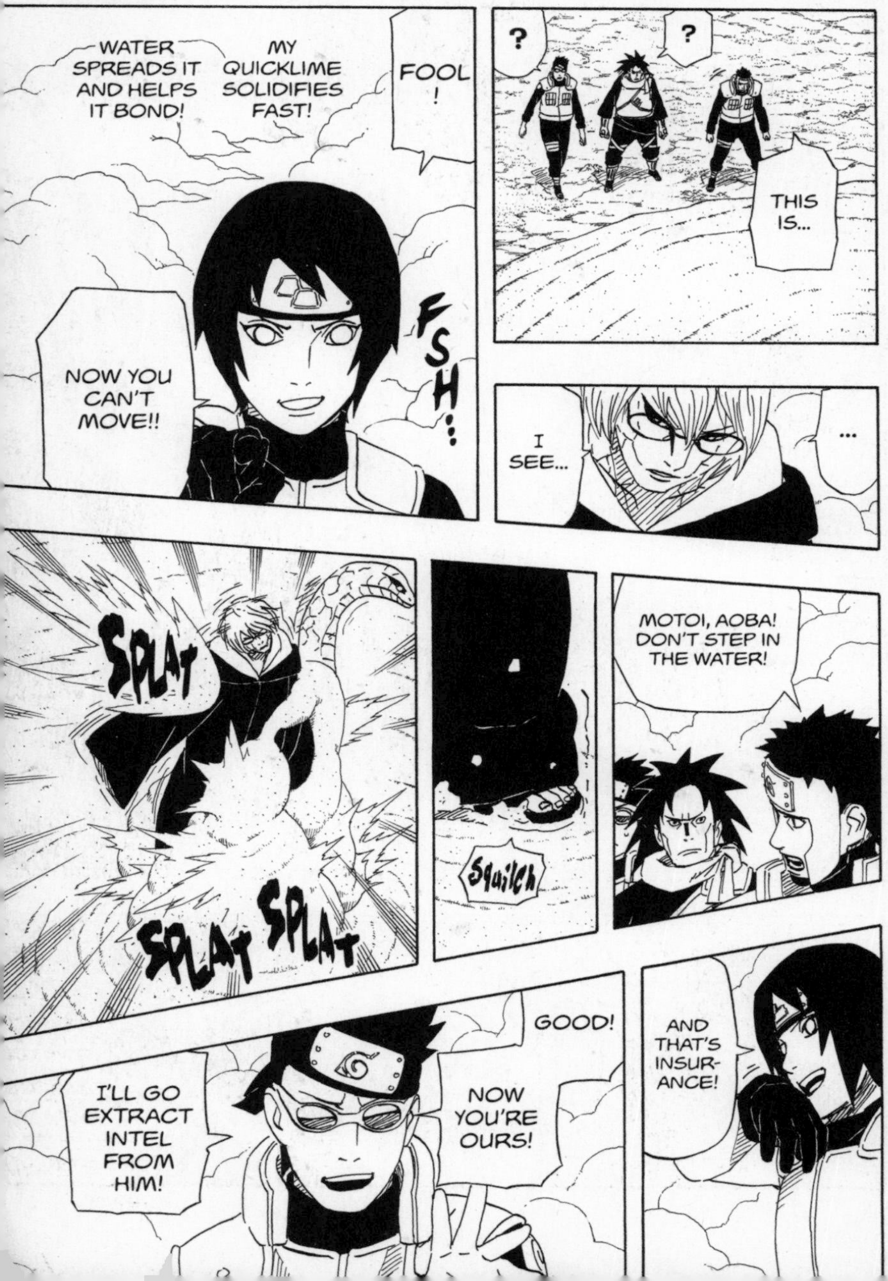

?
?
THIS IS...
...
I SEE...
FOOL!
MY QUICKLIME SOLIDIFIES FAST!
WATER SPREADS IT AND HELPS IT BOND!
FSH!!
NOW YOU CAN'T MOVE!!
MOTOI, AOBA! DON'T STEP IN THE WATER!
Squilch
SPLAT
SPLAT SPLAT
AND THAT'S INSUR-ANCE!
GOOD!
NOW YOU'RE OURS!
I'LL GO EXTRACT INTEL FROM HIM!

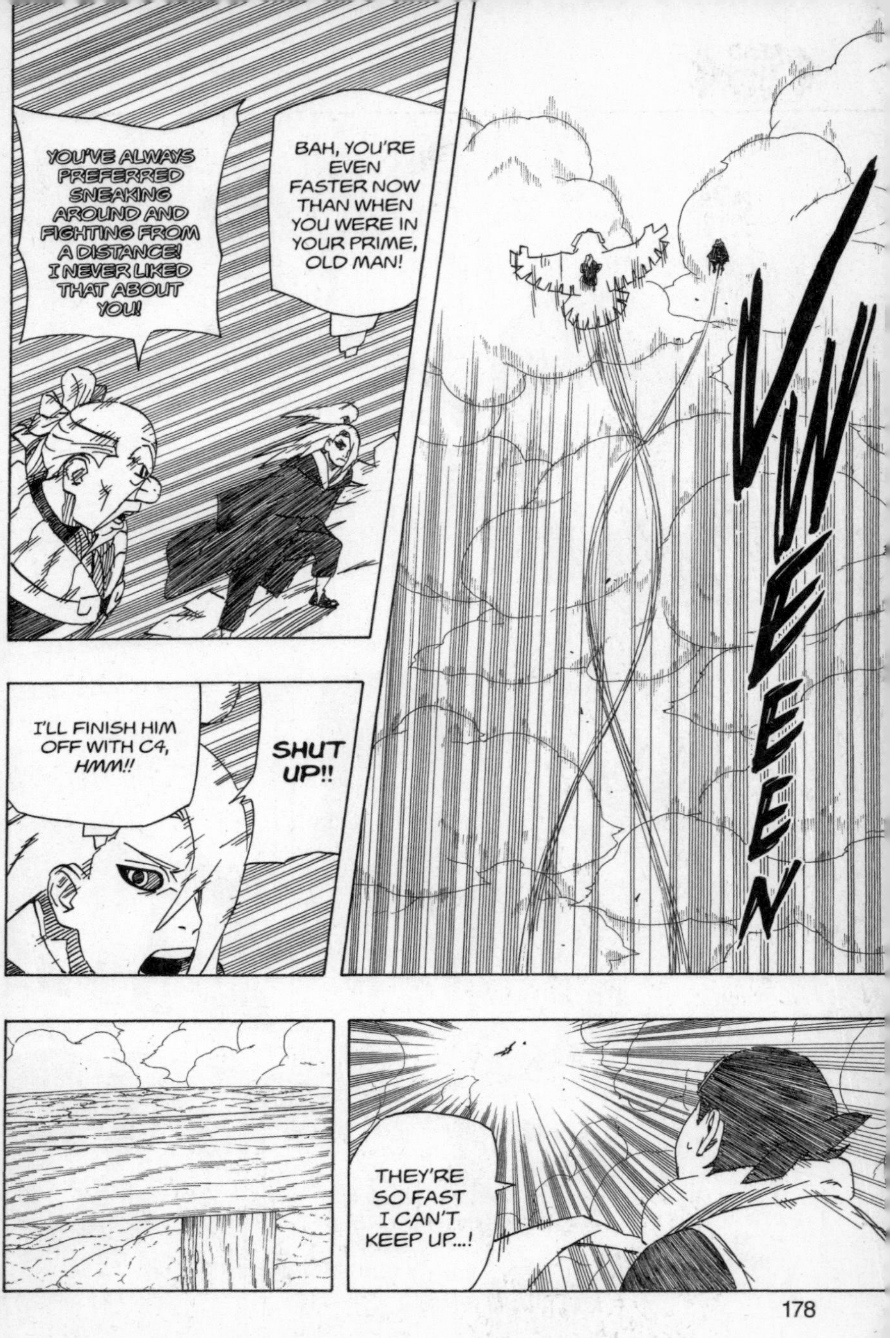
VWEEEEN
BAH, YOU'RE EVEN FASTER NOW THAN WHEN YOU WERE IN YOUR PRIME, OLD MAN!
YOU'VE ALWAYS PREFERRED SNEAKING AROUND AND FIGHTING FROM A DISTANCE! I NEVER LIKED THAT ABOUT YOU!
SHUT UP!!
I'LL FINISH HIM OFF WITH C4, HMM!!
THEY'RE SO FAST I CAN'T KEEP UP...!

READ THIS WAY

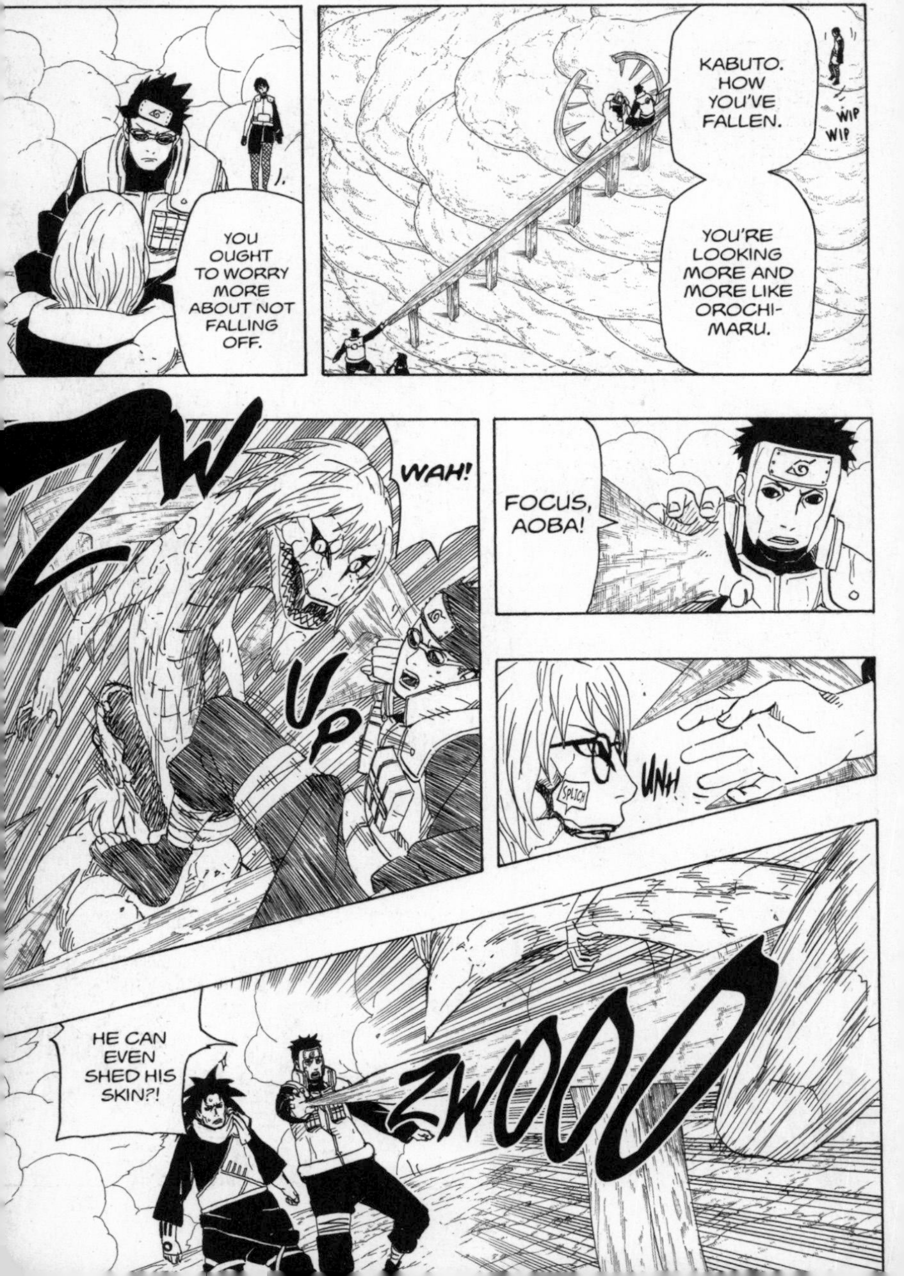
WIP WIP
KABUTO. HOW YOU'VE FALLEN.
YOU'RE LOOKING MORE AND MORE LIKE OROCHI-MARU.
YOU OUGHT TO WORRY MORE ABOUT NOT FALLING OFF.
FOCUS, AOBA!
UNH!
SPLICH
WAH!
ZW
UP
ZWOOO
HE CAN EVEN SHED HIS SKIN?!

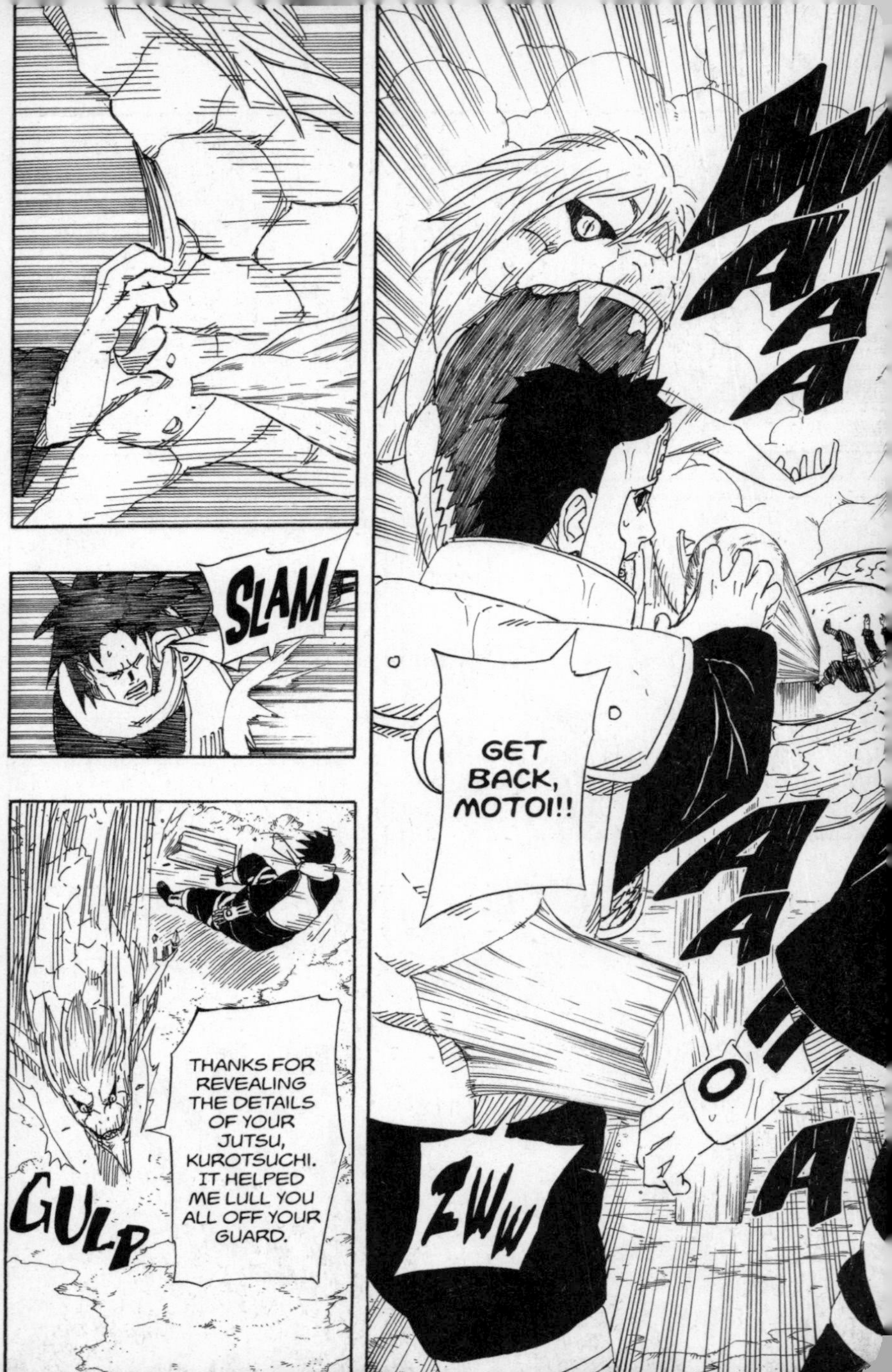
WAAAA
GET BACK, MOTOI!!
ZWW
SLAM
THANKS FOR REVEALING THE DETAILS OF YOUR JUTSU, KUROTSUCHI. IT HELPED ME LULL YOU ALL OFF YOUR GUARD.
GULP

READ THIS WAY

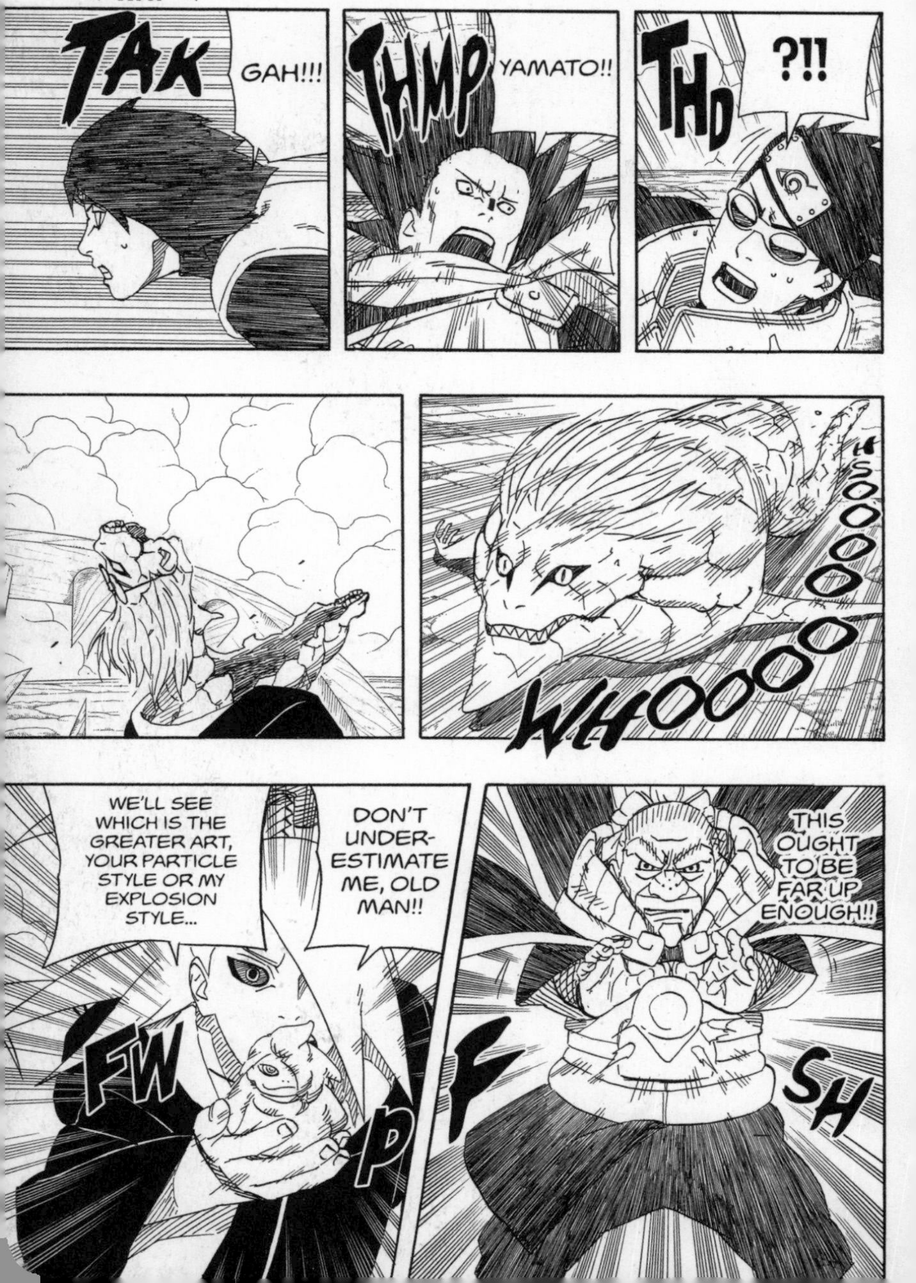
THD
?!!
THMP
YAMATO!!
TAK
GAH!!!
WHOOOOOOOOOOOSH
SH
THIS OUGHT TO BE FAR UP ENOUGH!!
DON'T UNDER-ESTIMATE ME, OLD MAN!!
WE'LL SEE WHICH IS THE GREATER ART, YOUR PARTICLE STYLE OR MY EXPLOSION STYLE...
FWP
F

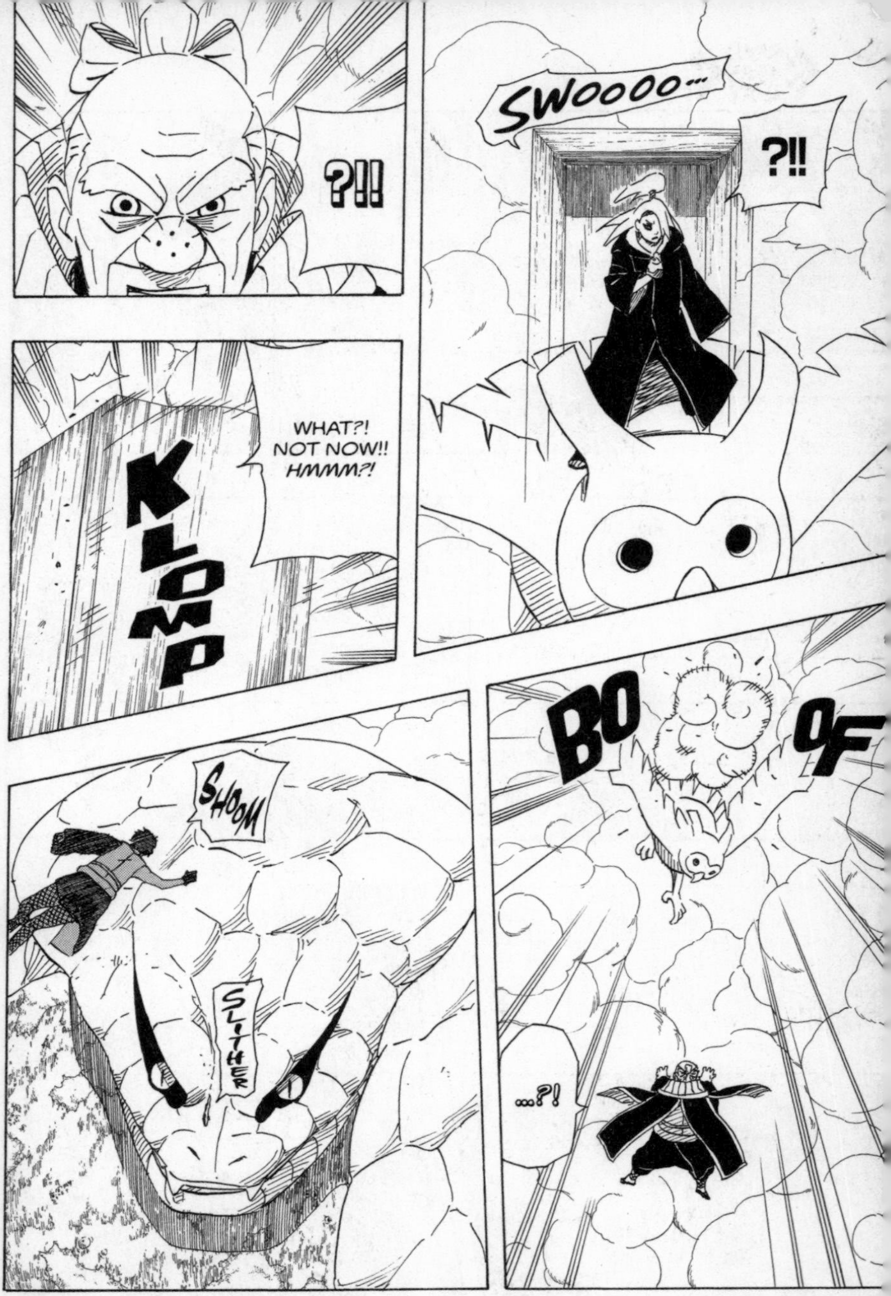
SWOOOO...
?!!
?!!
WHAT?!
NOT NOW!!
HMMM?!
KLOMP
BOOF
...?!
SHOOM
SLITHER

READ THIS WAY

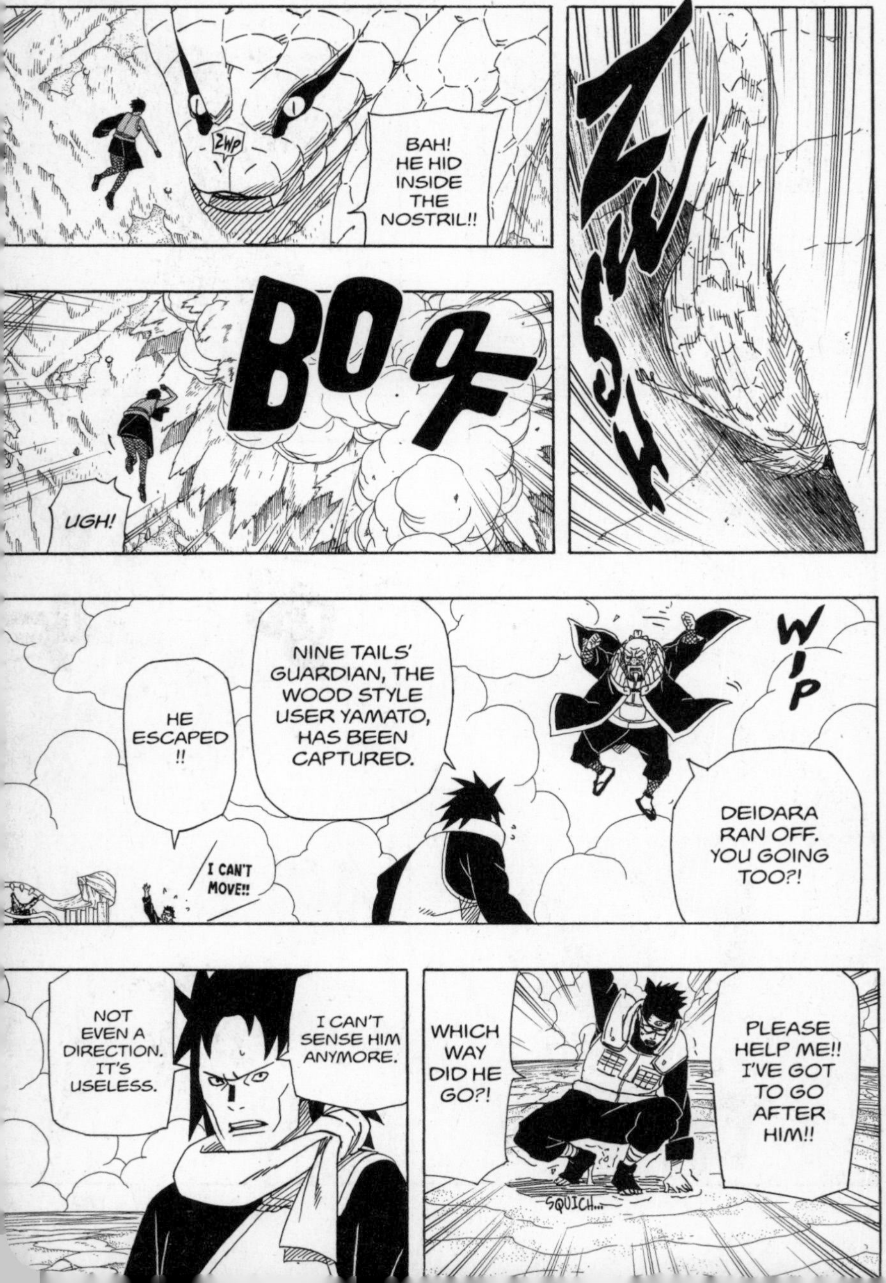

ZWSH
BAH! HE HID INSIDE THE NOSTRIL!!
ZWP
BOOF
UGH!
WIP
DEIDARA RAN OFF. YOU GOING TOO?!
NINE TAILS' GUARDIAN, THE WOOD STYLE USER YAMATO, HAS BEEN CAPTURED.
HE ESCAPED!!
I CAN'T MOVE!!
PLEASE HELP ME!! I'VE GOT TO GO AFTER HIM!!
WHICH WAY DID HE GO?!
SQUICH...
I CAN'T SENSE HIM ANYMORE.
NOT EVEN A DIRECTION. IT'S USELESS.

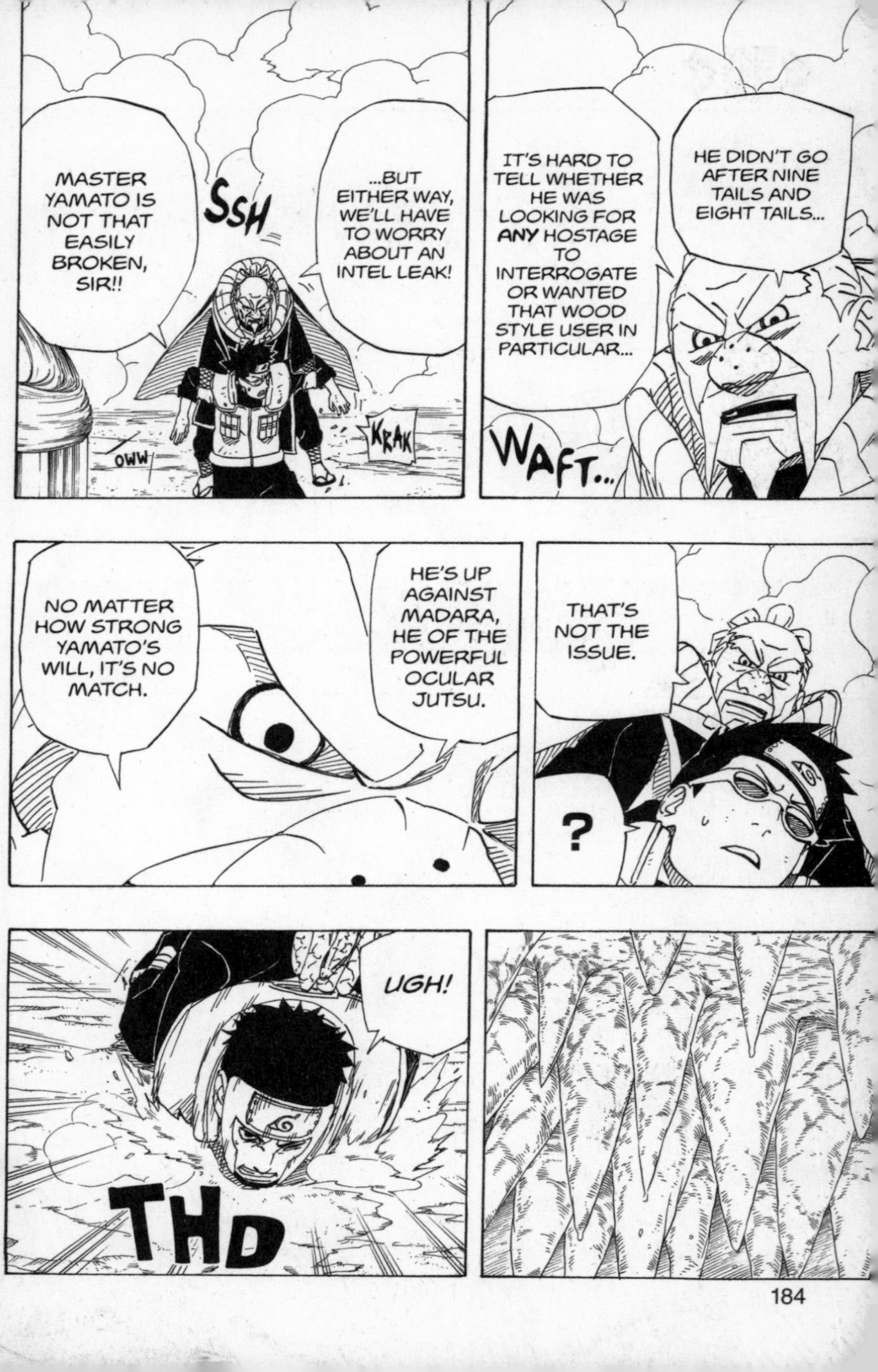
HE DIDN'T GO AFTER NINE TAILS AND EIGHT TAILS...
IT'S HARD TO TELL WHETHER HE WAS LOOKING FOR ANY HOSTAGE TO INTERROGATE OR WANTED THAT WOOD STYLE USER IN PARTICULAR...
WAFT...
...BUT EITHER WAY, WE'LL HAVE TO WORRY ABOUT AN INTEL LEAK!
SSH
MASTER YAMATO IS NOT THAT EASILY BROKEN, SIR!!
KRAK
OWW
THAT'S NOT THE ISSUE.
?
HE'S UP AGAINST MADARA, HE OF THE POWERFUL OCULAR JUTSU.
NO MATTER HOW STRONG YAMATO'S WILL, IT'S NO MATCH.
UGH!
THD

READ THIS WAY

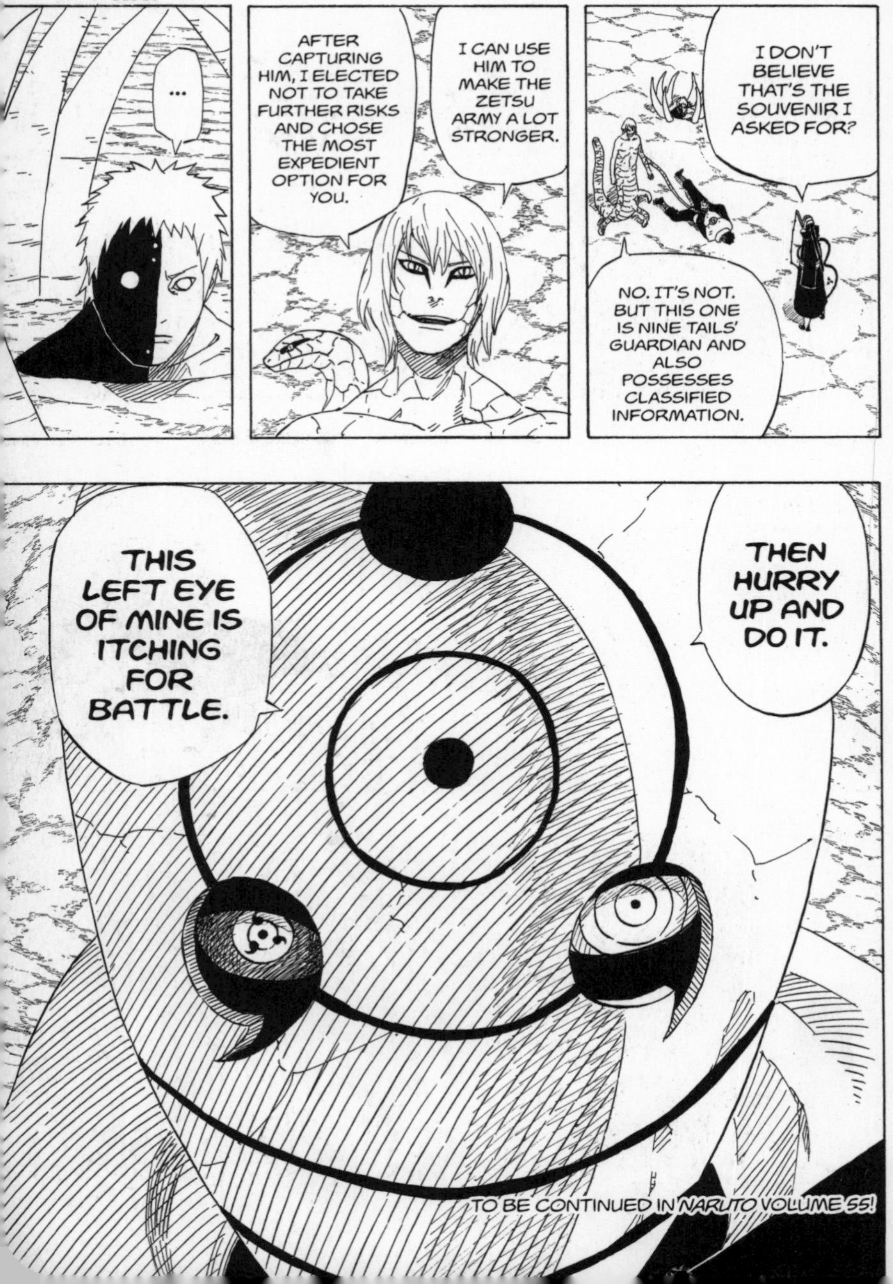

I DON'T BELIEVE THAT'S THE SOUVENIR I ASKED FOR?
NO. IT'S NOT. BUT THIS ONE IS NINE TAILS' GUARDIAN AND ALSO POSSESSES CLASSIFIED INFORMATION.
I CAN USE HIM TO MAKE THE ZETSU ARMY A LOT STRONGER.
AFTER CAPTURING HIM, I ELECTED NOT TO TAKE FURTHER RISKS AND CHOSE THE MOST EXPEDIENT OPTION FOR YOU.
...
THEN HURRY UP AND DO IT.
THIS LEFT EYE OF MINE IS ITCHING FOR BATTLE.
TO BE CONTINUED IN NARUTO VOLUME 55!

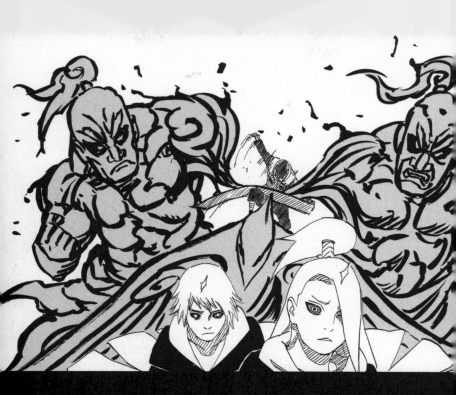

IN THE NEXT VOLUME...

THE GREAT WAR BEGINS

Evil masterminds Kabuto and Madara instigate a skirmish with Naruto and friends on Turtle Island. The Allied Shinobi Forces prepare to attack, but are they ready for Kabuto's horde of reanimated dead ninja?!

AVAILABLE MARCH 2012!
READ IT FIRST IN SHONEN JUMP MAGAZINE!

SHONEN JUMP
NARUTO
THE MOVIE
SHIPPUDEN
-Bonds- 絆

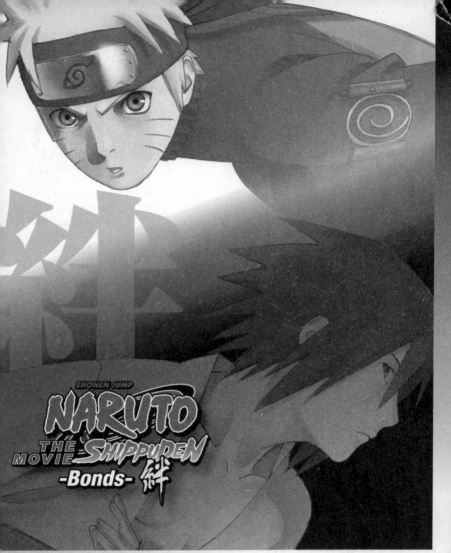

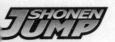

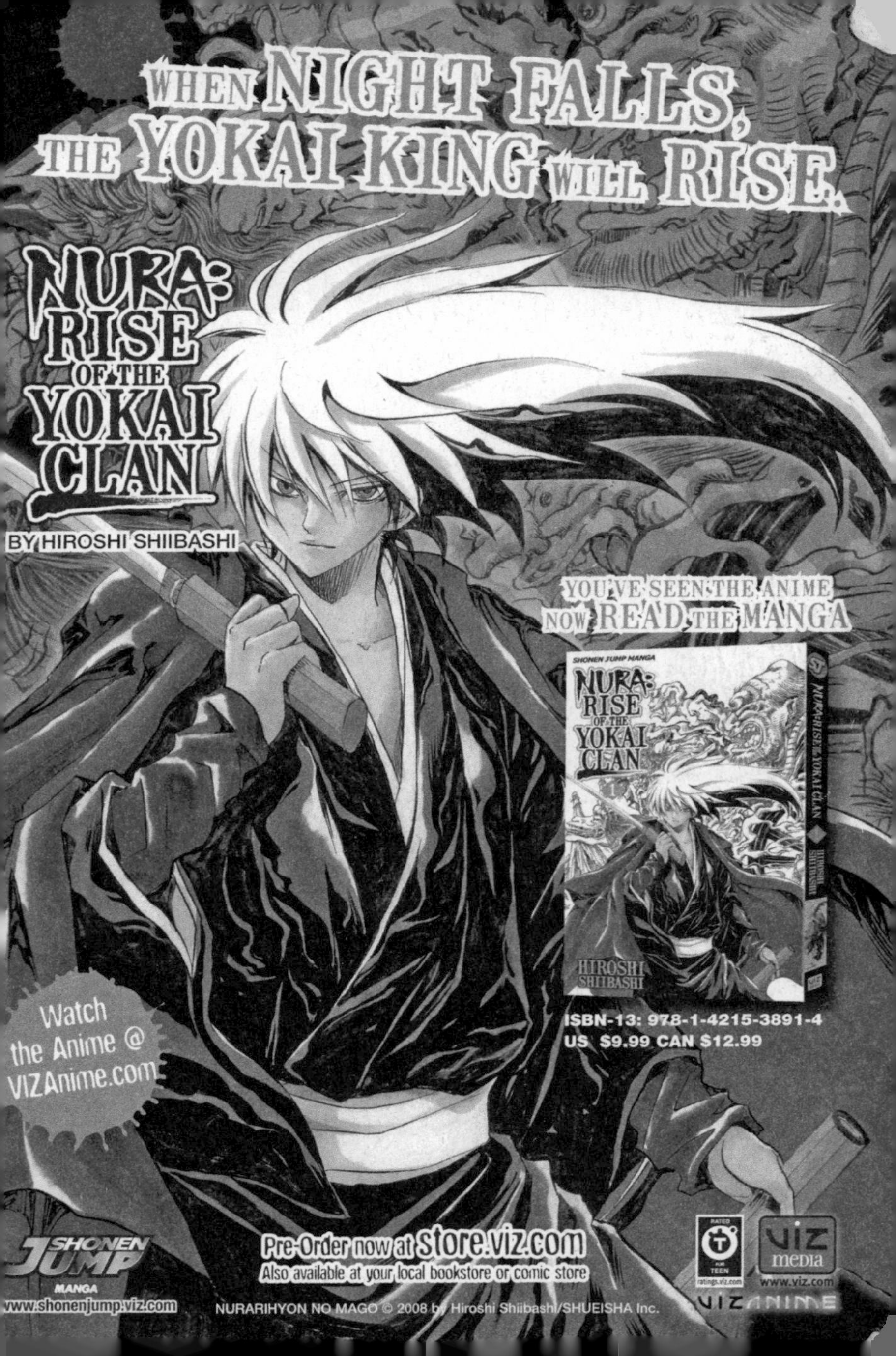
WHEN NIGHT FALLS, THE YOKAI KING WILL RISE.
NURA: RISE OF THE YOKAI CLAN
BY HIROSHI SHIIBASHI
YOU'VE SEEN THE ANIME NOW READ THE MANGA
SHONEN JUMP MANGA
NURA: RISE OF THE YOKAI CLAN
HIROSHI SHIIBASHI
ISBN-13: 978-1-4215-3891-4
US $9.99 CAN $12.99
Watch the Anime @ VIZAnime.com
Pre-Order now at store.viz.com
Also available at your local bookstore or comic store
SHONEN JUMP MANGA
www.shonenjump.viz.com
NURARIHYON NO MAGO © 2008 by Hiroshi Shiibashi/SHUEISHA Inc.
RATED T FOR TEEN
ratings.viz.com
VIZ media
www.viz.com
VIZ ANIME

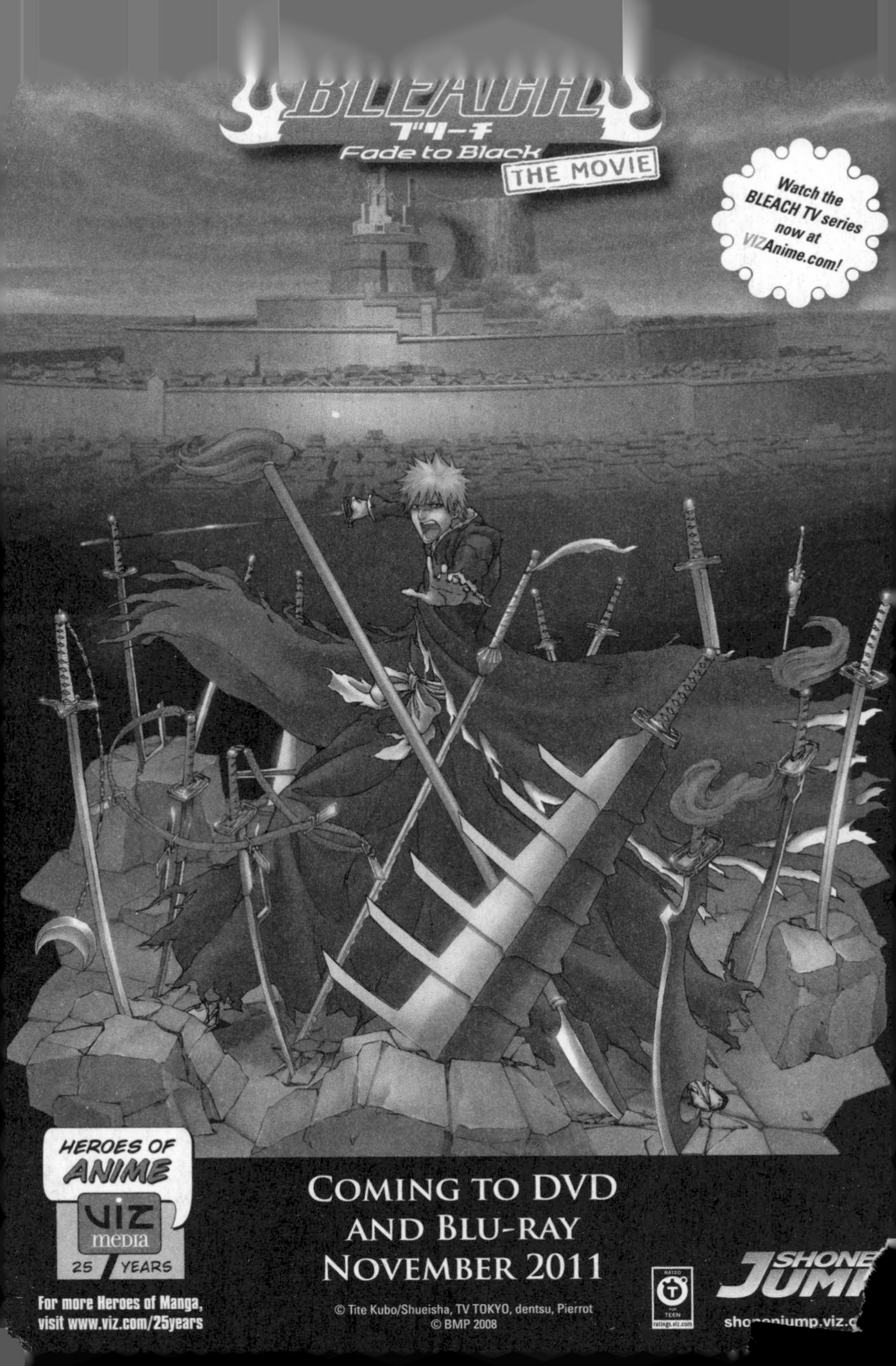
BLEACH
ブリーチ
Fade to Black
THE MOVIE
Watch the BLEACH TV series now at VIZAnime.com!
HEROES OF ANIME
viz media
25 YEARS
COMING TO DVD
AND BLU-RAY
NOVEMBER 2011
For more Heroes of Manga,
visit www.viz.com/25years
© Tite Kubo/Shueisha, TV TOKYO, dentsu, Pierrot
© BMP 2008
RATED T FOR TEEN
ratings.viz.com